Hyundai Excel Automotive Repair Manual

by Mike Stubblefield and John H Haynes
Member of the Guild of Motoring Writers

Models covered:
All Hyundai Excel models
1986 through 1994

 (8X9 – 1552)
ABCDE
FGHIJ
KLMNO
2

Haynes Publishing Group
Sparkford Nr Yeovil
Somerset BA22 7JJ England

Haynes North America, Inc
861 Lawrence Drive
Newbury Park
California 91320 USA

Acknowledgements

We are grateful for the help and cooperation of the Hyundai Motor Company for assistance with technical information and the vehicle photo, and the Champion Spark Plug Company, who supplied the illustrations of various spark plug conditions. Technical writers who contributed to this project include Larry Warren, Bob Henderson and Ken Freund.

A book in the **Haynes Automotive Repair Manual Series**

Printed in the USA

ISBN 1 56392 166 9

Library of Congress Catalog Card Number 95-78371

Contents

1989 Hyundai Excel 4-door sedan

About this manual

Its purpose

The purpose of this manual is to help you get the best value from your vehicle. It can do so in several ways. It can help you decide what work must be done, even if you choose to have it done by a dealer service department or a repair shop; it provides information and procedures for routine maintenance and servicing; and it offers diagnostic and repair procedures to follow when trouble occurs.

It is hoped that you will use the manual to tackle the work yourself. For many simpler jobs, doing it yourself may be quicker than arranging an appointment to get the vehicle into a shop and making the trips to leave it and pick it up. More importantly, a lot of money can be saved by avoiding the expense the shop must pass on to you to cover its labor and overhead costs. An added benefit is the sense of satisfaction and accomplishment that you feel after having done the job yourself.

Using the manual

The manual is divided into Chapters. Each Chapter is divided into numbered Sections, which are headed in bold type between horizontal lines. Each Section consists of consecutively numbered paragraphs.

At the beginning of each numbered section you will be referred to any illustrations which apply to the procedures in that section. The reference numbers used in illustration captions pinpoint the pertinent Section and the Step within that section. That is, illustration 3.2 means the illustration refers to Section 3 and Step (or paragraph) 2 within that Section.

Procedures, once described in the text, are not normally repeated. When it is necessary to refer to another Chapter, the reference will be given as Chapter and Section number i.e. Chapter 1/16). Cross references given without use of the word "Chapter" apply to Sections and/or paragraphs in the same Chapter. For example, "see Section 8" means in the same Chapter.

Reference to the left or right side of the vehicle is based on the assumption that one is sitting in the driver's seat, facing forward.

Even though extreme care has been taken during the preparation of this manual, neither the publisher nor the author can accept responsibility for any errors in, or omissions from, the information given.

NOTE

A Note provides information necessary to properly complete a procedure or information which will make the steps to be followed easier to understand.

CAUTION

A Caution indicates a special procedure or special steps which must be taken in the course of completing the procedure in which the **Caution** is found which are necessary to avoid damage to the assembly being worked on.

WARNING

A Warning indicates a special procedure or special steps which must be taken in the course of completing the procedure in which the **Warning** is found which are necessary to avoid injury to the person performing the procedure.

Introduction to the Hyundai Excel

Hyundai Excel models are available in 2 and 4-door hatchback and 4-door sedan body styles.

The transversely-mounted inline four-cylinder engine used in these models is equipped with a carburetor. The engine drives the front wheels through either a 4 or 5-speed manual or 3-speed automatic transaxle via independent driveaxles.

Independent suspension, featuring coil springs and struts or shock absorbers, is used at all four wheels. The rack and pinion steering unit is mounted behind the engine.

The brakes are disc at the front and drums at the rear, with power assist standard.

Vehicle identification numbers

Modifications are a continuing and unpublicized process in vehicle manufacturing. Since spare parts lists are compiled on a numerical basis, the individual vehicle numbers are essential to correctly identify the component required.

Vehicle Identification Number (VIN)

This very important identification number is stamped on a plate attached to the left side cowling just inside the windshield on the driver's side of the vehicle **(see illustration)**. The VIN also appears on the Vehicle Certificate of Title and Registration. It contains information such as where and when the vehicle was manufactured, the model year and the body style.

Manufacturers Plate

This plate is attached to the engine compartment firewall on the driver's side **(see illustration)**. It contains information on the vehicle model, engine and transaxle as well as the paint code.

Vehicle Certification Plate

The Vehicle Certification Plate (VC label) is affixed to the left front door pillar. The plate contains the name of the manufacturer, the month and year of production, the Gross Vehicle Weight Rating (GVWR) and the certification statement.

The Vehicle Identification Number (VIN) (arrow) is visible from outside the vehicle through the driver's side of the windshield

Engine ID number

The engine number is stamped into the block at the left (driver's) end of the exhaust manifold **(see illustration)**.

The Manufacturers Plate (arrow) is located on the firewall in the engine compartment

The engine ID number (arrow) is located on the block, adjacent to the exhaust manifold on the drivebelt end of the engine

Buying parts

Replacement parts are available from many sources, which generally fall into one of two categories – authorized dealer parts departments and independent retail auto parts stores. Our advice concerning these parts is as follows:

Retail auto parts stores: Good auto parts stores will stock frequently needed components which wear out relatively fast, such as clutch components, exhaust systems, brake parts, tune-up parts, etc. These stores often supply new or reconditioned parts on an exchange basis, which can save a considerable amount of money. Discount auto parts stores are often very good places to buy materials and parts needed for general vehicle maintenance such as oil, grease, filters, spark plugs, belts, touch-up paint, bulbs, etc. They also usually sell tools and general accessories, have convenient hours, charge lower prices and can often be found not far from home.

Authorized dealer parts department: This is the best source for parts which are unique to the vehicle and not generally available elsewhere (such as major engine parts, transmission parts, trim pieces, etc.).

Warranty information: If the vehicle is still covered under warranty, be sure that any replacement parts purchased – regardless of the source – do not invalidate the warranty!

To be sure of obtaining the correct parts, have engine and chassis numbers available and, if possible, take the old parts along for positive identification.

Maintenance techniques, tools and working facilities

Maintenance techniques

There are a number of techniques involved in maintenance and repair that will be referred to throughout this manual. Application of these techniques will enable the home mechanic to be more efficient, better organized and capable of performing the various tasks properly, which will ensure that the repair job is thorough and complete.

Fasteners

Fasteners are nuts, bolts, studs and screws used to hold two or more parts together. There are a few things to keep in mind when working with fasteners. Almost all of them use a locking device of some type, either a lockwasher, locknut, locking tab or thread adhesive. All threaded fasteners should be clean and straight, with undamaged threads and undamaged corners on the hex head where the wrench fits. Develop the habit of replacing all damaged nuts and bolts with new ones. Special locknuts with nylon or fiber inserts can only be used once. If they are removed, they lose their locking ability and must be replaced with new ones.

Rusted nuts and bolts should be treated with a penetrating fluid to ease removal and prevent breakage. Some mechanics use turpentine in a spout-type oil can, which works quite well. After applying the rust penetrant, let it work for a few minutes before trying to loosen the nut or bolt. Badly rusted fasteners may have to be chiseled or sawed off or removed with a special nut breaker, available at tool stores.

If a bolt or stud breaks off in an assembly, it can be drilled and removed with a special tool commonly available for this purpose. Most automotive machine shops can perform this task, as well as other repair procedures, such as the repair of threaded holes that have been stripped out.

Flat washers and lockwashers, when removed from an assembly, should always be replaced exactly as removed. Replace any damaged washers with new ones. Never use a lockwasher on any soft metal surface (such as aluminum), thin sheet metal or plastic.

Fastener sizes

For a number of reasons, automobile manufacturers are making wider and wider use of metric fasteners. Therefore, it is important to be able to tell the difference between standard (sometimes called U.S. or SAE) and metric hardware, since they cannot be interchanged.

All bolts, whether standard or metric, are sized according to diameter, thread pitch and length. For example, a standard 1/2 — 13 x 1 bolt is 1/2 inch in diameter, has 13 threads per inch and is 1 inch long. An M12 — 1.75 x 25 metric bolt is 12 mm in diameter, has a thread pitch of 1.75 mm (the distance between threads) and is 25 mm long. The two bolts are nearly identical, and easily confused, but they are not interchangeable.

In addition to the differences in diameter, thread pitch and length, metric and standard bolts can also be distinguished by examining the bolt heads. To begin with, the distance across the flats on a standard bolt head is measured in inches, while the same dimension on a metric bolt is sized in millimeters (the same is true for nuts). As a result, a standard wrench should not be used on a metric bolt and a metric wrench should not be used on a standard bolt. Also, most standard bolts have slashes radiating out from the center of the head to denote the grade or strength of the bolt, which is an indication of the amount of torque that can be applied to it. The greater the number of slashes, the greater the strength of the bolt. Grades 0 through 5 are commonly used on automobiles. Metric bolts have a property class (grade) number, rather than a slash, molded into their heads to indicate bolt strength. In this case, the higher the number, the stronger the bolt. Property class numbers 8.8, 9.8 and 10.9 are commonly used on automobiles.

Strength markings can also be used to distinguish standard hex nuts from metric hex nuts. Many standard nuts have dots stamped into one side, while metric nuts are marked with a number. The greater the number of dots, or the higher the number, the greater the strength of the nut.

Metric studs are also marked on their ends according to property class (grade). Larger studs are numbered (the same as metric bolts),

Grade 1 or 2   Grade 5   Grade 8

Bolt strength markings (top — standard/SAE/USS; bottom — metric)

Grade	Identification
Hex Nut Grade 5	3 Dots
Hex Nut Grade 8	6 Dots

Standard hex nut strength markings

Class	Identification
Hex Nut Property Class 9	Arabic 9
Hex Nut Property Class 10	Arabic 10

Metric hex nut strength markings

CLASS 10.9   CLASS 9.8   CLASS 8.8

Metric stud strength markings

while smaller studs carry a geometric code to denote grade.

It should be noted that many fasteners, especially Grades 0 through 2, have no distinguishing marks on them. When such is the case, the only way to determine whether it is standard or metric is to measure the thread pitch or compare it to a known fastener of the same size.

Standard fasteners are often referred to as SAE, as opposed to metric. However, it should be noted that SAE technically refers to a non-metric *fine thread* fastener only. Coarse thread non-metric fasteners are referred to as USS sizes.

Since fasteners of the same size (both standard and metric) may have different strength ratings, be sure to reinstall any bolts, studs or nuts removed from your vehicle in their original locations. Also, when re-placing a fastener with a new one, make sure that the new one has a strength rating equal to or greater than the original.

Tightening sequences and procedures

Most threaded fasteners should be tightened to a specific torque value (torque is the twisting force applied to a threaded component such as a nut or bolt). Overtightening the fastener can weaken it and cause it to break, while undertightening can cause it to eventually come loose. Bolts, screws and studs, depending on the material they are made of and their thread diameters, have specific torque values, many of which are noted in the Specifications at the beginning of each Chapter. Be sure to follow the torque recommendations closely. For fasteners not assigned a specific torque, a general torque value chart is presented here as a guide. These torque values are for dry (unlubricated) fasteners threaded into steel or cast iron (not aluminum). As was previously mentioned, the size and grade of a fastener determine the amount of torque that can safely be applied to it. The figures listed here are approximate

Metric thread sizes	Ft-lb	Nm/m
M-6	6 to 9	9 to 12
M-8	14 to 21	19 to 28
M-10	28 to 40	38 to 54
M-12	50 to 71	68 to 96
M-14	80 to 140	109 to 154
Pipe thread sizes		
1/8	5 to 8	7 to 10
1/4	12 to 18	17 to 24
3/8	22 to 33	30 to 44
1/2	25 to 35	34 to 47
U.S. thread sizes		
1/4 — 20	6 to 9	9 to 12
5/16 — 18	12 to 18	17 to 24
5/16 — 24	14 to 20	19 to 27
3/8 — 16	22 to 32	30 to 43
3/8 — 24	27 to 38	37 to 51
7/16 — 14	40 to 55	55 to 74
7/16 — 20	40 to 60	55 to 81
1/2 — 13	55 to 80	75 to 108

Standard (SAE and USS) bolt dimensions/grade marks

G Grade marks (bolt strength)
L Length (in inches)
T Thread pitch (number of threads per inch)
D Nominal diameter (in inches)

Metric bolt dimensions/grade marks

P Property class (bolt strength)
L Length (in millimeters)
T Thread pitch (distance between threads in millimeters)
D Diameter

for Grade 2 and Grade 3 fasteners. Higher grades can tolerate higher torque values.

Fasteners laid out in a pattern, such as cylinder head bolts, oil pan bolts, differential cover bolts, etc., must be loosened or tightened in sequence to avoid warping the component. This sequence will normally be shown in the appropriate Chapter. If a specific pattern is not given, the following procedures can be used to prevent warping.

Initially, the bolts or nuts should be assembled finger-tight only. Next, they should be tightened one full turn each, in a criss-cross or diagonal pattern. After each one has been tightened one full turn, return to the first one and tighten them all one-half turn, following the same pattern. Finally, tighten each of them one-quarter turn at a time until each fastener has been tightened to the proper torque. To loosen and remove the fasteners, the procedure would be reversed.

Component disassembly

Component disassembly should be done with care and purpose to help ensure that the parts go back together properly. Always keep track of the sequence in which parts are removed. Make note of special characteristics or marks on parts that can be installed more than one way, such as a grooved thrust washer on a shaft. It is a good idea to lay the disassembled parts out on a clean surface in the order that they were removed. It may also be helpful to make sketches or take instant photos of components before removal.

When removing fasteners from a component, keep track of their locations. Sometimes threading a bolt back in a part, or putting the washers and nut back on a stud, can prevent mix-ups later. If nuts and bolts cannot be returned to their original locations, they should be kept in a compartmented box or a series of small boxes. A cupcake or muffin tin is ideal for this purpose, since each cavity can hold the bolts and nuts from a particular area (i.e. oil pan bolts, valve cover bolts, engine mount bolts, etc.). A pan of this type is especially helpful when working on assemblies with very small parts, such as the carburetor, alternator, valve train or interior dash and trim pieces. The cavities can be marked with paint or tape to identify the contents.

Whenever wiring looms, harnesses or connectors are separated, it is a good idea to identify the two halves with numbered pieces of masking tape so they can be easily reconnected.

Gasket sealing surfaces

Throughout any vehicle, gaskets are used to seal the mating surfaces between two parts and keep lubricants, fluids, vacuum or pressure contained in an assembly.

Many times these gaskets are coated with a liquid or paste-type gasket sealing compound before assembly. Age, heat and pressure can sometimes cause the two parts to stick together so tightly that they are very difficult to separate. Often, the assembly can be loosened by striking it with a soft-face hammer near the mating surfaces. A regular hammer can be used if a block of wood is placed between the hammer and the part. Do not hammer on cast parts or parts that could be easily damaged. With any particularly stubborn part, always recheck to make sure that every fastener has been removed.

Avoid using a screwdriver or bar to pry apart an assembly, as they can easily mar the gasket sealing surfaces of the parts, which must remain smooth. If prying is absolutely necessary, use an old broom handle, but keep in mind that extra clean up will be necessary if the wood splinters.

After the parts are separated, the old gasket must be carefully scraped off and the gasket surfaces cleaned. Stubborn gasket material can be soaked with rust penetrant or treated with a special chemical to soften it so it can be easily scraped off. A scraper can be fashioned from a piece of copper tubing by flattening and sharpening one end. Copper is recommended because it is usually softer than the surfaces to be scraped, which reduces the chance of gouging the part. Some gaskets can be removed with a wire brush, but regardless of the method used, the mating surfaces must be left clean and smooth. If for some reason the gasket surface is gouged, then a gasket sealer thick enough to fill scratches will have to be used during reassembly of the components. For most applications, a non-drying (or semi-drying) gasket sealer should be used.

Hose removal tips

Warning: *If the vehicle is equipped with air conditioning, do not disconnect any of the A/C hoses without first having the system depressurized by a dealer service department or an air conditioning specialist.*

Hose removal precautions closely parallel gasket removal precautions. Avoid scratching or gouging the surface that the hose mates against or the connection may leak. This is especially true for radiator hoses. Because of various chemical reactions, the rubber in hoses can bond itself to the metal spigot that the hose fits over. To remove a hose, first loosen the hose clamps that secure it to the spigot. Then, with slip-joint pliers, grab the hose at the clamp and rotate it around the spigot. Work it back and forth until it is completely free, then pull it off. Silicone or other lubricants will ease removal if they can be applied between the hose and the outside of the spigot. Apply the same lubricant to the inside of the hose and the outside of the spigot to simplify installation.

As a last resort (and if the hose is to be replaced with a new one anyway), the rubber can be slit with a knife and the hose peeled from the spigot. If this must be done, be careful that the metal connection is not damaged.

If a hose clamp is broken or damaged, do not reuse it. Wire-type clamps usually weaken with age, so it is a good idea to replace them with screw-type clamps whenever a hose is removed.

Tools

A selection of good tools is a basic requirement for anyone who plans to maintain and repair his or her own vehicle. For the owner who has few tools, the initial investment might seem high, but when compared to the spiraling costs of professional auto maintenance and repair, it is a wise one.

Micrometer set   **Dial indicator set**

Dial caliper

Hand-operated vacuum pump

Timing light

Compression gauge with spark plug hole adapter

Damper/steering wheel puller

General purpose puller

Hydraulic lifter removal tool

Valve spring compressor

Valve spring compressor

Ridge reamer

Piston ring groove cleaning tool

Ring removal/installation tool

Ring compressor

Cylinder hone

Brake hold-down spring tool

Brake cylinder hone

Clutch plate alignment tool

Tap and die set

To help the owner decide which tools are needed to perform the tasks detailed in this manual, the following tool lists are offered: *Maintenance and minor repair, Repair/overhaul* and *Special*.

The newcomer to practical mechanics should start off with the maintenance and minor repair tool kit, which is adequate for the simpler jobs performed on a vehicle. Then, as confidence and experience grow, the owner can tackle more difficult tasks, buying additional tools as they are needed. Eventually the basic kit will be expanded into the repair and overhaul tool set. Over a period of time, the experienced do-it-yourselfer will assemble a tool set complete enough for most repair and overhaul procedures and will add tools from the special category when it is felt that the expense is justified by the frequency of use.

Maintenance and minor repair tool kit

The tools in this list should be considered the minimum required for performance of routine maintenance, servicing and minor repair work. We recommend the purchase of combination wrenches (box-end and open-end combined in one wrench). While more expensive than open end wrenches, they offer the advantages of both types of wrench.

Combination wrench set (1/4-inch to 1 inch or 6 mm to 19 mm)
Adjustable wrench, 8 inch
Spark plug wrench with rubber insert
Spark plug gap adjusting tool
Feeler gauge set
Brake bleeder wrench
Standard screwdriver (5/16-inch x 6 inch)
Phillips screwdriver (No. 2 x 6 inch)
Combination pliers — 6 inch
Hacksaw and assortment of blades
Tire pressure gauge
Grease gun
Oil can
Fine emery cloth
Wire brush

Battery post and cable cleaning tool
Oil filter wrench
Funnel (medium size)
Safety goggles
Jackstands (2)
Drain pan

Note: *If basic tune-ups are going to be part of routine maintenance, it will be necessary to purchase a good quality stroboscopic timing light and combination tachometer/dwell meter. Although they are included in the list of special tools, it is mentioned here because they are absolutely necessary for tuning most vehicles properly.*

Repair and overhaul tool set

These tools are essential for anyone who plans to perform major repairs and are in addition to those in the maintenance and minor repair tool kit. Included is a comprehensive set of sockets which, though expensive, are invaluable because of their versatility, especially when various extensions and drives are available. We recommend the 1/2-inch drive over the 3/8-inch drive. Although the larger drive is bulky and more expensive, it has the capacity of accepting a very wide range of large sockets. Ideally, however, the mechanic should have a 3/8-inch drive set and a 1/2-inch drive set.

Socket set(s)
Reversible ratchet
Extension — 10 inch
Universal joint
Torque wrench (same size drive as sockets)
Ball peen hammer — 8 ounce
Soft-face hammer (plastic/rubber)
Standard screwdriver (1/4-inch x 6 inch)
Standard screwdriver (stubby — 5/16-inch)
Phillips screwdriver (No. 3 x 8 inch)
Phillips screwdriver (stubby — No. 2)

Pliers — vise grip
Pliers — lineman's
Pliers — needle nose
Pliers — snap-ring (internal and external)
Cold chisel — 1/2-inch
Scribe
Scraper (made from flattened copper tubing)
Centerpunch
Pin punches (1/16, 1/8, 3/16-inch)
Steel rule/straightedge — 12 inch
Allen wrench set (1/8 to 3/8-inch or 4 mm to 10 mm)
A selection of files
Wire brush (large)
Jackstands (second set)
Jack (scissor or hydraulic type)

Note: *Another tool which is often useful is an electric drill motor with a chuck capacity of 3/8-inch and a set of good quality drill bits.*

Special tools

The tools in this list include those which are not used regularly, are expensive to buy, or which need to be used in accordance with their manufacturer's instructions. Unless these tools will be used frequently, it is not very economical to purchase many of them. A consideration would be to split the cost and use between yourself and a friend or friends. In addition, most of these tools can be obtained from a tool rental shop on a temporary basis.

This list primarily contains only those tools and instruments widely available to the public, and not those special tools produced by the vehicle manufacturer for distribution to dealer service departments. Occasionally, references to the manufacturer's special tools are inluded in the text of this manual. Generally, an alternative method of doing the job without the special tool is offered. However, sometimes there is no alternative to their use. Where this is the case, and the tool cannot be purchased or borrowed, the work should be turned over to the dealer service department or an automotive repair shop.

Valve spring compressor
Piston ring groove cleaning tool
Piston ring compressor
Piston ring installation tool
Cylinder compression gauge
Cylinder ridge reamer
Cylinder surfacing hone
Cylinder bore gauge
Micrometers and/or dial calipers
Hydraulic lifter removal tool
Balljoint separator
Universal-type puller
Impact screwdriver
Dial indicator set
Stroboscopic timing light (inductive pick-up)
Hand operated vacuum/pressure pump
Tachometer/dwell meter
Universal electrical multimeter
Cable hoist
Brake spring removal and installation tools
Floor jack

Buying tools

For the do-it-yourselfer who is just starting to get involved in vehicle maintenance and repair, there are a number of options available when purchasing tools. If maintenance and minor repair is the extent of the work to be done, the purchase of individual tools is satisfactory. If,

on the other hand, extensive work is planned, it would be a good idea to purchase a modest tool set from one of the large retail chain stores. A set can usually be bought at a substantial savings over the individual tool prices, and they often come with a tool box. As additional tools are needed, add-on sets, individual tools and a larger tool box can be purchased to expand the tool selection. Building a tool set gradually allows the cost of the tools to be spread over a longer period of time and gives the mechanic the freedom to choose only those tools that will actually be used.

Tool stores will often be the only source of some of the special tools that are needed, but regardless of where tools are bought, try to avoid cheap ones, especially when buying screwdrivers and sockets, because they won't last very long. The expense involved in replacing cheap tools will eventually be greater than the initial cost of quality tools.

Care and maintenance of tools

Good tools are expensive, so it makes sense to treat them with respect. Keep them clean and in usable condition and store them properly when not in use. Always wipe off any dirt, grease or metal chips before putting them away. Never leave tools lying around in the work area. Upon completion of a job, always check closely under the hood for tools that may have been left there so they won't get lost during a test drive.

Some tools, such as screwdrivers, pliers, wrenches and sockets, can be hung on a panel mounted on the garage or workshop wall, while others should be kept in a tool box or tray. Measuring instruments, gauges, meters, etc. must be carefully stored where they cannot be damaged by weather or impact from other tools.

When tools are used with care and stored properly, they will last a very long time. Even with the best of care, though, tools will wear out if used frequently. When a tool is damaged or worn out, replace it. Subsequent jobs will be safer and more enjoyable if you do.

Working facilities

Not to be overlooked when discussing tools is the workshop. If anything more than routine maintenance is to be carried out, some sort of suitable work area is essential.

It is understood, and appreciated, that many home mechanics do not have a good workshop or garage available, and end up removing an engine or doing major repairs outside. It is recommended, however, that the overhaul or repair be completed under the cover of a roof.

A clean, flat workbench or table of comfortable working height is an absolute necessity. The workbench should be equipped with a vise that has a jaw opening of at least four inches.

As mentioned previously, some clean, dry storage space is also required for tools, as well as the lubricants, fluids, cleaning solvents, etc. which will soon become necessary.

Sometimes waste oil and fluids, drained from the engine or cooling system during normal maintenance or repairs, present a disposal problem. To avoid pouring them on the ground or into a sewage system, pour the used fluids into large containers, seal them with caps and take them to an authorized disposal site or recycling center. Plastic jugs, such as old antifreeze containers, are ideal for this purpose.

Always keep a supply of old newspapers and clean rags available. Old towels are excellent for mopping up spills. Many mechanics use rolls of paper towels for most work because they are readily available and disposable. To help keep the area under the vehicle clean, a large cardboard box can be cut open and flattened to protect the garage or shop floor.

Whenever working over a painted surface, such as when leaning over a fender to service something under the hood, always cover it with an old blanket or bedspread to protect the finish. Vinyl covered pads, made especially for this purpose, are available at auto parts stores.

Booster battery (jump) starting

Certain precautions must be observed when using a booster battery to start a vehicle.
  a) Before connecting the booster battery, make sure the ignition switch is in the Off position.
  b) Turn off the lights, heater and other electrical loads.
  c) Your eyes should be shielded. Safety goggles are a good idea.
  d) Make sure the booster battery is the same voltage as the dead one in the vehicle.
  e) The two vehicles MUST NOT TOUCH each other!
  f) Make sure the transmission is in Neutral (manual) or Park (automatic).
  g) If the booster battery is not a maintenance-free type, remove the vent caps and lay a cloth over the vent holes.

Connect the red jumper cable to the *positive* (+) terminals of each battery.

Connect one end of the black jumper cable to the *negative* (–) terminal of the booster battery. The other end of this cable should be connected to a good ground on the vehicle to be started, such as a bolt or bracket on the engine block (see illustration). Use caution to ensure that the cable will not come into contact with the fan, drivebelts or other moving parts of the engine.

Start the engine using the booster battery, then, with the engine running at idle speed, disconnect the jumper cables in the reverse order of connection.

Make the booster battery cable connections in the numerical order shown (note that the negative cable of the booster battery is NOT attached to the negative terminal of the dead battery)

Jacking and towing

Jacking

Warning: *The jack supplied with the vehicle should only be used for raising the vehicle when changing a tire or placing jackstands under the frame. Never work under the vehicle or start the engine while the jack is being used as the only means of support.*

The vehicle must be on a level surface with the wheels blocked and the transaxle in Park (automatic) or Reverse (manual). Apply the park-ing brake if the front of the vehicle must be raised. Make sure no one is in the vehicle as it's being raised with the jack.

Remove the jack, lug nut wrench and spare tire (if needed) from the vehicle. If a tire is being replaced, use the lug wrench to remove the wheel cover. **Warning:** *Wheel covers may have sharp edges — be very careful not to cut yourself.* Loosen the lug nuts one-half turn, but leave them in place until the tire is raised off the ground.

Jacking points

Position the jack under the vehicle at the indicated jacking point. There's a front and rear jacking point on each side of the vehicle (**see illustration**).

Turn the jack handle clockwise until the tire clears the ground. Pull the tire off and replace it with the spare. Replace the lug nuts with the beveled edges facing in and tighten them snugly. Don't attempt to tighten them completely until the vehicle is lowered or it could slip off the jack.

Turn the jack handle counterclockwise to lower the vehicle. Remove the jack and tighten the lug nuts in a criss-cross pattern. If possible, tighten the nuts with a torque wrench (see Chapter 1 for the torque figures). If you don't have access to a torque wrench, have the nuts checked by a service station or repair shop as soon as possible.

Stow the tire, jack and wrench and unblock the wheels.

Towing

Vehicles with a manual transaxle

As a general rule, the vehicle should be towed with the front (drive) wheels off the ground. Be sure to release the parking brake. If the vehicle is being towed with the front wheels on the ground, place the transmission in Neutral. Also, the ignition key must be in the ACC position, since the steering lock mechanism isn't strong enough to hold the front wheels straight while towing.

Vehicles with an automatic transaxle

Caution: *Never tow a vehicle with an automatic transaxle from the rear with the front wheels on the ground. If the vehicle must be towed from the rear, place the front wheels on a towing dolly.*

Vehicles equipped with an automatic transaxle can be towed from the front only with all four wheels on the ground, provided that speeds don't exceed 30 mph and the distance is not over 50 miles. Before towing, check the transmission fluid level (see Chapter 1). If the level is below the HOT mark on the dipstick, add fluid or use a towing dolly. Release the parking brake, put the transaxle in Neutral and place the ignition key in the ACC position. A driver must be in the towed vehicle to steer and operate the brakes.

All vehicles

Equipment specifically designed for towing should be used. It should be attached to the main structural members of the vehicle, not the bumpers or brackets.

Safety is a major consideration when towing and all applicable state and local laws must be obeyed. A safety chain must be used at all times. Remember that power steering and brakes won't work with the engine off.

Automotive chemicals and lubricants

A number of automotive chemicals and lubricants are available for use during vehicle maintenance and repair. They include a wide variety of products ranging from cleaning solvents and degreasers to lubricants and protective sprays for rubber, plastic and vinyl.

Cleaners

Carburetor cleaner and choke cleaner is a strong solvent for gum, varnish and carbon. Most carburetor cleaners leave a dry-type lubricant film which will not harden or gum up. Because of this film it is not recommended for use on electrical components.

Brake system cleaner is used to remove grease and brake fluid from the brake system where clean surfaces are absolutely necessary. It leaves no residue and often eliminates brake squeal caused by contaminants.

Electrical cleaner removes oxidation, corrosion and carbon deposits from electrical contacts, restoring full current flow. It can also be used to clean spark plugs, carburetor jets, voltage regulators and other parts where an oil-free surface is desired.

Demoisturants remove water and moisture from electrical components such as alternators, voltage regulators, electrical connectors and fuse blocks. It is non-conductive, non-corrosive and non-flammable.

Degreasers are heavy-duty solvents used to remove grease from the outside of the engine and from chassis components. They can be sprayed or brushed on, and, depending on the type, are rinsed off either with water or solvent.

Lubricants

Motor oil is the lubricant formulated for use in engines. It normally contains a wide variety of additives to prevent corrosion and reduce foaming and wear. Motor oil comes in various weights (viscosity ratings) from 5 to 80. The recommended weight of the oil depends on the season, temperature and the demands on the engine. Light oil is used in cold climates and under light load conditions. Heavy oil is used in hot climates and where high loads are encountered. Multi-viscosity oils are designed to have characteristics of both light and heavy oils and are available in a number of weights from 5W-20 to 20W-50.

Gear oil is designed to be used in differentials, manual transaxles and other areas where high-temperature lubrication is required.

Chassis and wheel bearing grease is a heavy grease used where increased loads and friction are encountered, such as for wheel bearings, balljoints, tie rod ends and universal joints.

High temperature wheel bearing grease is designed to withstand the extreme temperatures encountered by wheel bearings in disc brake equipped vehicles. It usually contains molybdenun disulfide (moly), which is a dry-type lubricant.

White grease is a heavy grease for metal to metal applications where water is a problem. White grease stays soft under both low and high temperatures (usually from –100°F to +190°F), and will not wash off or dilute in the presence of water.

Assembly lube is a special extreme pressure lubricant, usually containing moly, used to lubricate high-load parts such as main and rod bearings and cam lobes for initial start-up of a new engine. The assembly lube lubricates the parts without being squeezed out or washed away until the engine oiling system begins to function.

Silicone lubricants are used to protect rubber, plastic, vinyl and nylon parts.

Graphite lubricants are used where oils cannot be used due to contamination problems, such as in locks. The dry graphite will lubricate metal parts while remaining uncontaminated by dirt, water, oil or acids. It is electrically conductive and will not foul electrical contacts in locks such as the ignition switch.

Moly penetrants loosen and lubricate frozen, rusted and corroded fasteners and prevent future rusting or freezing.

Heat-sink grease is a special electrically non-conductive grease that is used for mounting HEI ignition modules where it is essential that heat be transferred away from the module.

Sealants

RTV sealant is one of the most widely used gasket compounds. Made from silicone, RTV is air curing, it seals, bonds, waterproofs, fills surface irregularities, remains flexible, doesn't shrink, is relatively easy to remove, and is used as a supplementary sealer with almost all low and medium temperature gaskets.

Anaerobic sealant is much like RTV in that it can be used either to seal gaskets or to form gaskets by itself. It remains flexible, is solvent resistant and fills surface imperfections. The difference between an anaerobic sealant and an RTV-type sealant is in the curing. RTV cures when exposed to air, while an anaerobic sealant cures only in the absence of air. This means that an anaerobic sealant cures only after the assembly of parts, sealing them together.

Thread and pipe sealant is used for sealing hydraulic and pneumatic fittings and vacuum lines. It is usually made from a teflon compound, and comes in a spray, a paint-on liquid and as a wrap-around tape.

Chemicals

Anti-seize compound prevents seizing, galling, cold welding, rust and corrosion in fasteners. High temperature anti-seize, usually made with copper and graphite lubricants, is used for exhaust system and manifold bolts.

Anaerobic locking compounds are used to keep fasteners from vibrating or working loose, and cure only after installation, in the absence of air. Medium strength locking compound is used for small nuts, bolts and screws that you expect to be removing later. High strength locking compound is for large nuts, bolts and studs which you don't intend to be removing on a regular basis.

Oil additives range from viscosity index improvers to chemical treatments that claim to reduce internal engine friction. It should be noted that most oil manufacturers caution against using additives with their oils.

Gas additives perform several functions, depending on their chemical makeup. They usually contain solvents that help dissolve gum and varnish that build up on carburetor and intake parts. They also serve to break down carbon deposits that form on the inside surfaces of the combustion chambers. Some additives contain upper cylinder lubricants for valves and piston rings, and others chemicals to remove condensation from the gas tank.

Miscellaneous

Brake fluid is specially formulated hydraulic fluid that can withstand the heat and pressure encountered in brake systems. Care must be taken that this fluid does not come in contact with painted surfaces or plastics. An opened container should always be resealed to prevent contamination by water or dirt.

Weatherstrip adhesive is used to bond weatherstripping around doors, windows and trunk lids. It is sometimes used to attach trim pieces.

Undercoating is a petroleum-based tar-like substance that is designed to protect metal surfaces on the underside of the vehicle from corrosion. It also acts as a sound-deadening agent by insulating the bottom of the vehicle.

Waxes and polishes are used to help protect painted and plated surfaces from the weather. Different types of paint may require the use of different types of wax and polish. Some polishes utilize a chemical or abrasive cleaner to help remove the top layer of oxidized (dull) paint on older vehicles. In recent years many non-wax polishes that contain a wide variety of chemicals such as polymers and silicones have been introduced. These non-wax polishes are usually easier to apply and last longer than conventional waxes and polishes.

Safety first!

Regardless of how enthusiastic you may be about getting on with the job at hand, take the time to ensure that your safety is not jeopardized. A moment's lack of attention can result in an accident, as can failure to observe certain simple safety precautions. The possibility of an accident will always exist, and the following points should not be considered a comprehensive list of all dangers. Rather, they are intended to make you aware of the risks and to encourage a safety conscious approach to all work you carry out on your vehicle.

Essential DOs and DON'Ts

DON'T rely on a jack when working under the vehicle. Always use approved jackstands to support the weight of the vehicle and place them under the recommended lift or support points.

DON'T attempt to loosen extremely tight fasteners (i.e. wheel lug nuts) while the vehicle is on a jack — it may fall.

DON'T start the engine without first making sure that the transmission is in Neutral (or Park where applicable) and the parking brake is set.

DON'T remove the radiator cap from a hot cooling system — let it cool or cover it with a cloth and release the pressure gradually.

DON'T attempt to drain the engine oil until you are sure it has cooled to the point that it will not burn you.

DON'T touch any part of the engine or exhaust system until it has cooled sufficiently to avoid burns.

DON'T siphon toxic liquids such as gasoline, antifreeze and brake fluid by mouth, or allow them to remain on your skin.

DON'T inhale brake lining dust — it is potentially hazardous (see *Asbestos* below)

DON'T allow spilled oil or grease to remain on the floor — wipe it up before someone slips on it.

DON'T use loose fitting wrenches or other tools which may slip and cause injury.

DON'T push on wrenches when loosening or tightening nuts or bolts. Always try to pull the wrench toward you. If the situation calls for pushing the wrench away, push with an open hand to avoid scraped knuckles if the wrench should slip.

DON'T attempt to lift a heavy component alone — get someone to help you.

DON'T rush or take unsafe shortcuts to finish a job.

DON'T allow children or animals in or around the vehicle while you are working on it.

DO wear eye protection when using power tools such as a drill, sander, bench grinder, etc. and when working under a vehicle.

DO keep loose clothing and long hair well out of the way of moving parts.

DO make sure that any hoist used has a safe working load rating adequate for the job.

DO get someone to check on you periodically when working alone on a vehicle.

DO carry out work in a logical sequence and make sure that everything is correctly assembled and tightened.

DO keep chemicals and fluids tightly capped and out of the reach of children and pets.

DO remember that your vehicle's safety affects that of yourself and others. If in doubt on any point, get professional advice.

Asbestos

Certain friction, insulating, sealing, and other products — such as brake linings, brake bands, clutch linings, torque converters, gaskets, etc. — contain asbestos. *Extreme care must be taken to avoid inhalation of dust from such products since it is hazardous to health.* If in doubt, assume that they *do* contain asbestos.

Fire

Remember at all times that gasoline is highly flammable. Never smoke or have any kind of open flame around when working on a vehicle. But the risk does not end there. A spark caused by an electrical short circuit, by two metal surfaces contacting each other, or even by static electricity built up in your body under certain conditions, can ignite gasoline vapors, which in a confined space are highly explosive. Do not, under any circumstances, use gasoline for cleaning parts. Use an approved safety solvent.

Always disconnect the battery ground (–) cable *at the battery* before working on any part of the fuel system or electrical system. Never risk spilling fuel on a hot engine or exhaust component.

It is strongly recommended that a fire extinguisher suitable for use on fuel and electrical fires be kept handy in the garage or workshop at all times. Never try to extinguish a fuel or electrical fire with water.

Fumes

Certain fumes are highly toxic and can quickly cause unconsciousness and even death if inhaled to any extent. Gasoline vapor falls into this category, as do the vapors from some cleaning solvents. Any draining or pouring of such volatile fluids should be done in a well ventilated area.

When using cleaning fluids and solvents, read the instructions on the container carefully. Never use materials from unmarked containers.

Never run the engine in an enclosed space, such as a garage. Exhaust fumes contain carbon monoxide, which is extremely poisonous. If you need to run the engine, always do so in the open air, or at least have the rear of the vehicle outside the work area.

If you are fortunate enough to have the use of an inspection pit, never drain or pour gasoline and never run the engine while the vehicle is over the pit. The fumes, being heavier than air, will concentrate in the pit with possibly lethal results.

The battery

Never create a spark or allow a bare light bulb near the battery. The battery normally gives off a certain amount of hydrogen gas, which is highly explosive.

Always disconnect the battery ground (–) cable *at the battery* before working on the fuel or electrical systems.

If possible, loosen the filler caps or cover when charging the battery from an external source. Do not charge at an excessive rate or the battery may burst.

Take care when adding water and when carrying a battery. The electrolyte, even when diluted, is very corrosive and should not be allowed to contact clothing or skin.

Always wear eye protection when cleaning the battery to prevent the caustic deposits from entering your eyes.

Household current

When using an electric power tool, inspection light, etc., which operates on household current, always make sure that the tool is correctly connected to its plug and that, where necessary, it is properly grounded. Do not use such items in damp conditions and, again, do not create a spark or apply excessive heat in the vicinity of fuel or fuel vapor.

Secondary ignition system voltage

A severe electric shock can result from touching certain parts of the ignition system (such as the spark plug wires) when the engine is running or being cranked, particularly if components are damp or the insulation is defective. In the case of an electronic ignition system, the secondary system voltage is much higher and could prove fatal.

Conversion factors

Length (distance)

Inches (in)	X	25.4	= Millimetres (mm)	X 0.0394	= Inches (in)
Feet (ft)	X	0.305	= Metres (m)	X 3.281	= Feet (ft)
Miles	X	1.609	= Kilometres (km)	X 0.621	= Miles

Volume (capacity)

Cubic inches (cu in; in³)	X	16.387	= Cubic centimetres (cc; cm³)	X 0.061	= Cubic inches (cu in; in³)
Imperial pints (Imp pt)	X	0.568	= Litres (l)	X 1.76	= Imperial pints (Imp pt)
Imperial quarts (Imp qt)	X	1.137	= Litres (l)	X 0.88	= Imperial quarts (Imp qt)
Imperial quarts (Imp qt)	X	1.201	= US quarts (US qt)	X 0.833	= Imperial quarts (Imp qt)
US quarts (US qt)	X	0.946	= Litres (l)	X 1.057	= US quarts (US qt)
Imperial gallons (Imp gal)	X	4.546	= Litres (l)	X 0.22	= Imperial gallons (Imp gal)
Imperial gallons (Imp gal)	X	1.201	= US gallons (US gal)	X 0.833	= Imperial gallons (Imp gal)
US gallons (US gal)	X	3.785	= Litres (l)	X 0.264	= US gallons (US gal)

Mass (weight)

Ounces (oz)	X	28.35	= Grams (g)	X 0.035	= Ounces (oz)
Pounds (lb)	X	0.454	= Kilograms (kg)	X 2.205	= Pounds (lb)

Force

Ounces-force (ozf; oz)	X	0.278	= Newtons (N)	X 3.6	= Ounces-force (ozf; oz)
Pounds-force (lbf; lb)	X	4.448	= Newtons (N)	X 0.225	= Pounds-force (lbf; lb)
Newtons (N)	X	0.1	= Kilograms-force (kgf; kg)	X 9.81	= Newtons (N)

Pressure

Pounds-force per square inch (psi; lbf/in²; lb/in²)	X	0.070	= Kilograms-force per square centimetre (kgf/cm²; kg/cm²)	X 14.223	= Pounds-force per square inch (psi; lbf/in²; lb/in²)
Pounds-force per square inch (psi; lbf/in²; lb/in²)	X	0.068	= Atmospheres (atm)	X 14.696	= Pounds-force per square inch (psi; lbf/in²; lb/in²)
Pounds-force per square inch (psi; lbf/in²; lb/in²)	X	0.069	= Bars	X 14.5	= Pounds-force per square inch (psi; lbf/in²; lb/in²)
Pounds-force per square inch (psi; lbf/in²; lb/in²)	X	6.895	= Kilopascals (kPa)	X 0.145	= Pounds-force per square inch (psi; lbf/in²; lb/in²)
Kilopascals (kPa)	X	0.01	= Kilograms-force per square centimetre (kgf/cm²; kg/cm²)	X 98.1	= Kilopascals (kPa)

Torque (moment of force)

Pounds-force inches (lbf in; lb in)	X	1.152	= Kilograms-force centimetre (kgf cm; kg cm)	X 0.868	= Pounds-force inches (lbf in; lb in)
Pounds-force inches (lbf in; lb in)	X	0.113	= Newton metres (Nm)	X 8.85	= Pounds-force inches (lbf in; lb in)
Pounds-force inches (lbf in; lb in)	X	0.083	= Pounds-force feet (lbf ft; lb ft)	X 12	= Pounds-force inches (lbf in; lb in)
Pounds-force feet (lbf ft; lb ft)	X	0.138	= Kilograms-force metres (kgf m; kg m)	X 7.233	= Pounds-force feet (lbf ft; lb ft)
Pounds-force feet (lbf ft; lb ft)	X	1.356	= Newton metres (Nm)	X 0.738	= Pounds-force feet (lbf ft; lb ft)
Newton metres (Nm)	X	0.102	= Kilograms-force metres (kgf m; kg m)	X 9.804	= Newton metres (Nm)

Power

Horsepower (hp)	X	745.7	= Watts (W)	X 0.0013	= Horsepower (hp)

Velocity (speed)

Miles per hour (miles/hr; mph)	X	1.609	= Kilometres per hour (km/hr; kph)	X 0.621	= Miles per hour (miles/hr; mph)

Fuel consumption*

Miles per gallon, Imperial (mpg)	X	0.354	= Kilometres per litre (km/l)	X 2.825	= Miles per gallon, Imperial (mpg)
Miles per gallon, US (mpg)	X	0.425	= Kilometres per litre (km/l)	X 2.352	= Miles per gallon, US (mpg)

Temperature

Degrees Fahrenheit = (°C x 1.8) + 32   Degrees Celsius (Degrees Centigrade; °C) = (°F - 32) x 0.56

*It is common practice to convert from miles per gallon (mpg) to litres/100 kilometres (l/100km),
where mpg (Imperial) x l/100 km = 282 and mpg (US) x l/100 km = 235

Troubleshooting

Contents

This section provides an easy reference guide to the more common problems which may occur during the operation of your vehicle. These problems and possible causes are grouped under various components or systems; i.e. Engine, Cooling System, etc., and also refer to the Chapter and/or Section which deals with the problem.

Remember that successful troubleshooting is not a mysterious black art practiced only by professional mechanics. It's simply the result of a bit of knowledge combined with an intelligent, systematic approach to the problem. Always work by a process of elimination, starting with the simplest solution and working through to the most complex - and never overlook the obvious. Anyone can forget to fill the gas tank or leave the lights on overnight, so don't assume that you are above such oversights.

Finally, always get clear in your mind why a problem has occurred and take steps to ensure that it doesn't happen again. If the electrical system fails because of a poor connection, check all other connections in the system to make sure that they don't fail as well. If a particular fuse continues to blow, find out why - don't just go on replacing fuses. Remember, failure of a small component can often be indicative of potential failure or incorrect functioning of a more important component or system.

Engine

1   Engine will not rotate when attempting to start

1   Battery terminal connections loose or corroded. Check the cable terminals at the battery. Tighten the cable or remove corrosion as necessary.
2   Battery discharged or faulty. If the cable connections are clean and tight on the battery posts, turn the key to the On position and switch on the headlights and/or windshield wipers. If they fail to function, the battery is discharged.
3   Automatic transaxle not completely engaged in Park or Neutral or clutch pedal not completely depressed.
4   Broken, loose or disconnected wiring in the starting circuit. Inspect all wiring and connectors at the battery, starter solenoid and ignition switch.
5   Starter motor pinion jammed in flywheel ring gear. If manual transaxle, place transaxle in gear and rock the vehicle to manually turn the engine. Remove starter and inspect pinion and flywheel at earliest convenience (Chapter 5).
6   Starter solenoid faulty (Chapter 5).
7   Starter motor faulty (Chapter 5).
8   Ignition switch faulty (Chapter 12).

2   Engine rotates but will not start

1   Fuel tank empty.
2   Fault in the carburetor (Chapter 4).
3   Battery discharged (engine rotates slowly). Check the operation of electrical components as described in the previous Section.
4   Battery terminal connections loose or corroded (see previous Section).
5   Faulty fuel pump or fuel pump circuit (Chapter 4).
6   Fuel injection system faulty (fuel-injected models) (Chapter 4).
7   Excessive moisture on, or damage to, ignition components (Chapter 5).
8   Worn, faulty or incorrectly gapped spark plugs (Chapter 1).
9   Broken, loose or disconnected wiring in the starting circuit (see previous Section).
10   Distributor loose, causing ignition timing to change. Turn the distributor as necessary to start the engine, then set the ignition timing as soon as possible (Chapter 1).
11   Broken, loose or disconnected wires at the ignition coil or faulty coil (Chapter 5).

3   Starter motor operates without rotating engine

1   Starter pinion sticking. Remove the starter (Chapter 5) and inspect.
2   Starter pinion or flywheel teeth worn or broken. Remove the flywheel/driveplate access cover and inspect.

4   Engine hard to start when cold

1   Battery discharged or low. Check as described in Section 1.
2   Fault in the fuel or electrical systems (Chapters 4 and 5).
3   Carburetor/fuel injection system in need of repair or overhaul (Chapter 4).
4   Distributor rotor carbon tracked and/or damaged (Chapters 1 and 5).
5   Choke control stuck or inoperative (Chapters 1 and 4).

5   Engine hard to start when hot

1   Air filter clogged (Chapter 1).
2   Fault in the fuel or electrical systems (Chapters 4 and 5).
3   Fuel not reaching the carburetor (see Section 2).

6   Starter motor noisy or excessively rough in engagement

1   Pinion or flywheel gear teeth worn or broken. Remove the cover at the rear of the engine (if so equipped) and inspect.
2   Starter motor mounting bolts loose or missing.

7   Engine starts but stops immediately

1   Loose or faulty electrical connections at distributor, coil or alternator.
2   Fault in the fuel or electrical systems (Chapters 4 and 5).
3   Insufficient fuel reaching the carburetor/fuel injector(s). Check the fuel pump (Chapter 4).
4   Vacuum leak at the gasket surfaces of the intake manifold, or carburetor. Make sure all mounting bolts/nuts are tightened securely and all vacuum hoses connected to the carburetor and manifold are positioned properly and in good condition.

8   Engine lopes while idling or idles erratically

1   Vacuum leakage. Check the mounting bolts/nuts at the carburetor/throttle body and intake manifold for tightness. Make sure all vacuum hoses are connected and in good condition. Use a stethoscope or a length of fuel hose held against your ear to listen for vacuum leaks while the engine is running. A hissing sound will be heard. A soapy water solution will also detect leaks.
2   Fault in the fuel or electrical systems (Chapters 4 and 5).
3   Leaking EGR valve or plugged PCV valve (see Chapters 1 and 6).
4   Air filter clogged (Chapter 1).
5   Fuel pump not delivering sufficient fuel to the carburetor/fuel injector(s). Check the fuel pump (Chapter 4).
6   Carburetor out of adjustment (Chapter 4).
7   Leaking head gasket. Perform a compression check (Chapter 2).
8   Camshaft lobes worn (Chapter 2).

9   Engine misses at idle speed

1   Spark plugs worn or not gapped properly (Chapter 1).
2   Fault in the fuel or electrical systems (Chapters 4 and 5).
3   Faulty spark plug wires (Chapter 1).

10   Engine misses throughout driving speed range

4   Incorrect ignition timing (Chapter 1).
5   Check for cracked distributor cap, disconnected distributor wires and damaged distributor components (Chapter 1).
6   Defective spark plug wires (Chapter 1).

7   Faulty emissions system components (Chapter 6).
8   Low or uneven cylinder compression pressures. Remove the spark plugs and test the compression with a gauge (Chapter 2). .
9   Weak or faulty ignition system (Chapter 5).
10   Vacuum leaks at the carburetor/throttle body, intake manifold or vacuum hoses (see Section 8).

11   Engine stalls

1   Idle speed incorrect. Refer to the VECI label and Chapter 1.
2   Fuel filter clogged and/or water and impurities in the fuel system (Chapter 1).
3   Distributor components damp or damaged (Chapter 5).
4   Fault in the fuel system or sensors (Chapters 4 and 6).
5   Faulty emissions system components (Chapter 6).
6   Faulty or incorrectly gapped spark plugs (Chapter 1). Also check the spark plug wires (Chapter 1).
7   Vacuum leaks at the carburetor/fuel injection unit(s), intake manifold or vacuum hoses (see Section 8).

12   Engine lacks power

1   Incorrect ignition timing (Chapter 1).
2   Fault in the fuel or electrical systems (Chapters 4 and 5).
3   Excessive play in the distributor shaft. At the same time, check for a damaged rotor, faulty distributor cap, wires, etc. (Chapters 1 and 5).
4   Faulty or incorrectly gapped spark plugs (Chapter 1).
5   Carburetor not adjusted properly or excessively worn (Chapter 4).
6   Faulty coil (Chapter 5).
7   Brakes binding (Chapter 1).
8   Automatic transaxle fluid level incorrect (Chapter 1).
9   Clutch slipping (Chapter 8).
10   Fuel filter clogged and/or impurities in the fuel system (Chapter 1).
11   Emissions control system not functioning properly (Chapter 6).
12   Use of substandard fuel. Fill the tank with the proper octane fuel.
13   Low or uneven cylinder compression pressures. Test with a compression tester, which will detect leaking valves and/or a blown head gasket (Chapter 2).

13   Engine backfires

1   Emissions system not functioning properly (Chapter 6).
2   Fault in the fuel or electrical systems (Chapters 4 and 5).
3   Ignition timing incorrect (Chapter 1).
4   Faulty secondary ignition system (cracked spark plug insulator, faulty plug wires, distributor cap and/or rotor) (Chapters 1 and 5).
5   Carburetor in need of adjustment or worn excessively (Chapter 4).
6   Vacuum leaks at the carburetor/throttle body, intake manifold or vacuum hoses (see Section 8).
7   Valves sticking (Chapter 2).

14   Pinging or knocking engine sounds during acceleration or uphill

1   Incorrect grade of fuel. Fill the tank with fuel of the proper octane rating.
2   Fault in the fuel or electrical systems (Chapters 4 and 5).
3   Ignition timing incorrect (Chapter 1).
4   Carburetor in need of adjustment (Chapter 4).
5   Improper spark plugs. Check the plug type against the VECI label located in the engine compartment. Also check the plugs and wires for damage (Chapter 1).
6   Worn or damaged distributor components (Chapter 5).
7   Faulty emissions system (Chapter 6).
8   Vacuum leak. Check as described in Section 9.

15   Engine diesels (continues to run) after switching off

1   Idle speed too high. Refer to Chapter 1.
2   Fault in the fuel or electrical systems (Chapters 4 and 5).
3   Ignition timing incorrectly adjusted (Chapter 1).
4   Thermo-controlled air cleaner heat valve not operating properly (Chapters 1 and 6).
5   Excessive engine operating temperature. Probable causes of this are a malfunctioning thermostat, clogged radiator, faulty water pump (Chapter 3).
Engine electrical system

16   Battery will not hold a charge

1   Alternator drivebelt defective or not adjusted properly (Chapter 1).
2   Electrolyte level low or battery discharged (Chapter 1).
3   Battery terminals loose or corroded (Chapter 1).
4   Alternator not charging properly (Chapter 5).
5   Loose, broken or faulty wiring in the charging circuit (Chapter 5).
6   Short in the vehicle wiring causing a continual drain on battery (refer to Chapter 12 and the Wiring Diagrams).
7   Battery defective internally.

17   Ignition light fails to go out

1   Fault in the alternator or charging circuit (Chapter 5).
2   Alternator drivebelt defective or not properly adjusted (Chapter 1).

18   Ignition light fails to come on when key is turned on

1   Instrument cluster warning light bulb defective (Chapter 12).
2   Alternator faulty (Chapter 5).
3   Fault in the instrument cluster printed circuit, dashboard wiring or bulb holder (Chapter 12).
Fuel system

19   Excessive fuel consumption

1   Dirty or clogged air filter element (Chapter 1).
2   Incorrectly set ignition timing (Chapter 1).
3   Choke sticking or improperly adjusted (Chapter 1).
4   Emissions system not functioning properly (Chapter 6).
5   Fault in the fuel or electrical systems (Chapters 4 and 5).
6   Carburetor internal parts excessively worn or damaged (Chapter 4).
7   Low tire pressure or incorrect tire size (Chapter 1).

20   Fuel leakage and/or fuel odor

1   Leak in a fuel feed or vent line (Chapter 4).
2   Tank overfilled. Fill only to automatic shut-off.
3   Evaporative emissions system canister clogged (Chapter 6).
4   Vapor leaks from system lines (Chapter 4).
5   Carburetor internal parts excessively worn or out of adjustment (Chapter 4).

Cooling system

21   Overheating

1   Insufficient coolant in the system (Chapter 1).
2   Water pump drivebelt defective or not adjusted properly (Chapter 1).

3   Radiator core blocked or radiator grille dirty and restricted (Chapter 3).
4   Thermostat faulty (Chapter 3).
5   Fan blades broken or cracked (Chapter 3).
6   Radiator cap not maintaining proper pressure. Have the cap pressure tested by gas station or repair shop.
7   Ignition timing incorrect (Chapter 1).

22   Overcooling

Thermostat faulty (Chapter 3).

23   External coolant leakage

1   Deteriorated or damaged hoses or loose clamps. Replace hoses and/or tighten the clamps at the hose connections (Chapter 1).
2   Water pump seals defective. If this is the case, water will drip from the weep hole in the water pump body (Chapter 3).
3   Leakage from radiator core or header tank. This will require the radiator to be professionally repaired (see Chapter 3 for removal procedures).
4   Engine drain plug leaking (Chapter 1) or water jacket core plugs leaking (see Chapter 2).

24   Internal coolant leakage

Note: *Internal coolant leaks can usually be detected by examining the oil. Check the dipstick and inside of the cylinder head cover for water deposits and an oil consistency like that of a milkshake.*
1   Leaking cylinder head gasket. Have the cooling system pressure tested.
2   Cracked cylinder bore or cylinder head. Dismantle the engine and inspect (Chapter 2).

25   Coolant loss

1   Too much coolant in the system (Chapter 1).
2   Coolant boiling away due to overheating (see Section 15).
3   External or internal leakage (see Sections 23 and 24).
4   Faulty radiator cap. Have the cap pressure tested.

26   Poor coolant circulation

1   Inoperative water pump. A quick test is to pinch the top radiator hose closed with your hand while the engine is idling, then let it loose. You should feel the surge of coolant if the pump is working properly (Chapter 1).
2   Restriction in the cooling system. Drain, flush and refill the system (Chapter 1). If necessary, remove the radiator (Chapter 3) and have it reverse flushed.
3   Water pump drivebelt defective or not adjusted properly (Chapter 1).
4   Thermostat sticking (Chapter 3).

Clutch

27   Fails to release (pedal pressed to the floor - shift lever does not move freely in and out of Reverse)

1   On cable-operated models, worn or stretched cable. On later hydraulically operated models, low hydraulic fluid level (Chapter 1) or leaking seal in the master cylinder or release cylinder (Chapter 8).
2   Clutch plate warped or damaged (Chapter 8).
3   Worn or dry clutch release shaft bushing (Chapter 8).

28   Clutch slips (engine speed increases with no increase in vehicle speed)

1   Linkage out of adjustment (Chapter 8).
2   Clutch plate oil soaked or lining worn. Remove clutch (Chapter 8) and inspect.
3   Clutch plate not seated. It may take 30 or 40 normal starts for a new one to seat.

29   Grabbing (chattering) as clutch is engaged

1   Oil on clutch plate lining. Remove (Chapter 8) and inspect. Correct any leakage source.
2   Worn or loose engine or transaxle mounts. These units move slightly when the clutch is released. Inspect the mounts and bolts (Chapter 2).
3   Worn splines on clutch plate hub. Remove the clutch components (Chapter 8) and inspect.
4   Warped pressure plate or flywheel. Remove the clutch components and inspect.

30   Squeal or rumble with clutch fully disengaged (pedal depressed)

1   Worn, defective or broken release bearing (Chapter 8).
2   Worn or broken pressure plate springs (or diaphragm fingers) (Chapter 8).

31   Clutch pedal stays on floor when disengaged

Linkage or release bearing binding. Inspect the linkage or remove the clutch components as necessary.

Manual transaxle

32   Noisy in Neutral with engine running

1   Input shaft bearing worn.
2   Damaged main drive gear bearing.
3   Worn countershaft bearings.
4   Worn or damaged countershaft end play shims.

33   Noisy in all gears

1   Any of the above causes, and/or:
2   Insufficient lubricant (see the checking procedures in Chapter 1).

34   Noisy in one particular gear

1   Worn, damaged or chipped gear teeth for that particular gear.
2   Worn or damaged synchronizer for that particular gear.

35   Slips out of high gear

1   Transaxle loose on clutch housing (Chapter 7).
2   Shift rods (1986 through 1989 models) or shift cables (1990 and later models) interfering with the engine mounts or clutch lever (Chapter 7).
3   Shift rods or cables not working freely (Chapter 7).
4   Dirt between the transaxle case and engine or misalignment of the transaxle (Chapter 7).
5   Worn or improperly adjusted linkage (Chapter 7).

36 Difficulty in engaging gears

1 Clutch not releasing completely (see clutch adjustment in Chapter 1).
2 Loose, damaged or out-of-adjustment shift linkage. Make a thorough inspection, replacing parts as necessary (Chapter 7).

37 Oil leakage

1 Excessive amount of lubricant in the transaxle (see Chapter 1 for correct checking procedures). Drain lubricant as required.
2 Driveaxle oil seal or speedometer oil seal in need of replacement (Chapter 7).

Automatic transaxle

Note: *Due to the complexity of the automatic transaxle, it's difficult for the home mechanic to properly diagnose and service this component. For problems other than the following, the vehicle should be taken to a dealer service department or a transmission shop.*

38 General shift mechanism problems

1 Chapter 7 deals with checking and adjusting the shift linkage on automatic transaxles. Common problems which may be attributed to poorly adjusted linkage are:
 Engine starting in gears other than Park or Neutral.
 Indicator on shifter pointing to a gear other than the one actually being selected.
 Vehicle moves when in Park.
2 Refer to Chapter 7 to adjust the linkage.

39 Transaxle will not downshift with accelerator pedal pressed to the floor

 Chapter 7 deals with adjusting the throttle cable to enable the transaxle to downshift properly.

40 Transaxle slips, shifts rough, is noisy or has no drive in forward or reverse gears

1 There are many probable causes for the above problems, but the home mechanic should be concerned with only one possibility — fluid level.
2 Before taking the vehicle to a repair shop, check the level and condition of the fluid as described in Chapter 1. Correct fluid level as necessary or change the fluid and filter if needed. If the problem persists, have a professional diagnose the probable cause.

41 Fluid leakage

1 Automatic transaxle fluid is a deep red color. Fluid leaks should not be confused with engine oil, which can easily be blown by air flow to the transaxle.
2 To pinpoint a leak, first remove all built-up dirt and grime from around the transaxle. Degreasing agents and/or steam cleaning will achieve this. With the underside clean, drive the vehicle at low speeds so air flow will not blow the leak far from its source. Raise the vehicle and determine where the leak is coming from. Common areas of leakage are:
 a) Pan: Tighten the mounting bolts and/or replace the pan gasket as necessary (see Chapter 7).
 b) Filler pipe: Replace the rubber seal where the pipe enters the transaxle case.
 c) Transaxle oil lines: Tighten the connectors where the lines enter the transaxle case and/or replace the lines.
 d) Vent pipe: Transaxle overfilled and/or water in fluid (see checking procedures, Chapter 1).
 e) Speedometer connector: Replace the O-ring where the speedometer cable enters the transaxle case (Chapter 7).

Driveaxles

42 Clicking noise in turns

 Worn or damaged outer joint. Check for cut or damaged seals. Repair as necessary (Chapter 8).

43 Knock or clunk when accelerating after coasting

 Worn or damaged inner joint. Check for cut or damaged seals. Repair as necessary (Chapter 8)

44 Shudder or vibration during acceleration

1 Excessive joint angle. Have checked and correct as necessary (Chapter 8).
2 Worn or damaged CV joints. Repair or replace as necessary (Chapter 8).
3 Sticking CV joint assembly. Correct or replace as necessary (Chapter 8).

Rear axle

45 Noise

1 Road noise. No corrective procedures available.
2 Tire noise. Inspect tires and check tire pressures (Chapter 1).
3 Rear wheel bearings loose, worn or damaged (Chapter 1).

Brakes

Note: *Before assuming that a brake problem exists, make sure that the tires are in good condition and inflated properly (see Chapter 1), that the front end alignment is correct and that the vehicle is not loaded with weight in an unequal manner.*

46 Vehicle pulls to one side during braking

1 Defective, damaged or oil contaminated disc brake pads on one side. Inspect as described in Chapter 9.
2 Excessive wear of brake pad material or disc on one side. Inspect and correct as necessary.
3 Loose or disconnected front suspension components. Inspect and tighten all bolts to the specified torque (Chapter 10).
4 Defective caliper assembly. Remove the caliper and inspect for a stuck piston or other damage (Chapter 9).

47 Noise (high-pitched squeal with the brakes applied)

 Disc brake pads worn out. The noise comes from the wear sensor rubbing against the disc (does not apply to all vehicles) or the actual pad backing plate itself if the material is completely worn away. Replace the pads with new ones immediately (Chapter 9). If the pad material has worn completely away, the brake discs should be inspected for damage as described in Chapter 9.

48 Excessive brake pedal travel

1   Partial brake system failure. Inspect the entire system (Chapter 9) and correct as required.
2   Insufficient fluid in the master cylinder. Check (Chapter 1), add fluid and bleed the system if necessary (Chapter 9).
3   Rear brakes not adjusting properly. Make a series of starts and stops while the vehicle is in Reverse. If this does not correct the situation, remove the drums and inspect the self-adjusters (Chapter 9).

49 Brake pedal feels spongy when depressed

1   Air in the hydraulic lines. Bleed the brake system (Chapter 9).
2   Faulty flexible hoses. Inspect all system hoses and lines. Replace parts as necessary.
3   Master cylinder mounting bolts/nuts loose.
4   Master cylinder defective (Chapter 9).

50 Excessive effort required to stop vehicle

1   Power brake booster not operating properly (Chapter 9).
2   Excessively worn linings or pads. Inspect and replace if necessary (Chapter 9).
3   One or more caliper pistons or wheel cylinders seized or sticking. Inspect and rebuild as required (Chapter 9).
4   Brake linings or pads contaminated with oil or grease. Inspect and replace as required (Chapter 9).
5   New pads or shoes installed and not yet seated. It will take a while for the new material to seat against the drum (or rotor).

51 Pedal travels to the floor with little resistance

Little or no fluid in the master cylinder reservoir caused by leaking wheel cylinder(s), leaking caliper piston(s), loose, damaged or disconnected brake lines. Inspect the entire system and correct as necessary.

52 Brake pedal pulsates during brake application

1   Caliper improperly installed. Remove and inspect (Chapter 9).
2   Disc or drum defective. Remove (Chapter 9) and check for excessive lateral runout and parallelism. Have the disc or drum resurfaced or replace it with a new one.

Suspension and steering systems

53 Vehicle pulls to one side

1   Tire pressures uneven (Chapter 1).
2   Defective tire (Chapter 1).
3   Excessive wear in suspension or steering components (Chapter 10).
4   Front end in need of alignment.
5   Front brakes dragging. Inspect the brakes as described in Chapter 9.

54 Shimmy, shake or vibration

1   Tire or wheel out-of-balance or out-of-round. Have professionally balanced.

2   Loose, worn or out-of-adjustment rear wheel bearings (Chapter 1).
3   Shock absorbers and/or suspension components worn or damaged (Chapter 10).

55 Excessive pitching and/or rolling around corners or during braking

1   Defective shock absorbers. Replace as a set (Chapter 10).
2   Broken or weak springs and/or suspension components. Inspect as described in Chapter 10.

56 Excessively stiff steering

1   Lack of fluid in power steering fluid reservoir (Chapter 1).
2   Incorrect tire pressures (Chapter 1).
3   Front end out of alignment.

57 Excessive play in steering

1   Excessive wear in suspension or steering components (Chapter 10).
2   Steering gearbox damaged (Chapter 10).

58 Lack of power assistance

1   Steering pump drivebelt faulty or not adjusted properly (Chapter 1).
2   Fluid level low (Chapter 1).
3   Hoses or lines restricted. Inspect and replace parts as necessary.
4   Air in power steering system. Bleed the system (Chapter 10).

59 Excessive tire wear (not specific to one area)

1   Incorrect tire pressures (Chapter 1).
2   Tires out-of-balance. Have professionally balanced.
3   Wheels damaged. Inspect and replace as necessary.
4   Suspension or steering components excessively worn (Chapter 10).

60 Excessive tire wear on outside edge

1   Inflation pressures incorrect (Chapter 1).
2   Excessive speed in turns.
3   Front end alignment incorrect (excessive toe-in). Have professionally aligned.
4   Suspension arm bent or twisted (Chapter 10).

61 Excessive tire wear on inside edge

1   Inflation pressures incorrect (Chapter 1).
2   Front end alignment incorrect. Have professionally aligned.
3   Loose or damaged steering components (Chapter 10).

62 Tire tread worn in one place

1   Tires out-of-balance.
2   Damaged or buckled wheel. Inspect and replace if necessary.
3   Defective tire (Chapter 1).

Chapter 1 Tune-up and routine maintenance

Contents

1

Specifications

Recommended lubricants and fluids

Engine oil
Type .API grade SF or SF/CC multigrade and fuel efficient oil
Viscosity .... See accompanying chart
Capacity .... 3.59 qts (3.4 liters)
Fuel .... Unleaded gasoline, 87 octane or higher
Automatic transaxle fluid
Type .... Dexron II automatic transmission fluid
Capacity
1989 and earlier .... 6.0 qts (5.71 liters)
1990 on .... 6.4 qts (6.11 liters)

Anticipated atmospheric temperature range		SAE viscosity No.
°C	°F	
49	120	
38	100	20W
27	80	20 / 10W
16	60	40 / 50 / 30
		40
		50
0	32	5W *20
−12	10	30
−23	−10	40
−29	−20	

ENGINE OIL VISCOSITY CHART

Manual transaxle oil
  Type .... API GL-5 SAE 75/85W gear oil
  Capacity
    1989 and earlier .... 2.2 qts (2 liters)
    1990 on .... 1.9 qts (1.8 liters)
Brake and clutch fluid type.. DOT 3 brake fluid
Power steering system fluid .... Dexron II automatic transmission fluid
Rear wheel bearing grease .... NLGI No. 2 EP wheel bearing grease

Ignition system

Spark plug type and gap .... Champion RN9YC4 (.039-.043 in)
Ignition timing .... Refer to the *Emission Control Information* label in the engine compartment
Firing order 1 3 4 2

Cooling system

Coolant capacity... 6 qts (5 liters)
Thermostat rating
  Starts to open.. 190-degrees F (88-degrees C)
  Fully open .... 212-degrees F (100-degrees C)

Drivebelt deflection .... 1/4 to 3/8 in (7 to 9 mm)

Clutch

Cable-operated models
  Clutch pedal free play .... 1 in (25 mm)
  Adjusting nut-to-insulator clearance......................... 1/4 in (6.3 mm)
Hydraulically operated models
  Clutch pedal clevis pin free play .... 0.04 to 0.12 in (1 to 3 mm)

Brakes

Disc brake pad lining thickness (minimum) .... 1/8 in (3.175 mm)
Drum brake shoe lining thickness (minimum)................. 1/8 in (3.175 mm)
Steering and suspension
Steering wheel free play limit..................................... 1 in (26 mm)

Valve clearances (engine hot)

Intake valve.. 0.006 in (0.15 mm)
Exhaust valve... 0.010 in (0.25 mm)
Jet valve... 0.010 in (0.25 mm)

Firing order 1 - 3 - 4 - 2

Cylinder location and distributor rotation

Torque specifications

	Ft-lbs	Nm
Automatic transaxle		
Pan bolts	8	12
Filter bolts	5	7
Drain plug	25	35
Manual transaxle drain and filler plugs.............	25	35
Engine oil pan drain plug................................	33	44
Fuel filter eye bolt (fuel-injected models)...........	18 to 25	25 to 35
Rocker arm cover bolts...................................	1.4	2.0
Spark plugs...	15 to 21	20 to 30
Wheel lug nuts		
Steel wheel	50 to 57	67 to 77
Aluminum wheel	65 to 72	88 to 97
Rear wheel bearing spindle nut		
Castellated nut		
Step 1	15	
Step 2	loosen to 0	
Step 3	4	
Self-locking nut	108-145	

1   Introduction

This Chapter is designed to help the home mechanic maintain the Hyundai Excel with the goals of maximum performance, economy, safety and reliability in mind.

Included is a master maintenance schedule, followed by procedures dealing specifically with each item on the schedule. Visual checks, adjustments, component replacement and other helpful items are included. Refer to the accompanying illustrations of the engine compartment and the underside of the vehicle for the locations of various components.

Adhering to the mileage/time maintenance schedule and following the step-by-step procedures, which is simply a preventive maintenance program, will result in maximum reliability and vehicle service life. Keep in mind that it is a comprehensive program — maintaining some items but not others at the specified intervals will not produce the same results.

As you service the vehicle, you will discover that many of the procedures can — and should — be grouped together because of the nature of the particular procedure you're performing or because of the close proximity of two otherwise unrelated components to one another.

For example, if the vehicle is raised for chassis lubrication, you should inspect the exhaust, suspension, steering and fuel systems while you're under the vehicle. When you're rotating the tires, it makes good sense to check the brakes, since the wheels are already removed. Finally, let's suppose you have to borrow or rent a torque wrench. Even if you only need it to tighten the spark plugs, you might as well check the torque of as many critical fasteners as time allows.

The first step in this maintenance program is to prepare yourself before the actual work begins. Read through all the procedures you're planning to do, then gather up all the parts and tools needed. If it looks like you might run into problems during a particular job, seek advice from a mechanic or an experienced do-it-yourselfer.

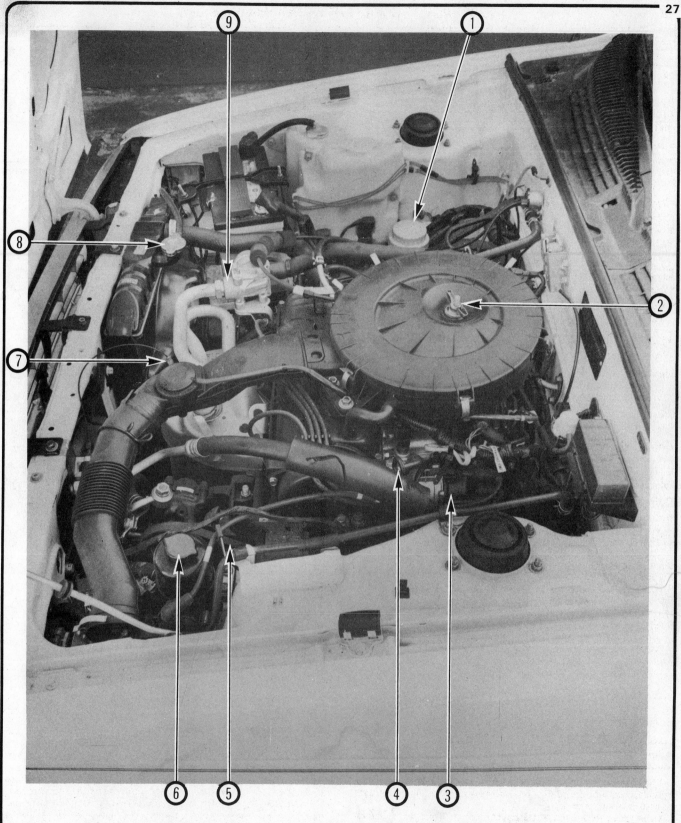

Engine compartment (viewed from the left side) checking points

1 Brake master cylinder
  fluid reservoir
2 Air cleaner
3 Distributor
4 Engine oil dipstick
5 Engine drivebelt

6 Power steering fluid reservoir
7 Oxygen sensor
8 Radiator cap
9 Automatic transaxle dipstick
  (under battery mount)

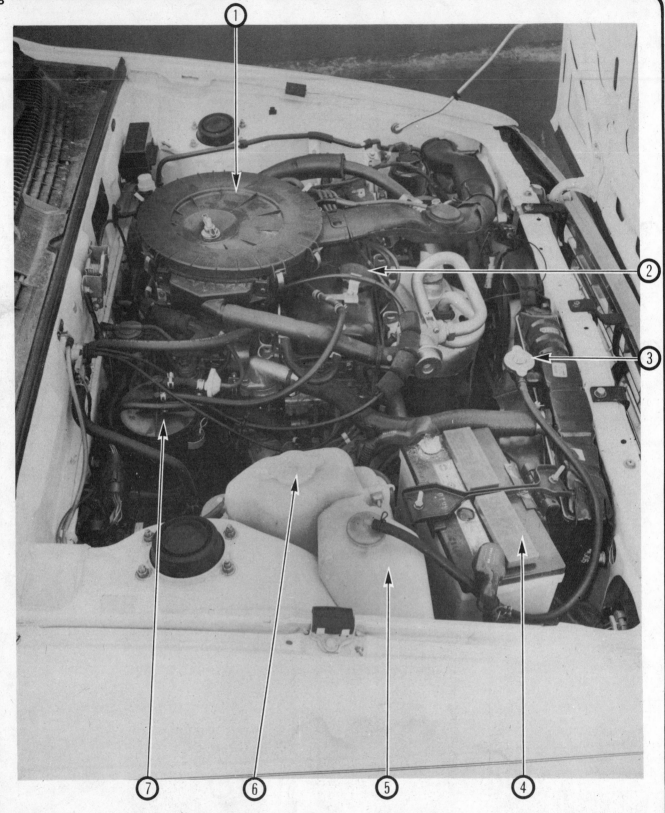

Engine compartment (viewed from the right side) checking points

1 Air cleaner
2 Engine oil filler cap
3 Radiator cap
4 Battery
5 Engine coolant reservoir
6 Windshield washer
   fluid reservoir
7 Evaporative emissions
   canister

1

Typical engine compartment under side components

1 Tie-rod boot
2 Suspension balljoint boot
3 Automatic transaxle drain plug
4 Automatic transaxle fluid pan
5 Engine oil drain plug
6 Brake caliper
7 Driveaxle boot
8 Steering gear boot
9 Exhaust pipe

Typical rear under side components

1 Parking brake cable
2 Brake hose (located above the suspension trailing arm, which hides it in this illustration)
3 Fuel tank filler hose
4 Fuel tank
5 Tank drain plug
6 Muffler
7 Drum Brake
8 Exhaust Pipe

2 Hyundai Excel Maintenance schedule

The following maintenance intervals are based on the assumption that the vehicle owner will be doing the maintenance or service work, as opposed to having a dealer service department do the work. Although the time/mileage intervals are loosely based on factory recommendations, most have been shortened to ensure, for example, that such items as filters, lubricants and fluids are checked/changed at intervals that promote maximum engine/driveline service life. Also, subject to the preference of the individual owner interested in keeping his or her vehicle in peak condition at all times, and with the vehicle's ultimate resale in mind, many of the maintenance procedures may be performed more often than recommended in the following schedule. We encourage such owner initiative.

When the vehicle is new it should be serviced initially by a factory authorized dealer service department to protect the factory warranty. In many cases the initial maintenance check is done at no cost to the owner (check with your dealer service department for more information).

Every 250 miles or weekly, whichever comes first

Check the engine oil level (Section 4)
Check the engine coolant level (Section 4)
Check the windshield washer fluid level (Section 4)
Check the water (electrolyte) in the battery (Section 4)
Check the brake fluid level (Section 4)
Check the tires and tire pressures (Section 5)

Every 3500 miles or 3 months, whichever comes first

All items listed above plus . . .
Check the power steering fluid level (Section 6)
Check the automatic transaxle fluid level (Section 7)
Change the engine oil and oil filter (Section 8)

Every 7500 miles or 6 months, whichever comes first

Inspect/replace the windshield wiper blades (Section 9)
Check/adjust the clutch pedal free play (Section 10)
Check and service the battery (Section 11)
Check/adjust the engine drivebelts (Section 12)
Inspect/replace all underhood hoses (Section 13)
Check the cooling system (Section 14)
Rotate the tires (Section 15)
Inspect the brakes (Section 16)

Every 15,000 miles or 12 months, whichever comes first

All items listed above plus . . .
Check/replace the air and PCV filters (Section 17)
Check the throttle positioner sensor system (Section 18)

Check/adjust the valve clearances (Section 19)
Check/adjust the engine idle speed (Section 20)
Replace the fuel filter (Section 21)
Inspect the fuel system (Section 22)
Inspect the steering and suspension
  components (Section 23)*
Check the driveaxle boots (Section 24)*
Inspect the exhaust system (Section 25)
Check the manual transaxle lubricant level (Section 26)

Every 30,000 miles or 24 months, whichever comes first

Check/replace the spark plugs (Section 27)
Inspect/replace the spark plug wires, distributor cap and
  rotor (Section 28)*
Check the carburetor choke (Section 29)
Check the thermostatically controlled air cleaner (Section 30)
Replace the drivebelts for the water pump and
  alternator (Section 12)
Drain, flush and refill the cooling system (Section 31)
Check/repack the rear wheel bearings (Section 32)
Drain the brake system and refill it with new fluid (Section 33)
If the vehicle is equipped with an automatic transaxle, change
  the fluid and filter (Section 34)**
If the vehicle is equipped with a manual transaxle, drain and refill
  it with new lubricant (Section 35)

Every 50,000 miles or 40 months, whichever comes first

Inspect the evaporative emissions control system and
  replace the canister (Section 36)
Check/adjust the ignition timing (Section 37)
Check/replace the PCV valve (Section 38)
Replace the oxygen sensor (Section 39)

Every 60,000 miles or 48 months, whichever comes first

Install a new timing belt (Chapter 2)

This item is affected by "severe" operating conditions as described below. If the vehicle in question is operated under "severe" conditions, perform all maintenance indicated with an asterisk (*) at 7500 mile/6 month intervals.

  Consider the conditions "severe" if most driving is done . . .
    In dusty areas
    When towing a trailer
    At low speeds or with extended periods of engine idling
    When outside temperatures remain below freezing and most
      trips are less than four miles

** *If most driving is done under one or more of the following conditions, change the automatic transaxle fluid every 15,000 miles:*
  In heavy city traffic where the outside temperature regularly
    reaches 90ºF (32ºC) or higher
  In hilly or mountainous terrain
  Frequent trailer pulling

1

3 Tune-up general information

The term *tune-up* is used in this manual to represent a combination of individual operations rather than one specific procedure.

If, from the time the vehicle is new, the routine maintenance schedule is followed closely and frequent checks are made of fluid levels and high wear items, as suggested throughout this manual, the engine will be kept in relatively good running condition and the need for additional work will be minimized.

More likely than not, however, there will be times when the engine is running poorly due to lack of regular maintenance. This is even more likely if a used vehicle, which has not received regular and frequent maintenance checks, is purchased. In such cases, an engine tune-up will be needed outside of the regular routine maintenance intervals.

The first step in any tune-up or diagnostic procedure to help correct a poor running engine is a cylinder compression check (see Chapter 2). This check will help determine the condition of internal engine components and should be used as a guide for tune-up and repair procedures. For instance, if a compression check indicates serious internal engine wear, a conventional tune-up will not improve the performance of the engine and would be a waste of time and money. Because of its importance, the compression check should be done by someone with the right equipment and the knowledge to use it properly.

The following procedures are those most often needed to bring a generally poor running engine back into a proper state of tune.

Minor tune-up

Clean, inspect and test the battery (Section 11)
Check all engine related fluids (Section 4)
Check and adjust the drivebelts (Section 12)
Replace the spark plugs (Section 27)
Inspect the distributor cap and rotor (Section 28)
Inspect the spark plug and coil wires (Section 28)
Check and adjust the idle speed (Section 20)
Check the PCV valve (Section 38)
Check the air filter (Section 17)
Check the cooling system (Section 14)
Check all underhood hoses (Section 13)

Major tune-up

All items listed under Minor tune-up, plus . . .
Check the EGR system (Chapter 6)
Check the ignition system (Chapter 5)
Check the charging system (Chapter 5)
Check the fuel system (Chapter 4)
Replace the air filter (Section 17)
Replace the distributor cap and rotor (Section 28)
Replace the spark plug wires (Section 28)

4 Fluid level checks

Note: *The following fluid level checks should be done on a 250 mile or weekly basis. Additional fluid level checks can be found in specific maintenance procedures which follow. Regardless of intervals, be alert for fluid leaks under the vehicle which would indicate a leak to be fixed immediately.*

Warning: *The electric cooling fan can activate at any time, even when the ignition is in the Off position. Disconnect the fan motor or negative battery cable when working in the vicinity of the fan.*

1   Fluids are an essential part of the lubrication, cooling, brake and windshield washer systems. Because the fluids gradually become depleted and/or contaminated during normal operation of the vehicle, they must be periodically replenished. See *Recommended lubricants and fluids* at the beginning of this Chapter before adding fluid to any of the following components. **Note:** *The vehicle must be on level ground when fluid levels are checked.*

Engine oil

Refer to illustrations 4.2, 4.4 and 4.6

2   The engine oil level is checked with a dipstick located at the front (drivebelt) end of the engine **(see illustration)**. It extends through a tube

4.2   The engine oil dipstick is located at the drivebelt end of the engine and is retained by an anti-rattle clip

4.4   The oil level should be between the MIN and MAX marks — if it isn't, add enough oil to bring the level to or near the MAX mark (it takes one full quart to raise the level from the MIN to the MAX mark)

and into the oil pan at the bottom of the engine.

3   The oil level should be checked before the vehicle has been driven, or about 15 minutes after the engine has been shut off. If the oil is checked immediately after driving the vehicle, some of the oil will remain in the upper engine components, resulting in an inaccurate reading on the dipstick.

4   Pull the dipstick out and wipe all the oil off the end with a clean rag or paper towel. Insert the clean dipstick all the way back into the tube, then pull it out again. Note the oil at the end of the dipstick. Add oil as necessary to keep the level between the MIN mark and the MAX mark on the dipstick **(see illustration)**.

5   Don't overfill the engine by adding too much oil, since it may result in oil fouled spark plugs, oil leaks or oil seal failures.

6   Oil is added to the engine after removing the cap from the rocker arm cover **(see illustration)**. An oil can spout or funnel may help to reduce spills.

7   Checking the oil level is an important preventive maintenance step. A consistently low oil level indicates oil leakage through damaged seals, defective gaskets or past worn rings or valve guides. If the oil looks milky in color or has water droplets in it, the cylinder head gasket may be blown or the head or block may be cracked. The engine should be checked immediately. The condition of the oil should also be noted. Whenever you check the oil level, slide your thumb and index finger up the dipstick before wiping off the oil. If you see small dirt or metal particles clinging to the dipstick, the oil should be changed (Section 8).

hose into the reservoir. As the engine cools, the coolant is automatically drawn back into the cooling system to maintain the correct level.

9   The coolant level in the reservoir should be checked regularly. **Warning:** *Do not remove the radiator cap to check the coolant level when the engine is warm.* The level in the reservoir varies with the temperature of the engine. When the engine is cold, the coolant level should be at or slightly above the LOW mark on the reservoir **(see illustration 4.8)**. Once the engine has warmed up, the level should be at or near the FULL mark. If it isn't, allow the engine to cool, then remove the cap from the reservoir and add a 50/50 mixture of ethylene glycol-based antifreeze and water.

10   Drive the vehicle and recheck the coolant level. If only a small amount of coolant is required to bring the system up to the proper level, water can be used. However, repeated additions of water will dilute the antifreeze and water solution. In order to maintain the proper ratio of antifreeze and water, always top up the coolant level with the correct mixture. An empty plastic milk jug or bleach bottle makes an excellent container for mixing coolant. Do not use rust inhibitors or additives.

11   If the coolant level drops consistently, there may be a leak in the system. Inspect the radiator, hoses, filler cap, drain plugs and water pump (see Section 14). If no leaks are noted, have the radiator cap pressure tested by a service station.

12   If you have to remove the radiator cap, wait until the engine has cooled, then wrap a thick cloth around the cap and turn it to the first stop. If coolant or steam escapes, let the engine cool down longer, then remove the cap.

13   Check the condition of the coolant as well. It should be relatively clear. If it's brown or rust colored, the system should be drained, flushed and refilled. Even if the coolant appears to be normal, the corrosion inhibitors wear out, so it must be replaced at the specified intervals.

Windshield washer fluid
Refer to illustration 4.14

14   Fluid for the windshield washer system is located in a plastic reservoir in the engine compartment **(see illustration)**.

15   In milder climates, plain water can be used in the reservoir, but it should be kept no more than 2/3 full to allow for expansion if the water freezes. In colder climates, use windshield washer system antifreeze, available at any auto parts store, to lower the freezing point of the fluid. Mix the antifreeze with water in accordance with the manufacturer's directions on the container. **Caution:** *Don't use cooling system antifreeze — it will damage the vehicle's paint.*

16   To help prevent icing in cold weather, warm the windshield with the defroster before using the washer.

4.6   Rotate the oil filler cap half a turn to remove it — always make sure the area around the opening is clean before unscrewing the cap; this prevents dirt from contaminating the engine

4.8   Make sure the coolant level in the reservoir is between the LOW and FULL marks — if it's below the LOW mark, add a sufficient quantity of the prescribed mixture of antifreeze and water

Engine coolant
Refer to illustration 4.8

Warning: *Do not allow antifreeze to come in contact with your skin or painted surfaces of the vehicle. Flush contaminated areas immediately with plenty of water. Don't store new coolant or leave old coolant lying around where it's accessible to children or pets — they're attracted by its sweet taste. Ingestion of even a small amount of coolant can be fatal! Wipe up garage floor and drip pan coolant spills immediately. Keep antifreeze containers covered and repair leaks in your cooling system as soon as they are noted.*

8   All vehicles covered by this manual are equipped with a pressurized coolant recovery system. A white plastic coolant reservoir located near the battery in the engine compartment is connected by a hose to the radiator filler neck **(see illustration)**. If the engine overheats, coolant escapes through a valve in the radiator cap and travels through the

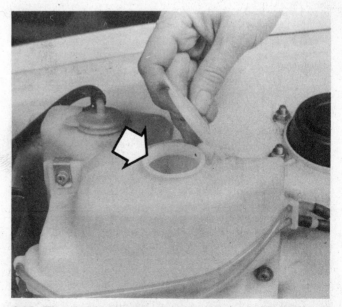

4.14   The windshield washer fluid reservoir (arrow) is located on the right side of the engine compartment, next to the coolant reservoir — be careful not to confuse these two reservoirs!

4.17   On conventional batteries, remove the cell caps to check the water level of the battery – if the level is too low, add distilled water only

4.19   The brake fluid level should be kept between the MAX and A marks (don't let it drop below B) on the translucent plastic reservoir – unscrew the cap to add fluid

Battery electrolyte
Refer to illustration 4.17

17   All vehicles with which this manual is concerned are equipped with a battery which is permanently sealed (except for vent holes) and has no filler caps. Water doesn't have to be added to these batteries at any time. If an aftermarket maintenance-type battery is installed, the caps on top of the battery should be removed periodically to check for a low water level **(see illustration)**. This check is most critical during the warm summer months.

Brake and clutch fluid
Refer to illustration 4.19

18   The brake master cylinder is mounted on the front of the power booster unit in the engine compartment. The smaller clutch master cylinder (later models) is normally located next to the brake master cylinder.
19   The fluid inside is readily visible. The level should be between the "A" MIN and MAX marks on the reservoir **(see illustration)**. If a low level is indicated, be sure to wipe the top of the reservoir cover with a clean rag to prevent contamination of the hydraulic system before removing the cover.
20   When adding fluid, pour it carefully into the reservoir to avoid spilling it onto surrounding painted surfaces. Be sure the specified fluid is used, since mixing different types of fluid can cause damage to the system. See *Recommended lubricants and fluids* at the front of this Chapter or your owner's manual. **Warning:** *Brake fluid can harm your eyes and damage painted surfaces, so use extreme caution when handling or pouring it. Do not use brake fluid that has been standing open or is more than one year old. Brake fluid absorbs moisture from the air. Excess moisture can cause a dangerous loss of braking effectiveness.*
21   At this time the fluid and master cylinder can be inspected for contamination. The system should be drained and refilled if deposits, dirt particles or water droplets are seen in the fluid (see Section 33 or Chapter 8).
22   After filling the reservoir to the proper level, make sure the cover is on tight to prevent fluid leakage.
23   The brake fluid level in the master cylinder will drop slightly as the pads and the brake shoes at each wheel wear down during normal operation. If the master cylinder requires repeated additions to keep it at the proper level, it's an indication of leakage in the brake system, which should be corrected immediately. Check all brake lines and connections (see Section 16 for more information).

24   The level in the clutch reservoir should remain relatively constant. If the level drops there's a leak (see Chapter 8).
25   If, upon checking the master cylinder fluid level, you discover the reservoir empty or nearly empty, the hydraulic system should be bled (Chapter 8 or 9).

5   Tire and tire pressure checks

Refer to illustrations 5.2, 5.3, 5.4a, 5.4b and 5.8
1   Periodic inspection of the tires may spare you the inconvenience of being stranded with a flat tire. It can also provide you with vital information regarding possible problems in the steering and suspension systems before major damage occurs.
2   The original tires on this vehicle are equipped with 1/2-inch side bands that will appear when tread depth reaches 1/16-inch, but they don't appear until the tires are worn out. Tread wear can be monitored with a simple, inexpensive device known as a tread depth indicator **(see illustration)**.
3   Note any abnormal tread wear **(see illustration)**. Tread pattern irregularities such as cupping, flat spots and more wear on one side

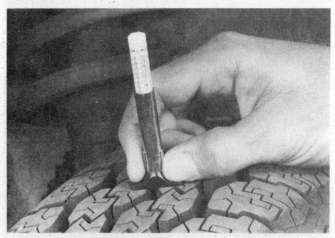

5.2   A tire thread depth indicator should be used to monitor tire wear – they are available at auto parts stores and service stations and cost very little

Condition	Probable cause	Corrective action	Condition	Probable cause	Corrective action
Shoulder wear	• Underinflation (both sides wear) • Incorrect wheel camber (one side wear) • Hard cornering • Lack of rotation	• Measure and adjust pressure. • Repair or replace axle and suspension parts. • Reduce speed. • Rotate tires.	Feathered edge **Toe wear**	• Incorrect toe	• Adjust toe-in.
Center wear	• Overinflation • Lack of rotation	• Measure and adjust pressure. • Rotate tires.	**Uneven wear**	• Incorrect camber or caster • Malfunctioning suspension • Unbalanced wheel • Out-of-round brake drum • Lack of rotation	• Repair or replace axle and suspension parts. • Repair or replace suspension parts. • Balance or replace. • Turn or replace. • Rotate tires.

5.3   This chart will help you determine the condition of your tires, the probable cause(s) of abnormal wear and the corrective action necessary

than the other are indications of front end alignment and/or balance problems. If any of these conditions are noted, take the vehicle to a tire shop or service station to correct the problem.

4   Look closely for cuts, punctures and embedded nails or tacks. Sometimes a tire will hold air pressure for a short time or leak down very slowly after a nail has embedded itself in the tread. If a slow leak persists, check the valve stem core to make sure it's tight (**see illustration**). Examine the tread for an object that may have embedded itself in the tire or for a ''plug'' that may have begun to leak (radial tire punctures are repaired with a plug that's installed in a puncture). If a puncture

is suspected, it can be easily verified by spraying a solution of soapy water onto the suspected area (**see illustration**). The soapy solution will bubble if there's a leak. Unless the puncture is unusually large, a tire shop or service station can usually repair the tire.

5   Carefully inspect the inner sidewall of each tire for evidence of brake fluid. If you see any, inspect the brakes immediately.

6   Correct air pressure adds miles to the lifespan of the tires, improves mileage and enhances overall ride quality. Tire pressure cannot be accurately estimated by looking at a tire, especially if it's a radial. A tire pressure gauge is essential. Keep an accurate gauge in the vehicle.

5.4a   If a tire loses air on a steady basis, check the valve core first to make sure it's snug (special inexpensive wrenches are commonly available at auto parts stores)

5.4b   If the valve core is tight, raise the corner of the vehicle with the low tire and spray a soapy water solution onto the tread as the tire is turned — slow leaks will cause small bubbles to appear

5.8   To extend the life of the tires, check the air pressure
at least once a week with an accurate gauge
(don't forget the spare!)

6.2   The power steering fluid filler cap/dipstick is located
on the left side of the engine compartment — unscrew the
cap to check the dipstick and/or add fluid

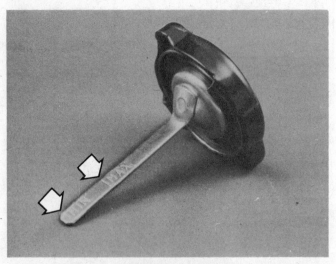

6.6   The power steering fluid level should be kept between
the MIN and MAX lines on the dipstick

The pressure gauges attached to the nozzles of air hoses at gas stations are often inaccurate.

7   Always check tire pressure when the tires are cold. Cold, in this case, means the vehicle has not been driven over a mile in the three hours preceding a tire pressure check. A pressure rise of four to eight pounds is not uncommon once the tires are warm.

8   Unscrew the valve cap protruding from the wheel or hubcap and push the gauge firmly onto the valve stem (see illustration). Note the reading on the gauge and compare the figure to the recommended tire pressure shown on the label attached to the inside of the glove compartment door. Be sure to reinstall the valve cap to keep dirt and moisture out of the valve stem mechanism. Check all four tires and, if necessary, add enough air to bring them up to the recommended pressure.

9   Don't forget to keep the spare tire inflated to the specified pressure (refer to your owner's manual or the tire sidewall).

6   Power steering fluid level check

Refer to illustrations 6.2 and 6.6

Warning: *The electric cooling fan can activate at any time, even when*

the ignition is in the Off position. Disconnect the fan motor or negative battery cable when working in the vicinity of the fan.

1   Unlike manual steering, the power steering system relies on fluid which may, over a period of time, require replenishing.

2   The fluid reservoir for the power steering pump is located on the inner fender panel near the front of the engine (see illustration).

3   For the check, the front wheels should be pointed straight ahead and the engine should be off.

4   Use a clean rag to wipe off the reservoir cap and the area around the cap. This will help prevent any foreign matter from entering the reservoir during the check.

5   Remove the cap and note the dipstick attached to it.

6   Wipe off the fluid with a clean rag, reinsert the dipstick, then withdraw it and read the fluid level. The level should be between the MIN and MAX marks (see illustration). Never allow the fluid level to drop below the MIN mark.

7   If additional fluid is required, pour the specified type directly into the reservoir, using a funnel to prevent spills.

8   If the reservoir requires frequent fluid additions, all power steering hoses, hose connections and the power steering pump should be carefully checked for leaks.

7   Automatic transaxle fluid level check

Refer to illustrations 7.4 and 7.6

Warning: *The electric cooling fan can activate at any time, even when the ignition is in the Off position. Disconnect the fan motor or negative battery cable when working in the vicinity of the fan.*

1   The level of the automatic transaxle fluid should be carefully maintained. Low fluid level can lead to slipping or loss of drive, while overfilling can cause foaming, loss of fluid and transaxle damage.

2   The transaxle fluid level should only be checked when the engine is at normal operating temperature. **Caution:** *If the vehicle has just been driven for a long time at high speed or in city traffic in hot weather, or if it has been pulling a trailer, an accurate fluid level reading cannot be obtained. Allow the fluid to cool down for about 30 minutes.*

3   Park on level ground, apply the parking brake and start the engine. While the engine is idling, depress the brake pedal and move the selector lever through all the gear ranges, beginning and ending in Park.

4   With the engine still idling, remove the dipstick (see illustration).

5   Wipe the fluid off the dipstick with a clean rag and reinsert it until the cap seats.

6   Pull the dipstick out again. The fluid level should be in the HOT

7.4 The automatic transmission dipstick (arrow) is located under the battery

7.6 Check the fluid with the transaxle at normal operating temperature — the level should be kept in the HOT range (between the two lines)

range **(see illustration)**. If the level is at the low side of the range, add the specified automatic transmission fluid through the dipstick tube with a funnel.

7   Add the fluid a little at a time and keep checking the level until it's correct.

8   The condition of the fluid should also be checked along with the level. If the fluid at the end of the dipstick is black or a dark reddish-brown color, or if it smells burned, the fluid should be changed (Section 33). If you're in doubt about the condition of the fluid, purchase some new fluid and compare the two for color and odor.

8 Engine oil and filter change

Refer to illustrations 8.3, 8.9, 8.14 and 8.18

1   Frequent oil changes are the most important preventive maintenance procedures that can be done by the home mechanic. As engine oil ages, it becomes diluted and contaminated, which leads to premature engine wear.

2   Although some sources recommend oil filter changes every other oil change, a new filter should be installed every time the oil is changed.

3   Gather together all necessary tools and materials before beginning this procedure **(see illustration)**.

4   You should have plenty of clean rags and newspapers handy to mop up any spills. Access to the underside of the vehicle is greatly improved if the vehicle can be lifted on a hoist, driven onto ramps or supported by jackstands. **Warning:** *Do not work under a vehicle which is supported only by a bumper, hydraulic or scissors-type jack.*

5   If this is your first oil change, get under the vehicle and familiarize yourself with the locations of the oil drain plug and the oil filter. The engine and exhaust components will be warm during the actual work, so note how they are situated to avoid touching them when working under the vehicle.

6   Warm the engine to normal operating temperature. If the new oil or any tools are needed, use this warm-up time to gather everything necessary for the job. Refer to *Recommended lubricants and fluids* at the beginning of this Chapter for the type of oil required.

7   With the engine oil warm (warm engine oil will drain better and more built-up sludge will be removed with it), raise and support the vehicle. Make sure it's safely supported!

8   Move all necessary tools, rags and newspapers under the vehicle. Set the drain pan under the drain plug. Keep in mind that the oil will initially flow from the pan with some force; position the pan accordingly.

9   Being careful not to touch any of the hot exhaust components,

8.3 These tools are required when changing the engine oil and filter

1 **Drain pan** — *It should be fairly shallow in depth, but wide in order to prevent spills*

2 **Rubber gloves** — *When removing the drain plug and filter it is inevitable that you will get oil on your hands (the gloves will prevent burns)*

3 **Breaker bar** — *Sometimes the oil drain plug is pretty tight and a long breaker bar is needed to loosen it*

4 **Socket** — *To be used with the breaker bar or a ratchet (must be the correct size to fit the drain plug)*

5 **Filter wrench** — *This is a metal band-type wrench, which requires clearance around the filter to be effective*

6 **Filter wrench** — *This type fits on the bottom of the filter and can be turned with a ratchet or breaker bar (different size wrenches are available for different types of filters)*

8.9   Use the proper size box-end wrench or six-point socket to remove the oil drain plug to avoid rounding it off

8.14   The oil filter is usually on very tight and will require a special wrench for removal — DO NOT use the wrench to tighten the new filter

use a wrench to remove the drain plug near the bottom of the oil pan (see illustration). Depending on how hot the oil is, you may want to wear gloves while unscrewing the plug the final few turns.

10   Allow the old oil to drain into the pan. It may be necessary to move the pan as the oil flow slows to a trickle.

11   After all the oil has drained, wipe off the drain plug with a clean rag. Small metal particles may cling to the plug and would immediately contaminate the new oil.

12   Clean the area around the drain plug opening and reinstall the plug. Tighten it securely with the wrench. If a torque wrench is available, use it to tighten the plug.

13   Move the drain pan into position under the oil filter.

14   Use the filter wrench to loosen the oil filter (see illustration). Chain or metal band filter wrenches may distort the filter canister, but it doesn't matter since the filter will be discarded anyway.

15   Completely unscrew the old filter. Be careful; it's full of oil. Empty the oil inside the filter into the drain pan.

16   Compare the old filter with the new one to make sure they're the same type.

17   Use a clean rag to remove all oil, dirt and sludge from the area where the oil filter mounts to the engine.

18   Apply a light coat of clean oil to the rubber gasket on the new oil filter (see illustration).

19   Attach the new filter to the engine, following the tightening directions printed on the filter canister or packing box. Most filter manufacturers recommend against using a wrench due to the possibility of over-tightening the filter and damaging the seal.

20   Remove all tools, rags, etc. from under the vehicle, being careful not to spill the oil in the drain pan, then lower the vehicle.

21   Move to the engine compartment and locate the oil filler cap.

22   Pour the fresh oil through the filler opening into the engine. A funnel should be used to prevent spills.

23   Pour four quarts of fresh oil into the engine. Wait a few minutes to allow the oil to drain into the pan, then check the level on the oil dipstick (see Section 4 if necessary). If the oil level is above the MIN mark, start the engine and allow the new oil to circulate.

24   Run the engine for only about a minute and then shut it off. Immediately look under the vehicle and check for leaks at the oil pan drain plug and around the oil filter. If either is leaking, tighten with a bit more force.

25   With the new oil circulated and the filter now completely full, recheck the level on the dipstick and add more oil as necessary.

26   During the first few trips after an oil change, make it a point to check frequently for leaks and proper oil level.

27   The old oil drained from the engine cannot be reused in its present state and should be disposed of. Oil reclamation centers, auto repair shops and gas stations will normally accept the oil, which can be refined and used again. After the oil has cooled it can be drained into a container (capped plastic jugs, topped bottles, milk cartons, etc.) for transport to a disposal site.

8.18   Lubricate the gasket with clean oil before installing the filter on the engine

9   Windshield wiper blade inspection and replacement

Refer to illustrations 9.5 and 9.6

1   The windshield wiper and blade assembly should be inspected periodically for damage, loose components and cracked or worn blade elements.

2   Road film can build up on the wiper blades and affect their efficiency, so they should be washed regularly with a mild detergent solution.

3   The action of the wiping mechanism can loosen bolts, nuts and fasteners, so they should be checked and tightened, as necessary, at the same time the wiper blades are checked.

4   If the wiper blade elements are cracked, worn or warped, or no longer clean adequately, they should be replaced with new ones.

5   Lift the arm assembly away from the glass for clearance, lift up on the release lever and detach the blade assembly from the arm (see illustration).

9.5   Lift up on the release lever and slide the blade assembly pin out of the arm

9.6   Use a small screwdriver to pry the lock up and over the end of the blade insert, then slide the insert out of the wiper arm, away from the lock

10.1   To check clutch pedal free play, measure the distance between the natural resting place of the pedal and the point at which you encounter resistance

6   Pry the metal lock on the end of the wiper arm up with a small screwdriver until it clears the metal tab on the end of the insert, then slide the insert away from the lock, out of the arm **(see illustration)**.
7   Slide the new insert into place until the hole in the end snaps over the tab.

10   Clutch pedal free play check and adjustment

Cable-operated models
Refer to illustrations 10.1 and 10.2
1   Push down on the clutch pedal and use a small steel ruler to measure the distance that it moves freely before the clutch resistance is felt **(see illustration)**. The freeplay should be within the specified limits. If it isn't, it must be adjusted.
2   Working within the engine compartment, turn the outer cable adjusting nut (located at the point where the cable enters the bulkhead) until the specific nut-to-insulator clearance is achieved **(see illustration)**.
3   Recheck the free play. Repeat the adjustment as necessary.

Hydraulically operated models
Refer to illustration 10.5
Caution: *When adjusting the clutch pedal clevis freeplay, be careful not to force the pushrod toward the master cylinder.*
4   Push down on the clutch pedal and use a small steel ruler to measure the distance that it moves freely before the clutch resistance is felt **(see illustration 10.1)**. The clevis pin free play should be within the specified limits. If it isn't, it must be adjusted.
5   Loosen the locknut and turn the master cylinder pushrod in either direction until clearance is achieved **(see illustration)**. Tighten the locknut. Repeat the adjustment if necessary.

10.2   Adjust the clutch pedal free play by turning the cable adjusting nut until the specified clearance (C) is achieved (cable operated models)

10.5 Loosen the locknut and turn the master cylinder pushrod in either direction (hydraulically operated models).

11   Battery check and maintenance

Refer to illustrations 11.1, 11.6, 11.7a, 11.7b and 11.7c
Warning: *Certain precautions must be followed when checking and servicing the battery. Hydrogen gas, which is highly flammable, is always present in the battery cells, so keep lighted tobacco and all other open flames and sparks away from the battery. The electrolyte inside the battery is actually dilute sulfuric acid, which will cause injury if splashed on your skin or in your eyes. It will also ruin clothes and painted surfaces. When removing the battery cables, always detach the negative cable first and hook it up last!*

1   Battery maintenance is an important procedure which will help ensure that you aren't stranded because of a dead battery. Several tools are required for this procedure (**see illustration**).

2   When checking/servicing the battery, always turn the engine and all accessories off.

3   A sealed (sometimes called maintenance-free), battery is standard equipment on these vehicles. The cell caps cannot be removed, no electrolyte checks are required and water cannot be added to the cells. However, if a standard aftermarket battery has been installed, the following maintenance procedure can be used.

4   Remove the caps and check the electrolyte level in each of the battery cells (see Section 4). It must be above the plates. There's usually a split-ring indicator in each cell to indicate the correct level. If the level is low, add distilled water only, then reinstall the cell caps. **Caution:** *Overfilling the cells may cause electrolyte to spill over during periods of heavy charging, causing corrosion and damage to nearby components.*

5   The external condition of the battery should be checked periodically. Look for damage such as a cracked case.

6   Check the tightness of the battery cable bolts (**see illustration**) to ensure good electrical connections. Inspect the entire length of each cable, looking for cracked or abraded insulation and frayed conductors.

7   If corrosion (visible as white, fluffy deposits) (**see illustration**) is evident, remove the cables from the terminals, clean them with a battery brush and reinstall them (**see illustrations**). Corrosion can be kept to a minimum by applying a layer of petroleum jelly or grease to the terminals.

8   Make sure the battery carrier is in good condition and the hold-down clamp is tight. If the battery is removed (see Chapter 5 for the removal and installation procedure), make sure that no parts remain in the bottom of the carrier when it's reinstalled. When reinstalling the hold-down clamp, don't overtighten the nuts.

9   Corrosion on the carrier, battery case and surrounding areas can be removed with a solution of water and baking soda. Apply the mixture with a small brush, let it work, then rinse it off with plenty of clean water.

10   Any metal parts of the vehicle damaged by corrosion should be coated with a zinc-based primer, then painted.

11   Additional information on the battery, charging and jump starting can be found in the front of this manual and in Chapter 5.

11.1   Tools and materials required for battery maintenance

1   ***Face shield/safety goggles*** — *When removing corrosion with a brush, the acidic particles can easily fly up into your eyes*

2   ***Baking soda*** — *A solution of baking soda and water can be used to neutralize corrosion*

3   ***Petroleum jelly*** — *A layer of this on the battery posts will help prevent corrosion*

4   ***Battery post/cable cleaner*** — *This wire brush cleaning tool will remove all traces of corrosion from the battery posts and cable clamps*

5   ***Treated felt washers*** — *Placing one of these on each post, directly under the cable clamps, will help prevent corrosion*

6   ***Puller*** — *Sometimes the cable clamps are very difficult to pull off the posts, even after the nut/bolt has been completely loosened. This tool pulls the clamp straight up and off the post without damage*

7   ***Battery post/cable cleaner*** — *Here is another cleaning tool which is a slightly different version of number 4 above, but it does the same thing*

8   ***Rubber gloves*** — *Another safety item to consider when servicing the battery; remember that's acid inside the battery!*

11.6   Use a wrench to check the tightness of battery cable bolts; when removing corroded bolts, it may be necessary to use special battery pliers

11.7a   Battery terminal corrosion

11.7b When cleaning the cable clamps, all corrosion must be removed (the inside of the clamp is tapered to match the taper on the post, so don't remove too much material)

11.7c Regardless of the type of tool used to clean the battery posts, a clean, shiny surface should result

1

12 Drivebelt check, adjustment and replacement

Refer to illustrations 12.3 and 12.5

Warning: *The electric cooling fan can activate at any time, even when the ignition is in the Off position. Disconnect the fan motor or negative battery cable when working in the vicinity of the fan.*

Check

1   The alternator and air conditioning compressor drivebelts, also referred to as V-belts or simply ''fan'' belts, are located at the left (driver's) end of the engine compartment. The condition and proper adjustment of the drivebelts is critical to the operation of the engine. Since they stretch and deteriorate as they get older, they must be inspected periodically.

2   The number of belts used on a particular vehicle depends on the accessories installed. One belt transmits power from the crankshaft to the alternator and water pump. If the vehicle is equipped with air conditioning, the A/C compressor is driven by another belt.

3   With the engine off, open the hood and locate the drivebelts at the left end of the engine. With a flashlight, check each belt for separation of the adhesive rubber on both sides of the core, core separation from the belt side, a severed core, separation of the ribs from the adhesive rubber, cracking or separation of the ribs, and torn or worn ribs or cracks in the inner ridges of the ribs (**see illustration**). Also check for fraying and glazing, which gives the belt a shiny appearance. Both sides of the belt should be inspected, which means you will have to twist the belt to check the underside. Use your fingers to feel the belt where you can't see it. If any of the above conditions are evident, replace the belt (go to Step 8).

4   To check the tension of each belt in accordance with factory specifications, install either a Nippondenso or Burroughs belt tension gauge on the belt. Measure the tension in accordance with the manufacturer's instructions and compare your measurement to the specified drivebelt tension for either a used or new belt. **Note:** *A ''used'' belt is defined as any belt which has been operated more than five minutes on the engine; a ''new'' belt is one that has been used for less than five minutes.*

5   If you don't have either of the special tools, and cannot borrow one, the following rule of thumb method is recommended: Push firmly on the belt with your thumb at a distance halfway between the pulleys and note how far the belt can be moved (deflected). Measure the deflection with a ruler (**see illustration**). The belt should deflect 1/4-inch if the distance from pulley center to pulley center is between 7 and 11-inches; the belt should deflect 1/2-inch if the distance from pulley center to pulley center is between 12 and 16-inches.

12.3 Check the drivebelts for signs of wear like these — if it looks worn, replace it

12.5 Measuring drivebelt deflection with a straightedge and ruler

Adjustment

6   If the alternator or power steering pump belt must be adjusted, loosen the adjustment bolt that secures the alternator or power steering pump to the slotted bracket and pivot the alternator or power steering pump (away from the engine block to tighten the belt, toward the block to loosen the belt). It's helpful to lever the alternator or power steering pump with a large pry bar when adjusting the belt because the pry bar enables you to precisely position the component until the adjuster bolt is tightened. Be very careful not to damage the aluminum housing of the alternator or power steering pump. Recheck the belt tension using one of the above methods. Repeat this Step until the alternator or power steering pump drivebelt tension is correct.

7   If the air conditioner compressor drivebelt must be adjusted, locate the idler pulley on the front right corner of the block, just above the compressor. Turn the idler pulley adjuster bolt. Measure the belt tension in accordance with one of the above methods. Repeat this step until the air conditioning compressor drivebelt is adjusted.

Replacement

8   To replace a belt, follow the above procedures for drivebelt adjustment but slip the belt off the crankshaft pulley and remove it. If you're replacing the alternator belt, you'll have to remove the air conditioning compressor belt first because of the way they're arranged on the crankshaft pulley. Because of this and because belts tend to wear out more or less together, it's a good idea to replace both belts at the same time. Mark each belt and its appropriate pulley groove so the replacement belts can be installed in the proper positions.

9   Take the old belts to the parts store in order to make a direct comparison for length, width and design.

10   After replacing a new-style V-ribbed drivebelt (use on later models), make sure that it fits properly in the ribbed grooves in the pulleys. It's essential that the belt be properly centered.

11   Adjust the belt(s) as described above.

---

13   Underhood hose check and replacement

Caution: *Replacement of air conditioning hoses must be left to a dealer service department or air conditioning shop that has the equipment to depressurize the system safely. Never remove air conditioning components or hoses until the system has been depressurized.*

General

1   High temperatures in the engine compartment can cause the deterioration of the rubber and plastic hoses used for engine, accessory and emission systems operation. Periodic inspection should be made for cracks, loose clamps, material hardening and leaks.

2   Information specific to the cooling system hoses can be found in Section 14.

3   Some, but not all, hoses are secured to the fittings with clamps. Where clamps are used, check to be sure they haven't lost their tension, allowing the hose to leak. If clamps aren't used, make sure the hose has not expanded and/or hardened where it slips over the fitting, allowing it to leak.

Vacuum hoses

4   It's quite common for vacuum hoses, especially those in the emissions system, to be color coded or identified by colored stripes molded into them. Various systems require hoses with different wall thicknesses, collapse resistance and temperature resistance. When replacing hoses, be sure the new ones are made of the same material.

5   Often the only effective way to check a hose is to remove it completely from the vehicle. If more than one hose is removed, be sure to label the hoses and fittings to ensure correct installation.

6   When checking vacuum hoses, be sure to include any plastic T-fittings in the check. Inspect the fittings for cracks and the hose where it fits over the fitting for distortion, which could cause leakage.

7   A small piece of vacuum hose (1/4-inch inside diameter) can be used as a stethoscope to detect vacuum leaks. Hold one end of the hose to your ear and probe around vacuum hoses and fittings, listening for the "hissing" sound characteristic of a vacuum leak. **Warning:** *When probing with the vacuum hose stethoscope, be very careful not to come into contact with moving engine components such as the drivebelts, cooling fan, etc.*

Fuel hose

Warning: *There are certain precautions which must be taken when inspecting or servicing fuel system components. Work in a well ventilated area and do not allow open flames (cigarettes, appliance pilot lights, etc.) or bare light bulbs near the work area. Mop up any spills immediately and do not store fuel soaked rags where they could ignite.*

8   Check all rubber fuel lines for deterioration and chafing. Check especially for cracks in areas where the hose bends and just before fittings, such as where a hose attaches to the fuel filter.

9   High quality fuel line, usually identified by the word *Fluroelastomer* printed on the hose, should be used for fuel line replacement. Never, under any circumstances, use unreinforced vacuum line, clear plastic tubing or water hose for fuel lines.

10   Spring-type clamps are commonly used on fuel lines. These clamps often lose their tension over a period of time, and can be "sprung" during removal. Replace all spring-type clamps with screw clamps whenever a hose is replaced.

Metal lines

11   Sections of metal line are often used for fuel line between the fuel pump and carburetor. Check carefully to be sure the line has not been bent or crimped and that cracks have not started in the line.

12   If a section of metal fuel line must be replaced, only seamless steel tubing should be used, since copper and aluminum tubing don't have the strength necessary to withstand normal engine vibration.

13   Check the metal brake lines where they enter the master cylinder and brake proportioning unit (if used) for cracks in the lines or loose fittings. Any sign of brake fluid leakage calls for an immediate thorough inspection of the brake system.

---

14   Cooling system check

Refer to illustration 14.4

1   Many major engine failures can be attributed to a faulty cooling system. If the vehicle is equipped with an automatic transmission, the cooling system also cools the transmission fluid and thus plays an important role in prolonging transmission life.

2   The cooling system should be checked with the engine cold. Do this before the vehicle is driven for the day or after the engine has been shut off for at least three hours.

3   Remove the radiator cap by turning it to the left until it reaches a stop. If you hear a hissing sound (indicating there is still pressure in the system), wait until it stops. Now press down on the cap with the palm of your hand and continue turning to the left until the cap can be removed. Thoroughly clean the cap, inside and out, with clean water. Also clean the filler neck on the radiator. All traces of corrosion should be removed. The coolant inside the radiator should be relatively transparent. If it's rust colored, the system should be drained and refilled (Section 31). If the coolant level isn't up to the top, add additional antifreeze/coolant mixture (see Section 4).

4   Carefully check the large upper and lower radiator hoses along with the smaller diameter heater hoses which run from the engine to the firewall. Inspect each hose along its entire length, replacing any hose which is cracked, swollen or shows signs of deterioration. Cracks may become more apparent if the hose is squeezed **(see illustration)**. Regardless of condition, it's a good idea to replace hoses with new ones every two years.

5   Make sure that all hose connections are tight. A leak in the cooling system will usually show up as white or rust colored deposits on the areas adjoining the leak. If wire-type clamps are used at the ends of the hoses, it may be a good idea to replace them with more secure screw-type clamps.

6   Use compressed air or a soft brush to remove bugs, leaves, etc. from the front of the radiator or air conditioning condenser. Be careful not to damage the delicate cooling fins or cut yourself on them.

7   Every other inspection, or at the first indication of cooling system problems, have the cap and system pressure tested. If you don't have a pressure tester, most gas stations and repair shops will do this for a minimal charge.

ALWAYS CHECK hose for chafed or burned areas that may cause an untimely and costly failure.

SOFT hose indicates inside deterioration. This deterioration can contaminate the cooling system and cause particles to clog the radiator.

HARDENED hose can fail at any time. Tightening hose clamps will not seal the connection or stop leaks.

SWOLLEN hose or oil soaked ends indicate danger and possible failure from oil or grease contamination. Squeeze the hose to locate cracks and breaks that cause leaks.

14.4 Hoses, like drivebelts, have a habit of failing at the worst possible time — to prevent the inconvenience of a blown radiator or heater hose, inspect them carefully as shown here

FRONT

15.2 The recommended tire rotation pattern for this vehicle

16.5 You will find an inspection hole like this in each caliper — placing a steel ruler across the hole should enable you to determine the thickness of the remaining pad material for both inner and outer pads (arrows)

15 Tire rotation

Refer to illustration 15.2

1   The tires should be rotated at the specified intervals and whenever uneven wear is noticed. Since the vehicle will be raised and the tires removed anyway, check the brakes (Section 16) at this time.

2   Radial tires must be rotated in a specific pattern **(see illustration)**.

3   Refer to the information in *Jacking and towing* at the front of this manual for the proper procedures to follow when raising the vehicle and changing a tire. If the brakes are to be checked, do not apply the parking brake as stated. Make sure the tires are blocked to prevent the vehicle from rolling.

4   Preferably, the entire vehicle should be raised at the same time. This can be done on a hoist or by jacking up each corner and then lowering the vehicle onto jackstands placed under the frame rails. Always use four jackstands and make sure the vehicle is firmly supported.

5   After rotation, check and adjust the tire pressures as necessary and be sure to check the lug nut tightness.

6   For further information on the wheels and tires, refer to Chapter 10.

16 Brake check

Note: *For detailed photographs of the brake system, refer to Chapter 9.*

1   In addition to the specified intervals, the brakes should be inspected every time the wheels are removed or whenever a defect is suspected. Any of the following symptoms could indicate a potential brake system defect: The vehicle pulls to one side when the brake pedal is depressed; the brakes make squealing or dragging noises when applied; brake travel is excessive; the pedal pulsates; brake fluid leaks, usually onto the inside of the tire or wheel.

2   Loosen the wheel lug nuts.

3   Raise the vehicle and place it securely on jackstands.

4   Remove the wheels (see *Jacking and towing* at the front of this book, or your owner's manual, if necessary).

Disc brakes

Refer to illustration 16.5

5   There are two pads — an outer and an inner — in each caliper. The pads are visible through small inspection holes in each caliper **(see illustration)** .

6   Check the pad thickness by looking at each end of the caliper and through the inspection hole in the caliper body. If the lining material is less than the specified thickness, replace the pads. **Note:** *Keep in mind that the lining material is riveted or bonded to a metal backing plate and the metal portion is not included in this measurement.*

7   If it is difficult to determine the exact thickness of the remaining pad material by the above method, or if you are at all concerned about the condition of the pads, remove the caliper(s), then remove the pads from the calipers for further inspection (refer to Chapter 9).

8   Once the pads are removed from the calipers, clean them with brake cleaner and remeasure them with a small steel pocket ruler or a vernier caliper.

9   Check the disc. Look for score marks, deep scratches and burned spots. If these conditions exist, the hub/disc assembly will have to be removed (see Chapter 9).

10   Before installing the wheels, check all brake lines and hoses for damage, wear, deformation, cracks, corrosion, leakage, bends and twists, particularly in the vicinity of the rubber hoses at the calipers. Check the clamps for tightness and the connections for leakage. Make

6.12   The rear brake shoe lining thickness is measured from the outer surface of the lining to the metal shoe (arrows)

16.14   Peel the wheel cylinder boot back carefully and check for leaking fluid, indicating the cylinder must be replaced or rebuilt

sure that all hoses and lines are clear of sharp edges, moving parts and the exhaust system. If any of the above conditions are noted, repair, reroute or replace the lines and/or fittings as necessary (refer to Chapter 9).

Rear drum brakes
Refer to illustrations 16.12 and 16.14

11   Refer to Section 32 and remove the rear brake drums. **Warning:** *Brake dust produced by lining wear and deposited on brake components contains asbestos, which is hazardous to your health. DO NOT blow it out with compressed air and DO NOT inhale it! DO NOT use gasoline or solvents to remove the dust. Brake system cleaner should be used to flush the dust into the drain pan. After the brake components are wiped clean with a damp rag, dispose of the contaminated rag(s) and solvent in a covered and labeled container. Try to use non-asbestos replacement parts whenever possible.*

12   Note the thickness of the lining material on the rear brake shoes **(see illustration)** and look for signs of contamination by brake fluid and grease. If the lining material is within 1/16-inch of the recessed rivets or metal shoes, replace the brake shoes with new ones. The shoes should also be replaced if they are cracked, glazed (shiny lining surfaces) or contaminated with brake fluid or grease. See Chapter 9 for the replacement procedure.

13   Check the shoe return and hold-down springs and the adjusting mechanism to make sure they're installed correctly and in good condition. Deteriorated or distorted springs, if not replaced, could allow the linings to drag and wear prematurely.

14   Check the wheel cylinders for leakage by carefully peeling back the rubber boots **(see illustration)**. If brake fluid is noted behind the boots, the wheel cylinders must be replaced (see Chapter 9).

15   Check the drums for cracks, score marks, deep scratches and hard spots, which will appear as small discolored areas. If imperfections cannot be removed with emery cloth, the drums must be resurfaced by an automotive machine shop (see Chapter 9 for more detailed information).

16   Refer to Chapter 9 and install the brake drums.

17   Install the wheels and tighten the wheel lug nuts finger tight.

18   Remove the jackstands and lower the vehicle.

19   Tighten the wheel lug nuts to the specified torque.

Parking brake

20   A simple method of checking the parking brake is to park the vehicle on a steep hill with the parking brake set and the transmission in Neutral. If the parking brake cannot prevent the vehicle from rolling, it is in need of adjustment (see Chapter 9).

---

17   Air filter and PCV filter replacement

Carbureted models
Refer to illustrations 17.2, 17.4 and 17.7

Warning: *The electric cooling fan can activate at any time, even when the ignition is in the Off position. Disconnect the fan motor or negative battery cable when working in the vicinity of the fan.*

1   At the specified intervals, the air filter and PCV filter (if equipped) should be replaced with new ones. The engine air cleaner also supplies filtered air to the PCV system.

2   The filter is located on top of the carburetor and is replaced by unscrewing the wing nut, detaching the clips from the top of the filter housing and lifting off the cover **(see illustration)**.

3   While the top plate is off, be careful not to drop anything down into the carburetor or air cleaner assembly.

4   Lift the air filter element out of the housing **(see illustration)** and wipe out the inside of the air cleaner housing with a clean rag.

5   Place the new filter in the air cleaner housing. Make sure it seats properly in the bottom of the housing.

6   The PCV filter is also located inside the air cleaner housing. Remove the top plate and air filter as previously described, then locate the PCV filter on the inside of the housing.

7   Remove the old filter **(see illustration)**.

8   Install the new PCV filter and the new air filter.

9   Install the top plate and any hoses which were disconnected. Don't overtighten the wing nut.

Fuel-injected models
Refer to illustration 17.13

Caution: *Use care when removing the air filter cover, since it contains the air-flow sensor that can be easily damaged.*

17.2   The top of the filter housing is removed by releasing the clips on the sides and unscrewing the wing nut on the top

17.4   Lift out the air filter element and wipe out the inside of the air cleaner housing with a clean rag

7.7 Removing the PCV filter

17.13 On fuel-injected models, the air filter is located inside this drum-like housing - release the clips to remove the filter

18.3 On 1986 and 1987 models, the cam-shaped actuator on the left side of the carburetor (arrow) must move smoothly through its arc and press progressively on the throttle position sensor, located directly to the rear of the actuator.

19.5 With the number one piston at Top Dead Center (TDC), adjust the valves marked A - with the number four piston at TDC, adjust the valves marked B

10   At the specified intervals, the air filter element should be replaced with a new one.
11   The air filter housing is attached to the right-hand inner fender panel. Loosen the air intake hose clamp screw and disconnect the hose from the air filter cover.
12   Unplug the electrical connector from the air-flow sensor.
13   Release the clips and remove the air filter cover, then lift the air filter element out of the housing and wipe out the housing with a clean rag **(see illustration)**.
14   Place the new filter element in the housing. Make sure it seats properly in the bottom of the housing.
15   Install the cover and secure the clips. Install the air intake hose and tighten the hose clamp screw securely. Plug in the electrical connector.

18.4 On 1988 and later models, check the lever for smooth operation and make sure the two retaining screws are tight

18   Throttle position sensor check (carbureted models)

Refer to illustrations 18.3 and 18.4
1   The throttle position sensor and linkage must work properly or vehicle driveability will be affected.
2   Have an assistant open and close the throttle while you watch the sensor and linkage.
3   On 1986 and 1987 models, the cam-shaped actuator must move smoothly throughout its arc, progressively depressing and releasing the throttle position sensor **(see illustration)**.
4   On 1988 and later models, check the lever for smooth operation and make sure the two retaining screws are tight **(see illustration)**.
5   If the linkage or the sensor bind, refer to Chapter 4 for more information on the throttle position sensor.

19   Valve clearance check and adjustment

Refer to illustrations 19.5, 19.7 and 19.12
Warning: The electric cooling fan can activate at any time, even when the ignition is in the Off position. Disconnect the fan motor or negative battery cable when working in the vicinity of the fan.
1   The valve clearances are checked and adjusted with the engine at normal operating temperature.
2   Remove the air cleaner assembly (Chapter 4).
3   Remove the rocker arm cover (Chapter 2).
4   Place the number one piston at Top Dead Center (TDC) on the compression stroke (Chapter 2). The number one cylinder rocker arms (closest to the timing belt end of the engine) should be loose (able to move up and down slightly) and the camshaft lobes should be facing away from the rocker arms.
5   With the crankshaft in this position the valves labeled A (plus the jet valves adjacent to the intake valves) can be check and adjusted **(see illustration)**. Always check and adjust the jet valve clearance first.
6   The intake valve and jet valve adjusting screws are located on a common rocker arm. Make sure the intake valve adjusting screw has been

9.7   There should be a slight drag as the feeler gauge is pulled between the jet valve adjustment screw and the valve stem

backed off two full turns, then loosen the locknut on the jet valve adjusting screw.

7   On models so equipped, turn the jet valve adjusting screw counterclockwise and insert the appropriate size feeler gauge between the valve stem and the adjusting screw. Carefully tighten the adjusting screw until you can feel a slight drag on the feeler gauge as you withdraw it from between the stem and adjusting screw **(see illustration)**.

8   On models so equipped since the jet valve spring is relatively weak, use special care not to force the jet valve open. Be particularly careful if the adjusting screw is hard to turn. Hold the adjusting screw with a screwdriver (to keep it from turning) and tighten the locknut. Recheck the clearance to make sure it hasn't changed.

9   Next, check and adjust the intake valve clearance. Insert the appropriate size feeler gauge between the intake valve stem and the adjusting screw. Carefully tighten the adjusting screw until you can feel a slight drag on the feeler gauge as you withdraw it from between the stem and adjusting screw.

10   Hold the adjusting screw with a screwdriver (to keep it from turning) and tighten the locknut. Recheck the clearance to make sure it hasn't changed.

11   Loosen the locknut on the exhaust valve adjusting screw. Turn the adjusting screw counterclockwise and insert the appropriate size feeler gauge between the valve stem and the adjusting screw. Carefully tighten the adjusting screw until you can feel a slight drag on the feeler gauge as you withdraw it from between the stem and adjusting screw.

12   Hold the adjusting screw with a screwdriver (to keep it from turning) and tighten the locknut **(see illustration)**. Recheck the clearance to make sure it hasn't changed.

13   Rotate the crankshaft until the number four piston is at TDC on the compression stroke. The number four cylinder rocker arms (closest to the transaxle end of the engine) are loose with the camshaft lobes facing away from the rocker arms.

14   Adjust the valves labeled B as described in Steps 4 through 8 **(see illustration 19.5).**

15   Install the rocker arm cover and the air cleaner assembly.

---

20   Engine idle speed check and adjustment

Carbureted models

Refer to illustration 20.8

1   Engine idle speed is the speed at which the engine operates when no accelerator pedal pressure is applied, as when stopped at a traffic light. This speed is critical
to the performance of the engine itself, as well as many engine subsystems.

2   Set the parking brake firmly set and block the wheels to prevent the vehicle from rolling. Put the transaxle in Neutral.

3   Hook up a hand held tachometer.

4   Start the engine and allow it to reach normal operating temperature.

5   Check, and adjust if necessary, the ignition timing (Section 37).

6   Allow the engine to idle for two minutes.

7   Check the engine idle speed on the tachometer and compare it to the *Emission Control Information* label in the engine compartment.

19.12   To make sure the adjusting screw doesn't move when the locknut is tightened, use a box-end wrench and have a good grip on the screwdriver

SAS 1

20.8   When adjusting the engine idle speed, make sure to turn only the SAS 1 screw - the other screws are preset at the factory and require special equipment for proper adjustment

8   If the idle speed is too low or too high, turn the speed adjusting screw (SAS 1) **(see illustration)** until the specified idle speed is obtained. Turn only the SAS 1 screw as the other adjustment screws are preset at the factory and require special equipment for proper adjustment.

Fuel-injected models

9   The engine idle speed on fuel-injected models requires several pieces of calibrated test equipment; therefore, the adjustment should be made by a dealer service department or qualified automotive repair facility.

---

21   Fuel filter replacement

Carbureted models

Refer to illustrations 21.1 and 21.2

Warning: *Gasoline is extremely flammable, so extra precautions must be taken when working on any part of the fuel system. Do not smoke or allow open flames or bare light bulbs near the work area. Also, do not work in a garage if a natural gas-type appliance with a pilot light is present.*

1   The fuel filter is located on the firewall, below the emissions canister **(see illustration)**.

2   For easier access, pull the filter out of the spring clip so both fittings can be reached **(see illustration)**.

3   Release the hose clamps at the filter fittings and slide them back up the hoses.

4   Disconnect the hoses and remove the filter. Now would be a good time to replace the hoses if they're deteriorated.

5   Push the hoses onto the new filter and position the clamps approximately 1/4-inch back from the ends.

6   Push the filter back into the spring clip. Check to make sure it is held securely and the hoses are not kinked.

7   Start the engine and check for fuel leaks at the filter.

21.1   The fuel filter is mounted on the firewall, below the evaporative emission system canister

21.2   Unsnap the fuel filter from the clip and pull it out for better access to the hoses

Fuel-injected models

Refer to illustration 21.11

Warning: *Fuel pressure must be released prior to disconnecting any component of the fuel injection system to prevent pressurized fuel from being sprayed when the lines are disconnected (see Chapter 4, Section 3, Step 21).*

8   The fuel filter is located on the bulkhead (firewall), next to the air filter air inlet hose.

9   Relieve the fuel pressure (see Chapter 4, Section 3, Step 21). Place a shop cloth over the top hose connection of the fuel filter to prevent fuel from splashing out when the upper fitting is loosened.

10   Secure the fuel filter upper fitting with a wrench, then loosen the top eye bolt. Remove the top eye bolt, gaskets and high-pressure hose from the fuel filter.

11   Secure the fuel filter lower fitting with a wrench, then loosen the lower eye bolt. Remove the lower eye bolt, gaskets and fuel main hose from the fuel filter **(see illustration)**.

12   Remove the fuel filter mounting bolts and remove the fuel filter from the bulkhead.

13   Be sure to install a new gasket (copper washer) on each side of the hose fittings and install both hoses onto the filter. Tighten the eye bolts to the torque listed in this Chapter's Specifications.

---

22   Fuel system check

Warning: *Certain precautions should be observed when inspecting or servicing the fuel system components. Work in a well ventilated area and do not allow open flames (cigarettes, appliance pilot lights, etc.) near the work area. Mop up spills immediately and do not store fuel soaked rags where they could ignite. It is a good idea to keep a dry chemical (Class B) fire extinguisher near the work area any time the fuel system is being serviced.*

1   If you smell gasoline while driving or after the vehicle has been sitting in the sun, inspect the fuel system immediately.

2   Remove the gas filler cap and inspect if for damage and corrosion. The gasket should have an unbroken sealing imprint. If the gasket is damaged or corroded, replace the cap.

3   Inspect the fuel feed and return lines for cracks. Check the metal fuel line connections to make sure they are tight.

4   Since some components of the fuel system - the fuel tank and part of the fuel feed and return lines, for example - are underneath the vehicle, they can be inspected more easily with the vehicle raised on a hoist. If that's not possible, raise the vehicle and secure it on jackstands. 5 With the vehicle raised and safely supported, inspect the gas tank and filler neck for punctures, cracks and other damage. The connection between the filler neck and the tank is particularly critical. Sometimes a rubber filler neck will leak because of loose clamps or deteriorated rubber. These are problems a home mechanic can usually rectify. **Warning:** *Do not, under any circumstances, try to repair a fuel tank (except rubber components). A welding torch or any open flame can easily cause fuel vapors inside the tank to explode.*

6   Carefully check all rubber hoses and metal lines leading away from the fuel tank. Check for loose connections, deteriorated hoses, crimped lines and other damage. Carefully inspect the lines from the

21.11 An exploded view of the fuel filter and hose connections (fuel-injected models)

EYE BOLT

GASKET

HIGH-PRESSURE HOSE

FUEL MAIN HOSE

05BBH

tank to the carburetor. Repair or replace damaged sections as necessary.

---

23   Steering and suspension check

Refer to illustration 23.6

Note: *For detailed illustrations of the steering and suspension components, refer to Chapter 10.*

With the wheels on the ground

1   With the vehicle stopped and the front wheels pointed straight ahead, rock the steering wheel gently back and forth. If free play is excessive, a front wheel bearing, main shaft yoke, intermediate shaft yoke, lower arm balljoint or steering system joint is worn or the steering gear is out of adjustment or broken. Refer to Chapter 10 for the appropriate repair procedure.

2   Other symptoms, such as excessive vehicle body movement over rough roads, swaying (leaning) around corners and binding as the steering wheel is turned, may indicate faulty steering and/or suspension components.

3   Check the shock absorbers by pushing down and releasing the vehicle several times at each corner. If the vehicle does not come back to a level position within one or two bounces, the shocks/struts are worn and must be replaced. When bouncing the vehicle up and down, listen for squeaks and noises from the suspension components. Additional information on suspension components can be found in Chapter 10.

With the vehicle raised

4   Raise the vehicle and support it securely on jackstands. See Jacking and towing at the front of this book for the proper jacking points.

5   Check the tires for irregular wear patterns (see Section 5) and proper inflation. See Section 5 in this chapter for information regarding

23.6   Push on the steering gear boot to check for cracks and lubricant leaks

24.2   Flex the driveaxle boots by hand to check for cracks or leaking grease

25.2   Check the rubber exhaust system hangers for cracks and deterioration – replace any that are in poor condition

26.1   The transaxle lubricant level should be even with the lower edge of the hole

tire wear and Section 32 or Chapter 10 for the wheel bearing replacement procedures.
6   Inspect the universal joint between the steering shaft and the steering gear housing. Check the steering gear housing for grease leakage or oozing. Make sure that the dust seals and boots are not damaged and that the boot clamps are not loose **(see illustration)**. Check the steering linkage for looseness or damage. Check the tie-rod ends for excessive play. Look for loose bolts, broken or disconnected parts and deteriorated rubber bushings on all suspension and steering components. While an assistant turns the steering wheel from side to side, check the steering components for free movement, chafing and binding. If the steering components do not seem to be reacting with the movement of the steering wheel, try to determine where the slack is located.
7   Inspect the balljoint boots for damage and leaking grease. Replace the boots with new ones if they are damaged (Chapter 10).

24   Driveaxle boot check

Refer to illustration 24.2
1   The driveaxle boots are very important because they prevent dirt, water and foreign material from entering and damaging the constant velocity (CV) joints. Oil and grease can cause the boot material to deteriorate prematurely, so it's a good idea to wash the boots with soap and water.
2   Inspect the boots for tears and cracks as well as loose clamps **(see illustration)**. If there is any evidence of cracks or leaking lubricant, they must be replaced as described in Chapter 8.

25   Exhaust system check

Refer to illustration 25.2
1   With the engine cold (at least three hours after the vehicle has been driven), check the complete exhaust system from its starting point at the engine to the end of the tailpipe. This should be done on a hoist where

unrestricted access is available.
2   Check the pipes and connections for evidence of leaks, severe corrosion or damage. Make sure that all brackets and hangers are in good condition and tight **(see illustration)**.
3   At the same time, inspect the underside of the body for holes, corrosion, open seams, etc. which may allow exhaust gases to enter the passenger compartment. Seal all body openings with silicone or body putty.
4   Rattles and other noises can often be traced to the exhaust system, especially the mounts and hangers. Try to move the pipes, muffler and catalytic converter. If the components can come in contact with the body or suspension parts, secure the exhaust system with new mounts.
5   Check the running condition of the engine by inspecting inside the end of the tailpipe. The exhaust deposits here are an indication of engine state-of-tune. If the pipe is black and sooty or coated with white deposits, the engine is in need of a tune-up, including a thorough fuel system inspection and adjustment.

26   Manual transaxle oil level check

Refer to illustration 26.1
1   The manual transaxle does not have a dipstick. To check the oil level, raise the vehicle and support it securely on jackstands. On the lower right front of the transaxle housing, you will see a plug. Remove it. If the lubricant level is correct, it should be up to the lower edge of the hole **(see illustration)**.
2   If the transaxle needs more lubricant (if the level is not up to the hole), use a syringe to add more. Stop filling the transaxle when the lubricant begins to run out the hole.
3   Install the plug and tighten it securely. Drive the vehicle a short distance, then check for leaks.

27   Spark plug replacement

Refer to illustrations 27.1, 27.4a, 27.4b, 27.6 and 27.10
1   Spark plug replacement requires a spark plug socket which fits onto a ratchet wrench. This socket is lined with a rubber grommet to protect the porcelain insulator of the spark plug and to hold the plug while you insert it into the spark plug hole. You will also need a wire-type feeler gauge to check and adjust the spark plug gap and a torque wrench

Common spark plug conditions

NORMAL

Symptoms: Brown to grayish-tan color and slight electrode wear. Correct heat range for engine and operating conditions.

Recommendation: When new spark plugs are installed, replace with plugs of the same heat range.

WORN

Symptoms: Rounded electrodes with a small amount of deposits on the firing end. Normal color. Causes hard starting in damp or cold weather and poor fuel economy.

Recommendation: Plugs have been left in the engine too long. Replace with new plugs of the same heat range. Follow the recommended maintenance schedule.

CARBON DEPOSITS

Symptoms: Dry sooty deposits indicate a rich mixture or weak ignition. Causes misfiring, hard starting and hesitation.

Recommendation: Make sure the plug has the correct heat range. Check for a clogged air filter or problem in the fuel system or engine management system. Also check for ignition system problems.

ASH DEPOSITS

Symptoms: Light brown deposits encrusted on the side or center electrodes or both. Derived from oil and/or fuel additives. Excessive amounts may mask the spark, causing misfiring and hesitation during acceleration.

Recommendation: If excessive deposits accumulate over a short time or low mileage, install new valve guide seals to prevent seepage of oil into the combustion chambers. Also try changing gasoline brands.

OIL DEPOSITS

Symptoms: Oily coating caused by poor oil control. Oil is leaking past worn valve guides or piston rings into the combustion chamber. Causes hard starting, misfiring and hesitation.

Recommendation: Correct the mechanical condition with necessary repairs and install new plugs.

GAP BRIDGING

Symptoms: Combustion deposits lodge between the electrodes. Heavy deposits accumulate and bridge the electrode gap. The plug ceases to fire, resulting in a dead cylinder.

Recommendation: Locate the faulty plug and remove the deposits from between the electrodes.

TOO HOT

Symptoms: Blistered, white insulator, eroded electrode and absence of deposits. Results in shortened plug life.

Recommendation: Check for the correct plug heat range, over-advanced ignition timing, lean fuel mixture, intake manifold vacuum leaks, sticking valves and insufficient engine cooling.

PREIGNITION

Symptoms: Melted electrodes. Insulators are white, but may be dirty due to misfiring or flying debris in the combustion chamber. Can lead to engine damage.

Recommendation: Check for the correct plug heat range, over-advanced ignition timing, lean fuel mixture, insufficient engine cooling and lack of lubrication.

HIGH SPEED GLAZING

Symptoms: Insulator has yellowish, glazed appearance. Indicates that combustion chamber temperatures have risen suddenly during hard acceleration. Normal deposits melt to form a conductive coating. Causes misfiring at high speeds.

Recommendation: Install new plugs. Consider using a colder plug if driving habits warrant.

DETONATION

Symptoms: Insulators may be cracked or chipped. Improper gap setting techniques can also result in a fractured insulator tip. Can lead to piston damage.

Recommendation: Make sure the fuel anti-knock values meet engine requirements. Use care when setting the gaps on new plugs. Avoid lugging the engine.

MECHANICAL DAMAGE

Symptoms: May be caused by a foreign object in the combustion chamber or the piston striking an incorrect reach (too long) plug. Causes a dead cylinder and could result in piston damage.

Recommendation: Repair the mechanical damage. Remove the foreign object from the engine and/or install the correct reach plug.

to tighten the new plugs to the specified torque (**see illustration**).

2   When replacing the plugs, purchase the new plugs in advance, adjust them to the proper gap and then replace each plug one at a time. **Note:** *When buying new spark plugs, it's essential that you obtain the correct plugs for your specific vehicle. This information can be found on the Vehicle Emissions Control Information (VECI) label located on the underside of the hood or in the owner's manual. If these two sources specify different plugs, purchase the spark plug type specified on the VECI label because that information is provided specifically for your engine.*

3   Inspect each of the new plugs for defects. If there are any signs of cracks in the porcelain insulator of a plug, don't use it.

4   Check the electrode gaps of the new plugs. Check the gap by inserting the wire gauge of the proper thickness between the electrodes at the tip of the plug (**see illustration**). The gap between the electrodes should be identical to that specified on the VECI label. If the gap is incorrect, use the notched adjuster on the feeler gauge body to bend the curved side electrode slightly (**see illustration**).

5   If the side electrode is not exactly over the center electrode, use the notched adjuster to align them. **Caution:** *If the gap of a new plug must be adjusted, bend only the base of the ground electrode do not touch the tip.*

Removal

6   To prevent the possibility of mixing up spark plug wires, work on one spark plug at a time. Remove the wire and boot from one spark plug. Grasp the boot — not the cable — as shown, give it a half twisting

motion and pull it off (**see illustration**).

7   If compressed air is available, blow any dirt or foreign material away from the spark plug area before proceeding (a common bicycle pump will also work).

8   Remove the spark plug.

9   Compare each old spark plug with those shown in the accompanying photos to determine the overall running condition of the engine.

27.4a   Spark plug manufacturers recommend using a wire-type gauge when checking the gap — if the wire does not slide between the electrodes with a slight drag, adjustment is required

27.1   Tools required for changing spark plugs

1   **Spark plug socket** — *This will have a rubber grommet inside to protect the spark plug porcelain insulator*
2   **Torque wrench** — *Although not mandatory, use of this tool is the best way to ensure that the plugs are tightened properly*
3   **Ratchet** — *Standard hand tool to fit the plug socket*
4   **Extension** — *Depending on model and accessories, you may need special extensions and universal joints to reach one or more of the plugs*
5   **Wire-type feeler gauge** — *This gauge for checking the gap comes in a variety of styles. Make sure the gap for your engine is included*

27.4b   To change the gap, bend the side electrode only, as indicated by the arrows, and be very careful not to crack or chip the porcelain insulator surrounding the center electrode

TWIST AND PULL

27.6   When removing the spark plug wires, pull only on the boot and use a twisting/pulling motion

27.10   A length of 3/16-inch ID rubber hose will save time and prevent damaged threads when installing the spark plugs

Installation

10 It's often difficult to insert spark plugs into their holes without cross-threading them. To avoid this possibility, fit a short piece of 3/16-inch ID rubber hose over the end of the spark plug **(see illustration)**. The flexible hose acts as a universal joint to help align the plug with the plug hole. Should the plug begin to cross-thread, the hose will slip on the spark plug, preventing thread damage. Tighten the plug securely.

11 Attach the plug wire to the new spark plug, again using a twisting motion on the boot until it is firmly seated on the end of the spark plug.

12 Follow the above procedure for the remaining spark plugs, replacing them one at a time to prevent mixing up the spark plug wires.

28 Spark plug wire, distributor cap and rotor check and replacement

Refer to illustrations 28.11a, 28.11b and 28.12

1 The spark plug wires should be checked whenever new spark plugs are installed.

28.11a Use a small screwdriver to pry off the distributor cap retaining clips

2 Begin this procedure by making a visual check of the spark plug wires while the engine is running. In a darkened garage (make sure there is ventilation) start the engine and observe each plug wire. Be careful not to come into contact with any moving engine parts. If there is a break in the wire, you will see arcing or a small spark at the damaged area. If arcing is noticed, make a note to obtain new wires, then allow the engine to cool and check the distributor cap and rotor.

3 The spark plug wires should be inspected one at a time to prevent mixing up the order, which is essential for proper engine operation. Each original plug wire should be numbered to help identify its location. If the number is illegible, a piece of tape can be marked with the correct number and wrapped around the plug wire.

4 Disconnect the plug wire from the spark plug. A removal tool can be used for this purpose or you can grasp the rubber boot, twist the boot half a turn and pull the boot free. Do not pull on the wire itself **(see illustration 27.6)**.

5 Check inside the boot for corrosion, which will look like a white crusty powder.

6 Push the wire and boot back onto the end of the spark plug. It should fit tightly onto the end of the plug. If it doesn't, remove the wire and use pliers to carefully crimp the metal connector inside the wire boot until the fit is snug.

7 Using a clean rag, wipe the entire length of the wire to remove built-up dirt and grease. Once the wire is clean, check for burns, cracks and other damage. Do not bend the wire sharply, because the conductor within the wire might break.

8 Disconnect the wire from the distributor. Again, pull only on the rubber boot. Check for corrosion and a tight fit. Press the wire back into the distributor.

9 Inspect the remaining spark plug wires, making sure that each one is securely fastened at the distributor and spark plug when the check is complete.

10 If new spark plug wires are required, purchase a set for your specific engine model. Pre-cut wire sets with the boots already installed are available. Remove and replace the wires one at a time to avoid mix-ups in the firing order.

11 Detach the distributor cap by prying off the two cap retaining clips **(see illustration)**. Look inside it for cracks, carbon tracks and worn, burned or loose contacts **(see illustration)**.

12 Pull the rotor off the distributor shaft and examine it for cracks and carbon tracks **(see illustration)**. Replace the cap and rotor if any damage or defects are noted.

13 It is common practice to install a new cap and rotor whenever new spark plug wires are installed, but if you wish to continue using the old cap, clean the terminals first.

14 When installing a new cap, remove the wires from the old cap one

28.11b Shown here are some of the common defects to look for when inspecting the distributor cap (if in doubt about its condition, install a new one)

28.12 The ignition rotor should be checked for wear and corrosion as indicated here (if in doubt about its condition, buy a new one)

29.3   The choke plate is located in the carburetor throat

at a time and attach them to the new cap in the exact same location — do not simultaneously remove all the wires from the old cap or firing order mix-ups may occur.

29   Carburetor choke check

Refer to illustration 29.3

Warning: *The electric cooling fan can activate at any time, even when the ignition is in the Off position. Disconnect the fan motor or negative battery cable when working in the vicinity of the fan.*

1   The choke operates only when the engine is cold, so this check should be performed before the engine has been started for the day.
2   Take off the top plate of the air cleaner assembly. It's held in place by a wing nut at the top and clips on the side. If any vacuum hoses must be disconnected, make sure you tag the hoses for reinstallation in their original positions. Place the top plate and wing nut aside, out of the way of moving engine components.
3   Look at the center of the air cleaner housing. You will notice a flat plate at the carburetor opening **(see illustration)**.
4   Press the accelerator pedal to the floor. The plate should close completely. Start the engine while you watch the plate at the carburetor. Don't position your face near the carburetor, as the engine could backfire, causing serious burns. When the engine starts, the choke plate should open slightly.
5   Allow the engine to continue running at an idle speed. As the engine warms up to operating temperature, the plate should slowly open, allowing more air to enter through the top of the carburetor.
6   After a few minutes, the choke plate should be fully open to the vertical position. Blip the throttle to make sure the fast idle cam disengages.
7   You'll notice that the engine speed corresponds with the plate opening. With the plate fully closed, the engine should run at a fast idle speed. As the plate opens and the throttle is moved to disengage the fast idle cam, the engine speed will decrease.
8   Refer to Chapter 4 for specific information on adjusting and servicing the choke components.

30   Thermostatically controlled air cleaner check (carbureted models)

Refer to illustration 30.3
Warning: *The electric cooling fan can activate at any time, even when the ignition is in the Off position. Disconnect the fan motor or negative battery cable when working in the vicinity of the fan.*
1   All engines are equipped with a thermostatically controlled air

Mirror

Air control valve

30.3   Use a mirror to observe movement of the air control valve

cleaner which draws air to the carburetor from different locations, depending on engine temperature.
2   This is a visual check, requiring use of a small mirror.
3   When the engine is cold, locate the air control valve inside the air cleaner assembly. It's inside the long snorkel of the air cleaner housing **(see illustration)**.
4   There is a flexible air duct attached to the end of the snorkel, leading to an area behind the headlight. Disconnect it at the snorkel. This will enable you to look through the end of the snorkel and see the air control valve inside.
5   Start the engine and look through the snorkel at the valve, which should move up to block off the air cleaner snorkel. With the valve closed, air cannot enter through the end of the snorkel, but instead enters the air cleaner through the flexible duct attached to the exhaust manifold and the heat stove passage.
6   As the engine warms up to operating temperature, the valve should move down to allow air to be drawn through the snorkel end. Depending on outside temperature, this may take 10-to-15 minutes. To speed up this check you can reconnect the snorkel air duct, drive the vehicle, then check to see if the valve is completely open.
7   If the thermostatically controlled air cleaner isn't operating properly, see Chapter 6 for more information.

31   Cooling system servicing (draining, flushing and refilling)

Warning: *Antifreeze is a corrosive and poisonous solution, so be careful not to spill any of the coolant mixture on the vehicle's paint or your skin. If this happens, rinse immediately with plenty of clean water. Consult local authorities regarding proper disposal procedures for antifreeze before draining the cooling system. In many areas, reclamation centers have been established to collect used oil and coolant mixtures. The electric cooling fan can activate at any time, even when the ignition is in the Off position. Disconnect the fan motor or negative battery cable when working in the vicinity of the fan.*

1   Periodically, the cooling system should be drained, flushed and refilled to replenish the antifreeze mixture and prevent formation of rust and corrosion, which can impair the performance of the cooling system and cause engine damage. When the cooling system is serviced, all hoses and the radiator cap should be checked and replaced if necessary.

Draining
Refer to illustrations 31.4 and 31.5
2   Apply the parking brake and block the wheels. If the vehicle has just been driven, wait several hours to allow the engine to cool down before beginning this procedure.
3   Once the engine is completely cool, remove the radiator cap.
4   Remove the splash cover located beneath the radiator. Then move a large container under the radiator drain to catch the coolant. Attach a 3/8-inch inner diameter hose to the drain fitting to direct the coolant into the container (some models are already equipped with a hose), then open the drain fitting (a pair of pliers may be required to turn it) **(see illustration)**.

31.4 On most models you will have to remove a cover for access to the radiator drain fitting located at the bottom of the radiator — before opening the valve, push a short section of 3/8-inch diameter hose onto the fitting (some models are already equipped with one) to prevent the coolant from splashing as it drains

31.5 After the coolant stops flowing from the radiator, remove the engine block coolant drain plug and allow the coolant to drain from the engine block

5   After the coolant stops flowing out of the radiator, move the container under the engine block drain plug **(see illustration)**. Loosen the plug and allow the coolant in the block to drain.

6   While the coolant is draining, check the condition of the radiator hoses, heater hoses and clamps (refer to Section 14 if necessary).

7   Replace any damaged clamps or hoses (refer to Chapter 3 for detailed replacement procedures).

Flushing

8   Once the system is completely drained, flush the radiator with fresh water from a garden hose until water runs clear at the drain. The flushing action of the water will remove sediments from the radiator but will not remove rust and scale from the engine and cooling tube surfaces.

9   These deposits can be removed by the chemical action of a cleaner. Follow the procedure outlined in the manufacturer's instructions. If the radiator is severely corroded, damaged or leaking, it should be removed (Chapter 3) and taken to a radiator repair shop.

10   Remove the overflow hose from the coolant recovery reservoir. Drain the reservoir and flush it with clean water, then reconnect the hose.

Refilling

11   Close and tighten the radiator drain. Install and tighten the block drain plug.

12   Place the heater temperature control in the maximum heat position.

13   Slowly add new coolant (a 50/50 mixture of water and antifreeze) to the radiator until it's full. Add coolant to the reservoir up to the lower mark.

14   Leave the radiator cap off and run the engine in a well-ventilated area until the thermostat opens (coolant will begin flowing through the radiator and the upper radiator hose will become hot).

15   Turn the engine off and let it cool. Add more coolant mixture to bring the level back up to the lip on the radiator filler neck.

16   Squeeze the upper radiator hose to expel air, then add more coolant mixture if necessary. Replace the radiator cap.

17   Start the engine, allow it to reach normal operating temperature and check for leaks.

---

32   Rear wheel bearing check, repack and adjustment

Check

Refer to illustration 32.1

1   In most cases the rear wheel bearings will not need servicing until the brake shoes are changed. However, the bearings should be checked whenever the rear of the vehicle is raised for any reason. Several items, including a torque wrench and special grease, are required for this procedure **(see illustration)**.

32.1 Tools and materials needed for rear wheel bearing maintenance

1   **Hammer** — *A common hammer will do just fine*

2   **Grease** — *Grease which is formulated specially for wheel bearings should be used*

3   **Wood block** — *If you have a scrap piece of 2x4, it can be used to drive the new seal into the hub*

4   **Needle-nose pliers** — *Used to straighten and remove the cotter pin in the spindle*

5   **Torque wrench** — *This is very important in this procedure; if the bearing is too tight, the wheel won't turn freely — if it is too loose, the wheel will 'wobble' on the spindle. Either way, it could mean extensive damage*

6   **Screwdriver** — *Used to remove the seal from the hub (a long screwdriver would be preferred)*

7   **Socket/breaker bar** — *Needed to loosen the nut on the spindle if it is extremely tight*

8   **Brush** — *Together with some clean solvent, this will be used to remove old grease from the hub and spindle*

2   With the vehicle securely supported on jackstands, spin each wheel and check for noise, rolling resistance and free play.
3   Grasp the top of each tire with one hand and the bottom with the other. Move the wheel in-and-out on the spindle. If there's any noticeable movement, the bearings should be checked and then repacked with grease or replaced if necessary.

Repack

Refer to illustrations 32.6, 32.7a, 32.7b, 32.8, 32.9, 32.11 and 32.15
4   Remove the tire/wheel assembly.
5   If necessary, back off the parking brake adjuster (Chapter 9).
6   Pry the dust cap out of the drum/hub assembly using a screwdriver or hammer and chisel **(see illustration)**.

7   Straighten the bent ends of the cotter pin, then pull the cotter pin out of the nut lock **(see illustration)**. Discard the cotter pin and use a new one during reassembly. Remove the nut lock **(see illustration)**. **Note:** *If no cotter pin is present, the vehicle is equipped with a self-locking nut.*
8   Remove the spindle nut and washer from the end of the spindle **(see illustration)**.
9   Pull the drum/hub assembly out slightly, then push it back into its original position. This should force the outer bearing off the spindle enough so it can be removed **(see illustration)**.
10   Pull the drum/hub off the spindle.
11   Use a seal puller or screwdriver to pry the seal out of the rear of the drum/hub **(see illustration)**. As this is done, note how the seal is installed.

32.6   Pry the dust cap out of the hub

32.7a   Wire cutters are useful for gripping the greasy cotter pin and pulling it out

32.7b   Pull the nut lock off the spindle nut

32.8   Remove the washer with a small screwdriver (the spindle nut has been removed in this illustration)

32.9   Remove the outer wheel bearing after pulling the drum/hub out slightly to dislodge it

32.11   Pry the seal out of the hub with a screwdriver or hooked seal puller such as this one (available at auto parts stores)

12 Remove the inner wheel bearing from the drum/hub.
13 Use solvent to remove all traces of the old grease from the bearings, hub and spindle. A small brush may prove helpful; however make sure no bristles from the brush embed themselves inside the bearing rollers. Allow the parts to air dry.
14 Carefully inspect the bearings for cracks, heat discoloration, worn rollers, etc. Check the bearing races inside the hub for wear and damage. If the bearing races are defective, the hubs should be taken to a machine shop with the facilities to remove the old races and press new ones in. Note that the bearings and races come as matched sets and old bearings should never be installed on new races.
15 Use wheel bearing grease to pack the bearings. Work the grease completely into the bearings, forcing it between the rollers, cone and cage from the back side (**see illustration**).
16 Apply a thin coat of grease to the spindle at the outer bearing seat, inner bearing seat, shoulder and seal seat.
17 Put a small quantity of grease inboard of each bearing race inside the hub. Using your finger, form a dam at these points to provide extra grease availability and to keep thinned grease from flowing out of the bearing.
18 Place the grease-packed inner bearing into the rear of the drum/hub and put a little more grease outboard of the bearing.
19 Place a new seal over the inner bearing and tap the seal evenly into place with a hammer and block of wood until it's flush with the hub.
20 Carefully place the drum/hub assembly onto the spindle and push the grease-packed outer bearing into position.

Adjustment - castellated nut
Refer to illustration 32.27
Note: *If equipped with a self-locking nut, install a new self-locking nut, torque to specs listed in this Chapter's Specifications, then proceed to Step 27.*
21 Install the washer and spindle nut. Tighten the nut only slightly (no more than 15 ft-lbs of torque).
22 Spin the drum/hub in a forward direction to seat the bearings and remove any grease or burrs which could cause excessive bearing play later.
23 Check to see that the tightness of the spindle nut is still approximately 15 ft-lbs.
24 Loosen the spindle nut until it's just loose, no more.
25 Tighten the nut until it's snug (4 ft-lbs). Install the nut lock, then install a new cotter pin through the hole in the spindle and the slots in the nut lock. If the slots don't line up, loosen the nut slightly until they do. The nut should not be loosened more than one-half flat to install the cotter pin.
26 Bend the ends of the cotter pin until they're flat against the nut. Cut off any extra length which could interfere with the dust cap.
27 Install the dust cap, tapping it into place with a hammer and a large punch (**see illustration**).
28 Install the tire/wheel assembly on the drum/hub and tighten the

lug nuts.
29 Grasp the top and bottom of the tire and check the bearings in the manner described earlier in this Section.
30 Lower the vehicle.

33 Brake fluid replacement

1 Because brake fluid absorbs moisture which could ultimately cause corrosion of the brake components, and air which could make the braking system less effective, the fluid should be replaced at the specified intervals. This job can be accomplished for a nominal fee by a properly equipped brake shop using a pressure bleeder. The task can also be done by the home mechanic with the help of an assistant. To bleed the air and old fluid and replace it with fresh fluid from sealed containers, refer to the brake bleeding procedure in Chapter 9.
2 If there is any possibility that incorrect fluid has been used in the system, drain all the fluid and flush the system with methylated spirits. Replace all piston seals and cups, as they will be affected and could possibly fail under pressure.

34 Automatic transaxle fluid and filter change

Refer to illustrations 34.7, 34.9 and 34.11
1 At the specified time intervals, the automatic transaxle fluid should be drained and replaced.
2 Before beginning work, purchase the specified transmission fluid (see *Recommended lubricants and fluids* at the front of this chapter).
3 Other tools necessary for this job include jackstands to support the vehicle in a raised position, a drain pan capable of holding at least eight pints, newspapers and clean rags.
4 The fluid should be drained immediately after the vehicle has been driven. Hot fluid is more effective than cold fluid at removing built up sediment. **Warning:** *Fluid temperature can exceed 350° in a hot transaxle. Wear protective gloves.*
5 After the vehicle has been driven to warm up the fluid, raise it and place it on jackstands for access to the transaxle drain plug.
6 Move the necessary equipment under the vehicle, being careful not to touch any of the hot exhaust components.
7 Place the drain pan under the drain plug in the transaxle and remove the drain plug (**see illustration**). Be sure the drain pan is in position, as fluid will come out with some force. Once the fluid is drained, reinstall the drain plug securely.
8 Remove the transaxle pan bolts, carefully pry the pan loose with a screwdriver and remove it.

32.15 Work the grease into the bearing rollers from the back side of the bearing race

32.27 Tap the grease cap into place with a large punch and a hammer, working around the outer circumference

34.7 Use a box-end wrench to remove the automatic transaxle drain plug without rounding it off

34.9   Remove the four bolts (arrows) and detach the filter

34.11   Be sure to reinstall the magnet in the fluid pan recess

9   Remove the four filter retaining bolts, and detach the filter from the transaxle **(see illustration)**. Be careful when lowering the filter as it contains residual fluid.
10   Place the new filter in position and install the bolts. Tighten the bolts to the specified torque.
11   Carefully clean the gasket surfaces of the fluid pan, removing all traces of old gasket material. Wash the pan in clean solvent and dry it with compressed air. Be sure to clean and reinstall the magnet **(see illustration)**.
12   Install a new gasket, place the fluid pan in position and install the bolts. Tighten the bolts to the specified torque.
13   Lower the vehicle.
14   With the engine off, add new fluid to the transaxle through the dipstick tube (see *Recommended lubricants and fluids* for the recommended fluid type and capacity). Use a funnel to prevent spills. It is best to add a little fluid at a time, continually checking the level with the dipstick (Section 7). Allow the fluid time to drain into the pan.
15   Start the engine and shift the selector into all positions from Park through Low, then shift into Park and apply the parking brake.
16   With the engine idling, check the fluid level. Add fluid up to the HOT level on the dipstick.

35   Manual transaxle oil change

Refer to illustration 35.1
1   Remove the drain plug and drain the oil **(see illustration)**.

2   Reinstall the drain plug. Tighten it to the specified torque.
3   Add new oil until it begins to run out of the filler hole (Section 26). See *Recommended lubricants and fluids* for the specified lubricant type.

36   Evaporative emissions control system check and canister replacement

Refer to illustration 36.2
1   The function of the evaporative emissions control system is to draw fuel vapors from the gas tank and fuel system, store them in a charcoal canister and route them to the intake manifold during normal engine operation.
2   The most common symptom of a fault in the evaporative emissions system is a strong fuel odor in the engine compartment. If a fuel odor is detected, inspect the charcoal canister, located in the engine compartment **(see illustration)**. Check the canister and all hoses for damage and deterioration.
3   At the specified intervals, the charcoal canister must be replaced with a new one. Disconnect the hoses, release the spring clip and lift the canister from the engine compartment. Installation is the reverse of removal.
4   The evaporative emissions control system is explained in more detail in Chapter 6.

35.1   The manual transaxle drain plug (arrow) is located on the right side of the case

36.2   The evaporative emissions (charcoal) canister is located on the firewall — check the hoses for cracks and other damage — release the spring clip (arrow) to remove the canister

37.1   Tools needed to check and adjust the ignition timing

1   Vacuum plugs — *Vacuum hoses will, in most cases, have to be disconnected and plugged. Molded plugs in various shapes and sizes are available for this*
2   Inductive pick-up timing light — *Flashes a bright concentrated beam of light when the number one spark plug fires. Connect the leads according to the instructions supplied with the light*
3   Distributor wrench — *On some models, the hold-down bolt for the distributor is difficult to reach and turn with conventional wrenches or sockets. A special wrench like this must be used*

37   Ignition timing check and adjustment

Refer to illustrations 37.1, 37.3 and 37.10

Note: *If the information in this Section differs from the Vehicle Emission Control Information label in the engine compartment of your vehicle, the label should be considered correct.*

1   Some special tools are required for this procedure **(see illustration)**. The engine must be at normal operating temperature and the air conditioner must be Off. Make sure the idle speed is correct (Section 20).
2   Apply the parking brake and block the wheels to prevent movement of the vehicle. The transmission must be in Park (automatic) or Neutral (manual).
3   Locate the timing marks at the drivebelt end of the engine (they should be visible from above after the hood is opened) **(see illustration)**. The crankshaft pulley or vibration damper has a notch in it and a plate with raised numbers is attached to the timing cover. Clean the plate with solvent so the numbers are visible.
4   Use chalk or white paint to mark the notch in the pulley/vibration damper.
5   Highlight the point on the timing plate that corresponds to the ignition timing specification on the Vehicle Emission Control Information label.
6   Hook up the timing light by following the manufacturer's instructions (an inductive pick-up timing light is preferred). Generally, the power leads are attached to the battery terminals and the pick-up lead is attached to the number one spark plug wire. The number one spark plug is the one closest to the drivebelt end of the engine. **Caution:** *If an inductive pick-up timing light isn't available, don't puncture the spark plug wire to attach the timing light pick-up lead. Instead, use an adapter between the spark plug and plug wire. If the insulation on the plug wire is damaged, the secondary voltage will jump to ground at the damaged point and the engine will misfire.*

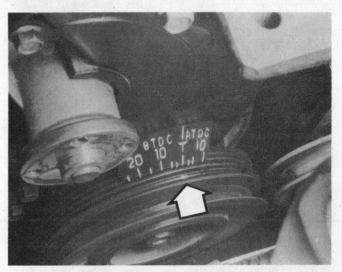

37.3   The timing marks are located on the drivebelt end of the engine (drivebelt is removed for clarity) — highlight the notch in the crankshaft pulley and the appropriate mark on the timing plate

37.7   On 1991 and later models, ground the timing adjustment terminal before checking or adjusting timing

37.11   After loosening the mounting nut, rotate the distributor housing to adjust the ignition timing

7   On 1991 and later models, connect a jumper wire between the terminal for ignition timing adjustment and ground **(see illustration)**.
8   Make sure the timing light wires are routed away from the drivebelts and fan, then start the engine.
9   Allow the idle speed to stabilize, then point the flashing timing light at the timing marks - be very careful of moving engine components!

38.1   The PCV valve (arrow) is screwed into the end of the rocker arm cover and is connected to the air cleaner by a hose

39.1   Prior to removing the oxygen sensor (1), unplug the wire at the connector (2), unscrew the bolts (3) and remove the exhaust manifold heat shield

10   The mark on the pulley/vibration damper will appear stationary.If it's aligned with the specified point on the timing plate, the ignition timing is correct.

11   If the marks aren't aligned, adjustment is required. Loosen the distributor mounting nut **(see illustration)** and turn the distributor very slowly until the marks are aligned.

12   Tighten the nut and recheck the timing.

13   Turn off the engine and remove the timing light (and jumper wire, if used).

38   Positive Crankcase Ventilation (PCV) valve check and replacement

Refer to illustration 38.1

1   The PCV valve is located in the rocker arm cover **(see illustration)**.

2   Disconnect the hose, unscrew the PCV valve from the cover, then reconnect the hose.

3   With the engine idling at normal operating temperature, place your finger over the valve opening. If there's no vacuum at the valve, check for a plugged hose or valve. Replace any plugged or deteriorated hoses.

4   Turn off the engine. Remove the PCV valve from the hose. Blow through the valve from the threaded end. If air will not pass through

the valve in this direction, replace it with a new one.

5   When purchasing a replacement PCV valve, make sure it's for your particular vehicle and engine size. Compare the old valve with the new one to make sure they're the same.

39   Oxygen sensor replacement

1986 through 1989 models
Refer to illustration 39.1

Warning: *The electric cooling fan can activate at any time, even when the ignition is in the Off position. Disconnect the fan motor or negative battery cable when working in the vicinity of the fan.*

1   Unplug the oxygen sensor wire at the connector located directly behind the top left corner of the radiator and remove the exhaust manifold heat shield bolts **(see illustration)**.

2   Lift the heat shield up for access and unscrew the oxygen sensor.

3   Screw the new oxygen sensor into the exhaust manifold. Tighten the sensor securely.

4   Place the heat shield in position and install the retaining bolts. Tighten the bolts securely.

5   Plug in the electrical connector.

1990 and later models

6   Unplug the oxygen sensor wire at the connector located behind the radiator.

7   Unscrew the oxygen sensor from the exhaust manifold.

8   Screw the new sensor into the exhaust manifold. Tighten the sensor securely.

9   Plug in the electrical connector.

Chapter 2 Part A Engine

Contents

Specifications

General
Firing order 1-3-4-2
Cylinder numbers (drivebelt end-to-transaxle end) 1–2–3–4

Camshaft
Camshaft end play . . . . 0.002 to 0.008 in (0.05 to 0.20 mm)
Cam lobe height
  Standard
    Intake . . . . 1.500 in (38.1 mm)
    Exhaust . . . . 1.5039 in (38.2 mm)
  Wear limit . . . . 0.020 in (0.5 mm)
Camshaft bearing oil clearance . . . . 0.002 to 0.0035 in (0.05 to 0.09 mm)

Cylinder head
Warpage limit . . . . 0.004 in (0.1 mm)

Timing belt
Timing belt deflection . . . . 0.28 to 0.35 in (7 to 9 mm)
Clearance between timing belt and seal line . . . . Approx. 0.55 in (14 mm)

Oil pump
Clearances
  Outer gear-to-front case . . . . 0.0039 to 0.0079 in (0.10 to 0.20 mm)
  Outer gear-to-crescent . . . . 0.0087 to 0.0134 in (0.22 to 0.34 mm)
  Inner gear-to-crescent . . . . 0.0083 to 0.0126 in (0.21 to 0.32 mm)
  Gear end play . . . . 0.0016 to 0.0039 in (0.04 to 0.10 mm)
Pressure regulator spring
  Free height . . . . 1.850 in (47 mm)
  Load . . . . 9.5 lb at 1.575 in (4.3 kg at 40 mm)

0793H

Firing order 1 - 3 - 4 - 2

**Cylinder location and
distributor rotation**

Torque specifications

Ft-lbs (unless otherwise indicated)

Rocker arm cover bolts	15 to 50 in-lbs
Intake and exhaust manifold nuts and bolts	
Carbureted models	12 to 14
Fuel-injected models	11 to 14
Air inlet surge tank bolts and nuts	11 to 14
Throttle body bolts	11 to 16
Camshaft sprocket bolt	47 to 54
Cylinder head bolts	
Cold engine	51 to 54
Warm engine	58 to 61
Crankshaft pulley bolts	130 in-lbs
Crankshaft pulley center bolt	51 to 72
Oil pump cover bolts	130 in-lbs
Oil pump-to-block bolts	130 in-lbs
Oil pan bolts	75 in-lbs
Flywheel/driveplate bolts	94 to 101
Timing belt cover bolts	84 to 110 in-lbs
Rocker arm shaft bolts	14 to 20
Cylinder head rear cover bolts	75 to 84 in-lbs
Timing belt tensioner bolt	14 to 20

1 General information

This Part of Chapter 2 is devoted to in-vehicle engine repair procedures. Information concerning engine removal and installation and engine block and cylinder head overhaul can be found in Part B of this Chapter.

The following repair procedures are based on the assumption that the engine is installed in the vehicle. If the engine has been removed from the vehicle and mounted on a stand, many of the steps outlined in this Part of Chapter 2 will not apply.

The Specifications included in this Part of Chapter 2 apply only to the procedures contained in this Part. Part B of Chapter 2 contains the Specifications necessary for cylinder head and engine block rebuilding.

2 Repair operations possible with the engine in the vehicle

Many major repair operations can be accomplished without removing the engine from the vehicle.

Clean the engine compartment and the exterior of the engine with some type of degreaser before any work is done. It will make the job easier and help keep dirt out of the internal areas of the engine.

Depending on the components involved, it may be helpful to remove the hood to improve access to the engine as repairs are performed (refer to Chapter 11 if necessary). Cover the fenders to prevent damage to the paint. Special pads are available, but an old bedspread or blanket will also work.

If vacuum, exhaust, oil or coolant leaks develop, indicating a need for gasket or seal replacement, the repairs can generally be made with the engine in the vehicle. The intake and exhaust manifold gaskets, oil pan gasket, crankshaft oil seals and cylinder head gasket are all accessible with the engine in place.

Exterior engine components, such as the intake and exhaust manifolds, the oil pan (and the oil pump), the water pump, the starter motor, the alternator, the distributor and the fuel system components can be removed for repair with the engine in place.

Since the camshaft and cylinder head can be removed without pulling the engine, valve component servicing can also be accomplished with the engine in the vehicle. Replacement of the timing belt and sprockets is also possible with the engine in the vehicle.

In extreme cases caused by a lack of necessary equipment, repair or replacement of piston rings, pistons, connecting rods and rod bearings is possible with the engine in the vehicle. However, this practice is not recommended because of the cleaning and preparation work that must be done to the components involved.

3 Top Dead Center (TDC) for number one piston — locating

Refer to illustrations 3.4, 3.6 and 3.7

Note: *The following procedure is based on the assumption that the spark plug wires and distributor are correctly installed. If you are trying to locate TDC to install the distributor correctly, piston position must be determined by feeling for compression at the number one spark plug hole, then aligning the ignition timing marks as described in step 6.*

1   Top Dead Center (TDC) is the highest point in the cylinder that each piston reaches as it travels up-and-down when the crankshaft turns. Each piston reaches TDC on the compression stroke and again on the exhaust stroke, but TDC generally refers to piston position on the compression stroke.

2   Positioning the piston(s) at TDC is an essential part of many procedures such as rocker arm removal, camshaft and timing belt/sprocket removal and distributor removal.

3   Before beginning this procedure, be sure to place the transmission in Neutral and apply the parking brake or block the rear wheels. Also, disable the ignition system by detaching the coil wire from the center terminal of the distributor cap and grounding it on the block with a jumper wire. Remove the spark plugs (see Chapter 1).

4   In order to bring any piston to TDC, the crankshaft must be turned using one of the methods outlined below. When looking at the drivebelt end of the engine, normal crankshaft rotation is *clockwise*.

    a)   The preferred method is to turn the crankshaft with a socket and ratchet attached to the bolt threaded into the drivebelt end of the crankshaft **(see illustration)**.

    b)   A remote starter switch, which may save some time, can also be used. Follow the instructions included with the switch. Once the piston is close to TDC, use a socket and ratchet as described in the previous paragraph.

    c)   If an assistant is available to turn the ignition switch to the Start position in short bursts, you can get the piston close to TDC without a remote starter switch. Make sure your assistant is out

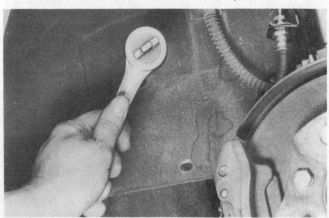

3.4 The crankshaft may be turned by placing a socket on the crankshaft pulley center bolt and slipping an extension through the left inner fender panel (wheel and tire removed for clarity)

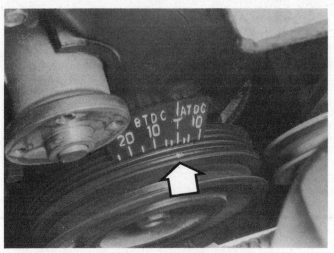

3.6 Align the notch in the pulley (arrow) with the T on the timing plate (drivebelts and water pump pulley removed for clarity)

3.8 When the number one piston is at Top Dead Center on the compression stroke, the distributor rotor should point straight down as shown here

of the vehicle, away from the ignition switch, then use a socket and ratchet as described in Paragraph a) to complete the procedure.

5   Detach the cap from the distributor and set it aside (see Chapter 1 if necessary).

6   Turn the crankshaft (see Paragraph 3 above) until the notch in the crankshaft pulley is aligned with the T on the timing plate (located at the front of the engine) **(see illustration)**.

7   Look at the distributor rotor — it should be pointing straight down **(see illustration)**.

8   If the rotor is 180° off, the number one piston is at TDC on the exhaust stroke. Go to Step 9.

9   To get the piston to TDC on the compression stroke, turn the crankshaft one complete turn (360°) clockwise. The rotor should now be pointing straight down. When the rotor is pointing at the number one spark plug wire terminal in the distributor cap and the ignition timing marks are aligned, the number one piston is at TDC on the compression stroke.

10   After the number one piston has been positioned at TDC on the compression stroke, TDC for any of the remaining pistons can be located by turning the crankshaft and following the firing order. With the distributor cap installed, use a felt tip pen or chalk to make a mark on the distributor body directly beneath each of the terminals on the distributor cap. Then number the marks to correspond with the cylinder numbers. As you turn the crankshaft, the rotor will also turn. When it's pointing directly at one of the marks on the distributor, the piston for that particular cylinder is at TDC on the compression stroke.

4 Rocker arm cover — removal and installation

Refer to illustration 4.3

1   Disconnect the negative cable from the battery.

2   Remove the air cleaner assembly (see Chapter 4).

3   Detach the spark plug wires and cable brackets from the rocker arm cover **(see illustration)**.

4   Clearly label and then disconnect any emission hoses which connect to or cross over the rocker arm cover.

5   Remove the six rocker arm cover bolts and lift the cover off. If the cover sticks to the cylinder head, tap on it with a soft-face hammer or place a block of wood against the cover and tap on the wood with a hammer.

6   Thoroughly clean the rocker arm cover and remove all traces of old gasket material.

7   Install a new gasket on the cover, using RTV to hold it in place. Place the cover on the engine and install the six cover bolts.

8   Working from the center out, tighten the bolts to the specified torque.

9   The remaining steps are the reverse of removal. When finished, run the engine and check for oil leaks.

4.3 Detach the spark plug wires and cable bracket

5 Rocker arm assembly — removal, inspection and installation

Removal

Refer to illustration 5.3

1   Remove the rocker arm cover (see Section 4).

2   Position the number one piston at Top Dead Center (see Section 3).

3   Loosen the rocker arm shaft mounting bolts **(see illustration)** 1/4-turn at a time each until the spring pressure is relieved.

5.3 Rocker shaft mounting bolts

5.6   Check the contact faces and adjusting screw tips (arrows) (jet valve model shown)

5.7   Back off the adjusters until they only protrude 1 mm (0.040-inch) (jet valve model shown)

4   Finish removing the bolts and lift each rocker arm shaft assembly from the engine.

Inspection
Refer to illustration 5.6

5   If you wish to disassemble and inspect the rocker arm assemblies (a good idea as long as you have them off), remove the retaining bolts and slip the rocker arms and springs off the shafts. Keep the parts in order so you can reassemble them in the same positions.

6   Thoroughly clean the parts and inspect them for wear and damage. Check the rocker arm faces that contact the camshaft and the adjusting screw tips **(see illustration)**. Replace any parts that are damaged or excessively worn. Also, make sure the oil holes in the shafts are not plugged.

Installation
Refer to illustration 5.7

7   Loosen the locknuts and back off the adjusters **(see illustration)** until they only protrude 1 mm (0.040-inch).

8   Lubricate all components with assembly lube or engine oil and reassemble them, referring to illustration 5.3. When installing the rocker arms, shafts and springs, note the markings and the difference between the left and right side parts. The free length of the RH springs (exhaust side) is approximately 1.85-inch (47 mm) while the LH springs (intake side) is approximately 3.03-inch (77 mm).

9   Position the rocker arm assemblies on the cylinder head and install the mounting bolts finger tight.

10   Tighten the bolts in several stages until the specified torque is reached.

11   Adjust the valve clearances (cold) as described in Chapter 1.

12   Temporarily install the rocker arm cover and run the engine until it is fully warmed up (coolant temp 176 to 203ºF).

13   Readjust the valves while the engine is still warm (see Chapter 1).

14   Reinstall the remaining parts in the reverse order of removal.

15   Run the engine and check for oil leaks and proper operation.

---

6   Valve springs, retainers and seals — replacement

Refer to illustrations 6.4, 6.5, 6.9, 6.10, 6.15 and 6.17

Note: *Broken valve springs and defective valve stem seals can be replaced without removing the cylinder heads. Two special tools and a compressed air source are normally required to perform this operation, so read through this Section carefully and rent or buy the tools before beginning the job. If compressed air isn't available, a length of nylon rope can be used to keep the valves from falling into the cylinder during this procedure.*

1   Refer to Section 4 and remove the rocker arm cover.

2   Remove the spark plug from the cylinder which has the defective component. If all of the valve stem seals are being replaced, all of the spark plugs should be removed.

3   Turn the crankshaft until the piston in the affected cylinder is at top dead center on the compression stroke (refer to Section 3 for instructions). If you're replacing all of the valve stem seals, begin with cylinder number one and work on the valves for one cylinder at a time. Move from cylinder-to-cylinder following the firing order sequence (see the Specifications).

4   Thread an adapter into the spark plug hole **(see illustration)** and connect an air hose from a compressed air source to it. Most auto parts stores can supply the air hose adapter. **Note:** *Many cylinder compression gauges utilize a screw-in fitting that may work with your air hose quick-disconnect fitting.*

5   Remove the rocker arm shaft (see Section 5), unless you are using a lever-type tool **(see illustration)**.

6   Apply compressed air to the cylinder. **Warning:** *The piston may be forced down by compressed air, causing the crankshaft to turn sud-*

6.4   This is what the air hose adapter that threads into the spark plug hole looks like — they're commonly available from auto parts stores

6.5   If you use a lever-type tool such as this one, leave the intake shaft in place while you replace the exhaust seals and vice-versa

6.9   Use needle-nose pliers (shown) or a small magnet to
remove the valve spring keepers — Be careful not to
drop them down into the engine!

6.10   Remove the valve guide seal with a pair of pliers

2A

denly. *If the wrench used when positioning the number one piston at TDC is still attached to the bolt in the crankshaft nose, it could cause damage or injury when the crankshaft moves.*

7   The valves should be held in place by the air pressure. If the valve faces or seats are in poor condition, leaks may prevent air pressure from retaining the valves — refer to the alternative procedure below.

8   If you don't have access to compressed air, an alternative method can be used. Position the piston at a point just before TDC on the compression stroke, then feed a long piece of nylon rope through the spark plug hole until it fills the combustion chamber. Be sure to leave the end of the rope hanging out of the engine so it can be removed easily. Use a large ratchet and socket to rotate the crankshaft in the normal direction of rotation until **slight** resistance is felt.

9   Stuff shop rags into the cylinder head holes above and below the valves to prevent parts and tools from falling into the engine, then use a valve spring compressor to compress the spring. Remove the keepers with small needle-nose pliers or a magnet (**see illustration**). Note: *A couple of different types of tools are available for compressing the valve springs with the head in place. One type grips the lower spring coils and presses on the retainer as the knob is turned, while the other type utilizes the rocker arm shaft for leverage. Both types work very well, although the lever type is usually less expensive.*

10   Remove the spring retainer and valve spring, then remove the guide seal (**see illustration**). Note: *If air pressure fails to hold the valve in the closed position during this operation, the valve face and/or seat*

is probably damaged. If so, the cylinder head will have to be removed for additional repair operations.

11   Wrap a rubber band or tape around the top of the valve stem so the valve won't fall into the combustion chamber, then release the air pressure. **Note:** *If a rope was used instead of air pressure, turn the crankshaft slightly in the direction opposite normal rotation.*

12   Inspect the valve stem for damage. Rotate the valve in the guide and check the end for eccentric movement, which would indicate that the valve is bent.

13   Move the valve up-and-down in the guide and make sure it doesn't bind. If the valve stem binds, either the valve is bent or the guide is damaged. In either case, the head will have to be removed for repair.

14   Reapply air pressure to the cylinder to retain the valve in the closed position, then remove the tape or rubber band from the valve stem. If a rope was used instead of air pressure, rotate the crankshaft in the normal direction of rotation until **slight** resistance is felt.

15   Lubricate the valve stem with engine oil and install a new guide seal (**see illustration**).

16   Install the spring in position over the valve.

17   Install the valve spring retainer. Compress the valve spring and carefully position the keepers in the groove. Apply a small dab of grease to the inside of each keeper to hold it in place if necessary (**see illustration**).

18   Remove the pressure from the spring tool and make sure the keepers are seated.

6.15   Gently tap the seal into place with a hammer and
deep socket or Hyundai tool no. 0922-21100

6.17   Apply a small dab of grease to each keeper before
installation to hold it in place on the valve stem
until the spring is released

**7.8a   The upper timing belt cover is attached
with three bolts (arrows)**

**7.8b   Arrows point to the locations of the lower timing
belt cover bolts (cover removed for clarity)**

19 Disconnect the air hose and remove the adapter from the spark plug hole. If a rope was used in place of air pressure, pull it out of the cylinder.
20 Refer to Section 5 and install the rocker shafts.
21 Install the spark plug(s) and hook up the wire(s).
22 Refer to Section 4 and install the rocker arm cover.
23 Start and run the engine, then check for oil leaks and unusual sounds coming from the rocker arm cover area.

7   Timing belt and sprockets — removal, inspection and installation

Removal

Refer to illustrations 7.8a, 7.8b, 7.9, 7.10, 7.11, 7.12, 7.14, 7.15a, and 7.15b

Caution: *Do not try to turn the crankshaft with the camshaft sprocket bolt and do not rotate the crankshaft counterclockwise.*

Note: *The valves will not collide with the pistons if the crankshaft is turned while the timing belt is removed.*

1   Position the number one piston at Top Dead Center (see Section 3).
2   Disconnect the negative cable from the battery.
3   Remove the air cleaner assembly and associated hoses (see Chapter 4).
4   Set the parking brake and block the rear wheels. Raise the front of the vehicle and support it securely on jackstands.
5   Remove the left engine mount (see Section 17).
6   Loosen the four water pump pulley bolts and then remove the drivebelts (see Chapter 1).
7   Unbolt and remove the water pump pulley.
8   Remove the three bolts that secure the upper timing belt cover **(see illustration)** and lift the cover off. Remove the four bolts that secure the lower cover **(see illustration)** and lift it off.
9   If you plan to reuse the timing belt, paint an arrow on it **(see illustration)** to indicate the direction of rotation (clockwise).
10 Loosen the adjusting bolt and move the timing belt tensioner towards the water pump as far as possible **(see illustration)**. Temporarily secure the tensioner by tightening the bolt.
11 Remove the splash pan from beneath the drivebelt end of the engine, then remove the large center bolt from the crankshaft pulley. It's very tight, so, to break it loose, wrap a rag around the pulley and

**7.9   If you plan to reuse the belt, paint an arrow on it to
indicate direction of rotation (clockwise)**

**7.10   Loosen the belt tensioner bolt (arrow) and pry the
tensioner towards the water pump (belt removed for clarity)**

7.11 Wrap a protective cloth around the pulley and attach a chain wrench — loosen the crankshaft pulley center bolt with a socket, extension and breaker bar

7.12 Remove the flywheel/driveplate cover for access and wedge a flat-blade screwdriver in the ring gear teeth at the right corner of the engine block (axle removed for clarity)

then attach a chain wrench. Slip a socket onto the bolt and then fit an extension through the hole in the inner fender. Carefully turn the extension with a breaker bar (**see illustration**).

12 If you are unable to loosen the bolt due to the chain wrench slipping, you can prevent the crankshaft from turning by having an assistant wedge a flat-blade screwdriver in the flywheel/driveplate ring gear teeth (**see illustration**). To do this, you must first remove the flywheel/driveplate cover (described in the transaxle removal procedures in Chapter 7).

13 Slip the timing belt off the sprockets and set it aside.

14 If you intend to remove the camshaft, unscrew the camshaft sprocket securing bolt and slide the sprocket off — a large screwdriver inserted through a hole in the sprocket will keep it from turning while you remove the bolt (**see illustration**).

15 If you intend to replace the crankshaft front oil seal, unscrew the four securing bolts for the crankshaft pulley (**see illustration**) and slide it off; then slide off the crankshaft sprocket and the belt guide flange (**see illustration**) located behind the crankshaft sprocket. When removing the flange, note the way it's installed (the chamfered side faces out).

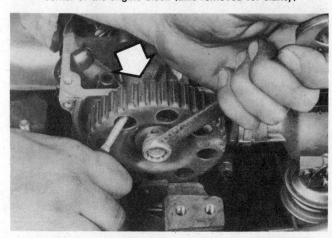

7.14 Slip a large screwdriver through the sprocket to prevent the camshaft from turning — be sure to pad the gasket surface (arrow) to prevent damage to the head

7.15a Remove the crankshaft pulley bolts (arrows)

7.15b When removing the belt guide, note how it's installed — the chamfered side (side with the tooth marks) faces out

Inspection

Refer to illustrations 7.16 and 7.17

16 Rotate the tensioner pulley by hand and move it side-to-side to detect roughness and excess play **(see illustration)**. Visually inspect the sprockets for any signs of damage and wear. Replace parts as necessary.

17 Inspect the timing belt **(see illustration)** for cracks, separation, wear, missing teeth and oil contamination. Replace the belt if it is in questionable condition.

7.16 Turn the tensioner pulley by hand to detect roughness and excess play

Installation

Refer to illustrations 7.18, 7.19a, 7.19b, 7.20, 7.23, 7.24 and 7.26

18 Reinstall the timing belt sprockets, if they were removed. Note that the camshaft sprocket is indexed by a dowel. Slip the belt guide flange onto the crankshaft before installing the lower sprocket — the chamfered side of the flange faces out. The crankshaft sprocket has two different size flats which match those on the crankshaft **(see illustration)**.

7.17 Carefully inspect the timing belt for the conditions shown here

7.18 Timing belt and related components — exploded view

1	Upper cover	7	Tensioner spring
2	Lower cover	8	Tensioner
3	Gasket	9	Timing belt
4	Damper pulley	10	Camshaft sprocket
5	Crankshaft pulley	11	Crankshaft sprocket
6	Tensioner spacer	12	Belt guide

19 Align the timing marks located on the camshaft and crankshaft sprockets (see illustrations).
20 Slip the timing belt onto the crankshaft sprocket. While maintaining tension on the rear (firewall) side of the belt, slip the belt onto the camshaft sprocket (see illustration).
21 Release the tensioner hold-down bolt to allow spring tension against the belt. Retighten the bolt.
22 Install the crankshaft pulley, taking care to align the locating pin with the small hole in the pulley. Install the crankshaft pulley bolts (both the pulley securing bolts and the center bolt) and tighten them to the specified torques. When tightening the bolts, hold the crankshaft in place using one of the methods discussed in Steps 11 and 12.
23 Using the bolt in the center of the crankshaft pulley, turn the crankshaft clockwise through two complete revolutions (720°). Recheck the alignment of the valve timing marks (see illustration). If the marks do not align properly, loosen the tensioner, slip the belt off the camshaft sprocket, align the marks, reinstall the belt, and check the alignment again.
24 Check for proper timing belt tension by pushing on the belt with thumb pressure. It should deflect to 1/4 of adjuster bolt head width (see illustration). If it is too tight or too loose, loosen the tensioner bolts and adjust the tensioner.
25 Tighten the tensioner bolts to the specified torque, starting with the adjustment bolt; then tighten the bolt which goes through the tension spring.

7.19a Line up the dowel on the crankshaft sprocket with the stationary mark on the oil pump (arrows)

2A

7.19b Align the triangular mark on the camshaft sprocket with the stationary mark on the cylinder head (arrows)

7.20 Maintain tension on the firewall side (right side of photo) of the belt during installation

7.23 Since you must view the camshaft sprocket marks at an angle, it may help to use a pointer to avoid mistakes

7.24 The belt is tensioned properly if it can be pressed in to 1/4 of the adjustment bolt head width

Thread diameter x Length   mm (in.)

7.26   Be sure to return the timing belt cover bolts to their proper locations

26 Reinstall the remaining parts in the reverse order of removal. Note that the timing belt cover bolts come in different lengths **(see illustration)**.

27 Start the engine, set the ignition timing (see Chapter 1) and road test the vehicle.

8 Front crankshaft oil seal — replacement

Refer to illustrations 8.2 and 8.4

1   Remove the timing belt and the crankshaft sprocket (see Section 7).

2   Wrap the tip of a small screwdriver with tape. Working from below the left inner fender, use the screwdriver to pry the seal out of its bore **(see illustration)**. Take care to prevent damaging the crankshaft and the seal bore.

3   Thoroughly clean and inspect the seal bore and sealing surface on the crankshaft. Minor imperfections can be removed with emery cloth. If there is a groove worn in the crankshaft sealing surface (from

8.4   Install the new front crankshaft oil seal by carefully tapping it into place with a socket and extension fit through the access hole in the left inner fender

8.2   Working from below the left inner fender, carefully pry the seal out with a small screwdriver

contact with the seal), installing a new seal will probably not stop the leak. Such wear normally indicates the internal engine components are also worn. Consider overhauling the engine.

4   Lubricate the new seal with engine oil and drive the seal into place with a hammer and socket **(see illustration)**.

5   Reinstall the timing belt and related components as described in Section 7.

6   Run the engine, checking for oil leaks.

9 Camshaft — removal, inspection and installation

Removal

Refer to illustrations 9.8, 9.10, 9.11, 9.12 and 9.13

1   Position the number one piston at Top Dead Center (see Section 3).

2   Disconnect the negative cable from the battery.

3   Drain the cooling system (see Chapter 1) and disconnect the upper radiator hose from the thermostat housing.

4   Detach the rocker arm cover (see Section 4).

5   Remove the distributor (see Chapter 5).

6   Remove the fuel pump (see Chapter 4).

7   Remove the timing belt and camshaft sprocket (see Section 7).

8   Wrap some tape around the end of a small screwdriver and use it to pry out the camshaft oil seal **(see illustration)**. Be careful not to

9.8   Carefully pry out the seal without scratching the metal surfaces

9.10   Remove the lower bolts (A) first and set the bracket aside, then the upper bolts (B) and finally the thrust case bolt (C)

9.11   Grip the camshaft between the third and fourth exhaust lobes and remove the thrust plate bolt

2A

damage the seal bore or the sealing surface on the camshaft.

9   Detach the rocker arm assembly (see Section 5).

10   Remove the cylinder head transaxle-end cover and the camshaft thrust case bolt (**see illustration**).

11   Hold the camshaft to keep it from turning and remove the camshaft thrust plate bolt (**see illustration**).

12   Pull the camshaft thrust case out of the cylinder head (**see illustration**).

13   To gain clearance, unbolt the windshield washer reservoir and set it aside. Slip the camshaft out of the cylinder head toward the transaxle end of the engine (**see illustration**).

Inspection

Refer to illustrations 9.16, 9.17 and 9.19

14   Thoroughly clean the camshaft, the rear cover plate and the gasket surfaces.

15   Visually inspect the camshaft for wear and/or damage to the distributor drive gear, lobe surfaces, bearing journals and seal contact surfaces. Visually inspect the camshaft bearing surfaces in the cylinder head for scoring and other damage.

16   Measure the camshaft lobe heights (**see illustration**) and compare them to the specifications.

9.12   Pull the thrust case out of the cylinder head — if it's stuck, slide the camshaft back and forth slightly to push it out

9.13   Guide the camshaft out of the cylinder head — be careful not to damage the bearings in the head

9.16   Measure the camshaft lobe heights

9.17   Measure the camshaft journal diameters

9.19   Measure camshaft end play with a feeler gauge

17   Measure the camshaft bearing journal diameters **(see illustration)**, then measure the inside diameter of the camshaft bearing surfaces in the cylinder head, using a telescoping gauge. Subtract the journal measurement from the bearing measurement to obtain the camshaft bearing oil clearance. Compare this clearance with the specifications.
18   Replace the camshaft if it fails any of the above inspections. **Note:** *If the distributor drive gear is faulty, replace the driven gear also. If the lobes are worn, replace the rocker arms along with the camshaft. Cylinder head replacement may be necessary if the camshaft bearing surfaces in the head are damaged or excessively worn.*
19   Install the crankshaft thrust case and thrust plate on the camshaft and tighten the bolt securely. Check the camshaft end play **(see illustration)** and compare it to the specifications.
20   If the end play is excessive, replace the thrust case and recheck the end play.
21   If the end play is still too great, check the outer end of the camshaft transaxle end journal for wear. If it is badly worn, replace the camshaft.

Installation

Refer to illustration 9.25
22   Liberally coat the journals and thrust portions of the camshaft with assembly lube or engine oil.
23   Carefully install the camshaft in the cylinder head. Insert the camshaft thrust case with the threaded hole up and align the threaded hole with the bolt hole in the cylinder head. Lock the thrust plate in position with the bolt.
24   Install the rear cover with a new gasket and tighten the bolts to

the specified torque.
25   Coat a new camshaft oil seal with engine oil and press it into place with a hammer and deep socket or Hyundai special tool no. 09221-21000 **(see illustration)**.
26   Install the camshaft sprocket and tighten the bolts to the specified torque.
27   Install the timing belt (see Section 7).
28   Install the rocker arm assembly (see Section 5).
29   Temporarily set the valve clearances prior to engine start-up (see Chapter 1).
30   Reinstall the remaining parts in the reverse order of removal.
31   Start the engine and allow it to warm up (176 to 203-degrees F) while you adjust the ignition timing (see Chapter 1).
32   Readjust the valve clearances as described in Chapter 1.
33   Reinstall the rocker arm cover and run the engine while checking for oil leaks.

---

10   Intake manifold – removal and installation

Refer to illustrations 10.4a, 10.4b, 10.4c, 10.4d and 10.8
1   Disconnect the negative cable from the battery.
2   Drain the cooling system (see Chapter 1). On fuel injected models, unbolt and remove the air inlet surge tank.
3   Remove the air cleaner – carbureted models – (see Chapter 4). On fuel injected models, relieve the fuel system pressure (see Chapter 4, Section 3, step 21).
4   Clearly label **(see illustration)** and then disconnect all hoses,

9.25   Tap the seal gently into place with a hammer and a large socket

10.4a   Label the wires and hoses with masking tape and a marking pen

**10.4b   Unplug the solenoid control valve connector
(carbureted models)**

**10.4c   Unsnap the emission control valves from the brackets
(carbureted models)**

2A

wires, brackets and emission lines which run to the carburetor/throttle body and intake manifold. Several components may be slipped out of brackets and laid over the carburetor **(see illustrations)**. On fuel-injected models, remove the distributor and ignition coil.

5   Disconnect the fuel lines from the carburetor or fuel rail and cap the fittings to prevent leakage (see Chapter 4). **Note:** *It may not be necessary to remove the fuel rail and injectors.*

6   Disconnect the throttle cable from the carburetor/throttle body (see Chapter 4).

7   Detach the cable which runs from the carburetor to the transmission (automatic transmission only) and the cruise control cable, on vehicles so equipped.

8   Unbolt the intake manifold and remove it from the engine **(see illustration)**. If it sticks, tap the manifold with a soft-face hammer. **Caution:** *Do not pry between gasket sealing surfaces or tap on the carburetor or fuel injection components.*

9   Thoroughly clean the manifold and cylinder head mating surfaces, removing all traces of gasket material.

10   Install the manifold, using a new gasket and tighten the nuts in several stages, working from the center out, until the specified torque is reached.

11   Reinstall the remaining parts in the reverse order of removal.

12   Add coolant, run the engine and check for leaks and proper operation.

---

11   Exhaust manifold – removal and installation

Refer to illustrations 11.3, 11.6, 11.7, 11.8 and 11.12
Warning: *Allow the engine to cool completely before following this procedure.*

1   Disconnect the negative cable from the battery.

2   Set the parking brake and block the rear wheels. Raise the vehicle and support it securely on jackstands.

3   Working from under the vehicle, remove the nuts that secure the

**10.4d   Detach the solenoid (A) from the firewall and disconnect
the hose from the back of the valve (B)
(carbureted models)**

**10.8   This is what the manifold/carburetor assembly should look
like when it's removed (carbureted models)**

11.3   Working under the vehicle, apply penetrating oil to the threads and remove the nuts (arrows) — note that one is hidden from view

11.6   Apply penetrating oil and unscrew the flare nuts (arrows)

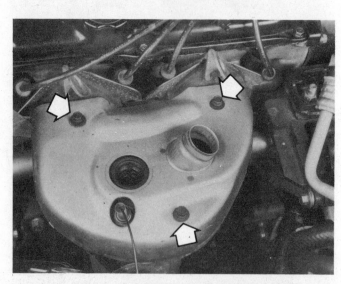

11.7   Remove the bolts from the heat shield (arrows)

exhaust system to the bottom of the exhaust manifold **(see illustration)**. Apply penetrating oil to the threads to make removal easier.

4   Remove the air cleaner assembly (see Chapter 4).

5   Unplug the oxygen sensor wire (see Chapter 1).

6   On models so equipped, apply penetrating oil and unscrew the flare nuts on the air injection tube **(see illustration)**. Remove the tube from the manifold.

7   Remove the three bolts that secure the heat shield **(see illustration)** to the exhaust manifold. Lift the heat shield off.

8   Apply penetrating oil to the threads and then remove the exhaust manifold mounting nuts **(see illustration)**, brackets and emission components.

9   Slip the manifold off the studs and remove it from the engine compartment.

10   Clean and inspect all threaded fasteners and repair as necessary.

11   Remove any traces of gasket material from the mating surfaces and inspect them for wear and cracks.

12   Fit a new gasket **(see illustration)**, install the manifold and tighten the nuts in several stages, working from the center out, to the specified torque.

13   Reinstall the remaining parts in the reverse order of removal.

14   Run the engine and check for exhaust leaks.

11.8   Remove the exhaust manifold mounting nuts (arrows)

11.12   The exhaust gasket is installed with the shields facing out as shown here

12.13   Install the new head gasket dry (no sealer) as shown — it can only go on one way due to the dowels (arrows)

12.10   Cylinder head bolt loosening sequence

12.14   Cylinder head bolt tightening sequence

12   Cylinder head — removal and installation

Refer to illustrations 12.10, 12.13 and 12.14

Caution: *Allow the engine to cool completely before following this procedure.*

1   Position the number one piston at Top Dead Center (see Section 3).
2   Disconnect the negative cable from the battery.
3   Drain the cooling system and remove the spark plugs (see Chapter 1).
4   Remove the intake manifold (see Section 10).
5   Remove the exhaust manifold (see Section 11).
6   Remove the distributor (see Chapter 5), including the cap and wires.
7   Remove the fuel pump (see Chapter 4).
8   Remove the timing belt (see Section 7).
9   Remove the rocker arm cover (see Section 4).
10   Using an 8 mm Allen head socket, loosen the cylinder head bolts, 1/4-turn at a time, in the sequence shown **(see illustration)** until they can be removed by hand.
11   Carefully lift the cylinder head straight up and place the head on wooden blocks to prevent damage to the sealing surfaces. If the head sticks to the engine block, dislodge it by placing a block of wood against the head casting and tapping the wood with a hammer. Cylinder head disassembly and inspection procedures are covered in Chapter 2, Part B. It's a good idea to have the head checked for warpage, even if you're just replacing the gasket.
12   Remove all traces of old gasket material from the block and head. Do not allow anything to fall into the engine. Clean and inspect all threaded fasteners and be sure the threaded holes in the block are clean and dry.
13   Place a new gasket **(see illustration)** and the cylinder head in position.
14   The cylinder head bolts should be tightened in several stages following the proper sequence **(see illustration)** to the specified torque.
15   Reinstall the timing belt (see Section 7).
16   Reinstall the remaining parts in the reverse order of removal.
17   Be sure to refill the cooling system and check all fluid levels. Rotate the crankshaft clockwise slowly by hand through two complete revolu-

tions. Recheck the camshaft timing marks (see Section 7).
18   Start the engine and set the ignition timing (see Chapter 1). Run the engine until normal operating temperature is reached. Check for leaks and proper operation. Shut off the engine, Remove the rocker arm cover and retorque the cylinder head bolts, unless the gasket manufacturer states otherwise. Recheck the valve adjustment.

13   Oil pan — removal and installation

Refer to illustrations 13.5a, 13.5b and 13.7

1   Disconnect the negative cable from the battery.
2   Raise the vehicle and support it securely on jackstands.
3   Remove the splash pan under the drivebelt end of the engine, then remove the dipstick and drain the engine oil (see Chapter 1).
4   Unbolt the front exhaust pipe from the exhaust manifold (see Section 11).

13.5a   Arrows point to oil pan bolts visible from below — others (not visible here) are located around the perimeter

13.5b   Tap the oil pan to break the seal

5   Remove the bolts (**see illustration**) and lower the oil pan from the vehicle. If the pan is stuck, tap it with a soft-face hammer (**see illustration**) or place a block of wood against the pan and tap the wood with a hammer.

6   Thoroughly clean the oil pan and sealing surfaces. Remove all traces of old gasket material. Check the oil pan sealing surface for distortion. Straighten or replace as necessary.

7   If the oil pan was sealed with RTV only (no gasket), you may apply a 4 mm bead of RTV sealer as shown (**see illustration**). If you are using a gasket, apply a thin coat of RTV sealer to the oil pan flange and affix the gasket.

8   Place the oil pan into position and install the bolts finger tight. Working side-to-side from the center out, tighten the bolts to the specified torque.

9   Reinstall the remaining parts in the reverse order of removal.

10   Refill the crankcase with the proper quantity and grade of oil and run the engine, checking for leaks. Road test the vehicle and check for leaks again.

13.7   If the oil pan was sealed with RTV only, apply RTV sealant in the groove and to the inside of the bolt holes

---

14   Oil pump — removal, inspection and installation

Removal

Refer to illustrations 14.3, 14.4, 14.5, 14.6 and 14.7

1   Remove the timing belt and crankshaft sprocket (see Section 7).

2   Remove the oil pan (see Section 13).

3   Unbolt the oil pickup tube (screen) from the bottom of the pump housing (**see illustration**).

4   Remove the pressure regulator plug, spring and plunger (**see illustration**).

5   Remove the timing belt tensioner (**see illustration**).

14.3   The oil pickup tube is attached to the bottom of the oil pump by two bolts (arrows)

14.4   Remove the pressure regulator plug, spring and plunger — if the plunger (arrow) sticks in the bore, remove it with a magnet

14.6 Note that the oil pump-to-block bolts come in different lengths

A 30 mm (1.181 in)
B 20 mm (0.787 in)
C 60 mm (2.362 in)

14.5 Remove the tensioner bolts, which are indicated by arrows (viewed from left inner fender)

6   Remove the oil pump-to-block bolts (**see illustration**) and carefully separate the front case from the engine.
7   Detach the cover from the rear of the case (**see illustration**) and remove the inner and outer oil pump gears.
8   Remove the crankshaft oil seal from the front case (see Section 8).

Inspection

Refer to Ilustrations 14.9, 14.10a, 14.10b, 14.10c, 14.10d and 14.10e

9   Clean all parts (**see illustration**) thoroughly and remove all traces of old gasket material from the sealing surfaces. Visually inspect all parts for wear, cracks and other damage. Replace parts as necessary.

14.7 Remove the screws (arrows) and lift off the oil pump cover

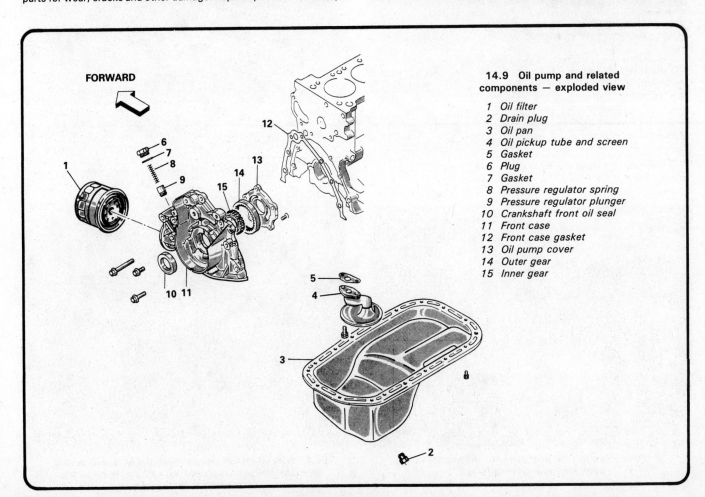

FORWARD

14.9 Oil pump and related components — exploded view

1 Oil filter
2 Drain plug
3 Oil pan
4 Oil pickup tube and screen
5 Gasket
6 Plug
7 Gasket
8 Pressure regulator spring
9 Pressure regulator plunger
10 Crankshaft front oil seal
11 Front case
12 Front case gasket
13 Oil pump cover
14 Outer gear
15 Inner gear

2A

14.10a Install the inner and outer gears as shown — the matchmarks (arrows) must be in the positions shown.

14.10b Measure the outer gear-to-front case clearance

14.10c Measure the inner gear-to-crescent clearance

14.10d Measure the outer gear-to-crescent clearance

14.10e Measure the gear end play with a precision straightedge and feeler gauge

14.13 When installing the pump on the engine, note that the crankshaft has machined flats which the oil pump inner gear must fit over

10 Install the oil pump outer and inner gears and measure the clearances **(see illustrations)**. Compare the clearances to the specifications. Measure the free height of the pressure regulator spring and compare the measurement to the specifications. Replace parts as necessary. Pack the pump cavity with petroleum jelly and install the cover. Tighten the bolts to the specified torque.

Installation

Refer to illustration 14.13

11 Replace the front crankshaft oil seal with a new seal (see Section 8).
12 Install the pressure regulator valve components and tighten the plug.
13 Using a new gasket, position the pump on the engine **(see illustration)**. Install the bolts in their proper locations, according to length **(see illustration 14.6)**. Tighten the bolts to the specified torque.
14 Reinstall the remaining parts in the reverse order of removal.
15 Add oil, start the engine and check for oil pressure and leaks.

---

15 Flywheel/driveplate — removal and installation

Refer to illustration 15.3

1 Raise the vehicle and support it securely on jackstands, then refer to Chapter 7 and remove the transaxle. If it's leaking, now would be a very good time to replace the front seal (the torque convertor must be removed to gain access to this seal).
2 Remove the pressure plate and clutch disc (manual transaxle equipped vehicles) (see Chapter 8). Now is a good time to check/replace the clutch components.
3 The bolt holes are staggered on the flywheel/driveplate and crankshaft to ensure correct alignment during reinstallation **(see illustration)**.
4 Remove the bolts that secure the flywheel/driveplate to the crankshaft. If the crankshaft turns, wedge a screwdriver in the ring gear teeth to jam the flywheel.
5 Remove the flywheel/driveplate from the crankshaft. Since the flywheel is fairly heavy, be sure to support it while removing the last bolt.
6 Clean the flywheel to remove grease and oil. Inspect the surface for cracks, rivet grooves, burned areas and score marks. Light scoring can be removed with emery cloth. Check for cracked and broken ring gear teeth. Lay the flywheel on a flat surface and use a straightedge to check for warpage. **Note:** *Ring gears are available separately and can be installed by an automative machine shop.*
7 Clean and inspect the mating surfaces of the flywheel/driveplate and the crankshaft. If the crankshaft rear seal is leaking, replace it before reinstalling the flywheel/driveplate (see Section 16).

15.3 The flywheel/driveplate bolt holes are staggered so they only line up one way

2A

8 Position the flywheel/driveplate against the crankshaft. Be sure to align the staggered bolt holes to ensure correct installation **(see illustration 15.3)**. Before installing the bolts, apply thread locking compound to the threads.
9 Wedge a screwdriver in the ring gear teeth to keep the flywheel/driveplate from turning as you tighten the bolts to the specified torque.
10 The remainder of installation is the reverse of the removal procedure.

---

16 Rear crankshaft oil seal — replacement

Refer to illustrations 16.2a, 16.2b, 16.5 and 16.6

1 The transaxle must be removed from the vehicle for this procedure (see Chapter 7).
2 The seal can be replaced without dropping the oil pan or removing the seal retainer. However, this method is not recommended because the lip of the seal is quite stiff and it's possible to cock the seal in the retainer bore or damage it during installation. If you want to take the chance, pry out the old seal **(see illustration)**. Apply moly-base grease to the crankshaft seal journal and the lip of the new seal and carefully tap the new seal into place **(see illustration)**. The lip is stiff so care-

16.2a The quick (but not recommended) way to replace the rear crankshaft oil seal is to simply pry the old one out

16.2b Lubricate the crankshaft journal and the lip of the new seal with moly-base grease and tap the new seal into place — the seal lip is stiff and can be easily damaged during installation if you're not careful

16.5   After removing the retainer from the engine, support it on wood blocks and drive out the old seal with a punch and hammer

16.6   Drive the new seal into the retainer with a block of wood or a section of pipe, if you have one large enough — make sure that you don't cock the seal in the retainer bore

fully work it onto the seal journal of the crankshaft with a smooth object like the end of an extension as you tap the seal into place. Don't rush it or you may damage the seal.

3   The following method is recommended but requires removal of the oil pan (see Section 13) and the seal retainer.

4   After the oil pan has been removed, remove the bolts, detach the seal retainer and peel off all the old gasket material.

5   Position the seal and retainer assembly on a couple of wood blocks on a workbench and drive the old seal out from the back side with a punch and hammer **(see illustration)**.

6   Drive the new seal into the retainer with a block of wood **(see illustration)** or a section of pipe slightly smaller in diameter than the outside diameter of the seal.

7   Lubricate the crankshaft seal journal and the lip of the new seal with moly-base grease. Position a new gasket on the engine block.

8   Slowly and carefully push the seal onto the crankshaft. The seal lip is stiff, so work it onto the crankshaft with a smooth object such as the end of an extension as you push the retainer against the block.

9   Install and tighten the retainer bolts to the specified torque. The bottom sealing flange of the retainer must not extend below the bottom sealing flange (oil pan rail) of the block.

10   The remaining steps are the reverse of removal.

11   Run the engine and check for oil leaks.

17.4   The front mount assembly is held in place by two through bolts — one at the bottom and one at the top (the bottom one is shown here)

17   Engine mounts — check and replacement

1   Engine mounts seldom require attention, but broken or deteriorated mounts should be replaced immediately or the added strain placed on the driveline components may cause damage or wear.

Check

Refer to illustration 17.4

2   During the check, the engine must be raised slightly to remove the weight from the mounts.

3   Raise the vehicle and support it securely on jackstands, then position a jack under the engine oil pan. Place a large block of wood between the jack head and the oil pan, then carefully raise the engine just enough to take the weight off the mounts. **Warning:** *DO NOT place any part of your body under the engine when it's supported only by a jack!*

4   Check the mounts to see if the rubber is cracked, hardened or separated from the metal backing. Sometimes the rubber will split right down the center. Check that the rod on the front mount is not bent **(see illustration)**.

5   Check for relative movement between the mount plates and the engine or frame (use a large screwdriver or pry bar to attempt to move the mounts). If movement is noted, lower the engine and tighten the mount fasteners.

6   Rubber preservative may be applied to the mounts to slow deterioration.

Replacement

Refer to illustrations 17.8a, 17.8b, 17.8c and 17.8d

7   Disconnect the negative battery cable from the battery, then raise the vehicle and support it securely on jackstands (if not already done).

8   Remove the fasteners and detach the mount from the frame and engine **(see illustrations)**. Do not disconnect more than one mount at a time, except during engine removal.

9   The mounts are available as inserts, which are pressed into place. Obtain new inserts and take them to an automotive machine shop or dealer service department to be pressed into the existing bracket.

10   Installation is the reverse of removal. Use thread locking compound on the mount bolts and be sure to tighten them securely.

17.8a The left mount is located adjacent to the upper timing belt cover — it is attached to the engine with two nuts and two bolts (arrows)

17.8b The left engine mount is attached to the bracket with a through-bolt that is secured by two retaining nuts on this side and one hidden by the mount (arrows)

2A

17.8c The transaxle mount is secured to the transaxle by a through-bolt and nut (arrows) — it is secured to the body by three bolts accessible from inside the right fender (see illustration 5.22 in part B of this chapter)

17.8d The rear mount is located above the steering rack — remove the mounting bolts and through-bolt (arrows)

Chapter 2   Part B
General engine overhaul procedures

Contents

Specifications

General
Cylinder compression pressure (at 250 rpm)	164 psi
Oil pressure (engine warm)	11 psi minimum at idle

Cylinder head
Warpage
Standard	0.002 in (0.05 mm)
Service limit	0.004 in (0.1 mm)

Valves and related components
Valve margin width
Intake	
Standard	0.039 in (1.0 mm)
Service limit	0.028 in (0.7 mm)
Exhaust	
Standard	0.059 in (1.5 mm)
Service limit	0.039 in (1.0 mm)
Valve stem diameter (intake and exhaust)	0.26 in (6.6 mm)

Valve stem-to-guide clearance
  Intake
    Standard .... 0.0012 to 0.0024 in (0.03 to 0.06 mm)
    Service limit .... 0.004 in (0.10 mm)
  Exhaust
    Standard .... 0.0020 to 0.0035 in (0.05 to 0.09 mm)
    Service limit .... 0.006 in (0.15 mm)
Valve spring
  Out-of-square limit .... 3°
  Pressure .... 53 lbs at 1.47 in (24 kg at 27.3 mm)
  Installed height .... 1.417 in (36 mm)
  Free length .... 1.756 in (44.6 mm)

Jet valves
Stem diameter .... 0.1693 in (4.30 mm)
Face/seat angle .... 45°
Spring
  Free length .... 1.165 in (29.60 mm)
  Load .... 5.5 lbs at 0.846 in (3.5 kg at 21.5 mm)

Crankshaft and connecting rods
Connecting rod journal
  Diameter .... 1.6535 in (42 mm)
  Out-of-round/taper limits .... 0.0004 in (0.01 mm)
  Bearing oil clearance .... 0.0004 to 0.0024 in (0.01 to 0.06 mm)
Connecting rod end play (side clearance) .... 0.004 to 0.010 in (0.10 to 0.25 mm)
Main bearing journal
  Diameter .... 1.8898 in (48 mm)
  Out-of-round/taper limits .... 0.0004 in (0.01 mm)
  Runout limit .... 0.0012 in (0.03 mm)
  Bearing oil clearance .... 0.0008 to 0.0028 in (0.02 to 0.07 mm)
Crankshaft end play .... 0.002 to 0.007 in (0.05 to 0.18 mm)

Cylinder bore
Diameter (nominal) .... 2.972 in (75.5 mm)
Out-of-round/taper limits .... 0.0008 in (0.02 mm)

Pistons and rings
Piston diameter (nominal)* .... 2.972 in (75.5 mm)
Piston-to-bore clearance .... 0.0008 to 0.0016 in (0.02 to 0.04 mm)
Piston ring end gap
  Compression rings
    Standard .... 0.008 to 0.014 in (0.20 to 0.35 mm)
    Service limit .... 0.039 in (0.10 mm)
  Oil ring
    Standard .... 0.008 to 0.028 in (0.20 to 0.70 mm)
    Service limit .... 0.039 in (0.10 mm)
Piston ring side clearance
  No. 1 (top) compression ring
    Standard .... 0.0012 to 0.0028 in (0.03 to 0.07 mm)
    Service limit .... 0.006 in (0.15 mm)
  No. 2 compression ring
    Standard .... 0.0008 to 0.0024 in (0.02 to 0.06 mm)
    Service limit .... 0.005 in (0.12 mm)

Measured 5/64-inch up from bottom of skirt

Torque specifications*	Ft-lbs	Nm
Main bearing cap bolts	36 to 39	49 to 53
Connecting rod cap nuts	23 to 25	31 to 34
Jet valves	13 to 16	18 to 22

* **Note:** *Refer to Part A for additional torque specifications.*

1 General information

Included in this portion of Chapter 2 are the general overhaul procedures for the cylinder head and internal engine components.

The information ranges from advice concerning preparation for an overhaul and the purchase of replacement parts to detailed, step-by-step procedures covering removal and installation of internal engine components and the inspection of parts.

The following Sections have been written based on the assumption that the engine has been removed from the vehicle. For information concerning in-vehicle engine repair, as well as removal and installation of the external components necessary for the overhaul, see Part A of this Chapter and Section 7 of this Part.

The Specifications included in this Part are only those necessary for the inspection and overhaul procedures which follow. Refer to Part A for additional Specifications.

2B

2 Engine overhaul — general information

Refer to illustrations 2.4a and 2.4b

It's not always easy to determine when, or if, an engine should be completely overhauled, as a number of factors must be considered.

High mileage is not necessarily an indication that an overhaul is needed, while low mileage doesn't preclude the need for an overhaul. Frequency of servicing is probably the most important consideration. An engine that's had regular and frequent oil and filter changes, as well as other required maintenance, will most likely give many thousands of miles of reliable service. Conversely, a neglected engine may require an overhaul very early in its life.

Excessive oil consumption is an indication that piston rings, valve seals and/or valve guides are in need of attention. Make sure that oil leaks aren't responsible before deciding that the rings and/or guides are bad. Perform a cylinder compression check to determine the extent of the work required (see Section 3).

Check the oil pressure with a gauge installed in place of the oil pressure sending unit **(see illustrations)** and compare it to the Specifications. If it's extremely low, the bearings and/or oil pump are probably worn out.

Loss of power, rough running, knocking or metallic engine noises, excessive valve train noise and high fuel consumption rates may also point to the need for an overhaul, especially if they're all present at the same time. If a complete tune-up doesn't remedy the situation, major mechanical work is the only solution.

An engine overhaul involves restoring the internal parts to the specifications of a new engine. During an overhaul, the piston rings are replaced and the cylinder walls are reconditioned (rebored and/or honed). If a rebore is done by an automotive machine shop, new oversize pistons will also be installed. The main bearings, connecting rod bearings and camshaft bearings are generally replaced with new ones and, if necessary, the crankshaft may be reground to restore the journals. Generally, the valves are serviced as well, since they're usually in less-than-perfect condition at this point. While the engine is being overhauled, other components, such as the distributor, starter and alternator, can be rebuilt as well. The end result should be a like new engine that will give many trouble free miles. **Note:** *Critical cooling system components such as the hoses, drivebelts, thermostat and water pump MUST be replaced with new parts when an engine is overhauled. The radiator should be checked carefully to ensure that it isn't clogged or leaking (see Chapter 3). Also, we don't recommend overhauling the oil pump — always install a new one when an engine is rebuilt.*

Before beginning the engine overhaul, read through the entire procedure to familiarize yourself with the scope and requirements of the job. Overhauling an engine isn't difficult, but it is time consuming. Plan on the vehicle being tied up for a minimum of two weeks, especially if parts must be taken to an automotive machine shop for repair or reconditioning. Check on availability of parts and make sure that any necessary special tools and equipment are obtained in advance. Most work can be done with typical hand tools, although a number of precision measuring tools are required for inspecting parts to determine if they must be replaced. Often an automotive machine shop will handle the inspection of parts and offer advice concerning reconditioning and replacement. **Note:** *Always wait until the engine has been completely disassembled and all components, especially the engine block, have been inspected before deciding what service and repair operations must be performed by an automotive machine shop. Since the block's condition will be the major factor to consider when determining whether to overhaul the original engine or buy a rebuilt one, never purchase parts or have machine work done on other components until the block has been thoroughly inspected.* As a general rule, time is the primary cost of an overhaul, so it doesn't pay to install worn or substandard parts.

As a final note, to ensure maximum life and minimum trouble from a rebuilt engine, everything must be assembled with care in a spotlessly clean environment.

3 Cylinder compression check

Refer to illustration 3.6

1 A compression check will tell you what mechanical condition the upper end (pistons, rings, valves, head gaskets) of your engine is in. Specifically, it can tell you if the compression is down due to leakage caused by worn piston rings, defective valves and seats or a blown head gasket. **Note:** *The engine must be at normal operating temperature and the battery must be fully charged for this check. Also, the choke valve must be all the way open to get an accurate compression reading (if the engine's warm, the choke should be open).*

2 Begin by cleaning the area around the spark plugs before you remove them (compressed air should be used, if available, otherwise a small brush or even a bicycle tire pump will work). The idea is to prevent dirt from getting into the cylinders as the compression check is being done.

3 Remove all of the spark plugs from the engine (Chapter 1).

4 Block the throttle wide open.

5 Detach the coil wire from the center of the distributor cap and ground it on the engine block. Use a jumper wire with alligator clips on each end to ensure a good ground.

2.4a The oil pressure sending unit (arrow) is located below the exhaust manifold between the engine mount bracket and the oil pump

2.4b An oil pressure gauge can be installed in the hole where the oil pressure sending unit is normally located

3.6 A compression gauge with a threaded fitting for the spark plug hole is preferred over the type that requires hand pressure to maintain the seal — be sure to open the throttle and choke valves as far as possible during the compression check!

6 Install the compression gauge in the number one spark plug hole **(see illustration).**
7 Crank the engine over at least seven compression strokes and watch the gauge. The compression should build up quickly in a healthy engine. Low compression on the first stroke, followed by gradually increasing pressure on successive strokes, indicates worn piston rings. A low compression reading on the first stroke, which doesn't build up during successive strokes, indicates leaking valves or a blown head gasket (a cracked head could also be the cause). Deposits on the undersides of the valve heads can also cause low compression. Record the highest gauge reading obtained.
8 Repeat the procedure for the remaining cylinders and compare the results to the Specifications.
9 Add some engine oil (about three squirts from a plunger-type oil can) to each cylinder, through the spark plug hole, and repeat the test.
10 If the compression increases after the oil is added, the piston rings are definitely worn. If the compression doesn't increase significantly, the leakage is occurring at the valves or head gasket. Leakage past the valves may be caused by burned valve seats and/or faces or warped, cracked or bent valves.
11 If two adjacent cylinders have equally low compression, there's a strong possibility that the head gasket between them is blown. The appearance of coolant in the combustion chambers or the crankcase would verify this condition.
12 If one cylinder is 20 percent lower than the others, and the engine has a slightly rough idle, a worn exhaust lobe on the camshaft could be the cause.
13 If the compression is unusually high, the combustion chambers are probably coated with carbon deposits. If that's the case, the cylinder head should be removed and decarbonized.
14 If compression is way down or varies greatly between cylinders, it would be a good idea to have a leak-down test performed by an automotive repair shop. This test will pinpoint exactly where the leakage is occurring and how severe it is.

4 Engine removal — methods and precautions

If you've decided that an engine must be removed for overhaul or major repair work, several preliminary steps should be taken.
Locating a suitable place to work is extremely important. Adequate work space, along with storage space for the vehicle, will be needed. If a shop or garage isn't available, at the very least a flat, level, clean work surface made of concrete or asphalt is required.
Cleaning the engine compartment and engine before beginning the removal procedure will help keep tools clean and organized.

An engine hoist or A-frame will also be necessary. Make sure the equipment is rated in excess of the combined weight of the engine and accessories. Safety is of primary importance, considering the potential hazards involved in lifting the engine out of the vehicle.
If the engine is being removed by a novice, a helper should be available. Advice and aid from someone more experienced would also be helpful. There are many instances when one person cannot simultaneously perform all of the operations required when lifting the engine out of the vehicle.
Plan the operation ahead of time. Arrange for or obtain all of the tools and equipment you'll need prior to beginning the job. Some of the equipment necessary to perform engine removal and installation safely and with relative ease are (in addition to an engine hoist) a heavy duty floor jack, complete sets of wrenches and sockets as described in the front of this manual, wooden blocks and plenty of rags and cleaning solvent for mopping up spilled oil, coolant and gasoline. If the hoist must be rented, make sure that you arrange for it in advance and perform all of the operations possible without it beforehand. This will save you money and time.
Plan for the vehicle to be out of use for quite a while. A machine shop will be required to perform some of the work which the do-it-yourselfer can't accomplish without special equipment. These shops often have a busy schedule, so it would be a good idea to consult them before removing the engine in order to accurately estimate the amount of time required to rebuild or repair components that may need work.
Always be extremely careful when removing and installing the engine. Serious injury can result from careless actions. Plan ahead, take your time and a job of this nature, although major, can be accomplished successfully.

5 Engine — removal and installation

Refer to illustrations 5.7, 5.20, 5.22, 5.23 and 5.26
Note: *Read through the entire Section before beginning this procedure. The engine and transaxle are removed as a unit and then separated outside the vehicle.*

Removal

1 If the vehicle is equipped with air conditioning, have the system discharged by a dealer service department or a service station.
2 Place protective covers on the front fenders.
3 Remove the hood (see Chapter 11).
4 Disconnect and remove the battery (see Chapter 5).
5 Remove the air cleaner assembly (see Chapter 4).
6 Drain and remove the radiator (see Chapter 3).
7 Carefully label, then disconnect all vacuum lines, coolant and emissions hoses and wire harness connectors. Masking tape and felt-tip pens work well for marking items **(see illustration).** If necessary, take instant photos or sketch the locations to ensure correct reinstallation.

5.7 Label both ends of each wire before disconnecting them

8   On fuel-injected models, relieve the fuel system pressure (see Chapter 4, Section 3, Step 21). Disconnect the fuel lines from the carburetor/fuel rail) (see Chapter 4) and cap them to prevent fuel leakage.

9   Detach the throttle cable (see Chapter 4).

10   Raise the vehicle and support it securely on jackstands.

11   On manual transaxle equipped vehicles, refer to Chapters 7 and 8 and detach the clutch cable, shift control rod and extension rod (1986 through 1989 models) or clutch hydraulic lines and shift cables (1990 and later models).

12   On automatic transaxle equipped vehicles, detach the shift control cable from the transaxle, then remove the bellhousing cover and the driveplate-to-converter bolts (see Chapter 7).

13   Detach the speedometer cable from the transaxle.

14   If equipped, remove the air conditioning compressor (see Chapter 3).

15   Remove the power steering pump and reservoir (if equipped) from the brackets without disconnecting the hoses and set them aside.

16   Remove the splash shield (if not already done) located at the drivebelt end of the engine.

17   Drain the engine oil and transaxle fluid and remove the oil filter (see Chapter 1).

18   Disconnect the exhaust pipe from the exhaust manifold (see Chapter 2, Part A).

19   Remove the driveaxles from the transaxle (see Chapter 8). Stuff clean rags into the openings to prevent the entry of foreign material.

20   Attach a short chain to the engine brackets and hook up the hoist (see illustration). Take up the slack until there is tension on the chain.

21   Support the transaxle with a floor jack. Place a block of wood on the jack pad to protect the transaxle. Warning: *Do not place any part of your body under the engine/transaxle when it's supported only by a hoist or other lifting device.*

22   Remove the plugs from the right front inner fender (see illustration).

23   Check for clearance and, if necessary, remove the brake master cylinder (see Chapter 9) and transaxle mount bracket (see illustration).

24   Remove the engine mount through bolts.

25   Confirm that all of the cables, hoses, wires and other items are disconnected from the engine.

26   Carefully push the transaxle down while lifting the engine up to clear obstructions (see illustration).

27   Lift the engine and transaxle high enough to clear the front of the vehicle and slowly move the hoist away.

28   Lower the hoist and set the transaxle on blocks — leave the hoist hooked up.

29   Remove the bolts and separate the engine from the transaxle. Refer to Chapter 7 if necessary.

30   Remove the clutch components and flywheel (or driveplate) (see Chapter 2, Part A) and the engine rear plate and mount the engine on a stand.

Installation

31   Check the engine/transaxle mounts. If they're worn or damaged, replace them.

32   On manual transaxle equipped vehicles, inspect the clutch components (see Chapter 8) and apply a very small amount of high temperature grease to the transaxle input shaft splines.

33   On automatic transaxle equipped vehicles, inspect the converter seal and bushing.

34   Carefully rejoin the transaxle and engine following the procedure outlined in Chapter 7. Caution: *Do not use the bolts to force the engine and transaxle into alignment. It may crack or damage major components.*

35   Install the transaxle-to-engine bolts and tighten them securely.

36   Attach the hoist to the engine and carefully lower the engine/transaxle assembly into the vehicle.

37   Install the mount bolts and tighten them securely.

5.20   Attach a chain to the hoist brackets on the engine with large bolts and washers, then connect the hoist hook to the chain

5.22   The transaxle mount bolts are behind plugs in the right inner fender (arrows)

5.23   On some models, it may be necessary to remove the master cylinder and unbolt the transaxle mount bracket (arrows) to remove the engine/transaxle assembly

5.26   Slowly lift the engine up while pushing the transaxle down

38 Reinstall the remaining components and fasteners in the reverse order of removal.
39 Add coolant, oil, power steering and transmission fluid/lubricant as needed (see Chapter 1).
40 Run the engine and check for proper operation and leaks. Shut off the engine and recheck the fluid levels.

6 Engine rebuilding alternatives

The do-it-yourselfer is faced with a number of options when performing an engine overhaul. The decision to replace the engine block, piston/connecting rod assemblies and crankshaft depends on a number of factors, with the number one consideration being the condition of the block. Other considerations are cost, access to machine shop facilities, parts availability, time required to complete the project and the extent of prior mechanical experience on the part of the do-it-yourselfer.

Some of the rebuilding alternatives include:

Individual parts — If the inspection procedures reveal that the engine block and most engine components are in reusable condition, purchasing individual parts may be the most economical alternative. The block, crankshaft and piston/connecting rod assemblies should all be inspected carefully. Even if the block shows little wear, the cylinder bores should be surface honed.

Short block — A short block consists of an engine block with a crankshaft and piston/connecting rod assemblies already installed. All new bearings are incorporated and all clearances will be correct. The existing camshaft, valve train components, cylinder head(s) and external parts can be bolted to the short block with little or no machine shop work necessary.

Long block — A long block consists of a short block plus an oil pump, oil pan, cylinder head(s), rocker arm cover(s), camshaft and valve train components, timing sprockets and chain or gears and timing cover. All components are installed with new bearings, seals and gaskets incorporated throughout. The installation of manifolds and external parts is all that's necessary.

Give careful thought to which alternative is best for you and discuss the situation with local automotive machine shops, auto parts dealers and experienced rebuilders before ordering or purchasing replacement parts.

7 Engine overhaul — disassembly sequence

Refer to illustrations 7.3a, 7.3b, 7.3c and 7.5

1 It's much easier to disassemble and work on the engine if it's mounted on a portable engine stand. A stand can often be rented quite cheaply from an equipment rental yard. Before the engine is mounted on a stand, the flywheel/driveplate should be removed from the engine.
2 If a stand isn't available, it's possible to disassemble the engine with it blocked up on the floor. Be extra careful not to tip or drop the engine when working without a stand.
3 If you're going to obtain a rebuilt engine, all external components **(see illustrations)** must come off first, to be transferred to the replacement engine, just as they will if you're doing a complete engine overhaul yourself. These include:

Alternator and brackets
Emissions control components
Distributor, spark plug wires and spark plugs
Thermostat and housing cover
Water pump
Carburetor
Intake/exhaust manifolds
Oil filter
Engine mounts
Clutch and flywheel/driveplate
Engine rear plate

Note: *When removing the external components from the engine, pay close attention to details that may be helpful or important during installation. Note the installed position of gaskets, seals, spacers, pins, brackets, washers, bolts and other small items.*

2B

7.3a Hyundai engine — drivebelt/timing belt end

7.3b Hyundai engine — exhaust manifold (radiator) side

7.3c Hyundai engine – intake manifold (firewall) side (carbureted models)

4   If you're obtaining a short block, which consists of the engine block, crankshaft, pistons and connecting rods all assembled, then the cylinder head, oil pan and oil pump will have to be removed as well. See *Engine rebuilding alternatives* for additional information regarding the different possibilities to be considered.

5   If you're planning a complete overhaul, the engine must be disassembled and the internal components (**see illustration**) removed in the following order:

  Rocker arm cover
  Intake and exhaust manifolds
  Rocker arms and shafts
  Timing belt cover
  Timing belt and sprockets
  Camshaft
  Cylinder head
  Oil pan
  Oil pump
  Rear main oil seal housing
  Piston/connecting rod assemblies
  Crankshaft and main bearings

6   Before beginning the disassembly and overhaul procedures, make sure the following items are available. Also, refer to *Engine overhaul — reassembly sequence* for a list of tools and materials needed for engine reassembly.

  Common hand tools
  Small cardboard boxes or plastic bags for storing parts
  Gasket scraper
  Ridge reamer
  Micrometers
  Telescoping gauges
  Dial indicator set
  Valve spring compressor
  Cylinder surfacing hone
  Piston ring groove cleaning tool
  Electric drill motor
  Tap and die set
  Wire brushes
  Oil gallery brushes
  Cleaning solvent

8 Cylinder head — disassembly

Refer to illustrations 8.2, 8.3, 8.4, 8.6 and 8.7

Note: *New and rebuilt cylinder heads are commonly available for most engines at dealerships and auto parts stores. Due to the fact that some specialized tools are necessary for the disassembly and inspection procedures, and replacement parts may not be readily available, it may be more practical and economical for the home mechanic to purchase a replacement head rather than taking the time to disassemble, inspect and recondition the original.*

1   Cylinder head disassembly involves removal of the intake and exhaust valves and related components. If they're still in place, remove the rocker arm shafts. Label the parts or store them separately so they can be reinstalled in their original locations.

2   Before the valves are removed, arrange to label and store them, along with their related components, so they can be kept separate and

2B

FORWARD

7.5 Engine internal components — exploded view

1 Flywheel*	8 Bellhousing cover	
2 Ring gear*	9 Rear main oil seal	
3 Adapter plate**	10 Oil seal housing	
4 Driveplate**	11 Gasket	
5 Adapter plate**	12 Main bearing cap	
6 NOT USED	13 Lower main bearing	
7 Rear plate	14 Crankshaft	
	15 Upper main bearing	

    * Vehicles with a manual transaxle
  ** Vehicles with an automatic transaxle

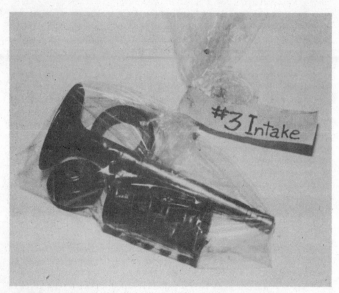

8.2   A small plastic bag, with an appropriate label, can be used to store the valve train components so they can be kept together and reinstalled in the correct guide

8.3   Use a valve spring compressor to compress the spring, then remove the keepers from the valve stem

8.4   If the valve won't pull through the guide, deburr the edge of the stem end and the area around the top of the keeper groove with a file

reinstalled in the same valve guides they are removed from **(see illustration)**.

3   Compress the springs on the first valve with a spring compressor and remove the keepers **(see illustration)**. Carefully release the valve spring compressor and remove the retainer, the spring and the spring seat (if used).

4   Pull the valve out of the head, then remove the oil seal from the guide. If the valve binds in the guide (won't pull through), push it back into the head and deburr the area around the keeper groove with a fine file or whetstone **(see illustration)**.

5   Repeat the procedure for the remaining valves. Remember to keep all the parts for each valve together so they can be reinstalled in the same locations.

6   Remove the jet valves **(see illustration)**. **Caution:** *When the jet valve socket is used, make certain that the wrench is not tilted with respect to the center of the jet valve. If the tool is tilted, the valve stem might be bent by the force exerted on the valve spring retainer, resulting in defective jet valve operaton or a damaged tool.*

7   When disassembling the jet valve, compress the spring with the Hyundai special tool (09222–21400) **(see illustration)**, remove the valve spring retainer lock, the retainer and the spring. **Caution:** *Do not mix up the jet valve parts after disassembly or gas leakage and malfunctioning may result.*

8   Pull off the valve stem seals with pliers and discard them.

9   Once the valves and related components have been removed and

8.6   Unscrew the jet valves with Hyundai special tool no. 09222-21300 or a deep socket

8.7   The jet valve spring should be compressed with special tool no. 09222-21400

stored in an organized manner, the head should be thoroughly cleaned and inspected. If a complete engine overhaul is being done, finish the engine disassembly procedures before beginning the cylinder head cleaning and inspection process.

9 Cylinder head — cleaning and inspection

Refer to illustrations 9.12, 9.14, 9.16, 9.17 and 9.18

1 Thorough cleaning of the cylinder head and related valve train components, followed by a detailed inspection, will enable you to decide how much valve service work must be done during the engine overhaul. **Note:** *If the engine was severely overheated, the cylinder head is probably warped (see Step 12).*

Cleaning

2 Scrape all traces of old gasket material and sealing compound off the head gasket, intake manifold and exhaust manifold sealing surfaces. Be very careful not to gouge the cylinder head. Special gasket removal solvents that soften gaskets and make removal much easier are available at auto parts stores.
3 Remove all built up scale from the coolant passages.
4 Run a stiff wire brush through the various holes to remove deposits that may have formed in them.
5 Run an appropriate size tap into each of the threaded holes to remove corrosion and thread sealant that may be present. If compressed air is available, use it to clear the holes of debris produced by this operation. **Warning:** *Wear eye protection when using compressed air!*
6 Clean the valve adjuster threads in each rocker arm with a wire brush.
7 Clean the cylinder head with solvent and dry it thoroughly. Compressed air will speed the drying process and ensure that all holes and recessed areas are clean. **Note:** *Decarbonizing chemicals are available and may prove very useful when cleaning cylinder heads and valve train components. They are very caustic and should be used with caution. Be sure to follow the instructions on the container.*
8 Clean the rocker arms, springs, wave washers and shafts with solvent and dry them thoroughly (don't mix them up during the cleaning process). Compressed air will speed the drying process and can be used to clean out the oil passages.
9 Clean all the valve springs, spring seats, keepers and retainers with solvent and dry them thoroughly. Do the components from one valve at a time to avoid mixing up the parts.
10 Scrape off any heavy deposits that may have formed on the valves, then use a motorized wire brush to remove deposits from the valve heads and stems. **Warning:** *Wear eye protection!* Again, make sure the valves don't get mixed up.

Inspection

Note: *Be sure to perform all of the following inspection procedures before concluding that machine shop work is required. Make a list of the items that need attention.*

Cylinder head

11 Inspect the head very carefully for cracks, evidence of coolant leakage and other damage. If cracks are found, check with an automotive machine shop concerning repair. If repair isn't possible, a new cylinder head should be obtained.
12 Using a straightedge and feeler gauge, check the head gasket mating surface for warpage **(see illustration)**. If the warpage exceeds the specified limit, it can be resurfaced at an automotive machine shop.
13 Examine the valve seats in each of the combustion chambers. If they're pitted, cracked or burned, the head will require valve service that's beyond the scope of the home mechanic.
14 Check the valve stem-to-guide clearance by measuring the lateral movement of the valve stem with a dial indicator attached securely to the head **(see illustration)**. The valve must be in the guide and approximately 1/16-inch off the seat. The total valve stem movement indicated by the gauge needle must be divided by two to obtain the actual clearance. After this is done, if there's still some doubt regarding the condition of the valve guides they should be checked by an automotive machine shop (the cost should be minimal).

Valves

15 Carefully inspect each valve face for uneven wear, deformation, cracks, pits and burned areas. Check the valve stem for scuffing and galling and the neck for cracks. Rotate the valve and check for any obvious indication that it's bent. Look for pits and excessive wear on the end of the stem. The presence of any of these conditions indicates the need for valve service by an automotive machine shop.
16 Measure the margin width on each valve **(see illustration)**. Any valve with a margin narrower than specified will have to be replaced with a new one.

2B

9.12 Check the cylinder head gasket surface for warpage by trying to slip a feeler gauge under the straightedge (see the Specifications for the maximum warpage allowed and use a feeler gauge of that thickness)

9.14 A dial indicator can be used to determine the valve stem-to-guide clearance (move the valve stem as indicated by the arrows)

9.16 The margin width on each valve must be as specified (if no margin exists, the valve cannnot be reused)

9.17   Measure the free length of each valve spring with a dial or vernier caliper

9.18   Check each valve spring for squareness

Valve components

17   Check each valve spring for wear (on the ends) and pits. Measure the free length and compare it to the Specifications **(see illustration)**. Any springs that are shorter than specified have sagged and should not be reused. The tension of all springs should be checked with a special fixture before deciding that they're suitable for use in a rebuilt engine (take the springs to an automotive machine shop for this check).

18   Stand each spring on a flat surface and check it for squareness **(see illustration)**. If any of the springs are distorted or sagged, replace all of them with new parts.

19   Check the spring retainers and keepers for obvious wear and cracks. Any questionable parts should be replaced with new ones, as extensive damage will occur if they fail during engine operation.

Rocker arm components

20   Refer to Chapter 2, Part A, for the rocker arm and shaft inspection procedures.

Jet valves

21   Make sure each jet valve slides smoothly in the jet valve body with no play. Do not interchange parts between jet valves. If any parts are worn or damaged, replace the entire jet valve assembly.

22   Check the valve head and valve seat for damage and evidence of seizure. Check the spring for distortion and cracks.

23   Any damaged or excessively worn parts must be replaced with new ones.

24   If the inspection process indicates that the valve components are in generally poor condition and worn beyond the limits specified, which is usually the case in an engine that's being overhauled, reassemble the valves in the cylinder head and refer to Section 10 for valve servicing recommendations.

10   Valves — servicing

1   Because of the complex nature of the job and the special tools and equipment needed, servicing of the valves, the valve seats and the valve guides, commonly known as a valve job, should be done by a professional.

2   The home mechanic can remove and disassemble the head, do the initial cleaning and inspection, then reassemble and deliver it to a dealer service department or an automotive machine shop for the actual service work. Doing the inspection will enable you to see what condition the head and valvetrain components are in and will ensure that you know what work and new parts are required when dealing with an automotive machine shop.

3   The dealer service department, or automotive machine shop, will remove the valves and springs, recondition or replace the valves and valve seats, recondition the valve guides, check and replace the valve springs, spring retainers and keepers (as necessary), replace the valve seals with new ones, reassemble the valve components and make sure

the installed spring height is correct. The cylinder head gasket surface will also be resurfaced if it's warped.

4   After the valve job has been performed by a professional, the head will be in like new condition. When the head is returned, be sure to clean it again before installation on the engine to remove any metal particles and abrasive grit that may still be present from the valve service or head resurfacing operations. Use compressed air, if available, to blow out all the oil holes and passages.

11   Cylinder head — reassembly

Refer to illustrations 11.3, 11.5, 11.6, 11.8, 11.9 and 11.12

1   Regardless of whether or not the head was sent to an automotive repair shop for valve servicing, make sure it's clean before beginning reassembly.

2   If the head was sent out for valve servicing, the valves and related components will already be in place. Begin the reassembly procedure with Step 8.

3   Install new seals on each of the intake valve guides. Using a hammer and a deep socket or seal installation tool, gently tap each seal into place until it's completely seated on the guide **(see illustration)**. Don't twist or cock the seals during installation or they won't seal properly on the valve stems.

4   Beginning at one end of the head, lubricate and install the first valve. Apply moly-base grease or clean engine oil to the valve stem.

5   Drop the spring seat over the valve guide and set the valve spring and retainer in place **(see illustration)**.

11.3   Valve seals require a special tool for installation (although a deep socket can be used if the tool isn't available) — don't hammer on the seals once they're seated!

11.5 Install the valve springs with the enamel coated ends away from the cylinder head as shown here

11.6 Apply a small dab of grease to each keeper as shown here before installation — it will hold them in place on the valve stem as the spring is released

11.8 Be sure to check the valve spring installed height (the distance from the top of the seat/shims to the top of the spring)

6 Compress the spring with a valve spring compressor and carefully install the keepers in the upper groove, then slowly release the compressor and make sure the keepers seat properly. Apply a small dab of grease to each keeper to hold it in place if necessary **(see illustration)**.

7 Repeat the procedure for the remaining valves. Be sure to return the components to their original locations — don't mix them up!

8 Check the installed valve spring height with a ruler graduated in 1/32-inch increments or a dial caliper. If the head was sent out for service work, the installed height should be correct (but don't automatically assume that it is). The measurement is taken from the top of each spring seat to the bottom of the retainer **(see illustration)**. If the height is greater than specified, shims can be added under the springs to correct it. **Caution:** *Don't, under any circumstances, shim the springs to the point where the installed height is less than specified.*

9 Using special tool number 09222–21500, drive the jet valve stem seal into place on the valve body **(see illustration)**. Do not reuse the old seals and don't try to install the seals with any other type of tool.

10 Apply engine oil to the jet valve stem when installing it in the valve body. Take care not to damage the valve stem seal lip. Make sure the jet valve stem slides smoothly in the body.

11 Compress the spring with special tool number 09222–21400 and install it together with the valve spring retainer. Install the retainer lock. Be careful not to damage the valve stem seal with the bottom of the retainer.

12 Install a new O-ring in the jet valve body groove and apply a thin coat of engine oil to it **(see illustration)**. Apply oil to the threads and seat as well.

11.9 A special tool is available for jet valve stem seal replacement

11.12 Be sure to use new O-rings when reinstalling the jet valves and apply engine oil to the O-rings, threads and seat area (arrows)

2B

12.1   A ridge reamer is required to remove the ridge from the top of each cylinder — do this before removing the pistons!

12.3   Check the connecting rod end play with a feeler gauge as shown

12.6   To prevent damage to the crankshaft journals and cylinder walls, slip sections of hose over the rod bolts before removing the pistons

13 Reinstall the jet valves and tighten them to the specified torque.

14 Apply moly-base grease to the rocker arm faces, the camshaft and the rocker shafts, then install the camshaft, rocker arms and shafts (refer to Part A).

12   Pistons/connecting rods — removal

Refer to illustrations 12.1, 12.3 and 12.6

Note: *Prior to removing the piston/connecting rod assemblies, remove the cylinder head and the oil pan by referring to the appropriate Sections in Chapter 2, Part A.*

1   Use your fingernail to feel if a ridge has formed at the upper limit of ring travel (about 1/4-inch down from the top of each cylinder). If carbon deposits or cylinder wear have produced ridges, they must be completely removed with a special tool **(see illustration)**. Follow the manufacturer's instructions provided with the tool. Failure to remove the ridges before attempting to remove the piston/connecting rod assemblies may result in piston breakage.

2   After the cylinder ridges have been removed, turn the engine upside-down so the crankshaft is facing up.

3   Before the connecting rods are removed, check the end play with feeler gauges. Slide them between the first connecting rod and the crankshaft throw until the play is removed **(see illustration)**. The end play is equal to the thickness of the feeler gauge(s). If the end play

exceeds the service limit, new connecting rods will be required. If new rods (or a new crankshaft) are installed, the end play may fall under the specified minimum (if it does, the rods will have to be machined to restore it — consult an automotive machine shop for advice if necessary). Repeat the procedure for the remaining connecting rods.

4   Check the connecting rods and caps for identification marks. If they aren't plainly marked, use a small center punch to make the appropriate number of indentations on each rod and cap (1, 2, 3, etc., depending on the cylinder they're associated with).

5   Loosen each of the connecting rod cap nuts 1/2-turn at a time until they can be removed by hand. Remove the number one connecting rod cap and bearing insert. Don't drop the bearing insert out of the cap.

6   Slip a short length of plastic or rubber hose over each connecting rod cap bolt to protect the crankshaft journal and cylinder wall as the piston is removed **(see illustration)**.

7   Remove the bearing insert and push the connecting rod/piston assembly out through the top of the engine. Use a wooden hammer handle to push on the upper bearing surface in the connecting rod. If resistance is felt, double-check to make sure that all of the ridge was removed from the cylinder.

8   Repeat the procedure for the remaining cylinders.

9   After removal, reassemble the connecting rod caps and bearing inserts in their respective connecting rods and install the cap nuts finger tight. Leaving the old bearing inserts in place until reassembly will help prevent the connecting rod bearing surfaces from being accidentally nicked or gouged.

10 Don't separate the pistons from the connecting rods (see Section 17 for additional information).

13   Crankshaft — removal

Refer to illustrations 13.1 and 13.4

Note: *The crankshaft can be removed only after the engine has been removed from the vehicle. It's assumed that the flywheel or driveplate, crankshaft pulley, timing belt, oil pan, oil pump and piston/connecting rod assemblies have already been removed. The rear main oil seal housing must be unbolted and separated from the block before proceeding with crankshaft removal.*

1   Before the crankshaft is removed, check the end play. Mount a dial indicator with the stem in line with the crankshaft and just touching one of the crank throws **(see illustration)**.

2   Push the crankshaft all the way to the rear and zero the dial indicator. Next, pry the crankshaft to the front as far as possible and check the reading on the dial indicator. The distance that it moves is the end play. If it's greater than specified, check the crankshaft thrust surfaces for wear. If no wear is evident, new main bearings should correct the end play.

3   If a dial indicator isn't available, feeler gauges can be used. Gently pry or push the crankshaft all the way to the front of the engine. Slip

13.1 Checking crankshaft end play with a dial indicator

13.4 The arrow on the main bearing cap indicates the front (timing belt end) of the engine

feeler gauges between the crankshaft and the front face of the thrust main bearing to determine the clearance.

4   Check the main bearing caps to see if they're marked to indicate their locations. They should be numbered consecutively from the front of the engine to the rear. If they aren't, mark them with number stamping dies or a center punch. Main bearing caps generally have a cast-in arrow, which points to the front of the engine **(see illustration)**. Loosen the main bearing cap bolts 1/4-turn at a time each, until they can be removed by hand.

5   Gently tap the caps with a soft-face hammer, then separate them from the engine block. If necessary, use the bolts as levers to remove the caps. Try not to drop the bearing inserts if they come out with the caps.

6   Carefully lift the crankshaft out of the engine. It may be a good idea to have an assistant available, since the crankshaft is quite heavy. With the bearing inserts in place in the engine block and main bearing caps, return the caps to their respective locations on the engine block and tighten the bolts finger tight.

14 Engine block — cleaning

Refer to illustrations 14.1, 14.8 and 14.10

Caution: *The core plugs (also known as freeze or soft plugs) may be difficult or impossible to retrieve if they're driven into the block coolant passages.*

1   Drill a small hole in the center of each core plug and pull them out with an auto body type dent puller **(see illustration)**.

2   Using a gasket scraper, remove all traces of gasket material from

the engine block. Be very careful not to nick or gouge the gasket sealing surfaces.

3   Remove the main bearing caps and separate the bearing inserts from the caps and the engine block. Tag the bearings, indicating which cylinder they were removed from and whether they were in the cap or the block, then set them aside.

4   Remove all of the threaded oil gallery plugs from the block. The plugs are usually very tight — they may have to be drilled out and the holes retapped. Use new plugs when the engine is reassembled.

5   If the engine is extremely dirty it should be taken to an automotive machine shop to be steam cleaned or hot tanked.

6   After the block is returned, clean all oil holes and oil galleries one more time. Brushes specifically designed for this purpose are available at most auto parts stores. Flush the passages with warm water until the water runs clear, dry the block thoroughly and wipe all machined surfaces with a light, rust preventive oil. If you have access to compressed air, use it to speed the drying process and to blow out all the oil holes and galleries. **Warning:** *Wear eye protection when using compressed air!*

7   If the block isn't extremely dirty or sludged up, you can do an adequate cleaning job with hot soapy water and a stiff brush. Take plenty of time and do a thorough job. Regardless of the cleaning method used, be sure to clean all oil holes and galleries very thoroughly, dry the block completely and coat all machined surfaces with light oil.

8   The threaded holes in the block must be clean to ensure accurate torque readings during reassembly. Run the proper size tap into each of the holes to remove rust, corrosion, thread sealant or sludge and restore damaged threads **(see illustration)**. If possible, use compressed air to clear the holes of debris produced by this operation. Now is a good time to clean the threads on the head bolts and the main bearing

14.1 The core plugs should be removed with a puller — if they're driven into the block, they may be impossible to retrieve

14.8 All bolt holes in the block — particularly the main bearing cap and head bolt holes — should be cleaned and restored with a tap (be sure to remove debris from the holes after this is done)

14.10   A large socket on an extension can be used to drive the new core plugs into the bores

15.4b   The ability to "feel" when the telescoping gauge is at the correct point will be developed over time, so work slowly and repeat the check until you are satisfied that the bore measurement is accurate

15.4c   The gauge is then measured with a micrometer to determine the bore size

15.4a   Measure the diameter of each cylinder just under the wear ridge (A), at the center (B) and at the bottom (C)

cap bolts as well.

9   Reinstall the main bearing caps and tighten the bolts finger tight.

10   After coating the sealing surfaces of the new core plugs with Permatex no. 2 sealant, install them in the engine block **(see illustration)**. Make sure they're driven in straight and seated properly or leakage could result. Special tools are available for this purpose, but a large socket, with an outside diameter that will just slip into the core plug, a 1/2-inch drive extension and a hammer will work just as well.

11   Apply non-hardening sealant (such as Permatex no. 2 or Teflon pipe sealant) to the new oil gallery plugs and thread them into the holes in the block. Make sure they're tightened securely.

12   If the engine isn't going to be reassembled right away, cover it with a large plastic trash bag to keep it clean.

15   Engine block — inspection

Refer to illustrations 15.4a, 15.4b and 15.4c

1   Before the block is inspected, it should be cleaned as described in Section 14.

2   Visually check the block for cracks, rust and corrosion. Look for stripped threads in the threaded holes. It's also a good idea to have the block checked for hidden cracks by an automotive machine shop that has the special equipment to do this type of work. If defects are found, have the block repaired, if possible, or replaced.

3   Check the cylinder bores for scuffing and scoring.

4   Measure the diameter of each cylinder at the top (just under the ridge area), center and bottom of the cylinder bore, parallel to the crankshaft axis **(see illustrations)**.

5   Next, measure each cylinder's diameter at the same three locations *across* the crankshaft axis. Compare the results to the Specifications.

6   If the required precision measuring tools aren't available, the piston-to-cylinder clearances can be obtained, though not quite as accurately, using feeler gauge stock. Feeler gauge stock comes in 12-inch lengths and various thicknesses and is generally available at auto parts stores.

7   To check the clearance, select a feeler gauge and slip it into the cylinder along with the matching piston. The piston must be positioned exactly as it normally would be. The feeler gauge must be between the piston and cylinder on one of the thrust faces (90° to the piston pin bore).

8   The piston should slip through the cylinder (with the feeler gauge in place) with moderate pressure.

9   If it falls through or slides through easily, the clearance is excessive and a new piston will be required. If the piston binds at the lower end of the cylinder and is loose toward the top, the cylinder is tapered. If tight spots are encountered as the piston/feeler gauge is rotated in the cylinder, the cylinder is out-of-round.

10   Repeat the procedure for the remaining pistons and cylinders.

11   If the cylinder walls are badly scuffed or scored, or if they're out-of-round or tapered beyond the limits given in the Specifications, have the engine block rebored and honed at an automotive machine shop. If a rebore is done, oversize pistons and rings will be required.

12   If the cylinders are in reasonably good condition and not worn to the outside of the limits, and if the piston-to-cylinder clearances can be maintained properly, then they don't have to be rebored. Honing is all that's necessary (Section 16).

16.3a A ''bottle brush'' hone will produce better results if you have never done cylinder honing before

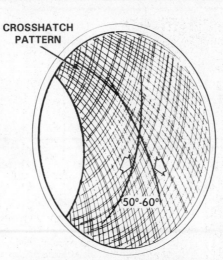

16.3b The cylinder hone should leave a smooth, crosshatch pattern with the lines intersecting at approximately a 60-degree angle

17.4a The piston ring grooves can be cleaned with a special tool, as shown here, . . .

2B

16 Cylinder honing

Refer to illustrations 16.3a and 16.3b

1   Prior to engine reassembly, the cylinder bores must be honed so the new piston rings will seat correctly and provide the best possible combustion chamber seal. **Note:** *If you don't have the tools or don't want to tackle the honing operation, most automotive machine shops will do it for a reasonable fee.*

2   Before honing the cylinders, install the main bearing caps and tighten the bolts to the specified torque.

3   Two types of cylinder hones are commonly available — the flex hone or ''bottle brush'' type and the more traditional surfacing hone with spring-loaded stones. Both will do the job, but for the less experienced mechanic the ''bottle brush'' hone will probably be easier to use. You'll also need some kerosene or honing oil, rags and an electric drill motor. Proceed as follows:

   a) Mount the hone in the drill motor, compress the stones and slip it into the first cylinder **(see illustration)**. Be sure to wear safety goggles or a face shield!

   b) Lubricate the cylinder with plenty of honing oil, turn on the drill and move the hone up-and-down in the cylinder at a pace that will produce a fine crosshatch pattern on the cylinder walls. Ideally, the crosshatch lines should intersect at approximately a 60° angle **(see illustration)**. Be sure to use plenty of lubricant and don't take off any more material than is absolutely necessary to produce the desired finish. **Note:** *Piston ring manufacturers may specify a smaller crosshatch angle than the traditional 60° — read and follow any instructions included with the new rings.*

   c) Don't withdraw the hone from the cylinder while it's running. Instead, shut off the drill and continue moving the hone up-and-down in the cylinder until it comes to a complete stop, then compress the stones and withdraw the hone. If you're using a ''bottle brush'' type hone, stop the drill motor, then turn the chuck in the normal direction of rotation while withdrawing the hone from the cylinder.

   d) Wipe the oil out of the cylinder and repeat the procedure for the remaining cylinders.

4   After the honing job is complete, chamfer the top edges of the cylinder bores with a small file so the rings won't catch when the pistons are installed. **Be very careful not to nick the cylinder walls with the end of the file.**

5   The entire engine block must be washed again very thoroughly with warm, soapy water to remove all traces of the abrasive grit produced during the honing operation. **Note:** *The bores can be considered clean when a lint-free white cloth — dampened with clean engine oil — used to wipe them out doesn't pick up any more honing residue, which will show up as gray areas on the cloth.* Be sure to run a brush through all oil holes and galleries and flush them with running water.

17.4b   . . . or a section of a broken ring

6   After rinsing, dry the block and apply a coat of light rust preventive oil to all machined surfaces. Wrap the block in a plastic trash bag to keep it clean and set it aside until reassembly.

17 Pistons/connecting rods — inspection

Refer to illustrations 17.4a, 17.4b, 17.10 and 17.11

1   Before the inspection process can be carried out, the piston/connecting rod assemblies must be cleaned and the original piston rings removed from the pistons. **Note:** *Always use new piston rings when the engine is reassembled.*

2   Using a piston ring installation tool, carefully remove the rings from the pistons. Be careful not to nick or gouge the pistons in the process.

3   Scrape all traces of carbon from the top of the piston. A hand-held wire brush or a piece of fine emery cloth can be used once the majority of the deposits have been scraped away. Do not, under any circumstances, use a wire brush mounted in a drill motor to remove deposits from the pistons. The piston material is soft and may be eroded away by the wire brush.

4   Use a piston ring groove cleaning tool to remove carbon deposits from the ring grooves. If a tool isn't available, a piece broken off the old ring will do the job. Be very careful to remove only the carbon deposits — don't remove any metal and do not nick or scratch the sides of the ring grooves **(see illustrations)**.

**17.10   Check the ring side clearance with a feeler gauge
at several points around the groove**

**17.11   Measure the piston diameter at a 90° angle to the
piston pin, 5/64-inch up from the bottom of the skirt**

5   Once the deposits have been removed, clean the piston/rod assemblies with solvent and dry them with compressed air (if available). Make sure the oil return holes in the back sides of the ring grooves are clear.

6   If the pistons and cylinder walls aren't damaged or worn excessively, and if the engine block is not rebored, new pistons won't be necessary. Normal piston wear appears as even vertical wear on the piston thrust surfaces and slight looseness of the top ring in its groove. New piston rings, however, should always be used when an engine is rebuilt.

7   Carefully inspect each piston for cracks around the skirt, at the pin bosses and at the ring lands.

8   Look for scoring and scuffing on the thrust faces of the skirt, holes in the piston crown and burned areas at the edge of the crown. If the skirt is scored or scuffed, the engine may have been suffering from overheating and/or abnormal combustion, which caused excessively high operating temperatures. The cooling and lubrication systems should be checked thoroughly. A hole in the piston crown is an indication that abnormal combustion (preignition) was occurring. Burned areas at the edge of the piston crown are usually evidence of spark knock (detonation). If any of the above problems exist, the causes must be corrected or the damage will occur again. The causes may include intake air leaks, incorrect fuel/air mixture, incorrect ignition timing and EGR system malfunctions.

9   Corrosion of the piston, in the form of small pits, indicates that coolant is leaking into the combustion chamber and/or the crankcase. Again, the cause must be corrected or the problem may persist in the rebuilt engine.

10   Measure the piston ring side clearance by laying a new piston ring in each ring groove and slipping a feeler gauge in beside it (**see illustration**). Check the clearance at three or four locations around each groove. Be sure to use the correct ring for each groove — they are different. If the side clearance is greater than specified, new pistons will have to be used.

11   Check the piston-to-bore clearance by measuring the bore (see Section 15) and the piston diameter. Make sure the pistons and bores are correctly matched. Measure the piston across the skirt 5/64-inch above the bottom of the piston, at a 90° angle to and in line with the piston pin (**see illustration**). Subtract the piston diameter from the bore diameter to obtain the clearance. If it's greater than specified, the block will have to be rebored and new pistons and rings installed.

12   Check the piston-to-rod clearance by twisting the piston and rod in opposite directions. Any noticeable play indicates excessive wear, which must be corrected. The piston/connecting rod assemblies should be taken to an automotive machine shop to have the pistons and rods resized and new pins installed.

13   If the pistons must be removed from the connecting rods for any reason, they should be taken to an automotive machine shop. While they are there have the connecting rods checked for bend and twist, since automotive machine shops have special equipment for this pur-

pose. **Note:** *Unless new pistons and/or connecting rods must be installed, do not disassemble the pistons and connecting rods.*

14   Check the connecting rods for cracks and other damage. Temporarily remove the rod caps, lift out the old bearing inserts, wipe the rod and cap bearing surfaces clean and inspect them for nicks, gouges and scratches. After checking the rods, replace the old bearings, slip the caps into place and tighten the nuts finger tight. **Note:** *If the engine is being rebuilt because of a connecting rod knock, be sure to install new rods.*

18   Crankshaft — inspection

Refer to illustration 18.6

1   Clean the crankshaft with solvent and dry it with compressed air (if available). Be sure to clean the oil holes with a stiff brush and flush them with solvent.

2   Check the main and connecting rod bearing journals for uneven wear, scoring, pits and cracks.

3   Rub a penny across each journal several times. If a journal picks up copper from the penny, it's too rough and must be reground.

4   Remove all burrs from the crankshaft oil holes with a stone, file or scraper.

5   Check the rest of the crankshaft for cracks and other damage. It should be magnafluxed to reveal hidden cracks — an automotive machine shop will handle the procedure.

6   Using a micrometer, measure the diameter of the main and connecting rod journals and compare the results to the Specifications (**see illustration**). By measuring the diameter at a number of points around

**18.6   Measure the diameter of each crankshaft journal at
several points to detect taper and out-of-round conditions**

each journal's circumference, you'll be able to determine whether or not the journal is out-of-round. Take the measurement at each end of the journal, near the crank throws, to determine if the journal is tapered.

7   If the crankshaft journals are damaged, tapered, out-of-round or worn beyond the limits given in the Specifications, have the crankshaft reground by an automotive machine shop. Be sure to use the correct size bearing inserts if the crankshaft is reconditioned.

8   Check the oil seal journals at each end of the crankshaft for wear and damage. If the seal has worn a groove in the journal, or if it's nicked or scratched, the new seal may leak when the engine is reassembled. In some cases, an automotive machine shop may be able to repair the journal by pressing on a thin sleeve. If repair isn't feasible, a new or different crankshaft should be installed.

9   Refer to Section 19 and examine the main and rod bearing inserts.

19   Main and connecting rod bearings — inspection

Refer to illustration 19.1

1   Even though the main and connecting rod bearings should be replaced with new ones during the engine overhaul, the old bearings should be retained for close examination, as they may reveal valuable information about the condition of the engine (see illustration).

19.1 Typical bearing failures

2   Bearing failure occurs because of lack of lubrication, the presence of dirt or other foreign particles, overloading the engine and corrosion. Regardless of the cause of bearing failure, it must be corrected before the engine is reassembled to prevent it from happening again.

3   When examining the bearings, remove them from the engine block, the main bearing caps, the connecting rods and the rod caps and lay them out on a clean surface in the same general position as their location in the engine. This will enable you to match any bearing problems with the corresponding crankshaft journal.

4   Dirt and other foreign particles get into the engine in a variety of ways. It may be left in the engine during assembly, or it may pass through filters or the PCV system. It may get into the oil, and from there into the bearings. Metal chips from machining operations and normal engine wear are often present. Abrasives are sometimes left in engine components after reconditioning, especially when parts are not thoroughly cleaned using the proper cleaning methods. Whatever the source, these foreign objects often end up embedded in the soft bearing material and are easily recognized. Large particles will not embed in the bearing and will score or gouge the bearing and journal. The

best prevention for this cause of bearing failure is to clean all parts thoroughly and keep everything spotlessly clean during engine assembly. Frequent and regular engine oil and filter changes are also recommended.

5   Lack of lubrication (or lubrication breakdown) has a number of interrelated causes. Excessive heat (which thins the oil), overloading (which squeezes the oil from the bearing face) and oil leakage or throw off (from excessive bearing clearances, worn oil pump or high engine speeds) all contribute to lubrication breakdown. Blocked oil passages, which usually are the result of misaligned oil holes in a bearing shell, will also oil starve a bearing and destroy it. When lack of lubrication is the cause of bearing failure, the bearing material is wiped or extruded from the steel backing of the bearing. Temperatures may increase to the point where the steel backing turns blue from overheating.

6   Driving habits can have a definite effect on bearing life. Full throttle, low speed operation (lugging the engine) puts very high loads on bearings, which tends to squeeze out the oil film. These loads cause the bearings to flex, which produces fine cracks in the bearing face (fatigue failure). Eventually the bearing material will loosen in pieces and tear away from the steel backing. Short trip driving leads to corrosion of bearings because insufficient engine heat is produced to drive off the condensed water and corrosive gases. These products collect in the engine oil, forming acid and sludge. As the oil is carried to the engine bearings, the acid attacks and corrodes the bearing material.

7   Incorrect bearing installation during engine assembly will lead to bearing failure as well. Tight fitting bearings leave insufficient bearing oil clearance and will result in oil starvation. Dirt or foreign particles trapped behind a bearing insert result in high spots on the bearing which lead to failure.

20   Engine overhaul — reassembly sequence

1   Before beginning engine reassembly, make sure you have all the necessary new parts, gaskets and seals as well as the following items on hand:

Common hand tools
A 1/2-inch drive torque wrench
Piston ring installation tool
Piston ring compressor
Short lengths of rubber or plastic hose
*   to fit over connecting rod bolts*
Plastigage
Feeler gauges
A fine-tooth file
New engine oil
Engine assembly lube or moly-base grease
Gasket sealant
Thread locking compound

2   In order to save time and avoid problems, engine reassembly must be done in the following general order:

Piston rings
Crankshaft and main bearings
Piston/connecting rod assemblies
Oil pump
Rear main oil seal housing
Oil pan
Cylinder head, camshaft and rocker arm assembly
Timing belt and sprockets
Timing belt cover
Intake and exhaust manifolds
Rocker arm cover
Engine rear plate
Flywheel/driveplate

21   Piston rings — installation

Refer to illustrations 21.3, 21.4, 21.5, 21.9a, 21.9b, 21.11 and 21.12

1   Before installing the new piston rings, the ring end gaps must be checked. It's assumed that the piston ring side clearance has been checked and verified correct (Section 17).

2   Lay out the piston/connecting rod assemblies and the new ring

2B

21.3   When checking piston ring end gap, the ring must be square in the cylinder bore (this is done by pushing the ring down with the top of a piston as shown)

21.4   With the ring square in the cylinder, measure the end gap with a feeler gauge

21.5   If the end gap is too small, clamp a file in a vise and file the ring ends (from the outside in only) to enlarge the gap slightly

sets so the ring sets will be matched with the same piston and cylinder during the end gap measurement and engine assembly.

3   Insert the top (number one) ring into the first cylinder and square it up with the cylinder walls by pushing it in with the top of the piston **(see illustration)**. The ring should be near the bottom of the cylinder, at the lower limit of ring travel.

4   To measure the end gap, slip feeler gauges between the ends of the ring until a gauge equal to the gap width is found **(see illustration)**. The feeler gauge should slide between the ring ends with a slight amount of drag. Compare the measurement to the Specifications. If the gap is larger or smaller than specified, double-check to make sure you have the correct rings before proceeding.

5   If the gap is too small, it must be enlarged or the ring ends may come in contact with each other during engine operation, which can cause serious damage to the engine. The end gap can be increased by filing the ring ends very carefully with a fine file. Mount the file in a vise equipped with soft jaws, slip the ring over the file with the ends contacting the file face and slowly move the ring to remove material from the ends. When performing this operation, file only from the outside in **(see illustration)**.

6   Excess end gap isn't critical unless it's greater than 0.039-inch. Again, double-check to make sure you have the correct rings for your engine.

7   Repeat the procedure for each ring that will be installed in the first cylinder and for each ring in the remaining cylinders. Remember to keep rings, pistons and cylinders matched up.

8   Once the ring end gaps have been checked/corrected, the rings can be installed on the pistons.

9   The oil control ring (lowest one on the piston) is usually installed first. It's composed of three separate components. Slip the spacer/expander into the groove **(see illustration)**. If an anti-rotation tang is used, make sure it's inserted into the drilled hole in the ring groove. Next, install the lower side rail. Don't use a piston ring installation tool on the oil ring side rails, as they may be damaged. Instead, place one end of the side rail into the groove between the spacer/expander and the ring land, hold it firmly in place and slide a finger around the piston while pushing the rail into the groove **(see illustration)**. Next, install the upper side rail in the same manner.

10   After the three oil ring components have been installed, check to make sure that both the upper and lower side rails can be turned smoothly in the ring groove.

11   The number two (middle) ring is installed next. It's usually stamped with a mark which must face up, toward the top of the piston **(see illustration)**. **Note:** *Always follow the instructions printed on the ring package or box — different manufacturers may require different approaches. Do not mix up the top and middle rings, as they have different cross sections.*

12   Use a piston ring installation tool and make sure the identification mark is facing the top of the piston, then slip the ring into the middle groove on the piston **(see illustration)**. Don't expand the ring any more than necessary to slide it over the piston.

13   Install the number one (top) ring in the same manner. Make sure

21.9a   Installing the spacer/expander in the oil control ring groove

21.9b   DO NOT use a piston ring installation tool when installing the oil ring side rails

21.11 The no. 1 (top) and no. 2 compression rings have different cross sections — be sure to install them in the correct locations with the marks facing UP

21.12 Installing the compression rings with a ring expander — the mark (arrow) must face up

the mark is facing up. Be careful not to confuse the number one and number two rings.

14 Repeat the procedure for the remaining pistons and rings.

22 Crankshaft — installation and main bearing oil clearance check

Refer to illustrations 22.11 and 22.15

1 Crankshaft installation is the first step in engine reassembly. It's assumed at this point that the engine block and crankshaft have been cleaned, inspected and repaired or reconditioned.

2 Position the engine with the bottom facing up.

3 Remove the main bearing cap bolts and lift out the caps. Lay them out in the proper order to ensure correct installation.

4 If they're still in place, remove the original bearing inserts from the block and the main bearing caps. Wipe the bearing surfaces of the block and caps with a clean, lint-free cloth. They must be kept spotlessly clean.

Main bearing oil clearance check

5 Clean the back sides of the new main bearing inserts and lay one in each main bearing saddle in the block. If one of the bearing inserts from each set has a large groove in it, make sure the grooved insert is installed in the block. Lay the other bearing from each set in the corresponding main bearing cap. Make sure the tab on the bearing insert fits into the recess in the block or cap. **Caution:** *The oil holes in the block must line up with the oil holes in the bearing insert. Do not hammer the bearing into place and don't nick or gouge the bearing faces. No lubrication should be used at this time.*

6 The flanged thrust bearing must be installed in the center cap and saddle **(see illustration 7.5).**

7 Clean the faces of the bearings in the block and the crankshaft main bearing journals with a clean, lint-free cloth.

8 Check or clean the oil holes in the crankshaft, as any dirt here can go only one way — straight through the new bearings.

9 Once you're certain the crankshaft is clean, carefully lay it in position in the main bearings.

10 Before the crankshaft can be permanently installed, the main bearing oil clearance must be checked.

11 Cut several pieces of the appropriate size Plastigage (they must be slightly shorter than the width of the main bearings) and place one piece on each crankshaft main bearing journal, parallel with the journal axis **(see illustration).**

12 Clean the faces of the bearings in the caps and install the caps in their respective positions (don't mix them up) with the arrows pointing toward the front of the engine. Don't disturb the Plastigage.

13 Starting with the center main and working out toward the ends, tighten the main bearing cap bolts, in three steps, to the specified torque. Don't rotate the crankshaft at any time during this operation.

14 Remove the bolts and carefully lift off the main bearing caps. Keep them in order. Don't disturb the Plastigage or rotate the crankshaft. If any of the main bearing caps are difficult to remove, tap them gently from side-to-side with a soft-face hammer to loosen them.

15 Compare the width of the crushed Plastigage on each journal to the scale printed on the Plastigage envelope to obtain the main bearing oil clearance **(see illustration).** Check the Specifications to make sure it's correct.

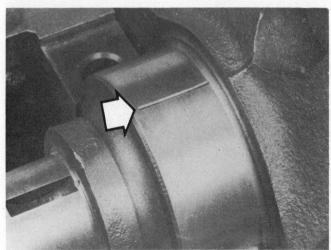

22.11 Lay the Plastigage strips (arrow) on the main bearing journals, parallel to the crankshaft centerline

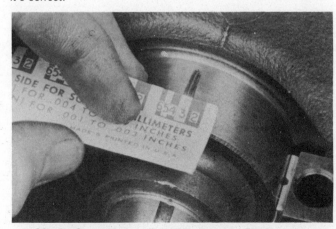

22.15 Compare the width of the crushed Plastigage to the scale on the envelope to determine the main bearing oil clearance (always take the measurement at the widest point of the Plastigage); be sure to use the correct scale — standard and metric scales are included

2B

16 If the clearance is not as specified, the bearing inserts may be the wrong size (which means different ones will be required). Before deciding that different inserts are needed, make sure that no dirt or oil was between the bearing inserts and the caps or block when the clearance was measured. If the Plastigage was wider at one end than the other, the journal may be tapered (refer to Section 18).

17 Carefully scrape all traces of the Plastigage material off the main bearing journals and/or the bearing faces. Use your fingernail or the edge of a credit card — don't nick or scratch the bearing faces.

Final crankshaft installation

18 Carefully lift the crankshaft out of the engine.

19 Clean the bearing faces in the block, then apply a thin, uniform layer of moly-base grease or engine assembly lube to each of the bearing surfaces. Be sure to coat the thrust faces as well as the journal face of the thrust bearing.

20 Make sure the crankshaft journals are clean, then lay the crankshaft back in place in the block.

21 Clean the faces of the bearings in the caps, then apply lubricant to them.

22 Install the caps in their respective positions with the arrows pointing toward the front of the engine.

23 Install the bolts.

24 Tighten all except the thrust bearing cap bolts to the specified torque (work from the center out and approach the final torque in three steps).

25 Tighten the thrust bearing cap bolts to 10-to-12 ft-lbs.

26 Tap the ends of the crankshaft forward and backward with a lead or brass hammer to line up the main bearing and crankshaft thrust surfaces.

27 Retighten all main bearing cap bolts to the specified torque, starting with the center main and working out toward the ends.

28 On manual transmission equipped models, install a new pilot bearing in the end of the crankshaft (see Chapter 8).

29 Rotate the crankshaft a number of times by hand to check for any obvious binding.

30 Recheck the crankshaft end play with a feeler gauge or a dial indicator as described in Section 13. The end play should be correct if the crankshaft thrust faces aren't worn or damaged and new bearings have been installed.

31 Refer to Section 23 and install the new rear main oil seal, then bolt the housing to the block.

23   Rear main oil seal installation

Refer to illustrations 23.3 and 23.5

1   The crankshaft must be installed first and the main bearing caps bolted in place, then the new seal should be installed in the housing and the housing bolted to the block.

2   Check the seal contact surface on the crankshaft very carefully for scratches and nicks that could damage the new seal lip and cause oil leaks. If the crankshaft is damaged, the only alternative is a new or different crankshaft.

3   The old seal can be removed from the housing by driving it out from the back side with a hammer and punch **(see illustration)**. Be sure to note how far it's recessed into the bore before removing it; the new seal will have to be recessed an equal amount. Be very careful not to scratch or otherwise damage the bore in the housing or oil leaks could develop.

4   Make sure the housing is clean, then apply a thin coat of engine oil to the outer edge of the new seal. The seal must be pressed squarely into the bore, so hammering it into place isn't recommended. If you don't have access to a press, sandwich the housing and seal between two smooth pieces of wood and press the seal into place with the jaws of a large vise. The pieces of wood must be thick enough to distribute the force evenly around the entire circumference of the seal. Work slowly and make sure the seal enters the bore squarely.

5   As a last resort, the seal can be tapped into the housing with a hammer. Use a block of wood to distribute the force evenly and make sure the seal is driven in squarely **(see illustration)**.

6   The seal lips must be lubricated with clean engine oil or moly-based grease before the seal/housing is slipped over the crankshaft and bolted to the block. Use a new gasket and sealant.

7   Tighten the bolts a little at a time until they're all secure.

24   Pistons/connecting rods — installation and rod bearing oil clearance check

Refer to illustrations 24.5, 24.9, 24.11, 24.13, 24.14 and 24.17

1   Before installing the piston/connecting rod assemblies, the cylinder walls must be perfectly clean, the top edge of each cylinder must be chamfered, and the crankshaft must be in place.

2   Remove the cap from the end of the number one connecting rod (refer to the marks made during removal). Remove the original bearing inserts and wipe the bearing surfaces of the connecting rod and cap with a clean, lint-free cloth. They must be kept spotlessly clean.

Connecting rod bearing oil clearance check

3   Clean the back side of the new upper bearing insert, then lay it in place in the connecting rod. Make sure the tab on the bearing fits into the recess in the rod. Don't hammer the bearing insert into place and be very careful not to nick or gouge the bearing face. Don't lubricate the bearing at this time.

4   Clean the back side of the other bearing insert and install it in the rod cap. Again, make sure the tab on the bearing fits into the recess in the cap, and don't apply any lubricant. It's critically important that the mating surfaces of the bearing and connecting rod are perfectly clean and oil free when they're assembled.

23.3   Support the housing on a couple of wood blocks and drive out the old seal with a punch or screwdriver and hammer

23.5   Drive the new seal into the housing with a block of wood or a section of pipe, if you have one large enough — make sure that you don't cock the seal in the bore

24.5   Position the ring gaps as shown here before installing the piston/connecting rod assemblies in the engine

24.9   The front mark must point towards the timing belt end of the engine when the pistons are installed

2B

5   Position the piston ring gaps at 90° intervals around the piston **(see illustration)**.

6   Slip a section of plastic or rubber hose over each connecting rod cap bolt.

7   Lubricate the piston and rings with clean engine oil and attach a piston ring compressor to the piston. Leave the skirt protruding about 1/4-inch to guide the piston into the cylinder. The rings must be compressed until they're flush with the piston.

8   Rotate the crankshaft until the number one connecting rod journal is at BDC (bottom dead center) and apply a coat of engine oil to the cylinder walls.

9   With the mark on top of the piston **(see illustration)** facing the front of the engine, gently insert the piston/connecting rod assembly into the number one cylinder bore and rest the bottom edge of the ring compressor on the engine block.

10   Tap the top edge of the ring compressor to make sure it's contacting the block around its entire circumference.

11   Gently tap on the top of the piston with the end of a wooden hammer handle **(see illustration)** while guiding the end of the connecting rod into place on the crankshaft journal. The piston rings may try to pop out of the ring compressor just before entering the cylinder bore, so keep some downward pressure on the ring compressor. Work slowly, and if any resistance is felt as the piston enters the cylinder, stop immediately. Find out what's hanging up and fix it before proceeding. Do not, for any reason, force the piston into the cylinder — you might break a ring and/or the piston.

12   Once the piston/connecting rod assembly is installed, the connecting rod bearing oil clearance must be checked before the rod cap is permanently bolted in place.

13   Cut a piece of the appropriate size Plastigage slightly shorter than

the width of the connecting rod bearing and lay it in place on the number one connecting rod journal, parallel with the journal axis **(see illustration)**.

14   Clean the connecting rod cap bearing face, remove the protective hoses from the connecting rod bolts and install the rod cap. Make sure the mating mark on the cap is on the same side as the mark on the connecting rod **(see illustration)**.

24.11   The piston can be driven (gently) into the cylinder bore with the end of a wooden hammer handle

24.13   Lay the Plastigage strips on each rod bearing journal, parallel to the crankshaft centerline

24.14   Match up the cylinder number marks and the bearing tab notches when installing the connecting rod caps

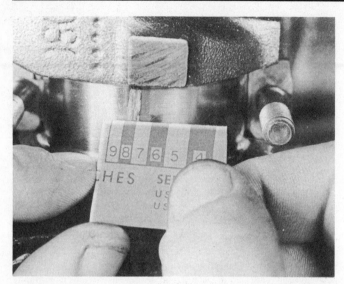

24.17 Measuring the width of the crushed Plastigage to determine the rod bearing oil clearance (be sure to use the correct scale — standard and metric scales are included)

15 Install the nuts and tighten them to the specified torque, working up to it in three steps. **Note:** *Use a thin-wall socket to avoid erroneous torque readings that can result if the socket is wedged between the rod cap and nut. If the socket tends to wedge itself between the nut and the cap, lift up on it slighty until it no longer contacts the cap.* Do not rotate the crankshaft at any time during this operation.
16 Remove the nuts and detach the rod cap, being very careful not to disturb the Plastigage.
17 Compare the width of the crushed Plastigage to the scale printed on the Plastigage envelope to obtain the oil clearance **(see illustration)**. Compare it to the Specifications to make sure the clearance is correct.
18 If the clearance is not as specified, the bearing inserts may be the wrong size (which means different ones will be required). Before deciding that different inserts are needed, make sure that no dirt or oil was between the bearing inserts and the connecting rod or cap when the clearance was measured. Also, recheck the journal diameter. If the Plastigage was wider at one end than the other, the journal may be tapered (refer to Section 18).

Final connecting rod installation

19 Carefully scrape all traces of the Plastigage material off the rod journal and/or bearing face. Be very careful not to scratch the bearing — use your fingernail or the edge of a credit card.
20 Make sure the bearing faces are perfectly clean, then apply a uniform layer of clean moly-base grease or engine assembly lube to both of them. You'll have to push the piston into the cylinder to expose the face of the bearing insert in the connecting rod — be sure to slip the protective hoses over the rod bolts first.
21 Slide the connecting rod back into place on the journal, remove the protective hoses from the rod cap bolts, install the rod cap and tighten the nuts to the specified torque. Again, work up to the torque in three steps.

22 Repeat the entire procedure for the remaining pistons/connecting rods.
23 The important points to remember are . . .
   a) Keep the back sides of the bearing inserts and the insides of the connecting rods and caps perfectly clean when assembling them.
   b) Make sure you have the correct piston/rod assembly for each cylinder.
   c) The mark on the piston must face the front of the engine.
   d) Lubricate the cylinder walls with clean oil.
   e) Lubricate the bearing faces when installing the rod caps after the oil clearance has been checked.
24 After all the piston/connecting rod assemblies have been properly installed, rotate the crankshaft a number of times by hand to check for any obvious binding.
25 As a final step, the connecting rod end play must be checked. Refer to Section 12 for this procedure.
26 Compare the measured end play to the Specifications to make sure it's correct. If it was correct before disassembly and the original crankshaft and rods were reinstalled, it should still be right. If new rods or a new crankshaft were installed, the end play may be inadequate. If so, the rods will have to be removed and taken to an automotive machine shop for resizing.

---

25   Initial start-up and break-in after overhaul

Warning: *Have a fire extinguisher handy when starting the engine for the first time.*
1   Once the engine has been installed in the vehicle, double-check the engine oil and coolant levels. Add transaxle fluid as needed.
2   With the spark plugs out of the engine and the ignition system disabled (see Section 3), crank the engine until the oil pressure light goes out.
3   Install the spark plugs, hook up the plug wires and restore the ignition system functions (Section 3).
4   Start the engine. It may take a few moments for the fuel system to build up pressure, but the engine should start without a great deal of effort. **Note:** *If backfiring occurs through the carburetor, recheck the valve timing and ignition timing.*
5   After the engine starts, it should be allowed to warm up to normal operating temperature. While the engine is warming up, make a thorough check for fuel, oil and coolant leaks. Check the automatic transaxle fluid level (if so equipped).
6   Shut the engine off and recheck the engine oil and coolant levels.
7   Drive the vehicle to an area with minimum traffic, accelerate at full throttle from 30 to 50 mph, then allow the vehicle to slow to 30 mph with the throttle closed. Repeat the procedure 10 or 12 times. This will load the piston rings and cause them to seat properly against the cylinder walls. Check again for oil and coolant leaks.
8   Drive the vehicle gently for the first 500 miles (no sustained high speeds) and keep a constant check on the oil level. It is not unusual for an engine to use oil during the break-in period.
9   At approximately 500 to 600 miles, change the oil and filter.
10 For the next few hundred miles, drive the vehicle normally. Do not pamper it or abuse it.
11 After 2000 miles, change the oil and filter again and consider the engine broken in.

Chapter 3 Cooling, heating and air conditioning systems

Contents

Specifications

General

Radiator cap pressure rating

    1986 through 1989 models .... 11.3 to 14.2 psi

    1990 models .... 11.3 to 15.6 psi

    1991 and later models .... 11.8 to 15.6 psi

Thermostat rating (opening temperature) .... 190°F (88°C)

Cooling system capacity .... See Chapter 1

Refrigerant capacity .... 1.9 to 2.2 lbs

Torque specifications

	Ft-lbs	Nm
Water pump-to-engine block		
Alternator brace bolt (head mark 7)	14 to 20	20 to 26
All others (head mark 4)	9 to 11	12 to 15
Water pump pulley bolts	6 to 7	8 to 10
Thermostat housing cover bolts	7.2 to 9.4	10 to 13

1 General information

Engine cooling system

All vehicles covered by this manual employ a pressurized engine cooling system with thermostatically controlled coolant circulation. An impeller type water pump mounted on the front (drivebelt end) of the block pumps coolant through the engine. The coolant flows around each cylinder and toward the rear of the engine. Cast-in coolant passages direct coolant around the intake and exhaust ports, near the spark plug areas and in close proximity to the exhaust valve guides.

A wax pellet type thermostat is located in a housing near the transaxle end of the engine. During warm up, the closed thermostat prevents coolant from circulating through the radiator. As the engine nears normal operating temperature, the thermostat opens and allows hot coolant to travel through the radiator, where it's cooled before returning to the engine.

The cooling system is sealed by a pressure type radiator cap, which raises the boiling point of the coolant and increases the cooling efficiency of the radiator. If the system pressure exceeds the cap pressure relief value, the excess pressure in the system forces the spring-loaded valve inside the cap off its seat and allows the coolant to escape through the overflow tube into a coolant reservoir. When the system cools, the excess coolant is automatically drawn from the reservoir back into the radiator.

The coolant reservoir does double duty as both the point at which fresh coolant is added to the cooling system to maintain the proper fluid level and as a holding tank for overheated coolant.

This type of cooling system is known as a closed design because coolant that escapes past the pressure cap is saved and reused.

Heating system

The heating system consists of a blower fan and heater core located in the heater box, the hoses connecting the heater core to the engine cooling system and the heater/air conditioning control head on the dashboard. Hot engine coolant is circulated through the heater core. When the heater mode is activated, a flap door opens to expose the heater box to the passenger compartment. A fan switch on the control head activates the blower motor, which forces air through the core, heating the air.

Air conditioning system

The air conditioning system consists of a condenser mounted in front of the radiator, an evaporator mounted adjacent to the heater core, a compressor mounted on the engine, a filter-drier which contains a high pressure relief valve and the plumbing connecting all of the above components.

A blower fan forces the warmer air of the passenger compartment through the evaporator core (sort of a radiator-in-reverse), transferring the heat from the air to the refrigerant. The liquid refrigerant boils off into low pressure vapor, taking the heat with it when it leaves the evaporator.

---

2 Antifreeze — general information

Warning: *Do not allow antifreeze to come in contact with your skin or painted surfaces of the vehicle. Rinse off spills immediately with plenty of water. Antifreeze, if consumed, can be fatal to children and pets, so wipe up garage floor and drip pan coolant spills immediately. Keep antifreeze containers covered and repair leaks in your cooling system as soon as they are noticed.*

The cooling system should be filled with a water/ethylene glycol based antifreeze solution, which will prevent freezing down to at least −20°F, or lower if local climate requires it. It also provides protection against corrosion and increases the coolant boiling point.

The cooling system should be drained, flushed and refilled at the specified intervals (see Chapter 1). Old or contaminated antifreeze solutions are likely to cause damage and encourage the formation of corrosion and scale in the system. Use distilled water with the antifreeze.

Before adding antifreeze, check all hose connections, because antifreeze tends to search out and leak through very minute openings. Engines don't normally consume coolant, so if the level goes down, find the cause and correct it.

The exact mixture of antifreeze-to-water which you should use depends on the relative weather conditions. The mixture should contain at least 50 percent antifreeze, but should never contain more than 70 percent antifreeze. Consult the mixture ratio chart on the antifreeze container before adding coolant. Hydrometers are available at most auto parts stores to test the coolant. Use antifreeze which meets the vehicle manufacturer's specifications.

---

3 Thermostat — check and replacement

Warning: *Do not remove the radiator cap, drain the coolant or replace the thermostat until the engine has cooled completely.*

Check

1 Before assuming the thermostat is to blame for a cooling system problem, check the coolant level, drivebelt tension (Chapter 1) and temperature gauge operation.
2 If the engine seems to be taking a long time to warm up (based on heater output or temperature gauge operation), the thermostat is probably stuck open. Replace the thermostat with a new one.
3 If the engine runs hot, use your hand to check the temperature of the upper radiator hose. If the hose isn't hot, but the engine is, the thermostat is probably stuck closed, preventing the coolant inside the

engine from escaping to the radiator. Replace the thermostat. **Caution:** *Don't drive the vehicle without a thermostat. The computer may stay in open loop and emissions and fuel economy will suffer.*
4 If the upper radiator hose is hot, it means that the coolant is flowing and the thermostat is open. Consult the Troubleshooting Section at the front of this manual for cooling system diagnosis.

Replacement

Refer to illustrations 3.10 and 3.13
5 Disconnect the negative battery cable from the battery.
6 Drain the cooling system (Chapter 1). If the coolant is relatively new or in good condition (see Chapter 1), save it and reuse it.
7 Follow the upper radiator hose to the engine to locate the thermostat housing.
8 Loosen the hose clamp, then detach the hose from the fitting. If it's stuck, grasp it near the end with a pair of Channelock pliers and twist it to break the seal, then pull it off. If the hose is old or deteriorated, cut it off and install a new one.
9 If the outer surface of the large fitting that mates with the hose is deteriorated (corroded, pitted, etc.) it may be damaged further by hose removal. If it is, the thermostat housing cover will have to be replaced.
10 Remove the bolts and detach the housing cover **(see illustrations)**. If the cover is stuck, tap it with a soft-face hammer to jar it loose. Be prepared for some coolant to spill as the gasket seal is broken.
11 Note how it's installed (which end is facing up), then remove the thermostat.
12 Stuff a rag into the engine opening, then remove all traces of old gasket material and sealant from the housing and cover with a gasket scraper. Remove the rag from the opening and clean the gasket mating surfaces with lacquer thinner or acetone.

3.10 Remove the two thermostat housing cover bolts (arrows) to gain access to the thermostat

3.13 Make sure the thermostat is installed correctly — if it's installed wrong, the engine will overheat and damage will result

13 Install the new thermostat in the housing. Make sure the correct end faces up — the spring end is normally directed into the engine (**see illustration**).

14 Apply a thin, uniform layer of RTV sealant to both sides of the new gasket and position it on the housing.

15 Install the cover and bolts. Tighten the bolts to the specified torque.

16 Reattach the hose to the fitting and tighten the hose clamp securely.

17 Refill the cooling system (Chapter 1).

18 Start the engine and allow it to reach normal operating temperature, then check for leaks and proper thermostat operation (as described in Steps 2 through 4).

4 Radiator — removal and installation

Refer to illustrations 4.5, 4.7, 4.9a and 4.9b

Warning: *Wait until the engine is completely cool before beginning this procedure.*

1 Disconnect the negative battery cable from the battery.

2 Drain the cooling system (see Chapter 1). If the coolant is relatively new or in good condition, save it and reuse it.

3 Loosen the hose clamps, then detach the radiator hoses from the fittings. If they're stuck, grasp each hose near the end with a pair of Channelock pliers and twist it to break the seal, then pull it off — be careful not to distort the radiator fittings! If the hoses are old or deteriorated, cut them off and install new ones.

4 Disconnect the reservoir hose from the radiator filler neck.

5 Unplug the fan wire harness connector (**see illustration**).

6 If the vehicle is equipped with an automatic transaxle, disconnect the cooler lines.

7 Plug the lines and fittings (**see illustration**).

8 On 1986 through 1989 models, remove the grille (see Chapter 11).

9 Remove the radiator mounting bolts as follows:

 a) On 1986 through 1989 models, remove the radiator upper and lower mounting bolts (**see illustrations**).

 b) On 1990 and later models, remove the upper insulator bolts and remove the upper insulators from the radiator mounting posts.

10 Carefully remove the radiator. On 1990 and later models, pull the radiator up to release the radiator mounting posts from the lower insulators. Don't spill coolant on the vehicle or scratch the paint.

11 With the radiator removed, it can be inspected for leaks and damage. If it needs repair, have a radiator shop or dealer service department perform the work as special techniques are required.

12 Bugs and dirt can be removed from the radiator with compressed air and a soft brush. Don't bend the cooling fins as this is done.

13 Installation is the reverse of the removal procedure.

14 After installation, fill the cooling system with the proper mixture of antifreeze and water. Refer to Chapter 1 if necessary.

15 Start the engine and check for leaks. Allow the engine to reach normal operating temperature, indicated by the upper radiator hose becoming hot. Recheck the coolant level and add more if required.

16 If you're working on an automatic transaxle equipped vehicle, check and add fluid as needed.

4.5 The engine cooling fan wire harness connector is located between the radiator and battery (arrow)

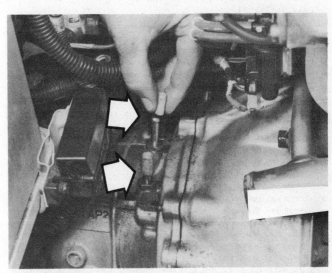

4.7 Disconnect the automatic transaxle fluid cooler lines at the transaxle fittings (arrows) and cap the lines and fittings

4.9b The lower bolt on the right side of the radiator (arrow) is located behind the grille

4.9a The top bolt on the right side (not visible) and the two bolts on the left (arrows) are accessible in the engine compartment

3

5.8   Unplug the wiring harness and remove the four bolts (arrows)

5.9   Hold the fan blades to keep them from turning and remove the nut (arrow)

5   Engine cooling fan — check and replacement

Refer to illustrations 5.8 and 5.9

Check

1   The engine cooling fan is controlled by a temperature switch mounted in the bottom of the radiator. When the coolant reaches a predetermined temperature, the switch provides a ground return for the fan motor circuit.
2   First, check the fuses (see Chapter 12).
3   To test the fan motor, unplug the motor connector and use jumper wires to connect the fan directly to the battery. If the fan still does not work, replace the motor.
4   If the motor tested OK, the fault lies in the coolant temperature switch or the wiring harness (see Chapter 12).
5   Test the temperature switch by unplugging the connector and grounding the wire from the fan motor with a jumper wire.
6   If the fan does not operate, check the wiring (see Chapter 12).

Replacement

7   Remove the radiator from the vehicle (see Section 4).
8   Unplug the wires and unbolt the fan shroud **(see illustration)**.
9   Remove the nut and detach the fan blade assembly from the motor shaft **(see illustration)**.
10 Take out the screws holding the fan motor to the bracket and detach the motor.
11 Installation is the reverse of removal. **Note:** *Air conditioned vehicles have an additional fan to cool the condenser, which is mounted to the left of the radiator. It can be checked by following Steps 2, 3 and 6. For replacement, follow Steps 8 through 11.*

6   Coolant temperature sending unit — check and replacement

Refer to illustration 6.3
Warning: *The engine must be completely cool before removing the sending unit.*

Check

1   If the coolant temperature gauge is inoperative, check the fuses first (Chapter 12).
2   If the temperature indicator shows excessive temperature after running a while, see the Troubleshooting Section in the front of the manual.
3   If the temperature gauge indicates Hot shortly after the engine is started cold, disconnect the wire(s) at the coolant temperature sending unit **(see illustration)**. If the gauge reading drops, replace the send-

ing unit. If the reading remains high, the wire to the gauge or light may be shorted to ground or the gauge is faulty.
4   If the coolant temperature gauge fails to indicate after the engine has been warmed up (approximately 10 minutes) and the fuses checked out OK, shut off the engine. Disconnect the green/yellow wire at the sending unit and using a jumper wire, connect it to a clean ground on the engine. Turn on the ignition without starting the engine. If the gauge now indicates Hot, replace the sending unit.
5   If the gauge still does not work, the circuit may be open or the gauge may be faulty. See Chapter 12 for additional information.

Replacement

6   With the engine completely cool, remove the cap from the radiator to release any pressure, then replace the cap. This reduces coolant loss during sending unit replacement.
7   Disconnect the wiring harness from the sending unit.
8   Prepare the new sending unit for installation by applying sealer to the threads.
9   Unscrew the sending unit from the engine and quickly install the new one to prevent coolant loss.
10 Tighten the sending unit securely and connect the wiring harness.
11 Refill the cooling system and run the engine. Check for leaks and proper gauge operation.

6.3   On 1989 and earlier models the coolant temperature sending unit (arrow) is located in the bottom of the intake manifold, behind the distributor (the distributor has been removed for clarity) – on later models it's screwed into the side of the intake manifold

7.2 Pull out the cap and remove the two bolts (arrows), then lift out the coolant reservoir

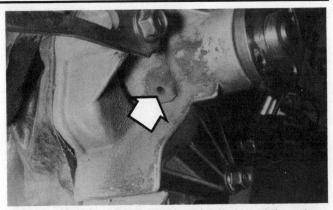

8.4 If coolant is leaking from the weep hole (arrow) the water pump must be replaced

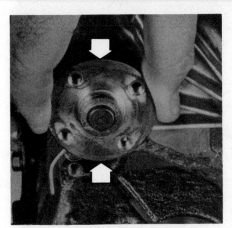

8.5 If there is play in the shaft, replace the water pump

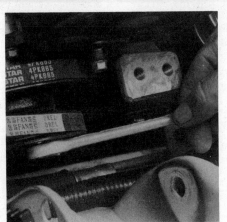

9.3 Loosen the water pump pulley bolts before removing the drivebelts

9.7 Remove the mounting bolts (arrows) (the bolt holding the alternator brace in place is longer than the other three)

3

7 Coolant reservoir - removal and installation

Refer to illustration 7.2

1   Lift the cap off the coolant resevoir and withdraw the overflow hose.

2   Remove the coolant reservoir-to-fender bolt and the windshield washer-to-coolant reservoir bolt **(see illustration)** and lift the coolant reservoir out. The windshield washer reservoir can remain in place.

3   Installation is the reverse of removal.

8 Water pump - check

Refer to illustrations 8.4 and 8.5

1   A failure in the water pump can cause serious engine damage due to overheating.

2   There are three ways to check the operation of the water pump while it's installed on the engine. If the pump is defective, it should be replaced with a new or rebuilt unit.

3   With the engine running at normal operating temperature, squeeze the upper radiator hose. If the water pump is working properly, a pressure surge should be felt as the hose is released. Warning: Keep your hands away from the fan blades!

4   Water pumps are equipped with weep or vent holes. If a failure occurs in the pump seal, coolant will leak from the hole. In most cases you'll need a flashlight to find the hole on the water pump from underneath to check for leaks **(see illustration)**.

5   If the water pump shaft bearings fail there may be a howling sound at the front of the engine while it's running. Shaft wear can be felt if the water pump pulley is rocked up and down **(see illustration)**. Don't mistake drivebelt slippage, which causes a squealing sound, for water pump bearing failure.

9 Water pump - removal and installation

Refer to illustrations 9.3 and 9.7

Warning: *Wait until the engine is completely cool before beginning this procedure.*

1   Disconnect the negative battery cable from the battery.

2   Drain the cooling system (Chapter 1). If the coolant is relatively new or in good condition, save it and reuse it.

3   Remove the left engine mount (see Chapter 2, Part A) and loosen the water pump pulley bolts **(see illustration)**.

4   Remove the drivebelts (Chapter 1) and the pulley at the end of the water pump shaft

5   Remove the timing belt and tensioner (see Chapter 2, Part A).

6   Remove the alternator bracket from the water pump.

7   Remove the bolts **(see illustration)** and detach the water pump from the engine. Note the locations of the various lengths and different types of bolts as they're removed to ensure correct installation.

8   Clean the bolt threads and the threaded holes in the engine to remove corrosion and sealant.

9   Compare the new pump to the old one to make sure they're identical.

10   Remove all traces of old gasket material from the engine with a gasket scraper.

11   Clean the engine and new water pump mating surfaces with lacquer thinner or acetone.

12   Install a new O-ring in the groove at the front end of the coolant pipe and lubricate the O-ring with coolant.

13   Apply a thin coat of RTV sealant to the engine side of the new gasket and to the gasket mating surface of the new pump, then carefully mate the gasket and the pump. Slip a couple of bolts through the pump mounting holes to hold the gasket in place.

14   Carefully attach the pump and gasket to the engine and thread

10.3 The heater blower unit is located below the glove compartment – unplug the wiring harness connectors and release the clips (arrows)

10.5 The fan is held on the moter shaft with a clip _ spread the clip and slip the fan off the shaft

the bolts into the holes finger tight. Note that the bolt on the left side of the pump (that attaches the alternator brace) is longer than the other three bolts.

15   Install the remaining bolts (be sure to reposition the alternator bracket at this time). Tighten them to the specified torque in 1/4-turn increments. Don't overtighten them or the pump may be distorted.
16   Reinstall all parts removed for access to the pump.
17   Refill the cooling system and check the drivebelt tension (Chapter 1). Run the engine and check for leaks.

10   Heater blower - removal and installation

Refer to illustrations 10.3 and 10.5
1   Disconnect the negative cable from the battery.
2   Remove the lower dash panel below the glove compartment (see Chapter 11).
3   Disconnect the wiring harnesses from the blower **(see illustration)**.
4   Remove the screws holding the blower motor to the heater housing and lift the unit out.
5   If you are replacing the motor, detach the fan and transfer it to the new motor **(see illustration)**.
6   Installation is the reverse of removal. Run the blower and check for proper operation.

11   Heater core- removal and installation

Refer to illustration 11.8
Warning: *The air conditioning system is under high pressure. Do not loosen any hose fittings or remove any components until after the system has been discharged by a dealer service department or service station. Always wear eye protection when disconnecting air conditioning system fittings.*
1   Disconnect the negative cable from the battery.
2   Drain the cooling system (see Chapter 1) and the heater core by setting the control lever to the HOT position.
3   Working in the engine compartment disconnect the heater hoses from the heater core connector tubes. On models equipped with air conditioning, disconnect the evaporator lines **(see Warning)**. A special spring lock coupling tool is needed on 1990 and later models.
4   Remove the console assembly, glove box, lower crashpad and center support bracket and the center facia assembly (see Chapter 11). On models equipped with air conditioning, remove the bolts retaining the air conditioning unit and move the unit aside.
5   Loosen the heating duct mounting screws and remove the lower heating ducts.
6   Disconnect the heater control cable (see Section 16) or vacuum lines as necessary.
7   Unbolt the heating unit and remove it from the vehicle.

11.8 Typical heater unit details

| 1 | Heater unit | 3 | Blower unit |
| 2 | Duct | 4 | Cover |

8   On 1989 and earlier models, remove the heater core cover, tubes and brackets **(see illustration)**. On 1990 and later models, remove the screws and clips and separate the heater core case halves.
9   Remove the defective heater core, then carefully install the new core and seal into the unit.
10   Reassemble the heater unit and check the operation of the air control doors. If any binding is experienced, correct the problem before installing the unit into the vehicle.
11   Reinstall the remaining parts in the reverse order of removal. Fill the cooling system with the correct type and amount of coolant (see Chapter 1). On models equipped with air conditioning, have the A/C system evacuated and recharged by the shop that discharged it.

12   Air conditioning system – check and maintenance

Refer to illustrations 12.7a and 12.7b
Warning: *The air conditioning system is under high pressure. Do not loosen any hose fittings or remove any components until after the system has been discharged by a dealer service department or service station. Always wear eye protection when disconnecting air conditioning system fittings.*

12.7a   1993 and earlier models are designed to use R-12 refrigerant, which is no longer available to the do-it-yourselfer

12.7b   If you have a 1994 model, R-134a refrigerant and recharge kits are available to do-it-yourselfers from auto parts stores – follow the instructions that come with the recharge kit

Note 1: *The air conditioning system on 1994 models uses the non-ozone-depleting refrigerant, referred to as R-134a. The R-134a refrigerant and its lubricating oil are not compatible with the R-12 system and under no circumstances should the two different types of refrigerant and lubricating oil be intermixed. If mixed, it could result in costly compressor failure due to improper lubrication.*

Note 2: *Because of recent Federal regulations proposed by the Environmental Protection Agency, R-12 refrigerant is no longer available to the do-it-yourselfer. If you are properly certified and can obtain R-12 refrigerant, refer to the Haynes Automotive Heating and Air Conditioning Manual for recharging instructions.*

1   The following maintenance checks should be performed on a regular basis to ensure that the air conditioner continues to operate at peak efficiency.

   a) Check the compressor drivebelt. If it's worn or deteriorated, replace it (see Chapter 1).

   b) Check the drivebelt tension and, if necessary, adjust it (see Chapter 1).

   c) Check the system hoses. Look for cracks, bubbles, hard spots and deterioration. Inspect the hoses and all fittings for oil bubbles and seepage. If there's any evidence of wear, damage or leaks, replace the hose(s).

   d) Inspect the condenser fins for leaves, bugs and other debris. Use a "fin comb" or compressed air to clean the condenser.

   e) Make sure the system has the correct refrigerant charge.

2   It's a good idea to operate the system for about 10 minutes at least once a month, particularly during the winter. Long term non-use can cause hardening, and subsequent failure, of the seals.

3   Because of the complexity of the air conditioning system and the special equipment necessary to service it, in-depth troubleshooting and repairs are not included in this manual. However, simple checks and component replacement procedures are provided in this Chapter.

4   The most common cause of poor cooling is simply a low system refrigerant charge. If a noticeable drop in cool air output occurs, one of the following quick checks will help you determine if the refrigerant level is low.

5   Warm the engine up to normal operating temperature.

6   Place the air conditioning temperature selector at the coldest setting and put the blower at the highest setting. Open the doors (to make sure the air conditioning system doesn't cycle off as soon as it cools the passenger compartment).

7   With the compressor engaged – the clutch will make an audible click and the center of the clutch will rotate – inspect the sight glass **(see illustration 12.2)**. If the refrigerant looks foamy, it's low. Charge the system or have it charged by a professional **(see illustrations)**.

13.2   Receiver-driver and related components

1	Pressure switch	3	Clamp bolt
2	Refrigerant lines	4	Sight glass

13   Air conditioning receiver/drier – removal and installation

Refer to illustration 13.2

Warning: *The air conditioning system is under high pressure. Do not loosen any fittings or remove any components until after the system has been discharged by a dealer service department or service station. Always wear eye protection when disconnecting refrigerant fittings.*

1   The receiver/drier, which acts as a reservoir and filter for the refrigerant, is located in the left front corner of the engine compartment.

2   Unplug the electrical connector from the pressure switch **(see illustration)**.

3   Detach the two refrigerant lines from the receiver/drier.

4   Immediately cap the open fittings to prevent the entry of dirt and moisture.

5   Unbolt the receiver/drier and lift it out of the engine compartment.

6   Install new O-rings on the lines and lubricate them with clean refrigerant oil.

7   Installation is the reverse of removal. **Note:** *Do not remove the sealing caps until you are ready to reconnect the lines. Do not mistake the inlet (marked IN) and the outlet (marked OUT) connections.*
8   If a new receiver/drier is installed, add 1.0 US fluid ounce (30 cc) of refrigerant oil to the system.
9   Have the system evacuated, charged and leak tested by the shop that discharged it.

14   Air conditioning compressor - removal and installation

Refer to illustrations 14.6 and 14.7

Warning: *The air conditioning system is under high pressure. Do not loosen any fittings or remove any components until after the system has been discharged by a dealer service department or service station. Always wear eye protection when disconnecting refrigerant fittings.*
1   Disconnect the negative cable from the battery.
2   Set the parking brake and block the rear tires.
3   Raise the front of the vehicle and support it securely on jackstands.
4   Unbolt the belly pan and remove the compressor drivebelt (see Chapter 1).
5   Disconnect the clutch wire from the compressor.
6   Detach the refrigerant lines from the back of the compressor **(see illustration)** and immediately cap the open fittings to prevent the entry of dirt and moisture.
7   Remove the mounting bolts **(see illustration)** and lower the compressor from the engine compartment. Note the location and thickness

of any shims and reinstall them in the same place. **Note:** *Keep the compressor level during handling and storage. If the compressor seized or you find metal particles in the refrigerant lines, the system must be flushed out by an air conditioning technician and the receiver/drier must be replaced.*
8   Prior to installation, turn the center of the clutch six times to disperse any oil that has collected in the head.
9   Install the compressor in the reverse order of removal.
10   If you are installing a new compressor, refer to the manufacturer's instructions for adding refrigerant oil to the system.
11   Have the system evacuated, charged and leak tested by the shop that discharged it.

15   Air conditioning condenser - removal and installation

Refer to illustrations 15.2, 15.3 and 15.4

Warning: *The air conditioning system is under high pressure. Do not loosen any fittings or remove any components until after the system has been discharged by a dealer service department or service station. Always wear eye protection when disconnecting refrigerant fittings.*
1   Remove the hood, grille and vertical brace (see Chapter 11).
2   Disconnect the refrigerant lines from the condenser. Be sure to use a back-up wrench to avoid twisting the lines **(see illustration)**.
3   Immediately cap the open fittings to prevent the entry of dirt and moisture **(see illustration)**.
4   Unbolt the condenser **(see illustration)** and lift it out of the vehicle. Store it upright to prevent oil loss.

14.6 Air conditioner compressor viewed from above showing refrigerant line fittings and upper mounting bolts (arrows)

14.7 Air conditioner compressor lower mounting bolts (arrows)

15.2 Use a back-up wrench to avoid twisting the lines

15.3 Immediately seal off the ends - tape works well

15.4 Remove the bolts and center brace (arrows) and lift the condenser out

5   Installation is the reverse of removal.
6   If a new condenser was installed, add 1.0 US ounce (30 cc) of refrigerant oil to the system.
7   Have the system evacuated, charged and leak tested by the shop that discharged it.

16   Air conditioner and heater control assembly - removal, installation and cable adjustment

Removal and installation
Refer to illustrations 16.4a, 16.4b, 16.4c and 16.5

1   Disconnect the negative cable from the battery.
2   Remove the trim panel which surrounds the control assembly (see Chapter 11).
3   Remove the glove compartment and the covers on the sides of the console under the dash.
4   Disconnect the control cables at the ends opposite from the control by detaching the cable clamps and separating the cables from the pins on the operating levers **(see illustrations)**.
5   Remove the control mounting screws **(see illustration)**.

16.4a **Mode control cable mounting details**

Tube
Clamp
Cable mounting boss
Cable
DEF mode pin
Cam

0065-11

16.4b **Fresh-recirc cable mounting details**

Cable mounting bracket
Tube
Fresh-recirc lever
Fresh mode pin
Clamp
Cable

0066-11

16.4c **Temperature cable mounting details**

Tube holder
Tube
Clamp
Cable mounting boss
Cable
Cool-warm pin
Cool-warm lever

0067-H

16.5 **Heater control mounting screw locations (arrows)**

3

16.8   Mode control in the defrost position for cable adjustment

**16.9   Fresh-recirc control in the outside air position
for cable adjustment**

**16.10   Place the temperature lever all the way to the left
for cable adjustment**

6   Carefully slip the unit out of the dash.
7   Installation is the reverse of removal.

Cable adjustment
Refer to illustrations 16.8, 16.9 and 16.10

Defrost-vent cable
8   Set the control to defrost **(see illustration)**. Move the lever all the way back, connect the cable to the lever and reinstall the clamp.

Fresh-recirc cable
9   Set the control in the outside-air position **(see illustration)**. Move the lever all the way back, connect the cable to the lever and reinstall the clamp.

Temperature control cable
10   Set the control to the left position **(see illustration)**. Move the water valve lever to the highest position, connect the cable to the lever and reinstall the clamp.

Chapter 4 Fuel and exhaust systems

Contents

4

Specifications

Electrical and power steering load idle-up speed

1986 models
  Canada
    Manual transaxle .... 900 ± 10 rpm
    Automatic transaxle .... 950 ± 10 rpm
  USA .... 850 rpm
1987 and later models
  First 300 miles .... 800 ± 50 rpm
  After 300 miles .... 850 ± 100 rpm

Air conditioner load idle-up
speed (1988 and later models) .... 875 ± 25 rpm

Solenoid valve resistance (1986 and 1987 models)*

Idle-up control solenoid valve .... Approx. 40 ohms
Deceleration solenoid valve (DSV) .... 49.7 ohms
Enrichment solenoid valve (ESV) .... 49.7 ohms
Jet mixture solenoid valve (JSV) .... 49.7 ohms
Bowl vent valve (BVV) .... 80 ohms

Specifications not available for 1988 and later models

Throttle position sensor (carbureted models only)

Resistance
  1986 and 1987 models
    Closed throttle .... Approx. 1.2 K-ohms
    Wide open models .... Approx. 4.9 K-ohms
  1988 and later models .... 3.5 to 6.5 K-ohms
Output voltage .... 250 mV

Dash pot adjustment engine speed .... 1800 rpm

Choke valve-to-bore clearance
(1988 and later models)** .... 0.055 to 0.063 in (1.4 to 1.6 mm)

Fast idle speed (1988 and later models)
Manual transaxle .... 2800 rpm
Automatic transaxle .... 2700 rpm

Choke heater (1988 and later models) .... Should be conductive (about 6 ohms resistance at 68~F)

Electric fuel pump pressure
With fuel pressure regulator hose
Connected .... 39 psi
Disconnected .... 40 to 49 psi

Fuel injector resistance .... 13 to 16 ohms

**Engine idling, vacuum hose detached

---

1 General information

Refer to illustrations 1.1a, 1.1b and 1.1c

From 1986 through 1989, both US and Canadian models were equipped with the Feedback Carburetor (FBC) system. In 1990, the US models changed over to a multi-point fuel injection (MPI) system, while the Canadian models continue to use the FBC carburetor.

Carbureted models

The fuel system consists of a fuel tank, two fuel filters (one in-tank and one in the engine compartment), a fuel pump, an air cleaner assembly and a two-barrel carburetor **(see illustrations)**.

The fuel pump is a mechanical type mounted on the cylinder head. The pump is driven off the camshaft by a pushrod.

The Feedback Carburetor (FBC) system is controlled by a computer which monitors changes in engine operation with various information sensors, compares this data to parameters stored in its memory and alters fuel delivery accordingly by means of actuators installed on the carburetor. Refer to Chapter 6 for more information.

Fuel injected-models

The multi-point fuel injection system consists of a fuel tank, two fuel filters (one in the tank and one in the fuel feed line), an electric fuel pump, a fuel pressure regulator, a fuel rail, injectors and an air cleaner assembly.

The fuel pump supplies pressurized fuel to the injectors. The regulator allows excess fuel to return to the fuel tank to maintain the pressure at a set limit.

This computerized fuel control system uses various input sensors to feed information to the Electronic Control Unit (ECU). The ECU uses this input to determine the amount of time to hold the injectors (placed at each intake valve) open. Refer to Section 13 for more information.

Exhaust system

All vehicles are equipped with an exhaust manifold, a catalytic converter, the connecting pipe between the converter and a main muffler assembly (the rear part of the exhaust pipe and the muffler itself). The exhaust system is suspended from the underside of the vehicle and insulated from vibration by a series of rubber hangers.

1.1a Feedback carburetor components (1986 and 1987 vehicles)

Dash pot and throttle opener

Choke breaker

Coolant outlet

Plug for float level check

Depression chamber

1.1b Feedback carburetor components (1986 and 1987 vehicles)

To canister

Jet mixture solenoid valve

Bowl vent valve

Fuel inlet

Mixture control valve (MCV)

Depression chamber

2-stage choke breaker

Electric choke

B

C

Acceleration pump

Throttle opener/dash pot

A

Mixture control valve (MCV)

Feedback solenoid valve (FBSV)

Depression chamber

Bowl vent valve (BVV)

View B

Feedback solenoid valve (FBSV)

Slow cut solenoid valve (SCSV)

Throttle opener/dash pot

Acceleration pump

Vacuum nipple A (VRV)

Vacuum nipple D (distributor)

Vacuum nipple E (EGR valve)

Enrichment

Throttle position sensor (TPS)

View A

View C

1.1c Feedback carburetor components (1988 and later models)

4

2   Fuel lines and fittings – inspection and replacement

Warning: *Gasoline is extremely flammable, so take extra precautions when working on any part of the fuel system. Do not smoke or allow open flames or bare light bulbs in or near the work area. Also, don't work in a garage if a natural gas appliance such as a water heater or clothes dryer is present.*

Inspection

1   Once in a while, you will have to raise the vehicle to service or replace some component (an exhaust pipe hanger, for example). Whenever you work under the vehicle, always inspect the fuel lines and fittings for possible damage or deterioration.
2   Check all hoses and pipes for cracks, kinks, deformation or obstructions.
3   Make sure all hose and pipe clips attach their associated hoses or pipes securely to the underside of the vehicle.
4   Verify all hose clamps attaching rubber hoses to metal fuel lines or pipes are snug enough to assure a tight fit between the hoses and pipes.

Replacement

5   If you must replace any damaged sections, use original equipment replacement hoses or pipes constructed from exactly the same material as the section you are replacing. Do not install substitutes constructed from inferior or inappropriate material or you could cause a fuel leak or a fire.
6   Always, before detaching or disassembling any part of the fuel line system, note the routing of all hoses and pipes and the orientation of all clamps and clips to assure that replacement sections are installed in exactly the same manner.
7   Before detaching any part of the fuel system, be sure to relieve the fuel tank pressure by removing the fuel filler cap.
8   While you're under the vehicle, it's a good idea to check the following related components:
   a)   Check the condition of the fuel filter – make sure that it's not clogged or damaged (see Chapter 1).
   b)   Inspect the evaporative emission control system. Verify that the overfill limiter, the fuel check valve and the purge control valve are operating properly (see Chapter 6).

3   Fuel pump – check

Refer to illustration 3.4

Warning: *Gasoline is extremely flammable, so take extra precautions when working on any part of the fuel system. Do not smoke or allow open flames or bare light bulbs in or near the work area. Also, don't work in a garage if a natural gas appliance such as a water heater or clothes dryer is present.*

1   If you suspect insufficient fuel delivery, first inspect all fuel lines to ensure that the problem is not simply a leak in a line (see Section 2).
2   If there are no leaks evident in the fuel lines, inspect the fuel pump itself. The following checks will tell you if the fuel pump is leaking and whether it is pumping fuel.
3   Before performing the following checks, detach the cable from the negative terminal of the battery and remove the air cleaner (see Section 8).

Mechanical fuel pump

Breather hole check

4   Locate the fuel pump (see Section 4), on the rear side of the cylinder head, between the left and right intake manifold runners. Note whether there is any fuel or oil leaking from the breather hole **(see illustration)**. If there is, either the oil seal or the diaphragm in the fuel pump is defective. Replace the fuel pump if leakage is noted (see Section 4).

3.4   Check the fuel pump breather hole (arrow) – if any gas or oil is leaking out, replace the pump (intake manifold removed for clarity)

3.19   Using a jumper wire, apply battery voltage to the fuel pump test connector

3.22   Install a fuel pressure gauge into the fitting directly above the fuel filter

Fuel pump output check

5   Hook up a remote starter switch in accordance with the manufacturer's instructions. If you don't have a remote starter switch, you will need an assistant to help you with this and the following procedure.
6   Trace the fuel outlet hose from the pump to the carburetor and detach it at the carburetor (see Section 4).
7   Attach the cable to the negative terminal of the battery.
8   Detach the wires from the ignition coil primary terminals (see Chapter 5).
9   Place a metal or approved gasoline container under the open end of the fuel pump outlet hose.
10   Direct the fuel pump outlet hose into the container while cranking the engine for a few seconds with the remote starter (or while an assistant cranks the engine with the ignition key).

4.5   Working from underneath the intake manifold side of the engine, detach the fuel inlet, outlet and return hoses from the fuel pump

4.6   Working from above, remove the fuel pump bolts, then carefully break the pump loose with your hand and detach it, along with the two gaskets and the insulator – note that the insulator is sandwiched between the two gaskets

11   If fuel is emitted in well defined spurts, the pump is operating satisfactorily. If fuel dribbles or trickles out the hose, the pump is defective. Replace it (see Section 4).

Inlet valve check

12   Detach the inlet hose from the fuel pump.
13   Attach a vacuum gauge to the inlet fitting.
14   Crank the engine with a remote starter switch (or have an assistant crank it with the ignition key).
15   A fairly steady vacuum, uninterrupted by alternating blowback pulses (sudden pulses of pressure), should be evident.
16   If blowback is evident, the fuel pump inlet valve is not seating properly. Replace the pump (see Section 4).
17   Replace the wires on the ignition coil primary terminals and reconnect the battery terminal.

Electric fuel pump (fuel-injected models)

Preliminary check
Refer to illustration 3.19

18   Depending on the symptom, the fuel pump and its related circuit have several items that must be checked in order to pinpoint the exact problem.
19   If the vehicle won't start and there is no sound of combustion, remove the fuel filler cap and listen for the sound of the fuel pump. Turn the ignition key OFF. Apply battery voltage to the fuel pump drive connector **(see illustration)** and listen for the sound from the electric fuel pump. If there is no sound from the fuel pump, pinch the fuel hose from the fuel filter to check if pressure is felt.
20   If the vehicle doesn't run, or if it starts but has poor driveability, check the fuel pressure (see Step 21).

Fuel pressure check
Refer to illustration 3.22

Note: *When reconnecting the fuel line always use new washers. Check to make sure the bolt does not have stripped threads. Also, this procedure requires a special fuel pressure gauge and fittings. If the special tools are not available, have the test performed by a dealer service department or other repair shop.*

21   Relieve the fuel pressure. Disconnect the fuel pump electrical connector at the fuel tank. Start the engine and after it stalls, turn the ignition key OFF.
22   Disconnect the fuel hose between the fuel filter and the fuel rail and install a fuel pressure gauge **(see illustration)**.
23   Start the engine and check for leakage around the gauge connections.
24   Read and record the fuel pressure, then disconnect the vacuum hose from the fuel pressure regulator and note the reading on the gauge. The fuel pressure should increase when you disconnect the vacuum hose. Compare your readings with the values listed in this Chapter's Specifications.

26   If the fuel pressure is low, pinch the fuel return line shut and watch the gauge. If the pressure doesn't rise, the fuel pump is defective or there is a restriction in the fuel feed line. If the pressure rises sharply, replace the fuel pressure regulator.

4   Fuel pump – removal and installation

Warning: *Gasoline is extremely flammable, so take extra precautions when working on any part of the fuel system. Do not smoke or allow open flames or bare light bulbs in or near the work area. Also, don't work in a garage where a natural gas appliance such as a water heater or clothes dryer is present.*

Mechanical fuel pump (carbureted models)
Refer to illustrations 4.5 and 4.6

1   Detach the cable from the negative battery terminal.
2   Remove the fuel tank filler cap to relieve fuel tank pressure.
3   Remove the air cleaner assembly (see Section 8).
4   Apply the parking brake and place blocks behind the rear wheels. Raise the front of the vehicle and support it with jackstands.
5   Working from underneath the rear (intake manifold side) of the engine, detach the fuel inlet, outlet and return hoses **(see illustration)** from the pump.
6   Working from above, remove the fuel pump mounting bolts **(see illustration)**.
7   Carefully break the fuel pump loose with your hand – do not use a pry bar – and remove the pump, gaskets and insulator. Note that the insulator is sandwiched between the two gaskets.
8   Using a scraper, remove the old gasket material from the insulator, the pump (if it will be reused), and the pump mating surface on the cylinder head.
9   Inspect the condition of the fuel inlet, outlet and return hoses. If they're damaged or worn, replace them (see Section 2).
10   Installation is the reverse of removal. Be sure to use new gaskets.

Electric fuel pump (fuel-injected models)

11   Remove the fuel tank from the vehicle (see Section 6).
12   Remove the nuts from the fuel pump cover and lift the fuel pump assembly from the tank.
13   Installation is the reverse of removal.

5   In-tank fuel filter/drain plug – removal and installation

Refer to illustrations 5.3a, 5.3b and 5.5

Warning: *Gasoline is extremely flammable, so take extra precautions when working on any part of the fuel system. Do not smoke or allow open flames or bare light bulbs in or near the work area. Also,*

4

5.3a   The drain plug is located on the bottom of the fuel tank

5.3b   To prevent damage to the in-tank fuel filter during removal and installation, be sure to pull the plug/filter assembly straight down until it clears the in-tank outlet pipe

5.5   When installing a new in-tank fuel filter, be sure to press down on the new filter until the claws of the filter fit snugly into the locking holes in the plug

6.5   Clearly label, then detach the fuel feed, return and vapor lines (arrows)

6.7   Remove the fuel tank strap bolts and the protector (if equipped) (arrows) and swing the straps down out of the way

don't work in a garage if a natural gas appliance such as a water heater or clothes dryer is present. Have a fire extinguisher handy.

Note: Although it's not a regularly scheduled maintenance item, occasionally cleaning the in-tank fuel filter will prevent it's becoming clogged. You can also use this procedure anytime you need to drain the fuel tank (for example, before you remove it). Since you will be draining the fuel tank in this procedure, make sure the tank is nearly empty before beginning.

1   Detach the cable from the negative battery terminal.
2   Raise the rear of the vehicle and support it securely on jackstands. Place blocks in front of the front wheels.
3   Place an approved gasoline container under the drain plug. Unscrew the plug and pull it straight down so it will clear the fuel tank outlet pipe **(see illustrations)**.
4   Thoroughly clean the filter with a brush and solvent.
5   If the filter is damaged, replace it by pulling the old filter out of the drain plug and pressing in the new filter until it's claws fit snugly into the locking holes in the plug **(see illustration)**.
6   Carefully slide the filter up over the fuel tank outlet pipe and tighten the drain plug securely.
7   Use a funnel to pour the drained fuel back into the fuel tank.
8   Reconnect the negative battery terminal.

6.12   The overfill limiter valve is located on the upper left side of the fuel tank – to replace it, detach the mounting bolt (arrow) and both hoses

6   Fuel tank – removal and installation

Refer to illustrations 6.5, 6.7 and 6.12

Note: *Since you will be draining the fuel tank in this procedure, make sure the tank is nearly empty before proceeding.*

Warning: *Gasoline is extremely flammable, so take extra precautions when working on any part of the fuel system. Do not smoke or allow open flames or bare light bulbs in or near the work area. Also, don't work in a garage if a natural gas appliance with a pilot light is present. While performing any work on the fuel tank it is advisable to wear safety glasses and to have a dry chemical (Class B) fire extinguisher on hand. If you spill any fuel on your skin, rinse it off immediately with soap and water.*

8.3 You don't have to detach the cold air snorkel from the air cleaner assembly – just detach the snorkel mouth from the bracket on the wall of the engine compartment

8.4 Although you don't really need to remove the air cleaner cover and filter element to remove the air cleaner assembly, now is a good time to inspect the filter (see Chapter 1) – remove the large and small breather hoses (arrows) – also remove the two 12 mm flange nuts (arrows) to detach the air cleaner assembly from the rocker arm cover bracket studs

Tank removal and installation

1   Remove the fuel tank filler cap to relieve fuel tank pressure.
2   Detach the cable from the negative terminal of the battery.
3   Remove the fuel tank drain plug/filter assembly (see Section 4) and allow the fuel to collect in an approved gasoline container.
4   Raise the vehicle and place it securely on jackstands.
5   Disconnect the fuel lines and the vapor return line **(see illustration)**. Clearly label the three lines and the fittings. Be sure to plug the hoses to prevent leakage and contamination of the fuel system.
6   Support the fuel tank with a floor jack or jackstands. Position a piece of wood between the jack head (or stands) and the fuel tank to protect the tank.
7   Remove the fuel tank strap bolts and, if equipped, the protector from the front of the tank **(see illustration)**.
8   Swing the fuel tank retaining straps down until they are hanging out of the way.
9   Lower the tank enough to disconnect the electrical connector from the fuel gauge sending unit, which is located on the upper right side of the fuel tank.
10   Remove the tank from the vehicle.
11   Installation is the reverse of removal.

Overfill limiter (two-way) valve replacement

Note: *The overfill limiter valve is located on the fuel tank. If it is defective, you can replace it using the following procedure.*
12   Remove the overfill limiter mounting bolt **(see illustration)**.
13   Detach the vapor hoses from the limiter and remove it.
14   Installation is the reverse of removal.

7   Fuel tank cleaning and repair – general information

1   All repairs to the fuel tank or filler neck should be carried out by a professional who has experience in this critical and potentially dangerous work. Even after cleaning and flushing of the fuel system, explosive fumes can remain and ignite during repair of the tank.
2   If the fuel tank is removed from the vehicle, it should not be placed in an area where sparks or open flames could ignite the fumes coming out of the tank. Be especially careful inside garages where a natural gas-type appliance is located, because the pilot light could cause an explosion.

8   Air cleaner assembly – removal and installation

Carbureted models
Refer to illustrations 8.3, 8.4, 8.6, 8.7, 8.8 and 8.9
Warning: *Gasoline is extremely flammable, so take extra precautions when working on any part of the fuel system. Do not smoke or* allow open flames or bare light bulbs in or near the work area. Also, don't work in a garage where a natural gas appliance such as a water heater or clothes dryer is present.

1   Detach the cable from the negative terminal of the battery.
2   Remove the air cleaner cover and filter element (see Chapter 1).
Note: *Always inspect the filter element for contamination or moisture when you remove it.*
3   Detach the cold air snorkel from its clip **(see illustration)**.
4   Detach the small and large breather hoses from the air cleaner **(see illustration)**.
5   Remove the two 12 mm flange nuts that attach the air cleaner to the rocker arm cover bracket studs **(see illustration 8.4)**.
6   If your vehicle is a 1986 or 1987 model, detach the small canister mounted on the firewall behind the air cleaner from its clamp **(see illustration)** and set it aside. **Caution:** *Don't pull any of the vacuum hoses loose from this canister or you will have a vacuum leak when you reinstall the air cleaner assembly.*

8.6 If your vehicle is a 1986 or 1987 model, pop this vacuum canister loose and set it aside (being careful not to detach any of the vacuum hoses attached to it)

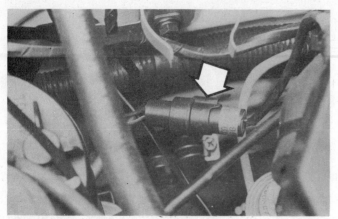

8.7   If your vehicle is a 1986 or 1987 model, unplug this electrical connector located underneath the vacuum canister you removed in the last step

8.8   Raise the air cleaner slightly and detach it from the heat riser tube (as they get older, these heat riser tubes have a tendency to fall off, so it's a good idea to put it aside in some place where you can find it when you reinstall the air cleaner)

8.9   Raise the left side of the air cleaner and detach this small vacuum hose from its clamp, then detach it from the underside of the case (arrow)

9.2   To detach the throttle cable from the bracket, loosen the adjusting nut (arrow)

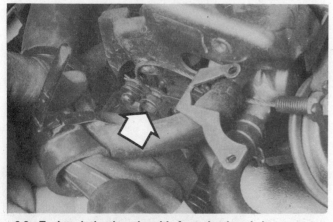

9.3   To detach the throttle cable from the throttle lever, rotate the lever to put slack in the cable, then push the cable plug toward the carburetor (there is a gap on the carburetor side of the lever where the cable can slide free)

9.4   Remove the trim panel under the dash (see Chapter 11) to reach the top of the accelerator pedal and detach the throttle cable at the point shown by the arrow

7   Disconnect the electrical connector **(see illustration)** located under the canister mounting clamp (not used on 1987 and 1988 vehicles).
8   Raise the air cleaner slightly and detach it from the heat riser tube **(see illustration)**.
9   Raise the left side of the air cleaner assembly and detach the small vacuum hose **(see illustration)** from the underside of the case.

10   Remove the air cleaner assembly.
11   Installation is the reverse of removal.

Fuel-injected models

12   Detach the cable from the negative terminal of the battery.
13   Remove the air cleaner cover and element (see Chapter 1). **Note:** *Always insect the filter element for contamination or moisture when you remove it.*
14   Remove the two bolts that attach the resonator to the air cleaner housing. Remove the resonator.
15   Remove the three bolts that attach the air cleaner to the right-hand inner fender panel. Remove the air cleaner assembly.
16   Installation is the reverse of removal.

9.5   To detach the throttle cable from the firewall, remove the two mounting bolts and separate the guide from the firewall

9   Throttle cable – removal and installation

Refer to illustrations 9.2, 9.3, 9.4 and 9.5

Warning: *Gasoline is extremely flammable, so take extra precautions when working on any part of the fuel system. Do not smoke or allow open flames or bare light bulbs in or near the work area. Also, don't work in a garage where a natural gas appliance such as a water heater or clothes dryer is present.*

1   Remove the air cleaner assembly (see Section 8).
2   Loosen the throttle cable adjusting nut **(see illustration)** and lift the cable housing off the bracket.
3   Detach the throttle cable from the throttle lever **(see illustration)**.
4   Detach the throttle cable from the accelerator pedal **(see illustration)**.
5   Detach the throttle cable guide from the firewall **(see illustration)**.
6   From outside the vehicle, pull the throttle cable through the firewall.
7   Installation is the reverse of removal. Don't leave any sharp bends in the cable.
8   After installing the cable, adjust free play, as follows:
 a) Run the engine until it reaches normal operating temperature. Verify the idle speed is correct and adjust it if necessary (see Chapter 1).
 b) Verify that the throttle cable has no slack in it.
 c) If the cable is slack, adjust it as follows:
 d) Turn the adjusting nut counterclockwise until the throttle lever is free.
 e) Remove any sharp bends from the accelerator cable.
 f) Loosen the locknut and turn the throttle cable adjusting nut clockwise to the point at which the throttle lever just begins to move, then back off the adjusting nut one turn and tighten the locknut securely.

10   Carburetor – on-vehicle check, adjustment and component replacement

Warning: *Gasoline is extremely flammable, so take extra precautions when working on any part of the fuel system. Do not smoke or allow open flames or bare light bulbs in or near the work area. Also, don't work in a garage where a natural gas appliance such as a water heater or clothes dryer is present.*

Note: *If your vehicle's engine is hard to start or does not start at all, has an unstable idle or poor driveability and you suspect the carburetor is malfunctioning, it's best to first take the vehicle to a dealer service department that has the Feedback Carburetor equipment necessary to diagnose this highly complicated system. The following procedures are intended to help the home mechanic verify proper operation of components, make minor adjustments, and replace some components. They are not intended as troubleshooting procedures.*

10.2a   Inspect the idle-up actuator hose (1) for cracks and deterioration – remove it from the vacuum-fitting before testing the actuator; take out the two screws (2) to remove the actuator; adjust the actuator with the adjustment screw (3)

10.2b   Inspect the hoses and wiring harness connected to the idle-up actuator (1) – to detach the solenoid mounting bracket from the engine, take out the two bolts (2)

Idle speed and mixture adjustment

1   Idle speed adjustment is covered in Chapter 1. Idle mixture adjustment cannot be performed by the home mechanic because an infrared gas analyzer is required. A dealer service department must perform this procedure.

Electrical and power steering load idle-up system check

Refer to illustrations 10.2a and 10.2b

Note: *1986 models are equipped with a throttle opener system; 1987 and later models are equipped with an idle-up system. These two systems are highly similar and, for simplicity, are both referred to below as idle-up-systems.*

2   Inspect the vacuum hoses and the idle-up control solenoid harness – make sure they're properly connected **(see illustrations)**.
3   Detach the vacuum hose from the fitting on the idle-up actuator/dashpot **(see illustration 10.2a)**.
4   Attach a vacuum pump to the idle-up actuator/dashpot vacuum fitting.
5   Hook up a tachometer in accordance with the manufacturer's instructions.
6   Start the engine and allow it to idle.
7   Apply 11.8 in-Hg vacuum with the vacuum pump. Engine speed should increase.
8   If engine speed does not increase, replace the idle-up actuator/dashpot, as discussed below. Stop the engine and remove the vacuum pump.

4

10.11   To detach the idle-up actuator rod from the free lever, pull the rod in the direction shown by the arrow

10.23   To adjust the idle-up actuator for proper idle speed under an air conditioning load, turn the throttle adjusting screw (arrow) until the tachometer indicates the specified speed

Idle-up actuator/dashpot replacement and adjustment

Replacement

Refer to illustration 10.11

9   Remove the throttle return spring from the throttle lever.
10   Remove the two idle-up actuator/dashpot attaching screws (**see illustration 10.2a**).
11   Detach the idle-up actuator rod from the free lever (**see illustration**) and remove the idle-up actuator.
12   Install the new idle-up actuator/dashpot and reattach the vacuum hose.
13   Adjust the idle-up actuator/dashpot as discussed below.

Adjustment

Note: *The following procedure adjusts the idle-up actuator's, control of the idle speed when electric or power steering loads are applied.*

14   Make sure that the curb idle speed is set as specified in Chapter 1. If it's not, readjust the idle speed to the specified speed before proceeding.
15   Unbolt the solenoid mounting bracket from the transaxle end of the cylinder head (**see illustration 10.2b**). Remove the electrical connector from the bottom of the idle-up control solenoid. Using jumper wires, connect one of the solenoid's terminals to the positive terminal of the battery and the other solenoid terminal to the negative terminal of the battery. This applies intake manifold vacuum to the idle-up actuator, which activates the actuator.
16   Open the throttle slightly – until engine speed reaches about 2000 rpm – then slowly close it.
17   Note the indicated engine speed. Adjust it, if necessary, to the specified rpm with the throttle opener adjustment screw (**see illustration 10.2a**).
18   Repeat Step 16 above and check the engine speed again.
19   Remove the jumper wire you attached in Step 15 and reattach the wire harness.

Idle-up air conditioning load actuator adjustment

Refer to illustration 10.23

Note: *The following procedure adjusts the idle-up actuator's, control of the idle speed when an air conditioning load is applied.*

20   Hook up a tachometer in accordance with the manufacturer's instructions.
21   Start the engine.
22   Turn on the air conditioner switch. This opens the solenoid valve, which allows intake manifold vacuum to move the actuator to its full open position. Note the indicated engine speed and compare your reading to the specified rpm.
23   If the engine speed is out of specification, adjust it with the throttle adjusting screw (**see illustration**).

10.28   To check the solenoid valve coils, unplug the connector and measure the resistance across the indicated pairs of terminals with an ohmmeter (for the bowl vent valve, measure between the indicated terminal and the negative post of the battery), then compare your readings with the specified resistance for each coil:

1   *Jet mixture solenoid valve*   3   *Deceleration solenoid valve*
2   *Enrichment solenoid valve*   4   *Bowl vent valve*

10.30   Before you can remove the deceleration, enrichment or jet mixture solenoid valves, you must detach the wire harness from the carburetor body at the locations indicated by arrows

10.31a   Location of the deceleration solenoid valve

10.31b   Location of the enrichment solenoid valve

10.31c   Location of the jet mixture solenoid valve

10.33   On 1986 and 1987 vehicles, detach the terminal blade (1) from the solenoid control valve connector by depressing the tang next to the terminal blade with a small screwdriver and pulling the blade out the bottom of the connector – to remove the bowl vent solenoid and valve assembly (2), take out the three mounting screws

10.37   To check the throttle position sensor, unplug the connector and measure the resistance between terminals 2 and 3

Fast idle cam

Lever

10.40   Verify the fast idle cam is released (the lever must not be resting on the cam)

Idle-up control solenoid valve check

24   Set the ignition switch in the Off position.
25   Remove the solenoid bracket from the transaxle end of the cylinder head and detach the electrical connector from the idle-up control solenoid **(see illustration 10.2b)**.
26   Check the solenoid valve coil with an ohmmeter. Compare your reading with the specified resistance. If the indicated resistance is not as specified, there is an open or short in the solenoid coil. Replace it.

Deceleration, enrichment, jet mixture solenoid valves and bowl vent valve check (1986 and 1987 models) and replacement

Refer to illustrations 10.28, 10.30, 10.31a, 10.31b, 10.31c and 10.33
27   Unplug the solenoid valve connector.
28   Check each solenoid valve coil with an ohmmeter between the indicated terminals **(see illustration)**. Compare your readings with the specified resistance. For the bowl vent valve, measure between the indicated terminal and the negative post of the battery. If the indicated resistance for any solenoid valve is not as specified, there's an open or short in it. Replace it (proceed to the next step). If there's a problem with the bowl vent valve, proceed to Step 33.
29   To remove the deceleration solenoid valve, you will need to remove the idle-up actuator **(see illustration 10.2a)**.
30   Detach the wire harness **(see illustration)**.
31   Remove the deceleration solenoid valve, enrichment solenoid valve or jet mixture solenoid valve **(see illustrations)** from the float cover.
32   Install the new solenoid valve and reattach the connector.

33   If your vehicle is a 1986 or 1987 model, detach the BVV wire harness terminal blade from the solenoid control valve electrical connector **(see illustration)**. If it's a 1988 and later model, simply unplug the BVV harness connector.
34   Remove the screws and detach the bowl vent solenoid and valve assembly from the float chamber cover **(see illustration 10.33)**.
35   Install the new bowl vent valve assembly on the float chamber cover and connect the harness.

Throttle position sensor (TPS) check and adjustment
Refer to illustrations 10.37, 10.40, 10.42 and 10.45

Check
36   Unplug the TPS connector.
37   Check the resistance between terminals 2 and 3 with an ohmmeter **(see illustration)**.

10.42   Back off the speed adjusting screws (SAS-1 and SAS-2) until the throttle valve is fully closed – be sure to count the number of turns (down to 1/4 -turn) so you can later return the screws to the same positions

10.45   To adjust the TPS output voltage on 1986 and 1987 models, turn the adjusting screw (arrow) until the output voltage is correct

38   Verify that the resistance changes smoothly as the throttle valve is slowly turned from a closed position to wide open. Note your readings and compare them to the specified resistance. If the resistance does not change smoothly, replace the sensor. If it is not within specifications, try adjusting the sensor. If you cannot adjust the sensor to specifications, replace the sensor. Be sure to adjust the new sensor.

Adjustment (1986 and 1987 models)

39   Warm up the engine.
40   Loosen the throttle cable (see section 9) and verify the fast idle cam is released **(see illustration)**.
41   Stop the engine.
42   Back off (turn counterclockwise) the speed adjusting screws (SAS-1 and SAS-2) **(see illustration)** until the throttle valve is fully

closed. Count the number of turns required by each screw to close the throttle valve and record these figures.
43   Attach a digital voltmeter between terminals 2 and 3 of the TPS connector **(see illustration 10.37)**. **Note:** *Don't disconnect the TPS connector from the main wire harness.*
44   Turn the ignition switch to On (don't start the engine), measure the TPS output voltage and compare your reading to the specified output voltage.
45   If the output voltage is incorrect, loosen the TPS adjusting screw and adjust the output voltage by turning the adjusting screw **(see illustration)**.
46   Turn the ignition switch to Off.
47   Retighten (turn clockwise) the SAS-1 and SAS-2 screws the same number of turns that you backed them off in Step 42 above.
48   Adjust the throttle cable free play (see Section 9).
49   Start the engine and verify the idle speed is within specifications (see Chapter 1).

Dash pot check and adjustment (1988 and later models)

Refer to illustrations 10.51 and 10.52

50   Before checking the dash pot:
   a) Start the engine and warm it up (coolant temperature must be between 176 and 203-degrees F).
   b) Turn off all lights and electrical accessories. Make sure that the cooling fan is off.
   c) Place the transmission in Neutral (manual transaxle) or Park (automatic transaxle).
   d) If the vehicle has power steering, make sure that the wheel are pointed straight ahead.

10.51   With the engine idling, open the throttle valve until the free lever contacts SAS-3

10.52   Close the throttle valve until SAS-2 contacts the free lever and note the indicated idle speed at that point

10.55   Verify that the alignment marks on the electric choke and bimetal assembly line up properly

10.57 The electric choke assembly:

1 *As the choke body temperature rises, the choke valve should open*
2 *When the engine coolant temperature has risen sufficiently and the choke opener is actuated, the fast idle cam should release*
3 *When the engine is warmed up, the electric choke should feel warm to the touch – if it doesn't, check the choke*

Below 18°C (65°F) (1st stage)

18°C (65°F) or higher (2nd stage)

10.59 The choke breaker system:

1 *Choke valve is fully closed when the engine is off*
2 *Choke valve opens slowly and slightly (about 0.059-inch) after the engine is started*
3 *Once the engine is warmed up and idling, the choke valve should not move when the yellow-striped vacuum hose is detached*
4 *After the engine temperature exceeds 65°F and vacuum hose is reattached, with engine idling, push choke valve closed with your finger – it should have a slightly larger opening than in 2 above (about 0.118-inch)*

51 With the engine idling, open the throttle valve the full stroke of the rod until the free lever contacts SAS-3 **(see illustration)**.
52 Close the throttle valve until the SAS-2 contacts the free lever **(see illustration)** and note the indicated engine idle speed at that moment.
53 If the indicated idle speed is not as specified, adjust the dash pot setting by turning SAS-3.
54 Release the free lever and verify that the engine returns to its idle speed slowly.

Electric choke system check (1988 and later models)
Refer to illustrations 10.55 and 10.57

Note: *The carburetor on all models has a tamperproof choke. The choke related parts are factory adjusted, so no further adjustments should be necessary unless you rebuild the carburetor, or a smog inspection indicates that choke related parts need to be adjusted.*

55 Verify that the alignment marks on the electric choke and bimetal assembly are lined up **(see illustration)**.

a) If they are misaligned in a clockwise direction, the engine will start better but the plugs are probably sooty.
b) If they are misaligned in a counterclockwise direction, the engine will be hard to start and will be more likely to stall.
56 Make sure that the engine coolant temperature is below 50-degrees F.
57 Start the engine and place your hand on the electric choke body to check the operation of the choke valve and fast idle cam **(see illustration)**.
a) The choke valve should open as the choke body temperature rises.
b) The fast idle cam should release as the engine coolant temperature rises and the choke opener operates.
58 If the electric choke body remains cool even after the engine is warmed up, check the choke heater (see below).

Choke breaker check (1988 and later models)
Refer to illustrations 10.59 and 10.62

59 While the engine coolant temperature is below 65-degrees F **(see illustration)**:

10.62   With the engine idling, close the choke valve lightly with your finger until the valve stops, measure the choke valve to choke bore clearance and compare your measurement to the specified value

10.71   Set the lever (1) on the second highest step of the fast idle cam (2)

a) The choke should be fully closed before you start the engine. If it isn't, either the bimetal assembly or the linkage operation is faulty.
b) After you start the engine (fully depress the accelerator pedal) and run it at idle, the choke should open slowly and slightly (immediately after starting), with a gap of about 0.059-inch If it doesn't, either the delay valve is clogged or the diaphragm for chamber A is ruptured **(see illustration 10.59)**.
c) Detach the yellow-striped vacuum hose and run the engine at idle. The choke valve shouldn't move. If it does, the thermo valve is faulty.
60   After the engine coolant temperature goes above 65-degrees F:
a) Attach the yellow striped vacuum hose and run the engine at idle.
b) Lightly close the choke valve with your finger. It should stop at a slightly larger opening than it did in Step 59b above (about 0.118-inch). If it doesn't, either the thermo valve is faulty or the diaphragm for chamber B is ruptured **(see illustration 10.59)**.
61   After inspecting the choke breaker system, detach the vacuum hose from the choke breaker and make the following check.
62   With the engine idling, close the choke valve lightly with your finger until the choke valve stops. Measure the choke valve-to-bore clearance **(see illustration)** and compare your measurement to the specification.
63   If the clearance is not as specified, take the vehicle to the dealer to have the internal choke linkage adjusted or the bimetal assembly replaced.

10.70   Detach the white-striped vacuum hose from the choke opener

10.73   If the fast idle speed is out of specification, adjust it with the fast idle adjusting screw (arrow)

Fast idle check and adjustment (1988 and later models)
Refer to illustrations 10.70, 10.71 and 10.73

64   Start the engine and warm up the coolant to between 176 and 203-degrees F.
65   Make sure that all lights, the cooling fan and all electrical accessories are off.
66   Place the transmission in Neutral (manual transaxle) or Park (automatic transaxle).
67   If the vehicle is equipped with power steering, make sure that the wheels are pointed straight ahead.
68   Remove the air cleaner assembly (see Section 8).
69   Hook up a tachometer in accordance with the manufacturer's instructions.
70   Detach the white-striped vacuum hose from the choke opener **(see illustration)**.
71   Set the lever on the second highest step of the fast idle cam **(see illustration)**.
72   Start the engine and check the fast idle speed. Compare your reading with the specified value.
73   If the fast idle speed is out of specification, adjust it with the fast idle adjusting screw **(see illustration)**.
a) If you turn the fast idle screw in a clockwise direction, the valve opening will be larger and the fast idle speed should increase.
b) If you turn the fast idle screw conuterclockwise, the valve opening will be smaller and the fast idle speed should decrease.

10.74 To check the electric choke heater, unplug the connector and check the continuity of the heater with an ohmmeter

Choke heater inspection (1988 and later models)
Refer to illustration 10.74

74   Unplug the electric choke heater connector and check the heater with an ohmmeter **(see illustration)**. It should indicate about 6 ohms.
75   If the resistance is not as specified, replace the bimetal assembly (electric choke body).

---

11   Carburetor – removal and installation

Warning: *Gasoline is extremely flammable so take extra precautions when working on any part of the fuel system. Do not smoke or allow open flames or bare light bulbs in or near the work area. Also, don't work in a garage if a natural gas appliance such as a water heater or clothes dryer is present.*

Removal
1   Remove the fuel filler cap to relieve fuel tank pressure.
2   Remove the air cleaner assembly (see Section 8).
3   Disconnect the throttle cable from the throttle lever (see Section 9).
4   If the vehicle is equipped with an automatic transmission, disconnect the TV cable from the throttle lever (see Chapter 7B).
5   Clearly label all vacuum hoses and fittings, then disconnect the hoses.
6   Disconnect the fuel line from the carburetor.
7   Label the wires and terminals, then unplug all wire harness connectors.
8   Remove the mounting bolts and detach the carburetor from the intake manifold. The bolts extend all the way through the carburetor. Remove the carburetor mounting gasket. Stuff a shop rag into the intake manifold opening.

Installation
9   Use a gasket scraper to remove all traces of gasket material and sealant from the intake manifold (and the carburetor, if it's being reinstalled), then remove the shop rag from the manifold openings. Clean the mating surfaces with lacquer thinner or acetone.
10   Place a new gasket on the intake manifold.
11   Position the carburetor on the gasket and install the mounting fasteners.
12   To prevent carburetor distortion or damage, tighten the fasteners in a criss-cross pattern, 1/4-turn at a time.
13   The remaining installation steps are the reverse of removal.
14   Check and, if necessary, adjust the idle speed (see Chapter 1).
15   If the vehicle is equipped with an automatic transmission, refer to Chapter 7B for the TV cable adjustment procedure.
16   Start the engine and check carefully for fuel leaks.

12.8a   An exploded view of a 1988 and later carburetor

1	Throttle return spring	8	Hose
2	Damper spring	9	Screw
3	Throttle return spring bracket	10	Float chamber cover assembly
4	Idle-up actuator/dash pot	11	Float chamber cover gasket
5	Bracket	12	Mixing body and throttle body assembly
6	Hose		
7	Vacuum delay valve		

---

12   Carburetor – diagnosis and overhaul

Refer to illustrations 12.8a, 12.8b and 12.8c
Warning: *Gasoline is extremely flammable, so take extra precautions when working on any part of the fuel system. Do not smoke or allow open flames or bare light bulbs in or near the work area. Also, don't work in a garage if a natural gas appliance such as a water heater or clothes dryer is present.*

Diagnosis
1   A thorough road test and check of carburetor adjustments should be done before any major carburetor service work. Specifications for some adjustments are listed on the Vehicle Emissions Control Information (VECI) label found in the engine compartment.
2   Carburetor problems usually show up as flooding, hard starting, stalling, severe backfiring and poor acceleration. A carburetor that's leaking fuel and/or covered with wet looking deposits definitely needs attention.
3   Some performance complaints directed at the carburetor are actually a result of loose, out-of-adjustment or malfunctioning engine or electrical components. Others develop when vacuum hoses leak, are disconnected or are incorrectly routed. The proper approach to analyzing carburetor problems should include the following items:
   a) Inspect all vacuum hoses and actuators for leaks and correct installation (see Chapters 1 and 6).

4

12.8b   An exploded view of a 1988 and later carburetor's float chamber cover assembly

13	Pin	34	Spring
14	Float	35	Body
15	Needle valve	36	Spring
16	Needle valve seat	37	Diaphragm
17	O-ring	38	Valve
18	Packing	39	Mixture control valve (MCV) assembly
19	Retainer	40	Gasket
20	Feedback solenoid valve (FBSV)	41	Cover
21	O-ring	42	Spring
22	O-ring	43	Diaphragm
23	Retainer	44	Body
24	Slow cut solenoid valve (SCSV)	45	Spring
		46	Diaphragm
25	O-ring	47	Bracket
26	O-ring	48	Cover
27	Plate	49	Spring
28	Bimetal assembly	50	Diaphragm
29	Packing	51	Body
30	Connector	52	Main air jet (primary)
31	Cover	53	Pilot jet (primary)
32	Diaphragm	54	Pilot jet (secondary)
33	Spring seat	55	Float chamber cover

12.8c   An exploded view of a 1988 and later carburetor's mixing chamber/throttle body assembly

56	Steel ball	78	Mixing body
57	Weight	79	Vacuum hose
58	Ball	80	Depression chamber
59	Plug	81	Throttle position sensor (TPS)
60	O-ring		
61	Ball	82	Lever
62	Screw	83	Adjusting screw
63	Gasket	84	Throttle Lever
64	Main jet (primary)	85	Cam follower
65	Main jet (secondary)	86	Fast idle adjusting screw
66	Cover	87	Free lever
67	Spring	88	Abutment plate
68	Diaphragm	89	Idle speed adjusting screw (SAS-2)
69	Enrichment jet valve		
70	Enrichment jet	90	Spring
71	Spring	91	Secondary lever
72	Ball	92	Idle speed adjusting screw (SAS-1)
73	Pump cover assembly		
74	Diaphragm	93	Plug
75	Spring	94	Mixture adjusting screw (MAS)
76	Pump body		
77	Gasket	95	Throttle body

13.1 The ECU is located under the dashboard on the driver's side of the vehicle

13.3 Location of the engine coolant temperature sensor

b) Tighten the intake manifold and carburetor mounting nuts/bolts evenly and securely.
c) Perform a cylinder compression test (see Chapter 2).
d) Clean or replace the spark plugs as necessary (see Chapter 1).
e) Check the spark plug wires (see Chapter 1).
f) Inspect the ignition primary wires.
g) Check the ignition timing (follow the instructions printed on the Vehicle Emissions Control Information label).
h) Check the fuel pump pressure/volume (see Chapter 4).
i) Check the heat control valve in the air cleaner for proper operation (see Chapter 1).
j) Check/replace the air filter element (see Chapter 1).
k) Check the PCV system (see Chapter 6).
l) Check/replace the fuel filter (see Chapter 1). Also, the strainer in the tank could be restricted.
m) Check for a plugged exhaust system.
n) Check EGR valve operation (see Chapter 6).
o) Check the choke-it should be completely open at normal engine operating temperature (see Chapter 1).
p) Check for fuel leaks and kinked or dented fuel lines (see Chapters 1 and 4).
q) Check accelerator pump operation with the engine off (remove the air cleaner cover and operate the throttle as you look into the carburetor throat – you should see a stream of gasoline enter the carburetor).
r) Check for incorrect fuel or bad gasoline.
s) Check the valve clearances and camshaft lobe lift (see Chapters 1 and 2).
t) Have a dealer service department or repair shop check the electronic engine and carburetor controls.

4   Diagnosing carburetor problems may require that the engine be started and run with the air cleaner off. While running the engine without the air cleaner, backfires are possible. This situation is likely to occur if the carburetor is malfunctioning, but just the removal of the air cleaner can lean the fuel/air mixture enough to produce an engine backfire. **Warning:** *Do not position any part of your body, especially your face, directly over the carburetor during inspection and servicing procedures. Wear eye protection!*

Overhaul

5   Once it's determined that the carburetor needs an overhaul, several options are available. If you're going to attempt to overhaul the

13.2 The air flow sensor also functions as a barometric pressure sensor and an intake air temperature sensor

carburetor yourself, first obtain a good quality carburetor rebuild kit (which will include all necessary gaskets, internal parts, instructions and a parts list). You'll also need some special solvent and a means of blowing out the internal passages of the carburetor with air.
6   An alternative is to obtain a new or rebuilt carburetor. They are readily available from dealers and auto parts stores. Make absolutely sure the exchange carburetor is identical to the original. A tag is usually attached to the top of the carburetor or a number is stamped on the float bowl. It will help determine the exact type of carburetor you have. When obtaining a rebuilt carburetor or a rebuild kit, make sure the kit or carburetor matches your application exactly. Seemingly insignificant differences can make a large difference in engine performance.
7   If you choose to overhaul your own carburetor, allow enough time to disassemble it carefully, soak the necessary parts in the cleaning solvent (usually for at least one-half day or according to the instructions listed on the carburetor cleaner) and reassemble it, which will usually take much longer than disassembly. When disassembling the carburetor, match each part with the illustration in the carburetor kit and lay the parts out in order on a clean work surface. Overhauls by inexperienced mechanics can result in an engine which runs poorly or not at all. To avoid this, use care and patience when disassembling the carburetor so you can reassemble it correctly.
8   Because carburetor designs are constantly modified by the manufacturer in order to meet increasingly more stringent emissions regulations, it isn't feasible to include a step-by-step overhaul of each type. You'll receive a detailed, well illustrated set of instructions with any carburetor overhaul kit; they will apply in a more specific manner to the carburetor on your vehicle. Exploded views of the carburetors are included here **(see illustrations)**.

---

13   Multi-Point Injection (MPI) system

Refer to illustrations 13.1, 13.2, 13.3, 13.5, 13.6 and 13.7
Note: *Refer to Chapter 6 for diagnosis and trouble code information.*

Electronic Control Unit

1   The Electronic Control Unit is a microcomputer with electrical connectors for receiving input/output signals and for power supply. The control unit regulates the amount of fuel that is injected, as well as the idle speed, fuel pump operation and the feedback of the mixture ratio. It's located under the dash, to the left of the steering column **(see illustration)**.

Air flow sensor

2   The air flow sensor measures the mass flow rate of intake air. The control circuit emits an electrical output signal which varies in relation to the amount of heat dissipated from a hot wire placed in the stream of intake air **(see illustration)**.

Engine coolant temperature sensor

3   The engine coolant temperature sensor is located in the right side of the cylinder head **(see illustration)**, monitors changes in the coolant temperature and transmits a signal to the ECU. Refer to Chapter 3 for the replacement procedure.

13.5   The throttle position sensor is mounted on the side of the throttle body

Oxygen sensor

4   Mounted in the exhaust manifold (under the vehicle), the oxygen sensor monitors the quantity of oxygen in the exhaust gases. Refer to Chapter 1 for the replacement procedure.

Throttle position sensor

5   The throttle position sensor actuates in response to accelerator pedal movement. It's mounted on the side of the throttle body and is equipped with contacts that detect the angle of the throttle plate **(see illustration)**. To replace the sensor, unplug the electrical connector, remove the Phillips-head screws and detach the sensor from the throttle body. When installing, be sure to align the sensor with the throttle shaft.

Vehicle speed sensor

6   The vehicle speed sensor provides a vehicle speed signal to the ECU. It's mounted on the back of the speedometer head **(see illustration)**. See Chapter 12 for the instrument cluster removal and installation procedure.

Fuel injectors

7   The fuel injectors supply the cylinders with fuel **(see illustration)**. The injector is a small, precision solenoid valve. As the ECU outputs an injection signal to each fuel injector, the coil built into the injector pulls the needle valve back and fuel is sprayed through the nozzle into the intake manifold. The amount of fuel injected is controlled by the ECU by varying the injection pulse duration. The injectors can be checked by unplugging the electrical connectors and measuring the resistance across the terminals, comparing your reading with the values listed in this Chapter's Specifications. To remove the fuel rail and injectors, relieve the fuel pressure (see Section 3, Step 21), then disconnect the fuel feed and return lines from the fuel rail. Disconnect the electrical connectors from the injectors, unplug the vacuum hose from the fuel pressure regulator and remove the fuel rail mounting bolts. Lift the fuel rail up, being careful not to drop any of the injectors. Before reinstalling the injectors/fuel rail assembly, replace the O-rings on the ends of each injector with new ones.

Idle position switch

8   The idle position switch is attached to the throttle body. The switch is used to stabilize idle speed when the engine load is heavy

from accessories such as the power steering pump, air conditioning compressor, high draw on the alternator, etc.

Fuel pump

9   The fuel pump, which is located in the fuel tank, is a wet type pump where the vane rollers are directly coupled to a motor which is filled with fuel. See Sections 3 and 4 for more information.

---

14   Exhaust system servicing – general information

Warning: *Inspection and repair of exhaust system components should be done only after enough time has elapsed after driving the vehicle to allow the system components to cool completely. Also, when working under the vehicle, make sure it is securely supported on jackstands.*

1   The exhaust system consists of the exhaust manifold, the catalytic converter, the muffler, the tailpipe and all connecting pipes, brackets, hangers and clamps. The exhaust system is attached to the body with mounting brackets and rubber hangers. If any of the parts are improperly installed, excessive noise and vibration will be transmitted to the body.

2   Conduct regular inspections of the exhaust system to keep it safe and quiet. Look for any damaged or bent parts, open seams, holes, loose connections, excessive corrosion or other defects which could allow exhaust fumes to enter the vehicle. Deteriorated exhaust system components should not be repaired; they should be replaced with new parts.

3   If the exhaust system components are extremely corroded or rusted together, welding equipment will probably be required to remove them. The convenient way to accomplish this is to have a muffler repair shop remove the corroded sections with a cutting torch. If, however, you want to save money by doing it yourself (and you don't have a welding outfit with a cutting torch), simply cut off the old components with a hacksaw. If you have compressed air, special pneumatic cutting chisels can also be used. If you do decide to tackle the job at home, be sure to wear safety goggles to protect your eyes from metal chips and work gloves to protect your hands.

4   Here are some simple guidelines to follow when repairing the exhaust system:
   a) Work from the back to the front when removing exhaust system components.
   b) Apply penetrating oil to the exhaust system component fasteners to make them easier to remove.
   c) Use new gaskets, hangers and clamps when installing exhaust systems components.
   d) Apply anti-seize compound to the threads of all exhaust system fasteners during reassembly.
   e) Be sure to allow sufficient clearance between newly installed parts and all points on the underbody to avoid overheating the floor pan and possibly damaging the interior carpet and insulation. Pay particularly close attention to the catalytic converter and heat shield.

5   To replace the front catalytic converter refer to Chapter 2A and remove the exhaust manifold and converter as an assembly. Then unbolt the converter from the manifold. Installation is the reverse of removal.

13.6   The vehicle speed sensor, mounted on the rear of the speedometer head, relays the vehicle speed to the ECU

13.7   The fuel injectors receive a signal from the control unit and the needle valve opens to inject fuel into the intake manifold – the amount of fuel injected is determined by the pulse duration

Chapter 5 Engine electrical systems

Contents

5

Specifications

Distributor air gap . . . .   0.03 in (0.8 mm)

Ignition coil

Early models
  Primary resistance . . . .   1.2 ohms
  Secondary resistance. . . . .   13.7 k-ohms
External resistor resistance. . . . .   1.35 ohms
Later models
  Primary resistance. . . . .   0.72 to 0.88 ohms
  Secondary resistance.. . . . .   10.3 to 13.9 k-ohms

---

1   General information

The engine electrical systems include all ignition, charging and starting components. Because of their engine-related functions, these components are discussed separately from chassis electrical devices such as the lights, the instruments, etc. (which are included in Chapter 12).

Always observe the following precautions when working on the electrical systems:

a) Be extremely careful when servicing engine electrical components. They are easily damaged if checked, connected or handled improperly.
b) Never leave the ignition switch on for long periods of time with the engine off.
c) Don't disconnect the battery cables while the engine is running.
d) Maintain correct polarity when connecting a battery cable from another vehicle during jump starting.
e) Always disconnect the negative cable first and hook it up last or

the battery may be shorted by the tool being used to loosen the cable clamps.

It's also a good idea to review the safety-related information regarding the engine electrical systems located in the *Safety first* section near the front of this manual before beginning any operation included in this Chapter.

There are two different distributors used on 1990 and later models. The distributor used in conjunction with the Feedback Carburetor (FBC) system is equipped with vacuum advance and has many internal components. The distributor used on the 1990 and later US models equipped with the multi-point fuel injection (MPI) system is less complicated and has an electronic advance system.

2   Battery – emergency jump starting

Refer to the *Booster battery (jump) starting* procedure at the front of this manual.

3.1   To remove the battery . . .

1   Detach the cable from the negative terminal
2   Detach the cable from the positive terminal
3   Remove the nuts and detach the clamp

3   Battery — removal and installation

Refer to illustration 3.1

1   **Caution:** *Always disconnect the negative cable first and hook it up last or the battery may be shorted by the tool being used to loosen the cable clamps.* Disconnect both cables from the battery terminals **(see illustration).**
2   Remove the battery hold down clamp.
3   Lift out the battery. Be careful — it's heavy.
4   While the battery is out, inspect the carrier (tray) for corrosion (see Chapter 1).
5   If you are replacing the battery, make sure that you get one that's identical, with the same dimensions, amperage rating, cold cranking rating, etc.
6   Installation is the reverse of removal.

4   Battery cables — check and replacement

1   Periodically inspect the entire length of each battery cable for damage, cracked or burned insulation and corrosion. Poor battery cable connections can cause starting problems and decreased engine performance.
2   Check the cable-to-terminal connections at the ends of the cables for cracks, loose wire strands and corrosion. The presence of white, fluffy deposits under the insulation at the cable terminal connection is a sign that the cable is corroded and should be replaced. Check the terminals for distortion, missing mounting bolts and corrosion.
3   When removing the cables, **always disconnect the negative cable first and hook it up last** or the battery may be shorted by the tool used to loosen the cable clamps. Even if only the positive cable is being replaced, be sure to disconnect the negative cable from the battery first (see Chapter 1 for further information regarding battery cable removal).
4   Disconnect the old cables from the battery, then trace each of them to their opposite ends and detach them from the starter solenoid and ground terminals. Note the routing of each cable to ensure correct installation.
5   If you are replacing either or both of the old cables, take them with you when buying new cables. It is vitally important that you replace the cables with identical parts. Cables have characteristics that make them easy to identify: positive cables are usually red, larger in cross-section and have a larger diameter battery post clamp; ground cables are usually black, smaller in cross-section and have a slightly smaller diameter clamp for the negative post.
6   Clean the threads of the solenoid or ground connection with a wire brush to remove rust and corrosion. Apply a light coat of battery terminal corrosion inhibitor, or petroleum jelly, to the threads to prevent future corrosion.

7   Attach the cable to the solenoid or ground connection and tighten the mounting nut/bolt securely.
8   Before connecting a new cable to the battery, make sure that it reaches the battery post without having to be stretched.
9   Connect the positive cable first, followed by the negative cable.

5   Ignition system – general information and precautions

The ignition system includes the ignition switch, the battery, the igniter, the coil, the primary (low voltage) and secondary (high voltage) wiring circuits, the distributor and the spark plugs.

When working on the ignition system, take the following precautions:

a) Do not keep the ignition switch on for more than 10 seconds if the engine will not start.
b) Always connect a tachometer in accordance with the manufacturer's instructions. Some tachometers may be incompatible with this ignition system. Consult a dealer service department before buying a tachometer for use with this vehicle.
c) Never allow the ignition coil terminals to touch ground. Grounding the coil could result in damage to the igniter and/or the ignition coil.
d) Do not disconnect the battery when the engine is running.
e) Make sure the igniter is properly grounded.

6   Ignition system — check

1   If the engine won't start, the following quick checks should pinpoint the problem.
2   Attach an inductive timing light to each plug wire, one at a time, and crank the engine.

a) If the light flashes, voltage is reaching the plug.
b) If the light does not flash, proceed to the next step.

3   Inspect the spark plug wire(s), distributor cap, rotor and spark plug(s) (see Chapter 1).
4   If the engine still won't start, check the ignition coil (see Section 7).

7   Ignition coil — check and replacement

Check

Refer to illustrations 7.2, 7.3a and 7.3b
1   Detach the cable from the negative terminal of the battery.
2   Locate the coil at the left front corner of the engine compartment **(see illustration).**

7.2   The ignition coil and ballast resistor assembly is located in the left front corner (driver's side) of the engine compartment, immediately behind the air cleaner intake snorkel (removed in this photo for clarity)

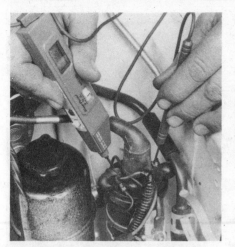

7.3a   To test the coil, measure the primary resistance (as shown here), . . .

7.3b   . . . then measure the secondary resistance (as shown here) and compare the readings to the specified resistances — if the indicated resistance is incorrect, replace the coil

7.5   To replace the coil, detach the wires (arrows), then remove the coil bracket mounting bolts (arrows — inner bolt obscured by radio noise suppression device) and lift the coil up far enough up to get at the ballast resistor

3   Using an ohmmeter, check the coil:
  a) Measure the resistance between the positive and negative terminals **(see illustration)**. Compare your reading with the specified primary coil resistance.
  b) Detach the high tension lead from the coil. Measure the resistance between the positive terminal and high tension terminal **(see illustration)**. Compare your reading with the specified secondary coil resistance.
4   If either of the above tests yield resistance values outside the specified resistance, replace the coil.

Replacement

Refer to illustrations 7.5 and 7.7

5   Detach the wire harness leads from the positive and negative coil primary terminals **(see illustration)**.
6   Remove the coil mounting bracket bolts and lift the coil and ballast resistor assembly up far enough to get at the ballast resistor clamp screw.
7   Loosen the ballast resistor clamp screw **(see illustration)** and set the ballast resistor aside. It's not necessary to detach the radio noise suppression device from the ballast resistor.
8   Loosen the coil clamp screw and remove the coil.
9   Installation is the reverse of removal.

8   Distributor – removal and installation

Refer to illustrations 8.6, 8.8a and 8.8b

Removal

1   Detach the cable from the negative battery terminal.
2   Unplug the coil high tension lead from the distributor cap.
3   On carbureted models, detach the vacuum hose(s) from the advance unit.
4   Look for a raised "1" on the distributor cap. This marks the location for the number one cylinder spark plug wire terminal. If the cap does not have a mark for the number one terminal, locate the number one spark plug and trace the wire back to the terminal on the cap.
5   Remove the distributor cap (see Chapter 1) and turn the engine over until the rotor is pointing toward the number one spark plug terminal (see locating TDC procedure in Chapter 2).
6   Make a mark on the edge of the distributor base directly below the rotor tip and in line with it **(see illustration)**. Also, mark the distributor base and the engine block to ensure that the distributor is installed correctly.
7   Remove the distributor hold down nut and washer, then pull the distributor straight out to remove it. **Caution:** *DO NOT turn the crankshaft while the distributor is out of the engine, or the alignment marks will be useless.*

5

7.7   To remove the ballast resistor, detach the leads (arrows) at both ends, loosen the clamp screw (arrow) and slide the resistor out

8.6   Before removing the distributor, paint or scribe an alignment mark on the edge of the distributor base directly beneath the rotor tip — DO NOT use a lead pencil

8.8a After you have pulled the distributor out of the cylinder head, unplug the two leads (arrows) from the igniter, . . .

9.4 To detach the vacuum unit from the distributor, remove the two screws (arrows), . . .

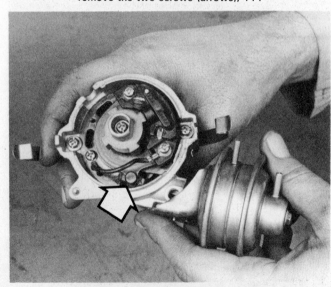

9.5 . . . then tilt it down, detach it from the pin (arrow) on the breaker base and pull it out

8.8b . . . then remove the small wire harness retaining clip screw from the side of the distributor base

8   Detach the leads from the igniter (see illustration) and remove the igniter lead clip screw from the distributor base (see illustration).

Installation

Note: *If the crankshaft has been moved while the distributor is out, the number one piston must be repositioned at TDC. This can be done by feeling for compression pressure at the number one plug hole as the crankshaft is turned. Once compression is felt, align the notch in the drivebelt pulley with the T on the timing scale.*

9   Insert the distributor into the engine in exactly the same relationship to the block that it was in when removed.
10   To mesh the helical gears on the camshaft and the distributor, it may be necessary to turn the rotor slightly. Recheck the alignment marks between the distributor base and the block to verify that the distributor is in the same position it was in before removal. Also check the rotor to see if it's aligned with the mark you made on the edge of the distributor base.
11   Loosely install the nut.
12   Plug in the igniter electrical leads.
13   Install the distributor cap.
14   On carbureted models, reattach the vacuum hose(s) to the advance unit.
15   Reattach the spark plug wires to the plugs (if removed).
16   Connect the cable to the negative terminal of the battery.
17   Check the ignition timing (see Chapter 1) and tighten the distributor hold down nut securely.

9   Vacuum advance unit – replacement (carbureted models)

Refer to illustrations 9.4 and 9.5
1   Remove the distributor (see Section 8).
2   Carefully clamp the distributor in a bench vise. Pad the jaws of the vise to avoid damage to the housing. Do not overtighten the vise — the distributor housing is an aluminum casting and will crack if squeezed too hard.
3   Pull the rotor off the shaft (see Chapter 1).
4   Remove the two vacuum unit mounting screws (see illustration).
5   Remove the controller link from the pin on the breaker base (see illustration), then detach the vacuum unit.
6   Installation is the reverse of removal.

10   Igniter – replacement (carbureted models)

Refer to illustration 10.3
1   Remove the distributor (see Section 8).
2   Remove the rotor.
3   Remove the two igniter mounting screws and detach the black

10.3   To detach the igniter, remove the two mounting screws (arrows) (one of them also holds the ground wire in place)

11.3   Remove the screws (arrows) to detach the signal rotor shaft and breaker plate

ground wire from the igniter **(see illustration)**. Remove the igniter.
4   Installation is the reverse of removal. Be sure to connect one end of the ground wire to the igniter mounting screw and the other end to the breaker plate.
5   Adjust the air gap (see Section 12) before reinstalling the distributor.

11   Centrifugal advance mechanism – component replacement (carbureted models)

Removal

Refer to illustrations 11.3, 11.4, 11.5, 11.6a, 11.6b and 11.7
1   Remove the distributor and detach the vacuum unit (see Section 9).
2   Remove the igniter (see Section 10).
3   Remove the signal rotor shaft screw and the two breaker plate screws **(see illustration)**.
4   Remove the signal rotor shaft and breaker plate assembly **(see illustration)**.
5   If you're replacing either the signal rotor or the signal rotor shaft, pull the two apart. If you're unable to pull the rotor off the shaft, support the breaker plate assembly and gently tap the shaft out of the signal rotor with a soft-face hammer **(see illustration)**.
6   Using a pair of needle-nose pliers, remove the two spring retainers, then remove the two governor springs **(see illustrations)**.

11.4   Pull the signal rotor shaft/breaker plate assembly off the distributor shaft

5

Rotor shaft
Signal rotor
Breaker plate

11.5   If you can't pull the signal rotor off the shaft, support the breaker plate assembly as shown, then gently tap the shaft out of the signal rotor with a soft-face hammer

11.6a   Using a pair of needle-nose pliers, remove the two spring retainers . . .

11.6b   . . . and the two governor springs

11.7   Remove the two governor weights

11.10   Make sure the governor weight pins (arrows) fit into the slots in the signal rotor shaft arm (apply a small amount of lightweight grease to the pins)

11.11   The projection on the breaker plate must fit into the groove in the distributor housing (arrows)

11.13   When you press the signal rotor onto the rotor shaft, be sure to align the flats (arrows)

12.2   To adjust the air gap between the igniter and the signal rotor, loosen the igniter mounting screws, insert a feeler gauge of the specified thickness between the igniter and one of the signal rotor projections, push the igniter against the gauge and tighten the mounting screws

13.4 Distributor and related components (fuel-injected models)

1   Breather
2   Distributor cap
3   Contact carbon
4   Rotor
5   Packing
6   Cover
7   Rotor shaft
8   Disc
9   Spacer
10   Plate
11   Unit
12   Bearing
13   Distributor shaft
14   Distributor housing
15   Lead wire
16   O-ring
17   Drive gear
18   Spring pin

7   Remove the two governor weights **(see illustration)**.

Installation

Refer to illustrations 11.10, 11.11 and 11.13

8   Apply a very small amount of lightweight grease to the pivot pins, then install the governor weights.

9   Attach the governor springs and spring retainers.
10   Lubricate the shaft with lightweight grease, then slide the signal rotor shaft onto the distributor shaft. Make sure the pins on the governor weights are aligned with the slots in the signal rotor shaft arm **(see illustration)**. Don't forget to install the screw.
11   Install the breaker plate in the housing. Make sure the breaker

plate projection fits into the groove in the housing **(see illustration)**.

12   Tighten the two breaker plate screws.

13   If you disassembled the signal rotor/signal rotor shaft assembly to replace either part, push the signal rotor onto the shaft. The flat face of the signal rotor must face up (the four projections must protrude down). Be sure to match the flat side of the signal rotor bore with the machined flat on the signal rotor shaft **(see illustration)**. If you try to assemble it without matching the two flat surfaces, you will damage the rotor and/or the shaft.

14   Install the igniter (see Section 10).

15   Adjust the air gap (see Section 12).

16   The remainder of installation is the reverse of removal.

12 Air gap – adjustment (carbureted models)

Refer to illustration 12.2

1   Anytime you replace the igniter – or remove it in order to get at the signal rotor or centrifugal advance mechanism – be sure to adjust the air gap before reinstalling the distributor cap.

2   Loosen the igniter mounting screws. Place a feeler gauge of the specified thickness between one of the four projections on the signal rotor and the igniter **(see illustration)**.

3   Gently push the igniter toward the signal rotor until it's a snug – not tight – fit against the feeler gauge.

4   Tighten the igniter mounting screws.

5   Check the adjustment by noting the amount of drag on the feeler gauge when you pull it out of the gap between the signal rotor and the igniter. You should feel a slight amount of drag. If you feel excessive drag on the gauge, the gap is probably too small. If you don't feel any drag on the gauge when you pull it out, the air gap is too large.

13 Distributor - disassembly and assembly (fuel-injected models)

Refer to illustration 13.4

1   Remove the distributor (see Section 8).

2   Carefully clamp the distributor in a bench vise. Pad the jaws of the vise to avoid damage to the housing. Do not overtighten the vise – the distributor housing is an aluminum casting and will crack if squeezed too hard.

3   Pull the rotor off the shaft (see Chapter 1).

4   Remove the packing rubber then lift off the cover **(see illustration)**.

5   Remove the screw and remove the rotor shaft.

6   Carefully remove the disc from the slot in the pickup unit, then remove the spacer.

7   Detach the lead wire connector.

8   Remove the three screws and remove the plate and unit.

9   Assembly is the reverse of disassembly. Install the disc into the slot in the pickup unit and in alignment with the spacer. Install the cover and align the indention with the housing notch.

14 Charging system – general information and precautions

The charging system includes the alternator, with an integral voltage regulator, the battery, a fusible link and the wiring between all the components. The charging system supplies electrical power for the ignition system, the lights, the radio, etc. The alternator is driven by a drivebelt at the front (driver's side) of the engine.

The purpose of the voltage regulator is to limit the alternator's voltage to a preset value. This prevents power surges, circuit overloads, etc., during peak voltage output.

The fusible link is a short length of insulated wire integral with the engine compartment wiring harness. The link is four wire gauges smaller in diameter than the circuit it protects. Production fusible links and their identification flags are identified by the flag color. See Chapter 12 for additional information regarding fusible links.

The charging system doesn't ordinarily require periodic maintenance. However, the drivebelt, battery and wires and connections should be inspected at the intervals outlined in Chapter 1.

The dashboard warning light should come on when the ignition key is turned to Start, then go off immediately. If it remains on, there is a malfunction in the charging system (see Section 14).

Be very careful when making electrical circuit connections to a vehicle equipped with an alternator and note the following:

a) When reconnecting wires to the alternator from the battery, be sure to note the polarity.

b) Before using arc welding equipment to repair any part of the vehicle, disconnect the wires from the alternator and the battery terminals.

c) Never start the engine with a battery charger connected.

d) Always disconnect both battery leads before using a battery charger.

e) The alternator is turned by an engine drivebelt which could cause serious injury if your hands, hair or clothes become entangled in it with the engine running.

f) Because the alternator is connected directly to the battery, it could arc or cause a fire if overloaded or shorted out.

g) Wrap a plastic bag over the alternator and secure it with rubberbands before steam cleaning the engine.

15 Charging system – check

1   If a malfunction occurs in the charging circuit, don't automatically assume that the alternator is causing the problem. First check the following items:

a) Check the drivebelt tension and condition (Chapter 1). Replace it if it's worn or deteriorated.

b) Make sure the alternator mounting and adjustment bolts are tight.

c) Inspect the alternator wiring harness and the connectors at the alternator and voltage regulator. They must be in good condition and tight.

d) Check the fusible link (if equipped) located between the starter solenoid and the alternator. If it's burned, determine the cause, repair the circuit and replace the link (the vehicle won't start and/or the accessories won't work if the fusible link blows). Sometimes a fusible link may look good, but still be bad. If in doubt, remove it and check for continuity.

e) Start the engine and check the alternator for abnormal noises (a shrieking or squealing sound indicates a bad bearing).

f) Check the specific gravity of the battery electrolyte. If it's low, charge the battery (doesn't apply to maintenance free batteries).

g) Make sure the battery is fully charged (one bad cell in a battery can cause overcharging by the alternator).

h) Disconnect the battery cables (negative first, then positive). Inspect the battery posts and the cable clamps for corrosion. Clean them thoroughly if necessary (see Chapter 1). Reconnect the cable to the positive terminal.

i) With the key off, connect a test light between the negative battery post and the disconnected negative cable clamp.

   1)   If the test light does not come on, reattach the clamp and proceed to the next step.

   2)   If the test light comes on, there is a short (drain) in the electrical system of the vehicle. The short must be repaired before the charging system can be checked.

   3)   Disconnect the alternator wiring harness.

      (a)   If the light goes out, the alternator is bad.

      (b)   If the light stays on, pull each fuse until the light goes out (this will tell you which component is shorted).

2   Using a voltmeter, check the battery voltage with the engine off. If should be approximately 12-volts.

3   Start the engine and check the battery voltage again. It should now be approximately 14-to-15 volts.

4   Turn on the headlights. The voltage should drop, and then come back up, if the charging system is working properly.

5   If the voltage reading is more than the specified charging voltage, replace the voltage regulator (refer to Section 16). If the voltage is less, the alternator diode(s), stator or rectifier may be bad or the voltage regulator may be malfunctioning.

16 Alternator – removal and installation

Refer to illustrations 16.6a, 16.6b and 16.7

1   Detach the cable from the negative terminal of the battery.

5

16.6a   The alternator mounting bolt (arrow) attaches the lower side of the alternator to a bracket integral with the oil filter housing (this photo depicts the bolt as seen from underneath the vehicle but you can remove it from above with a deep socket and extension)

16.6b   After loosening the alternator adjustment bolt (arrow) to remove the drivebelt, remove the bolt

16.7   If you have difficulty detaching the electrical connectors from the back of the alternator while it's still bolted to the engine, remove the alternator, then detach the connectors (arrows), open the wire harness clip (arrow) and lift the alternator up through the space between the exhaust manifold and the condenser

17.2   To detach the voltage regulator/brush holder assembly, remove the two mounting screws (arrows) and pull the regulator/brush holder straight out

17.3   Measure the brushes with a small ruler – if they're shorter than 3/16-inch, install new ones

2   If the vehicle is equipped with air conditioning, remove the left (driver's side) electric cooling fan (see Chapter 3).

3   Raise the vehicle and place it securely on jackstands.

4   Working from underneath the vehicle you should be able to detach the electrical connectors from the alternator. If you can't reach the wires, you can detach them after you unbolt the alternator (see Step 7).

5   Loosen the power steering pump drivebelt. Loosen the alternator adjustment and pivot bolts and detach the drivebelt (see Chapter 1).

6   Remove the adjustment and pivot bolts **(see illustrations)** and

detach the alternator from the engine.

7   If you haven't detached the wires yet, rotate the alternator so the back side faces up and detach the wires **(see illustration)**.

8   If you are replacing the alternator, take the old one with you when purchasing a replacement unit. Make sure the new/rebuilt unit looks identical to the old alternator. Look at the terminals – they should be the same in number, size and location as the terminals on the old alternator. Finally, look at the identification numbers – they will be stamped into the housing or printed on a tag attached to the housing. Make sure the numbers are the same on both alternators.

9   Many new/rebuilt alternators DO NOT have a pulley installed, so you may have to switch the pulley from the old unit to the new/rebuilt one. When buying an alternator, find out the shop's policy regarding pulleys – some shops will perform this service free of charge.

10   Installation is the reverse of removal.

11   After the alternator is installed, adjust the drivebelt tension (see Chapter 1).

12   Check the charging voltage to verify proper operation of the alternator (see Section 14).

17   Voltage regulator/alternator brushes – replacement

Refer to illustrations 17.2, 17.3 and 17.4
Note: *If you are replacing the brushes (but not the regulator itself), the following procedure requires that you unsolder the old brush leads from the regulator and solder the new ones into place. Unless you are skilled with a soldering gun, have this procedure performed by someone who is. If you overheat and damage the regulator, you could end up spending a lot more money than necessary.*

1   Remove the alternator.

2   Remove the voltage regulator mounting screws **(see illustration)**.

3   Remove the regulator/brush holder assembly and measure the length of the brushes **(see illustration)**. If they are less than 3/16-inch long, replace them with new ones. **Note:** *If you're simply replacing the*

17.4 To detach worn brushes from the voltage regulator/brush holder assembly, carefully unsolder the brush leads and extract each brush and lead from the holder

20.3 To remove the starter motor, reach up from underneath the vehicle and detach the wires from the terminals (arrows) on the back end of the solenoid, . . .

20.4 . . . then, working from above, remove the two bolts (arrows) and detach the starter motor from the engine

voltage regulator, skip the next step – the new regulator assembly includes a new set of brushes so the following step is unnecessary.
4   Unsolder the brush wiring connections **(see illustration)** and remove the brushes and springs.
5   Installation is the reverse of removal. Be sure to solder the new brush leads properly.

18 Starting system – general information and precautions

The sole function of the starting system is to turn over the engine quickly enough to allow it to start.

The starting system consists of the battery, the starter motor, the starter solenoid and the wires connecting them. The solenoid is mounted directly on the starter motor.

The solenoid/starter motor assembly is installed on the lower part of the engine, next to the transmission bellhousing.

When the ignition key is turned to the Start position, the starter solenoid is actuated through the starter control circuit. The starter solenoid then connects the battery to the starter. The battery supplies the electrical energy to the starter motor, which does the actual work of cranking the engine.

The starter motor on a vehicle equipped with a manual transmission can only be operated when the clutch pedal is depressed; the starter on a vehicle equipped with an automatic transmission can only be operated when the transmission selector lever is in Park or Neutral.

Always observe the following precautions when working on the starting system:
a) Excessive cranking of the starter motor can overheat it and cause serious damage. Never operate the starter motor for more than 30 seconds at a time without pausing to allow it to cool for at least two minutes.
b) The starter is connected directly to the battery and could arc or cause a fire if mishandled, overloaded or shorted out.
c) Always detach the cable from the negative terminal of the battery before working on the starting system.

19 Starter motor – testing in vehicle

Note: *Before diagnosing starter problems, make sure the battery is fully charged.*
1   If the starter motor does not turn at all when the switch is operated, make sure that the shift lever is in Neutral or Park (automatic transmission) or that the clutch pedal is depressed (manual transmission).
2   Make sure that the battery is charged and that all cables, both at the battery and starter solenoid terminals, are clean and secure.
3   If the starter motor spins but the engine is not cranking, the overrunning clutch in the starter motor is slipping and the starter motor must be replaced.
4   If, when the switch is actuated, the starter motor does not operate at all but the solenoid clicks, then the problem lies with either the battery, the main solenoid contacts or the starter motor itself (or the engine is seized).
5   If the solenoid plunger cannot be heard when the switch is actuated, the battery is bad, the fusible link is burned (the circuit is open) or the solenoid itself is defective.
6   To check the solenoid, connect a jumper lead between the battery (+) and the ignition switch wire terminal (the small terminal) on the solenoid. If the starter motor now operates, the solenoid is OK and the problem is in the ignition switch, neutral start switch or the wiring.
7   If the starter motor still does not operate, remove the starter/solenoid assembly for disassembly, testing and repair.
8   If the starter motor cranks the engine at an abnormally slow speed, first make sure that the battery is charged and that all terminal connections are tight. If the engine is partially seized, or has the wrong viscosity oil in it, it will crank slowly.
9   Run the engine until normal operating temperature is reached, then disconnect the coil wire from the distributor cap and ground it on the engine.
10   Connect a voltmeter positive lead to the positive battery post and connect the negative lead to the negative post.
11   Crank the engine and take the voltmeter readings as soon as a steady figure is indicated. Do not allow the starter motor to turn for more than 30 seconds at a time. A reading of 9 volts or more, with the starter motor turning at normal cranking speed, is normal. If the reading is 9 volts or more but the cranking speed is slow, the motor is faulty. If the reading is less than 9 volts and the cranking speed is slow, the solenoid contacts are probably burned, the starter motor is bad, the battery is discharged or there is a bad connection.

20 Starter motor – removal and installation

Refer to illustrations 20.3 and 20.4
Note: *On some vehicles, it may be necessary to remove the exhaust pipe(s) or frame crossmember to gain access to the starter motor. In extreme cases it may even be necessary to unbolt the mounts and raise the engine slightly to get the starter out.*
1   Detach the cable from the negative terminal of the battery.
2   Raise the vehicle and support it securely on jackstands.

5

21.3   To separate the solenoid from the starter motor, remove the nut and detach the lead (arrow), . . .

3   Clearly label, then disconnect the wires from the terminals on the starter motor and solenoid **(see illustration)**.
4   Remove the mounting bolts **(see illustration)** and detach the starter.
5   Installation is the reverse of removal.

21   Starter solenoid – removal and installation

Refer to illustrations 21.3 and 21.4
1   Disconnect the cable from the negative terminal of the battery.

21.4   . . . then remove the solenoid mounting screws (arrows) and pull the solenoid straight off the starter flange

2   Remove the starter motor (see Section 19).
3   Disconnect the large motor lead from the solenoid terminal **(see illustration)**.
4   Remove the screws which secure the solenoid to the starter motor **(see illustration)**.
5   Pull the solenoid from the starter body flange.
6   Installation is the reverse of removal.

Chapter 6 Emissions control systems

Contents

6

---

1 General information

To prevent pollution of the atmosphere from incompletely burned and evaporating gases, and to maintain good driveability and fuel economy, a number of emission control systems and devices are incorporated. They include the:

Positive Crankcase Ventilation (PCV) system
Evaporative emission control system
Heated Air Intake (HAI) system
Jet air system
Exhaust Gas Recirculation (EGR) system
Secondary air supply system
Catalytic converter
Deceleration devices
Fuel injection system (later models)

The Sections in this Chapter include general descriptions, checking procedures within the scope of the home mechanic and component replacement procedures (when possible) for each of the systems listed above.

Before assuming that an emissions control system is malfunctioning, check the fuel and ignition systems carefully. The diagnosis of some emission control devices requires specialized tools, equipment and training. If checking and servicing become too difficult or

if a procedure is beyond your ability, consult a dealer service department. Remember, the most frequent cause of emissions problems is simply a loose or broken vacuum hose or wire, so always check the hose and wiring connections first.

This doesn't mean, however, that emission control systems are particularly difficult to maintain and repair. You can quickly and easily perform many checks and do most of the regular maintenance at home with common tune-up and hand tools. Note: Because of a Federally mandated extended warranty which covers the emission control system components, check with your dealer about warranty coverage before working on any emissions-related systems. Once the warranty has expired, you may wish to perform some of the component checks and/or replacement procedures in this Chapter to save money.

Pay close attention to any special precautions outlined in this Chapter. It should be noted that the illustrations of the various systems may not exactly match the system installed on your vehicle because of changes made by the manufacturer during production or from year-to-year.

A Vehicle Emissions Control Information label is located in the engine compartment. This label contains important emissions specifications and adjustment information, as well as a vacuum hose schematic with emissions components identified. When servicing the engine or emissions systems, the VECI label in your particular vehicle should always be checked for up-to-date information.

3.3   The canister absorbs and stores fuel tank and carburetor float bowl vapors when the engine is off — when it's started, the vapors are routed through a series of valves and lines into the intake manifold

3.5   The purge control valve is closed during idle to prevent vaporized fuel from entering the intake manifold

2   Positive Crankcase Ventilation (PCV) system

1   The Positive Crankcase Ventilation (PCV) system reduces hydrocarbon emissions by scavenging crankcase vapors. It does this by circulating fresh air from the air cleaner through the crankcase, where it mixes with blow-by gases and is then rerouted through a PCV valve to the intake manifold.

2   The main components of the PCV system are the PCV valve, a fresh air filtered inlet and the vacuum hoses connecting these two components with the engine.

3   To maintain idle quality, the PCV valve restricts the flow when the intake manifold vacuum is high. During acceleration and high load conditions, vacuum is low, so the PCV passage opens more to facilitate flow. If abnormal operating conditions (such as piston ring problems) arise, the system is designed to allow excessive amounts of blow-by gases to flow back through the crankcase vent tube into the air cleaner to be consumed by normal combustion.

4   Checking and replacement of the PCV valve and filter is covered in Chapter 1.

3   Evaporative emission control system

Warning: *Gasoline is extremely flammable, so take extra precautions when working on any part of the fuel system. Don't smoke or allow open flames or bare light bulbs in or near the work area. Also, don't work in a garage in which a natural gas appliance such as a water heater or clothes dryer is present.*

General description

Refer to illustrations 3.3, 3.4, 3.5, 3.6, 3.8 and 3.9

1   The evaporative emission control system is designed to prevent the escape of fuel vapors from the fuel system into the atmosphere.

3.4   The bowl vent valve controls carburetor float bowl vapors — when the engine is on, the bowl vent valve closes to connect the float bowl to the carburetor air vent — when the key is off, the bowl vent valve opens to allow fuel vapors to flow to the canister

3.6   The thermo valve closes the purge control valve during engine warm-up and opens the purge control valve once the coolant temperature rises above a pre-set value

2   The evaporative emission control system consists of a canister, a bowl vent valve, a purge control valve, an overfill limiter, a thermo valve, a fuel check valve and a specially designed fuel filler cap. The purpose of each of these components, and how to check them, is described briefly in this Section.

Canister

3   When the engine is inoperative, fuel vapors generated inside the fuel tank and the carburetor float chamber are absorbed and stored in the canister. When the engine is running, the fuel vapors absorbed in the canister are drawn into the intake manifold through the purge control valve and an orifice **(see illustration)**.

Bowl vent valve

4   The bowl vent valve controls the carburetor bowl vapors. When the engine is running, intake vacuum acts on a diaphragm to close the bowl vent valve so that the bowl is connected to an air vent **(see illustration)**. During engine operation, the diaphragm is kept open by a solenoid valve — even when intake manifold vacuum falls to a value equal to atmospheric pressure — as long as the ignition key is turned on. When the key is turned off, the solenoid valve closes, the bowl vent valve opens to connect the carburetor bowl to the canister, allowing fuel vapors to migrate to the canister where they are stored until the next time the key is turned on.

Purge control valve

5   The purge control valve **(see illustration)** is closed during idle to prevent vaporized fuel from entering the intake manifold. At higher engine speeds, the purge control valve opens.

Thermo valve

6   The thermo valve **(see illustration)**, which monitors the engine coolant temperature at the intake manifold, closes the purge control valve when the engine coolant temperature is lower than the pre-set

3.8   The overfill limiter contains two valves: the pressure valve opens when fuel tank internal pressure builds up; the vacuum valve opens when fuel tank internal pressure is low

3.9   The fuel check valve, located in the fuel vapor line between the canister and the overfill limiter, prevents fuel leaks in the event of a vehicle rollover

3.12   To check the bowl vent valve (BVV), detach the vapor hose from the BVV, attach a hand vacuum pump to the fitting and apply a vacuum to the BVV — with the engine operating, the BVV should hold vacuum — with the engine off, it should leak vacuum

3.14   The purge control valve is located on top of the canister — to remove it, detach the two hoses (arrows)

temperature. This reduces CO and HC emissions under engine warm-up conditions. The thermo valve opens the purge control valve when the engine coolant temperature is above the pre-set temperature. The thermo valve also controls the choke breaker, EGR valve and choke opener.

Fuel filler cap
7   The fuel filler cap is equipped with a vacuum relief valve to prevent the escape of fuel vapor into the atmosphere.

Overfill limiter
8   The overfill limiter **(see illustration)** consists of two valves:
a)   The pressure valve, which opens when fuel tank internal pressure exceeds normal pressure.
b)   The vacuum valve, which opens when fuel tank internal pressure is lower than normal pressure.

Fuel check valve
9   The fuel check valve **(see illustration)**, which is connected in the fuel vapor line between the canister and the overfill limiter (it's mounted in the engine compartment on the firewall), prevents fuel leaks in the event of a vehicle rollover. The valve contains two balls. Under normal conditions, the fuel vapor passage in the valve is open, but, should the vehicle roll over, one of the balls closes the fuel passage, preventing fuel leakage.

Checking
Refer to illustrations 3.12, 3.14 and 3.15
Canister
10   See Chapter 1 for canister check and replacement procedures.

Bowl vent valve
11   Remove the air cleaner (see Chapter 4).
12   Detach the bowl vapor hose from the bowl vent valve (BVV) and attach a hand vacuum pump to the BVV fitting **(see illustration)**.
13   Apply a vacuum of 3 in-Hg to the BVV. With the engine operating, it should hold vacuum. With the engine off, it should leak vacuum.

3.15   To check the purge control valve, attach a hand vacuum pump to the valve vacuum fitting and blow in air lightly from the canister side — you should not be able to blow air through the valve at a vacuum less than 1.4 in-Hg

Purge control valve
14   Remove the purge control valve **(see illustration)**.
15   Attach a hand vacuum pump to the vacuum fitting on the valve **(see illustration)**.
16   Blow in air lightly from the canister side. The valve's operating vacuum should be more than 1.4 in-Hg.

Fuel filler cap
17   Inspect the gasket on the underside of the cap for deformation and deterioration. If damage is evident, replace the cap.

6

4.2   The Heated Air Intake (HAI) system: when the engine is cold, the temperature sensor allows intake manifold vacuum to the vacuum motor, which opens the air control valve, allowing hot air to be drawn into the air cleaner through the heat cowl and air duct

4   Heated Air Intake (HAI) system

General Description

Refer to illustration 4.2

1   All vehicles are equipped with a Heated Air Intake (HAI) system to permit leaner carburetion, which reduces HC and CO emissions, improves warm-up characteristics and minimizes carburetor icing.

2   The air cleaner is equipped with an air control valve inside the snorkel to regulate the temperature of intake air, which is admitted to the carburetor through the fresh air duct, the heat cowl and air duct, or through both routes **(see illustration).**

3   The air control valve is operated by a vacuum motor. A temperature sensor in the air cleaner controls when the vacuum motor receives intake manifold vacuum. When intake air is below about 86°F, the temperature sensor allows intake manifold vacuum to to the vacuum motor. This draws the air control valve up and causes hot air to be drawn through the heat cowl and air duct. When intake air is above about 113°F, the temperature sensor does not allow vacuum to the vacuum motor and the air control valve remains down. This causes cold air to be drawn through the fresh air duct. When intake air temperature is between about 86°F and 113°F, the air control valve is partially open and intake air is a blend of air drawn through both routes.

Checking

Refer to illustrations 4.5 and 4.8

HAI system

For information on checking the HAI system for proper operation, refer to Chapter 1.

Air control valve and vacuum motor

4   Remove the air cleaner (see Chapter 4).

5   Detach the vacuum hose from the air control valve and attach a hand vacuum pump to the valve fitting **(see illustration).**

6   Apply vacuum with the vacuum pump. Note the readings and look down the snorkel of the air cleaner to observe the position of the air control valve. Under 3.6 in-Hg, the air control valve should be down all the way. Over 7.6 in-Hg, the air control valve should be up all the way. If either does not happen, the vacuum motor, the air control valve, or the linkage that connects the two is faulty.

7   Detach the hand vacuum pump, reattach the vacuum hose, and reinstall the air cleaner.

Temperature sensor

8   Attach a hand vacuum pump to the temperature sensor fitting **(see illustration)** and apply vacuum.

   a) When the engine is cold (the temperature in the air cleaner is below 86°F), the temperature sensor should hold vacuum.

4.5   To check the air control valve and vacuum motor, remove the air cleaner, detach the vacuum hose from the vacuum motor, attach a hand vacuum pump to the valve and apply vacuum — the air valve inside the air cleaner snorkel should move up at a vacuum greater than 7.6 in-Hg

4.8   To check the temperature sensor, attach a hand vacuum pump to the temperature sensor and apply vacuum — when the engine is cold, the temperature sensor should hold vacuum; when the engine is at normal operating temperature, the sensor should leak vacuum

5.1 The jet valve (arrow) allows a super lean mixture to be admitted into the combustion chamber during the intake stroke

b) When the engine is idling at normal operating temperature (the temperature in the air cleaner is above 113°F), the temperature sensor should leak vacuum.

5 Jet air system

Refer to illustration 5.1

General description

1   In addition to the intake and exhaust valves, each combustion chamber is equipped with a smaller *jet valve* **(see illustration)** which allows a super lean mixture to be admitted into the combustion chamber during the intake stroke. This super lean mixture swirls as it enters the combustion chamber. The swirl continues throughout the compression stroke and improves flame propagation after ignition, assuring efficient combustion.

2   Air is admitted through intake openings located near the primary throttle valve of the carburetor, then routed to the jet valve via a passage through the intake manifold and cylinder head, where it is drawn through the jet valve opening into the combustion chamber.

3   The jet valve is operated by a forked rocker arm which also actuates the intake valve (they share the same cam lobe). This design ensures that the intake and jet valve open simultaneously.

Checking

4   To adjust the jet valves, see Chapter 1.

Component replacement

5   To overhaul or replace the jet valves, see Chapter 2, Part B.

6 Exhaust Gas Recirculation (EGR) system

General description

Refer to illustration 6.1

1   The Exhaust Gas Recirculation (EGR) system **(see illustration)** is designed to reduce oxides of nitrogen in the vehicle exhaust. The EGR system recirculates a portion of the exhaust gas from an exhaust port in the cylinder head into a port located in the intake manifold.

2   On 1986 and 1987 vehicles, EGR flow is controlled by an EGR valve, a sub-EGR valve and a thermo valve.

a) The EGR valve is controlled by carburetor vacuum in response to throttle valve opening; EGR flow is suspended at idle and during wide open throttle conditions.

b) The vacuum applied to the EGR valve is controlled by a thermo valve, which senses engine temperature. The thermo valve interrupts the vacuum signal to the EGR valve during warm-up when less NOx is generated and less EGR promotes better driveability.

c) The sub-EGR valve (not shown in illustration 6.1) opens and closes with the throttle valve via a linkage to regulate EGR flow through the EGR valve in response to the throttle valve position.

3   On 1988 and 1989 vehicles, the EGR system operates similarly, except no sub-EGR valve is used and a vacuum regulator valve (VRV) is used to modulate the vacuum signal to the EGR valve.

Checking (1986 and 1987 models)

Refer to illustrations 6.13 and 6.16

EGR system

4   Check all EGR system vacuum hoses for proper routing and installation.

6

6.1 The Exhaust Gas Recirculation (EGR) system (1988 and 1989 system shown)

EGR valve

EGR passage

A

E

D

Vacuum regulator valve

Thermo valve

Venturi

6.13   When checking the EGR valve on 1986 and 1987 vehicles, you must pull the sub-EGR valve open by hand

6.16   On 1986 and 1987 vehicles, attach a hand vacuum pump to the EGR valve and apply vacuum — if the idle speed becomes unstable, the EGR valve is OK; if the idle speed remains unchanged, replace the EGR valve

6.20   On 1988 and later models, attach a hand vacuum pump to the EGR valve and apply vacuum – the EGR valve should hold vacuum; you should also be able to blow through the valve (as indicated by arrows) when vacuum is applied

6.24   To check the Vacuum Regulator Valve (VRV), detach the white-striped hose from the VRV, attach a hand vacuum pump to it and apply vacuum — the VRV should leak vacuum with the engine stopped and should hold vacuum with the engine at 3500 rpm

5   Start the engine when it's cold and run it at idle speed.
6   Verify that an increase in engine speed from idle to 2500 rpm doesn't cause the EGR valve to operate. If the EGR valve operates, replace the thermo valve.
7   Warm up the engine until coolant temperature reaches about 185 to 205°F.
8   Verify that an increase in engine speed from idle to 2500 rpm causes the EGR valve to operate. It if doesn't operate, the problem may lie in the thermo valve or the EGR valve. Check them, as discussed below.

Thermo valve
9   Detach the green striped hose from the thermo valve.
10   Attach a vacuum pump to the thermo valve and apply vacuum. If vacuum does not hold, the thermo valve is defective. Replace it.
11   Detach the vacuum pump from the thermo valve and reattach the green striped hose to the thermo valve.

EGR valve
12   Detach the green striped hose from the vacuum fitting on the carburetor and attach a vacuum pump to the end of the hose.
13   While pulling the sub-EGR valve open by hand **(see illustration)**, apply 9.4 in-Hg vacuum with the hand pump.
   a) If the idle speed becomes unstable, the EGR valve is operating properly.
   b) If the idle speed remains unchanged, the EGR valve is not operating. Replace it.
14   Detach the vacuum pump and reattach the green striped hose to the carburetor.
15   Detach the yellow striped hose from the EGR valve.
16   Attach a vacuum pump to the EGR valve vacuum fitting from which

you disconnected the yellow striped hose **(see illustration)**.
17   While pulling the sub-EGR valve open by hand **(see illustration 6.13)**, apply 6.6 in-Hg vacuum with the vacuum pump.
   a) If the idle speed becomes unstable, the EGR valve is operating properly.
   b) If the idling speed remains unchanged, the valve is not operating. Replace the EGR valve.
18   Detach the vacuum pump from the EGR valve and reattach the yellow striped hose to the EGR valve.

Checking (1988 and later models)
Refer to illustrations 6.20, 6.24 and 6.27

EGR valve
19   Remove the EGR valve and check it for sticking, carbon deposits or other damage. If necessary, clean the valve with solvent to ensure tight valve seat contact.
20   Attach a hand vacuum pump to the vacuum fitting on the EGR valve **(see illustration)**.
21   Apply a vacuum of 22 in-Hg and verify that the EGR valve holds vacuum.
22   With vacuum applied, blow air into one passage of the EGR:
   a) With 2.6 in-Hg applied, air should not blow through.
   b) With 7.28 in-Hg applied, air should blow through.
23   If the EGR valve fails either test, replace it.

Vacuum Regulator Valve (VRV)
24   Detach the white-striped vacuum hose from the VRV and attach a hand vacuum pump to the VRV **(see illustration)**.
25   Apply 17 in-Hg vacuum and verify that the VRV operates as follows:

6.27 To check the thermo valve, detach all vacuum hoses, attach a hand vacuum pump to B and apply vacuum — when the engine is cold, the thermo valve should leak vacuum; when the engine is at normal operating temperature, the valve should hold vacuum

a) With the engine stopped, the VRV should leak vacuum.
b) With the engine at 3500 rpm, the VRV should hold vacuum.

Thermo valve
26 Detach all vacuum hoses from the thermo valve. Be sure to note where each is attached so you can return it to its proper location.
27 Attach a hand vacuum pump to fitting B (see illustration) and apply vacuum to verify that the thermo valve operates as follows:
a) Below 145 ± 5°F, the thermo valve should leak vacuum.
b) Above 149 ± 4°F, the thermo valve should hold vacuum.

---

7 Secondary air supply system

Refer to illustrations 7.1 and 7.3

General description
1 The secondary air supply system (see illustration) delivers air to

7.3 To remove the secondary air control valve, detach the hose from the air cleaner (1) (already removed in photograph), unscrew the threaded fitting for the metal tube to the exhaust (2), remove the vacuum hose (3) and unscrew the mounting bolts (4) — when checking the valve, remove the vacuum hose (3)

the front catalytic converter through a reed valve(s) to promote further oxidation of exhaust emissions during engine warm-up, deceleration and heavy engine loads. The reed valve(s) is actuated by vacuum generated by exhaust pulsation.
2 The system is controlled by the secondary air control valve, a solenoid valve and the vehicle's Electronic Control Unit (ECU).

Checking
3 Remove the secondary air control valve (see illustration).
4 Blow air into the fitting where the air cleaner hose was connected. Air shouldn't flow through the valve.

7.1 Secondary air supply system (1986 49-state system shown)

5   Attach a hand vacuum pump to the secondary air control valve fitting **(see illustration 7.3)**.

6   Apply a vacuum of 5.9 in-Hg and blow into the valve:
   a) You should be able to blow air through the valve from the fitting where the air cleaner hose was attached.
   b) You should not be able to blow air through the threaded hole where the exhaust manifold tube was attached.

7   If the secondary air control valve does not perform as described, replace it.

8   Catalytic converter

Note: *Because of a Federally mandated extended warranty which covers emissions-related components such as the catalytic converter, check with a dealer service department before replacing the converter at your own expense.*

General description

1   The catalytic converter is an emission control device added to the exhaust system to reduce pollutants from the exhaust gas stream. There are two types of converters. The rear converter is a conventional oxidation catalyst unit. It reduces the levels of hydrocarbons (HC) and carbon monoxide (CO). The front converter is a three-way catalyst unit. It lowers the levels of oxides of nitrogen (NOx) as well as hydrocarbons (HC) and carbon monoxide (CO).

Checking

2   The test equipment for a catalytic converter is expensive and highly sophisticated. If you suspect that the converter on your vehicle is malfunctioning, take it to a dealer service department or an authorized emissions inspection facility for diagnosis and repair.

3   Whenever the vehicle is raised for servicing of underbody components, check the converter for leaks, corrosion, dents and other damage. Check the welds/flange bolts that attach the front and rear ends of the converter to the exhaust system. If damage is discovered, the converter should be replaced.

4   Although catalytic converters don't break too often, they do become plugged. The easiest way to check for a restricted converter is to use a vacuum gauge to diagnose the effect of a blocked exhaust on intake vacuum.
   a) Open the throttle until the engine speed is about 2000 RPM.
   b) Release the throttle quickly.
   c) If there is no restriction, the gauge will quickly drop to not more than 2 in-Hg or more above its normal reading.

   d) If the gauge does not show 5 in-Hg or more above its normal reading, or seems to momentarily hover around its highest reading for a moment before it returns, the exhaust system, or the converter, is plugged (or an exhaust pipe is bent or dented, or the core inside the muffler has shifted).

Component replacement

5   Because the front converter is welded to the exhaust system, converter replacement requires removal of the exhaust pipe assembly (see Chapter 4). Take the vehicle, or the exhaust pipe system, to a dealer service department or a muffler shop.

6   The rear converter is bolted to the exhaust system. Refer to exhaust system removal and installation in Chapter 4.

9   Deceleration devices (1986 and 1987 models)

Deceleration spark advance system
Refer to illustration 9.1

1   Ignition timing is advanced during deceleration by a vacuum advance unit on the distributor **(see illustration)**. This unit normally has carburetor ported vacuum applied to it, but when the vehicle is decelerating, the Electronic Control Unit (ECU) sends a signal to a solenoid valve which opens to apply the higher vacuum from the intake manifold. This advances the ignition timing, reducing HC emissions.

Dash pot

2   The carburetor is equipped with a dash pot which slows the rate at which the throttle valve closes to its normal idling position, thereby reducing HC emissions.

3   For further information on the dash pot, refer to Chapter 4.

10   Mixture Control Valve (MCV) (1988 and later models)

Refer to illustration 10.6

General Description

1   When the throttle is closed suddenly during deceleration or shifting, the remaining fuel in the intake manifold causes a temporarily overrich mixture. To prevent this, the mixture control valve (MCV) temporarily supplies air from another passage to correct the air-fuel ratio and reduce HC emissions.

9.1   The deceleration spark advance system decreases HC emissions during deceleration by advancing ignition timing with a solenoid operated vacuum advance unit on the distributor

10.6 To remove the Mixture Control Valve (MCV), unscrew the three mounting screws (arrows)

Mixture control valve

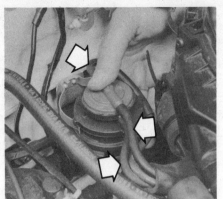

12.3 To remove the High Altitude Compensator (HAC) valve, detach the vacuum hoses (arrows) and unclip it from the bracket on the firewall

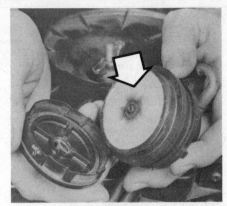

12.4 Peel the HAC air filter out, clean it with compressed air, inspect it and, if necessary, replace it

Checking

2 Remove the air cleaner (see chapter 4).
3 Warm up the engine.
4 Open and close the throttle valve quickly and note the presence or absence of air suction noise.
  a) Immediately after opening the throttle and closing it abruptly, the MCV should open and you should hear air suction noise (a hissing sound).
  b) After the engine returns to idle, the hissing sound should disappear.

Replacement

5 Remove the carburetor (see Chapter 4).
6 Unscrew the three mounting screws (**see illustration**) and remove the MCV assembly.
7 Installation is the reverse of removal.

11 Idle-up system

1 The Idle-up system consists of a dash pot assembly, a solenoid valve, a blower motor switch, a tail light switch and an oil pump pressure switch in the power steering system.
2 When the blower motor, tail light switch or oil pump switch is turned on during engine idle, the solenoid valve is opened, allowing vacuum from the intake manifold to act on the dash pot. This vacuum acting on the dash pot opens the throttle valve slightly via the idle-up lever on the throttle shaft. Thus, engine idle speed increases whenever power steering or electrical loads are high.
3 For further information on the idle-up system, see Chapter 4.

12 High altitude compensation system

General description

1 To meet Federal emission laws at all altitudes, all 49-state vehicles and some California vehicles are equipped with a high altitude compensation system. This system consists of a high altitude compensator (HAC) valve, a vacuum switching valve (49-state vehicles), a check valve and a distributor equipped with a high altitude vacuum advance device.
2 At high altitude, the system maintains the air-fuel mixture at its sea level ratio by supplying additional air into the carburetor. The system also supplies additional vacuum to the high altitude vacuum advance device on the distributor to compensate for high altitude.

Checking

Refer to illustrations 12.3, 12.4 and 12.5

3 Remove the HAC valve (**see illustration**) and look for deforma-

12.5 To check the HAC valve, detach the vacuum hose from the lower fitting, attach a hand vacuum pump and apply vacuum- the HAC should leak vacuum; reattach the lower hose, detach the upper hose, attach the vacuum pump to the upper fitting and apply vacuum – the HAC valve should hold vacuum

tion and cracks. Replace the HAC valve if either of these conditions exists.
4 Clean the air filter in the HAC valve (**see illustration**) and reinstall the valve.
5 At altitudes below 3900 feet:
  a) Detach the vacuum hose from the HAC lower fitting and attach a hand vacuum pump to it (**see illustration**).
  b) Apply vacuum with the pump. The HAC valve should leak vacuum. If it doesn't, replace the valve. Reattach the vacuum hose to the lower fitting.
  c) Detach the vacuum hose from the HAC valve upper fitting and attach a hand vacuum pump to it.
  d) Apply vacuum. The HAC valve should hold vacuum. If it doesn't, replace the valve.
6 At altitudes above 3900 feet:
  a) Detach either vacuum hose from the HAC valve and attach a hand vacuum pump to the fitting.
  b) Apply vacuum. The HAC valve should hold vacuum. If it doesn't, replace the valve.

13 Feedback carburetor (FBC) system

Refer to illustration 13.2

General description

1 The feedback carburetor (FBC) system consists of four components or groups of components:
  a) Information sensors
  b) Electronic control unit (ECU)
  c) Output actuators
  d) Feedback carburetor

6

2   Two systems are used on the vehicles covered by this manual. The original system is installed on 1986 and 1987 vehicles; the newer system is used on 1988 and later models. Although similar in operation, the two systems differ in the number and type of sensors and actuators used. A simplified drawing of an FBC system is shown in the accompanying illustration.

Information sensors

3   Both systems use information sensors to monitor various engine operating conditions and relay this data to the computer. They include:

   a) Exhaust oxygen sensor
   b) Coolant temperature sensor
   c) Engine speed sensor
   d) Throttle position sensor
   e) Closed throttle (idle) switch
   f) Intake air temperature sensor (not used on newer system)

Electronic Control Unit (ECU)

4   The ECU, which is located under the dash, just forward of the console, processes the constant information it receives from the abovelisted information sensors, compares this information to the values stored in its memory, calculates the new values necessary to maintain an ideal air-fuel ratio, converts this information into a digital signal and sends this signal to the output actuators located on or near the carburetor.

Output actuators

5   The output actuators (mainly solenoid valves) adjust the carburetor as operating conditions change. When energized by signals from the ECU, actuators turn on, turn off, reroute or alter the intensity of vacuum signals affecting the adjustment of devices installed on the carburetor. Output actuators include:

   a) 1986 and 1987 vehicles
      1   Enrichment solenoid valve
      2) Deceleration solenoid valve
      3) Jet mixture control solenoid valve
      4) Idle-up (throttle opener) control solenoid valve
      5) Secondary air control solenoid valve
   b) 1988 and later vehicles:
      1) Feedback solenoid valve (FBSV)
      2) Slow cut solenoid valve (SCSV)
      3) Distributor advance control solenoid valve
      4) Distributor cold advance control solenoid valve
      5) Throttle opener control solenoid valve
      6) Air conditioner power relay
      7) Mixture heater relay

Feedback carburetor

6   The FBC system (all sensors, actuators, the carburetor, the ECU and all components related to the system or whose proper function depends on the proper operation of this system) is covered by a Federally mandated extended warranty (five-years or 50,000 miles when this book was published – see your dealer for details). Therefore, all system malfunctions can and should be referred to your dealer as long as the vehicle is still under warranty.

7   Because of the complexity of the feedback carburetor system and because of the special electronic instrument needed to check and troubleshoot the entire system, servicing is beyond the scope of the home mechanic.

8   Where possible, the procedures for checking some of the components described above have been included in Chapter 4. However, because of the interrelationship of these devices, we do not recommend that you tackle feedback carburetor related problems unless you have the proper equipment and know what you are doing.

---

14   Multi-Point Injection (MPI) system – general diagnosis

General information

The Multi-Point Injection system controls the fuel injection system, the spark advance system, the self diagnosis system, the cooling fans etc. by means of the Electronic Control Unit (ECU).

The ECU receives signals from various sensors which monitor changing engine operations such as intake air volume, intake air temperature, coolant temperature, engine RPM, acceleration/deceleration, exhaust temperature etc. These signals are utilized by the ECU to determine the correct injection duration and ignition timing.

The Sections in this Chapter include general descriptions and checking procedures, within the scope of the home mechanic and component replacement procedures (when possible). Before assuming the fuel and ignition systems are malfunctioning check the emission control system thoroughly (see Chapter 6). The emission system and the fuel system are closely interrelated but can be checked seperately. The diagnosis of some of the fuel and emission control devices requires specialized tools, equipment and training. If checking and servicing become too difficult or if a procedure is beyond your ability, consult a dealer service department. Remember, the most frequent cause of fuel and emissions problems is simply a loose or broken vaccum hose or wire, so always check the hose and wiring connections first.

Note: *Because of a federally mandated extended warranty which covers the emission control system components (and any other components which have a primary purpose other than emission con-*

13.2   A simplified drawing of the feedback carburetor system

trol but have significant effects on emissions), check with your dealer about warranty coverage before working on any emission related systems. Once the warranty has expired, you may wish to perform some of the component checks and/or replacement procedures in this Chapter to save you money.

Precautions

a) Always disconnect the power by either turning off the ignition switch or disconnecting the battery terminals before disconnecting EFI electrcical connectors.

b) When installing a battery, be particularly careful to avoid reversing the positive and negative cables.

c) Do not subject EFI or emission related components or the ECU to severe impact during removal or installation.

d) Do not be careless during troubleshooting. Even slight terminal contact can invalidate a testing procedure and even damage one of the numerous transistor circuits.

e) Never attempt to work on the ECU or open the ECU cover. The ECU is protected by a government mandated extended warranty that will be nullified if you tamper with it.

f) If you are inspecting electronic control system components during rainy weather, make sure water does not enter any part. When washing the engine compartment, do not spray these parts or their connectors with water.

Self-diagnosis system

Refer to illustration 14.1

The self-diagnosis system is useful to diagnose malfunctions in major sensors and actuators of the MPI system.

1 Connect the voltmeter to the self-diagnosis connector in the fuse panel **(see illustration)**.

2 Turn the ignition key ON. Watch the pointer on the voltmeter carefully. The pointer will move up and back to zero. The first pattern is always extended (slow), indicating the first digit of the code. After the extended deflection(s) will come fast deflection(s) indicating the second digit of the code. The voltmeter will continue to deflect (pulse) signals until the entire code has been released by the ECU. For example, if there is a problem with the vehicle speed sensor, the meter will indicate two slow deflections followed by four fast deflections, or Code 24. Refer to the code chart for a complete list of diagnostic codes.

After the tests have been performed and the repairs completed, erase the memory by disconnecting the battery negative terminal for 15 seconds or more.

DIAGNOSIS TERMINAL

14.1 The self-diagnosis terminal is located on the fuse panel

SELF-DIAGNOSIS SYSTEM TROUBLE CODES		
Display code	**Circuit or system**	**Probable cause**
Code 9 (9 fast deflections)	Normal state	All components functioning properly
Code 11 (1 slow deflection, pause, 1 fast deflection)	Oxygen sensor	Check the harness for any open wires or shorts. Also check the injectors and the fuel pressure.
Code 12 (1 slow deflection, pause, 2 fast deflections)	Air flow sensor	The air flow sensor ground circuit(s) may be shorted or open.
Code 13 (1 slow deflection, pause, 3 fast deflections)	Air temperature sensor	The air temperature sensor ground circuit(s) may be shorted or open.
Code 14 (1 slow deflection, pause, 4 fast deflections)	Throttle position sensor	The throttle position sensor circuit is open.
Code 15 (1 slow deflection, pause, 5 fast deflections)	Motor position sensor	The motor position sensor circuit is open.
Code 21 (2 slow deflections, pause, 1 fast deflection)	Engine coolant temperature	The engine coolant temperature sensor circuit or sensor is faulty.
Code 22 (2 slow deflections, pause, 2 fast deflections)	Crank angle sensor	The crank angle sensor circuit or sensor is faulty.
Code 23 (2 slow deflections, pause, 3 fast deflections)	Number 1 cylinder TDC sensor	The TDC sensor circuit or sensor is faulty.
Code 24 (2 slow deflections, pause, 4 fast deflections)	Vehicle speed sensor	The vehicle speed sensor circuit or sensor is faulty.
Code 25 (2 slow deflections, pause, 5 fast deflections)	Barometric pressure sensor	The barometric pressure sensor circuit or sensor is faulty.
Code 41 (4 slow deflections, pause, 1 fast deflection)	Fuel injector	The fuel injector circuit or injector(s) is/are faulty.
Code 42 (4 slow deflections, pause, 2 fast deflections)	Fuel pump	The fuel pump circuit, control relay or pump is faulty.
Code 43 (4 slow deflections, pause, 3 fast deflections)	EGR system	The EGR circuit or valve is faulty.

6

Chapter 7 Part A Manual transaxle

Contents

Specifications

Torque specifications

	Ft-lbs	Nm
Transaxle-to-engine bolts		
8 x 14 mm	7 to 9	10 to 12
8 x 20 mm	11 to 16	15 to 22
8 x 60 mm	22 to 25	30 to 34
10 x 40 mm	31 to 40	43 to 55
10 x 55 mm	16 to 23	22 to 32
10 x 65 mm	31 to 40	43 to 55
Drain and filler plugs	See Chapter 1	
Shift rod set screw	24	32
Starter motor bolt	16 to 23	22 to 32

2.5a Early model manual transaxle shift mechanism components - exploded view

1	Shift lever	4	Fulcrum ball
2	Boot	5	Dust boot
3	Insulator	6	Rubber insulator

7	Extension rod	10	Lock wire
8	Bushing	11	Set screw
9	Dust cover	12	Shift rod

1 General information

The vehicles covered by this manual are equipped with either a four or five speed manual transaxle or a three speed automatic transaxle. Information on the manual transaxle is included in this Part of Chapter 7. Service procedures for the automatic transaxle are contained in Chapter 7, Part B.

The manual transaxle is a compact, two piece, lightweight aluminum alloy housing containing both the transmission and differential assemblies.

Because of the complexity, unavailability of replacement parts and special tools required, internal repair of the manual transaxle by the home mechanic is not recommended. For readers who wish to tackle a transaxle rebuild, exploded views and a brief *Manual transaxle overhaul – general information* Section are provided. The bulk of information in this Chapter is devoted to removal and installation procedures.

2 Manual transaxle shift assembly – removal and installation

1986 through 1989 models
Refer to illustrations 2.5a and 2.5b

1 Remove the shift knob (if required) and center console.
2 On models so equipped, remove the rear heat floor duct.

Dust cover

Lock wire

Bushing

Shift rod

Set screw

2.5b   Later model manual transaxle shift mechanism components – exploded view (up to 1989)

Extension rod

Shift knob

Shift lever

Shift lever cover

Insulator

Bushing

Rubber insulator

Dust cover

2.11   Shift cable installation details (1990 and later models)

2.17a   Dimensions A and B on both sides of the shift lever must be equal

ADJUSTER

2.17b   Adjust the cable length by turning the nuts (labeled "Adjuster")

3   On early models, remove the shift assembly bracket nuts.

4   Raise the vehicle and support it securely on jackstands.

5   Disconnect the extension rod from the transaxle **(see illustrations)**.

6   Remove the lock wire from the shift rod set screw. Loosen (early models) or remove (later models) the set screw and detach the shift rod from the transaxle.

7   On early models, remove the heat shield from the body for clearance when removing the shift assembly.

8   Remove the extension rod and shift lever assembly by lowering it from the vehicle.

9   Installation is the reverse of removal.

1990 and later models

Refer to illustrations 2.11, 2.17a and 2.17b

10   Remove the center console (see Chapter 11).

11   Remove the cotter pins securing the shift cables to the shift lever assembly **(see illustration)**.

12   Unbolt the shift lever assembly and remove it.

13   Unbolt the retainer from the bulkhead.

14   Raise the vehicle and support it securely on jackstands.

15   Remove the cotter pins securing the shift cables to the transaxle assembly.

7A

16   Remove the shift cable assembly.
17   Installation is the reverse of removal. Make sure the shifter operates freely and selects all gears. If not, the cable lengths can be adjusted at the shift-lever ends **(see illustrations)**.

3   Manual transaxle – removal and installation

Refer to illustration 3.10

Removal

1   Disconnect the negative cable from the battery.
2   Raise the vehicle and support it securely on jackstands.
3   Drain the transaxle fluid (Chapter 1).
4   Disconnect the shift and clutch linkage from the transaxle.
5   Detach the speedometer cable and wire harness connectors from the transaxle.

3.10   Remove the bolts (arrows) and detach the bellhousing cover for access to the lower transaxle-to-engine bolts

4.4a   Four speed transaxle components – exploded view (1986 through 1989 models)

1 Back-up light switch	14 Gasket
2 Gasket	15 Poppet springs
3 Steel ball	16 Poppet balls
4 Bolt	17 Reverse idler gear shaft
5 Locking plate	18 Reverse idler gear
6 Speedometer gear assembly	19 Bolts
7 Bolt	20 Reverse shift lever assembly
8 Transaxle case	21 Reverse shift rail
9 Outer bearing race	22 Spring pins
10 Spacers	23 1st/2nd shift rail
11 Breather	24 1st/2nd shift fork
12 Gasket	25 3rd/4th shift rail
13 Poppet plugs	26 3rd/4th shift fork

27 Interlock plungers
28 Output shaft assembly
29 Spacer
30 Differential assembly
31 Intermediate gear assembly
32 Bolts
33 Bearing retainer
34 Input shaft assembly
35 Bearing outer race
36 Clutch housing

6 Remove the exhaust system components as necessary for clearance.

7 Support the engine. This can be done from above with an engine hoist, or by placing a jack (with a block of wood as an insulator) under the engine oil pan. The engine must remain supported at all times while the transaxle is out of the vehicle!

8 Remove any chassis or suspension components that will interfere with transaxle removal (Chapter 10).

9 Disconnect the driveaxles from the transaxle (Chapter 8).

10 Support the transaxle with a jack, then remove the bolts securing the transaxle to the engine. You'll have to remove the bellhousing cover to gain access to the lower transaxle-to-engine bolts (see illustration).

11 Remove the transaxle mount nuts and bolts. Unbolt and remove the transaxle mount bracket.

12 Make a final check that all wires and hoses have been disconnected from the transaxle, then carefully pull the transaxle and jack away from the engine.

13 Once the input shaft is clear, lower the transaxle and remove it from under the vehicle.

14 With the transaxle removed, the clutch components are now accessible and can be inspected. In most cases, new clutch components should be routinely installed when the transaxle is removed.

Installation

15 If removed, install the clutch components (Chapter 8.)

16 With the transaxle secured to the jack with a chain, raise it into position behind the engine, then carefully slide it forward, engaging the input shaft with the clutch plate hub splines. Do not use excessive force to install the transaxle — if the input shaft does not slide into place, readjust the angle of the transaxle so it is level and/or turn the input shaft so the splines engage properly with the clutch plate hub.

17 Install the transaxle-to-engine bolts. Tighten the bolts securely.

18 Install the transaxle mount bracket and the mount nuts or bolts.

19 Install the chassis and suspension components which were removed. Tighten all nuts and bolts securely.

20 Remove the jacks supporting the transaxle and engine.

21 Install the various items removed previously, referring to Chapter 8

7A

4.4b Typical five speed transaxle components – exploded view
(1986 through 1989 models shown)

1	5th gear actuator	8	Input shaft assembly
2	Collar	9	Bearing retainer
3	O-ring	10	Spacer
4	Seat	11	Bearing outer race
5	Locking plate	12	Intermediate gear assembly
6	Select rail fork assembly	13	Speedometer gear assembly
7	Seat	14	Reverse idler gear shaft

15 Reverse idler gear
16 Reverse shift gear
17 Output shaft assembly
18 Outer bearing race
19 Spacer
20 Differential assembly
21 Reverse shift rail
22 1st/2nd shift rail
23 1st/2nd shift fork
24 3rd/4th shift fork
25 Spring pin
26 3rd/4th shift rail
27 5th gear lug
28 Selector spacer
29 Poppet ball
30 Poppet spring
31 Plug
32 Interlock plunger
33 Interlock plunger
34 Transaxle bracket
35 Clutch cable bracket
36 Backup light switch
37 Gasket
38 Steel ball
39 Transaxle case
40 Breather
41 5th gear actuator switch
42 Clutch housing

for installation of the driveaxles and Chapter 4 for information regarding the exhaust system components.

22 Make a final check that all wires, hoses, linkages and the speedometer cable have been connected and that the transaxle has been filled with lubricant to the proper level (Chapter 1).

23 Connect the negative battery cable. Road test the vehicle for proper operation and check for leaks.

---

4   Manual transaxle overhaul — general information

Refer to illustrations 4.4a and 4.4b

Overhauling a manual transaxle is a difficult job for the do-it-yourselfer. It involves the disassembly and reassembly of many small parts. Numerous clearances must be precisely measured and, if necessary, changed with select fit spacers and snap-rings. As a result, if transaxle problems arise, it can be removed and installed by a competent do-it-yourselfer, but overhaul should be left to a transmission repair shop. Rebuilt transaxles may be available — check with your dealer parts department and auto parts stores. At any rate, the time and money involved in an overhaul is almost sure to exceed the cost of a rebuilt unit.

Nevertheless, it's not impossible for an inexperienced mechanic to rebuild a transaxle if the special tools are available and the job is done in a deliberate step-by-step manner so nothing is overlooked.

The tools necessary for an overhaul include internal and external snap-ring pliers, a bearing puller, a slide hammer, a set of pin punches, a dial indicator and possibly a hydraulic press. In addition, a large, sturdy workbench and a vise or transaxle stand will be required.

During disassembly of the transaxle, make careful notes of how each piece comes off, where it fits in relation to other pieces and what holds it in place. Exploded views are included **(see illustrations)** to show where the parts go — but actually noting how they are installed when you remove the parts will make it much easier to get the transaxle back together.

Before taking the transaxle apart for repair, it will help if you have some idea what area of the transaxle is malfunctioning. Certain problems can be closely tied to specific areas in the transaxle, which can make component examination and replacement easier. Refer to the *Troubleshooting* section at the front of this manual for information regarding possible sources of trouble.

Chapter 7 Part B Automatic transaxle

Contents

Specifications

Clearances

Shift lever assembly adjusting sleeve-to-lever end clearance	0.677 to 0.705 in (17.2 to 17.9 mm)
Throttle valve (TV) cable clearance	0.04 ± 0.02 in (1 ± 0.5 mm)

Torque specifications

	Ft-lbs	Nm
Transaxle-to-engine bolts		
8 x 14 mm	7 to 9	10 to 12
8 x 20 mm	11 to 16	15 to 22
8 x 60 mm	22 to 25	30 to 34
10 x 40 mm	31 to 40	43 to 55
10 x 55 mm	16 to 23	22 to 32
10 x 65 mm	31 to 40	43 to 55
Torque converter-to-driveplate bolts	25 to 30	34 to 42
Drain and filler plugs	See Chapter 1	
Throttle valve lower cable bracket bolt	10	14
Neutral start switch bolts	8	11
Fluid pan bolts	See Chapter 1	
Starter motor bolts	16 to 23	22 to 32

7B

---

1 General information

All vehicles covered in this manual come equipped with either a four or five speed manual transaxle or an automatic transaxle. All information on the automatic transaxle is included in this Part of Chapter 7. Information for the manual transaxle can be found in Part A of this Chapter.

Due to the complexity of the automatic transaxle and the need for specialized equipment to perform most service operations, this Chapter contains only general diagnosis, routine maintenance, adjustment and removal and installation procedures.

If the transaxle requires major repair work, it should be left to a dealer service department or an automotive or transmission repair shop. You can, however, remove and install the transaxle yourself and save the expense, even if the repair work is done by a transmission shop.

2 Diagnosis — general

Note: *Automatic transaxle malfunctions may be caused by four general conditions: poor engine performance, improper adjustments, hydraulic malfunctions or mechanical malfunctions. Diagnosis of these problems should always begin with a check of the easily repaired items: fluid level and condition (Chapter 1), shift linkage adjustment and throttle linkage adjustment. Next, perform a road test to determine if the problem has been corrected or if more diagnosis is necessary. If the problem persists after the preliminary tests and corrections are completed, additional diagnosis should be done by a dealer service department or transmission repair shop. Refer to the Troubleshooting section at the front of this manual for transaxle problem diagnosis.*

Preliminary checks

1   Drive the vehicle to warm the transaxle to normal operating temperature.
2   Check the fluid level as described in Chapter 1:
  a) If the fluid level is unusually low, add enough fluid to bring the level within the designated area of the dipstick, then check for external leaks.
  b) If the fluid level is abnormally high, drain off the excess, then check the drained fluid for contamination by coolant. The presence of engine coolant in the automatic transmission fluid indicates that a failure has occurred in the internal radiator walls that separate the coolant from the transmission fluid (see Chapter 3).
  c) If the fluid is foaming, drain it and refill the transaxle, then check for coolant in the fluid or a high fluid level.
3   Check the engine idle speed. **Note:** *If the engine is malfunctioning, do not proceed with the preliminary checks until it has been repaired and runs normally.*
4   Check the throttle valve cable for freedom of movement. Adjust it if necessary (Section 6). **Note:** *The throttle valve cable may function properly when the engine is shut off and cold, but it may malfunction once the engine is hot. Check it cold and at normal engine operating temperature.*
5   Inspect the shift control cable (Section 5). Make sure that it's properly adjusted and that the linkage operates smoothly.

Fluid leak diagnosis

6   Most fluid leaks are easy to locate visually. Repair usually consists of replacing a seal or gasket. If a leak is difficult to find, the following procedure may help.
7   Identify the fluid. Make sure it's transmission fluid and not engine oil or brake fluid (automatic transmission fluid is a deep red color).
8   Try to pinpoint the source of the leak. Drive the vehicle several miles, then park it over a large sheet of cardboard. After a minute or two, you should be able to locate the leak by determining the source of the fluid dripping onto the cardboard.
9   Make a careful visual inspection of the suspected component and the area immediately around it. Pay particular attention to gasket mating surfaces. A mirror is often helpful for finding leaks in areas that are hard to see.
10   If the leak still cannot be found, clean the suspected area thoroughly with a degreaser or solvent, then dry it.
11   Drive the vehicle for several miles at normal operating temperature and varying speeds. After driving the vehicle, visually inspect the suspected component again.
12   Once the leak has been located, the cause must be determined before it can be properly repaired. If a gasket is replaced but the sealing flange is bent, the new gasket will not stop the leak. The bent flange must be straightened.
13   Before attempting to repair a leak, check to make sure that the following conditions are corrected or they may cause another leak. **Note:** *Some of the following conditions cannot be fixed without highly specialized tools and expertise. Such problems must be referred to a transmission shop or a dealer service department.*

Gasket leaks

14   Check the pan periodically. Make sure the bolts are tight, no bolts are missing, the gasket is in good condition and the pan is flat (dents in the pan may indicate damage to the valve body inside).
15   If the pan gasket is leaking, the fluid level or the fluid pressure may be too high, the vent may be plugged, the pan bolts may be too tight,

the pan sealing flange may be warped, the sealing surface of the transaxle housing may be damaged, the gasket may be damaged or the transaxle casting may be cracked or porous. If sealant instead of gasket material has been used to form a seal between the pan and the transaxle housing, it may be the wrong sealant.

Seal leaks

16   If a transaxle seal is leaking, the fluid level or pressure may be too high, the vent may be plugged, the seal bore may be damaged, the seal itself may be damaged or improperly installed, the surface of the shaft protruding through the seal may be damaged or a loose bearing may be causing excessive shaft movement.
17   Make sure the dipstick tube seal is in good condition and the tube is properly seated. Periodically check the area around the speedometer gear or sensor for leakage. If transmission fluid is evident, check the O-ring for damage. Also inspect the side gear shaft oil seals for leakage.

Case leaks

18   If the case itself appears to be leaking, the casting is porous and will have to be repaired or replaced.
19   Make sure the oil cooler hose fittings are tight and in good condition.

Fluid comes out vent pipe or fill tube

20   If this condition occurs, the transaxle is overfilled, there is coolant in the fluid, the case is porous, the dipstick is incorrect, the vent is plugged or the drain back holes are plugged.

3 Oil seal replacement

Refer to illustrations 3.4 and 3.6

1   Oil leaks frequently occur due to wear of the driveaxle oil seals, and/or the speedometer drive gear O-ring. Replacement of these seals is relatively easy, since the repairs can usually be performed without removing the transaxle from the vehicle.
2   The driveaxle oil seals are located at the sides of the transaxle, where the driveaxles are attached. If leakage at the seal is suspected, raise the vehicle and support it securely on jackstands. If the seal is leaking, lubricant will be found on the sides of the transaxle.
3   Refer to Chapter 8 and remove the driveaxles.
4   Using a screwdriver or pry bar, carefully pry the oil seal out of the transaxle bore **(see illustration)**.
5   If the oil seal cannot be removed with a screwdriver or pry bar, a special oil seal removal tool (available at auto parts stores) will be required.
6   Using a large section of pipe or a large deep socket as a drift, install the new oil seal **(see illustration)**. Drive it into the bore squarely and make sure it's completely seated.
7   Install the driveaxle(s). Be careful not to damage the lip of the new seal.
8   The speedometer cable and driven gear housing is located on the transaxle housing. Look for lubricant around the cable housing to determine if the O-ring is leaking.
9   Disconnect the speedometer cable from the transaxle.
10   Install a new O-ring on the driven gear housing and reinstall the speedometer cable assembly.

3.4   Insert the tip of a large screwdriver (arrow) behind the oil seal and very carefully pry it out

3.6 Apply a thin layer of grease to the outer edge of the new seal and carefully tap it into the bore with a large socket and a hammer

4.1 Pry on the transaxle mount with a large screwdriver to check for movement

4 Transaxle mount — check and replacement

Refer to illustration 4.1

1   Insert a large screwdriver or pry bar between the mount and transaxle bracket and pry it back and forth **(see illustration)**.
2   The transaxle bracket should not move away from the mount. If it does, replace the mount.
3   To replace a mount, support the transaxle with a jack, remove the nut and through bolt and the bracket-to-transaxle bolts, then detach the mount. It may be necessary to lower the transaxle slightly to provide enough clearance to remove the mount.
4   Installation is the reverse of removal.

5 Shift linkage — removal, installation and adjustment

Removal
Refer to illustrations 5.2 and 5.5

1   Disconnect the negative cable from the battery.
2   Working in the engine compartment, remove the air cleaner assembly and disconnect the shift cable at the bracket and transaxle lever **(see illustration)**.
3   Raise the vehicle and support it securely on jackstands.
4   Working under the vehicle, remove the shift cable assembly mounting bolt and nuts.
5   Remove the selector lever assembly mounting nuts **(see illustration)**.

7B

5.2 On 1989 and earlier models, the shift cable is attached to the lever on the transaxle by a cotter pin and washers and to the bracket by a spring clip or two large nuts (one on either side of the bracket)

5.5 Typical shift linkage components – exploded view (1986 through 1989 models shown)

1   *Handle set screw*
2   *Handle*
3   *Console (not shown)*
4   *Shift indicator light bulb*
5   *Indicator panel*
6   *Bolt*
7   *Shift cable adjusting nuts*
8   *Cable mounting bolt*
9   *Cable mounting bracket nuts*
10 *Selector lever assembly mounting nuts*
11 *Selector lever assembly*
12 *Gasket*
13 *Shift cable*
14 *Selector lever*

5.9 Make sure the toothed washer is installed as shown so the cable won't slip

6   Working inside the vehicle, remove the set screw, grasp the selector lever handle, press the lockout button in and pull up sharply to remove the handle. Remove the center console (Chapter 11). Disconnect the shift cable and remove the selector lever assembly **(see illustration 5.5)**.

7   Remove the shift cable from under the vehicle.

Installation
Refer to illustration 5.9

8   Install the selector lever assembly. Tighten the mounting nuts securely.

9   Install the shift cable and connect it to the transaxle and selector lever. Make sure the toothed washer is correctly positioned on the transaxle mounting bracket **(see illustration)**.

Adjustment
Refer to illustration 5.11

10   Place the selector lever in Neutral.

11   Turn the lever adjusting sleeve to achieve the specified sleeve-to-lever end clearance. Make sure the angled surface of the sleeve faces the driver's side after adjustment **(see illustration)**. Apply a small dab of multi-purpose grease to the outer edge and the angled surface of the sleeve.

12   Install the console and the selector lever handle.

13   If necessary, eliminate any slack in the shift cable by turning the adjusting nuts on the transaxle shift lever **(see illustration 5.5)**.

14   Check the operation of the transaxle in each selector lever position (try to start the engine in each gear — the starter should operate in Park and Neutral only). Adjust the Neutral start switch if necessary (Section 7).

---

6   Throttle valve (TV) cable — check and adjustment

Refer to illustration 6.3

1   The throttle valve (TV) cable adjustment is very important to proper transaxle operation. The cable positions a valve inside the transaxle which controls shift speed, shift quality and part throttle downshift sensitivity. If the cable is adjusted too short, early shifts and slippage between shifts may occur. If the cable is adjusted too long, shifts may be delayed and part throttle downshifts may be erratic.

2   Start and run the engine until it reaches normal operating temperature. Make sure the choke is off and the carburetor throttle lever is at the normal curb idle position. Turn off the engine.

3   Pull up on the cable cover B **(see illustration)** to expose the stopper and cover A, then loosen the lower cable bracket bolt.

4   Move the lower cable until the stopper is the specified distance from cover A.

5   Tighten the cable bracket bolt to the specified torque and recheck the clearance.

6   Open the throttle lever to the wide open position and make sure the cable does not bind.

5.11 Turn the shift lever sleeve to achieve the specified clearance to the end of the lever (A) — the angled face (B) must face the driver's side of the vehicle after adjustment

6.3 Pull up on the Throttle Valve (TV) inner cable cover B and check the stopper-to-cover A clearance — loosen the lower cable bracket bolt to make adjustments

7 Neutral start switch — removal, installation and adjustment

Refer to illustration 7.3

Removal

1 Remove the battery.
2 Place the selector lever in Neutral.
3 Remove the nut and separate the manual control lever from the shaft on the transaxle (see illustration).
4 Unplug the Neutral start switch wire harness connector.
5 Remove the two Neutral start switch mounting bolts.
6 Lift the switch off the transaxle.

Installation

7 Place the new switch in position and install the mounting bolts loosely.
8 Install the manual control lever and nut. Tighten the nut securely.
9 Plug in the wire harness connector.

Adjustment

10 Rotate the Neutral start switch until the shorter of the two shift levers is aligned with the flange on the switch body, then tighten the bolts to the specified torque (see illustration 7.3).
11 Check the operation of the transaxle in each selector lever position (try to start the engine in each gear — the starter should operate in Park and Neutral only). Readjust the switch if the engine starts in any other gears.

8 Automatic transaxle — removal and installation

Refer to illustration 8.5

Removal

1 Disconnect the negative cable from the battery.
2 Raise the vehicle and support it securely on jackstands.
3 Drain the transaxle fluid (Chapter 1).
4 Remove the torque converter cover.
5 Mark the torque converter and the driveplate with white paint so they can be installed in the same position (see illustration).
6 Remove the three torque converter-to-driveplate bolts. Turn the crankshaft pulley bolt for access to each bolt.
7 Remove the starter motor (Chapter 5).
8 Disconnect the driveaxles from the transaxle (Chapter 8).
9 Disconnect the speedometer cable.
10 Disconnect the wire harness from the transaxle.
11 On models so equipped, disconnect the vacuum hose(s).
12 Remove any exhaust components which will interfere with transaxle removal (chapter 4).
13 Disconnect the TV cable.
14 Disconnect the shift linkage.
15 Support the engine using a hoist from above or a jack and a block of wood under the oil pan to spread the load.
16 Support the transaxle with a jack — preferably a special jack made for this purpose. Safety chains will help steady the transaxle on the jack.
17 Remove any chassis or suspension components which will interfere with transaxle removal.
18 Remove the bolts securing the transaxle to the engine.
19 Remove the nuts and bolts and detach the transaxle mount.
20 Lower the transaxle slightly and disconnect and plug the transaxle cooler lines.
21 Move the transaxle back to disengage it from the engine block dowel pins and make sure the torque converter is detached from the driveplate. Secure the torque converter to the transaxle so it will not fall out during removal. Lower the transaxle from the vehicle.

Installation

22 Prior to installation, make sure that the torque converter hub is securely engaged in the pump.
23 With the transaxle secured to the jack, raise it into position. Be sure to keep it level so the torque converter does not slide out. Connect the fluid cooler lines.
24 Turn the torque converter to line up the holes with the holes in the driveplate. The white paint mark on the torque converter and the

7.3 Turn the Neutral start switch until the flange is lined up with the shorter of the two control levers (A), then tighten the bolts

8.5 Mark the driveplate and the torque converter with white paint so they can be reinstalled in the same relationship

7B

driveplate made in Step 5 must line up.
25 Move the transaxle forward carefully until the dowel pins and the torque converter are engaged.
26 Install the transaxle-to-engine bolts. Tighten them securely. Install the transaxle mount.
27 Install the torque converter-to-driveplate bolts. Tighten the bolts to the specified torque.
28 Install the transaxle and any suspension and chassis components which were removed. Tighten the bolts and nuts to the specified torque.
29 Remove the jacks supporting the transaxle and the engine.
30 Install the starter motor (Chapter 5).
31 Connect the vacuum hose(s) (if equipped).
32 Connect the shift and TV linkage.
33 Plug in the transaxle electrical connectors.
34 Install the torque converter cover.
35 Connect the driveaxles (Chapter 8).
36 Connect the speedometer cable.
37 Adjust the shift linkage (Section 5).
38 Install any exhaust system components that were removed or disconnected.
39 Lower the vehicle.
40 Fill the transaxle (Chapter 1), run the vehicle and check for fluid leaks.

Chapter 8   Clutch and driveaxles

Contents

Specifications

Clutch
Pedal free play .... See Chapter 1
Clutch disc lining minimum thickness... .... 1/16 in (1.58 mm) above rivet heads

Driveaxles
Inner CV joint assembled length....................................... 3.0 ± 0.04 in (75 ± 1 mm)
Distance from outer CV joint to dynamic damper .... 15 in (383.5 mm)

Torque specifications

	Ft-lbs	Nm
Pressure plate-to-flywheel bolts....................................	11 to 15	15 to 20
Driveaxle hub nut..	144 to 187	195 to 253
Wheel lug nuts	See Chapter 1	

1   General information

The information in this Chapter deals with the components from the rear of the engine to the drive wheels, except for the transaxle, which is dealt with in the previous Chapter. For the purposes of this Chapter, these components are grouped into two categories; clutch and driveaxles. Separate Sections within this Chapter offer general descriptions and checking procedures for components in each of the two groups.

Since nearly all the procedures covered in this Chapter involve working under the vehicle, make sure it's securely supported on sturdy jackstands or on a hoist where the vehicle can be easily raised and lowered.

2   Clutch – description and check

Refer to illustration 2.1

1   All vehicles with a manual transaxle use a single dry plate, diaphragm spring type clutch **(see illustration)**. The clutch disc has a splined hub which allows it to slide along the splines of the transaxle input shaft. The clutch and pressure plate are held in contact by spring pressure exerted by the diaphragm in the pressure plate.

2   The clutch release mechanism includes a clutch pedal, a clutch cable (1986 through 1989 models) or clutch hydraulic system (1990 and later models) that operates the clutch release fork and the release bearing.

3   When pressure is applied to the clutch pedal to release the clutch, the clutch cable or hydraulic system moves the outer end of the clutch release fork. As the release fork pivots, the shaft fingers push against the release bearing. The release bearing pushes against the fingers of the diaphragm spring of the pressure plate assembly, which in turn releases the clutch plate.

4   Terminology can be a problem when discussing the clutch components because common names are in some cases different from those used by the manufacturer. For example, the driven plate is also called the clutch plate or disc, the clutch release bearing is sometimes called a throwout bearing, the release cylinder is sometimes called the release lever.

5   Other than to replace components with obvious damage, some preliminary check should be performed to diagnose clutch problems.

a) On 1986 through 1989 models, the first check should be of the clutch cable adjustment. If there is too much slack in the cable, the clutch won't release completely, making gear engagement difficult or impossible. Refer to Section 5 for the adjustment procedure.

b) On 1990 and later models, the first check should be of the fluid level in the clutch master cylinder. If the fluid level is low, add fluid as necessary and inspect the hydraulic system for leaks. If the master cylinder reservoir has run dry, bleed the system as described in Section 8 and retest the clutch operation.

c) To check "clutch spin down time," run the engine at normal idle speed with the transaxle in Neutral (clutch pedal up – engaged). Disengage the clutch (pedal down), wait several seconds and shift the transaxle into Reverse. No grinding noise should be heard. A grinding noise would most likely indicate a problem in the pressure plate or the clutch disc.

d) To check for complete clutch release, run the engine (with the parking brake applied to prevent movement) and hold the clutch pedal approximately 1/2-inch from the floor. Shift the transaxle between 1st gear and Reverse several times. If the shift is rough, component failure is indicated, or as stated above, the cable is out of adjustment.

e) Visually inspect the pivot bushing at the top of the clutch pedal to make sure there is no binding or excessive play.

f) A clutch pedal that is difficult to operate is most likely caused by a faulty clutch cable. Check the cable where it enters the housing for frayed wires, rust and other signs of corrosion. If it looks good, lubricate the cable with penetrating oil. If pedal operation improves, the cable is worn out and should be replaced.

---

3 Clutch components – removal, inspection and installation

Warning: *Dust produced by clutch wear and deposited on clutch components may contain asbestos, which is hazardous to your health. DO NOT blow it out with compressed air and DO NOT inhale it. DO NOT use gasoline or petroleum-based solvents to remove the dust. Brake system cleaner should be used to flush the dust into a drain pan. After the clutch components are wiped clean with a rag, dispose of the contaminated rags and cleaner in a covered, marked container.*

Removal

Refer to illustration 3.5

1   Access to the clutch components is normally accomplished by removing the transaxle, leaving the engine in the vehicle. If, of course, the engine is being removed for major overhaul, then check the clutch for wear and replace worn components as necessary. However, the relatively low cost of the clutch components compared to the time and trouble spent gaining access to them warrants their replacement anytime the engine or transaxle is removed, unless they are new or in near perfect condition. The following procedures are based on the

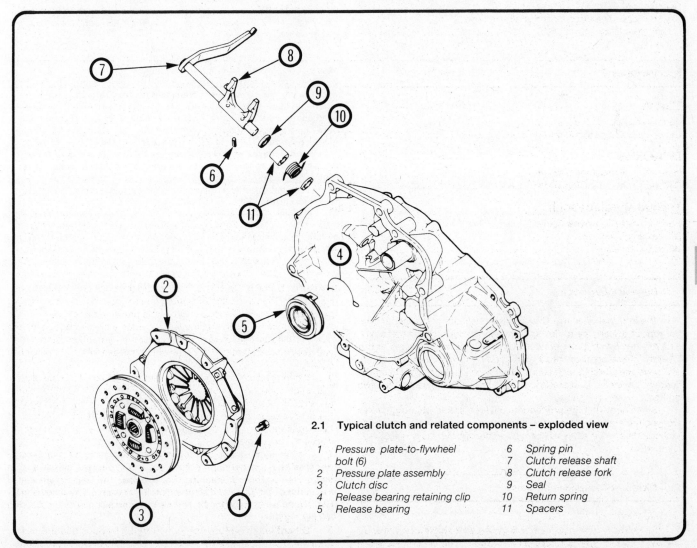

2.1 Typical clutch and related components – exploded view

1 Pressure plate-to-flywheel bolt (6)	6 Spring pin
2 Pressure plate assembly	7 Clutch release shaft
3 Clutch disc	8 Clutch release fork
4 Release bearing retaining clip	9 Seal
5 Release bearing	10 Return spring
	11 Spacers

3.5 Make an index mark across the pressure plate and flywheel (just in case you're going to reuse the same pressure plate)

3.9 The clutch disc

1 Lining — this will wear
down in use
2 Marks — ''Flywheel Side''
or something similar

3 Rivets — secure the lining
and will damage the pressure
plate if allowed to contact it

NORMAL FINGER WEAR   EXCESSIVE FINGER WEAR

EXCESSIVE WEAR

EXCESSIVE FINGER WEAR   BROKEN OR BENT FINGERS

3.11a Replace the pressure plate if the fingers are worn excessively, broken or bent

3.11b Also examine the pressure plate friction surface for score marks, cracks and evidence of overheating (blue discolored areas)

assumption the engine will stay in place.

2   Referring to Chapter 7 Part A, remove the transaxle from the vehicle. Support the engine while the transaxle is out. Preferably, an engine hoist should be used to support it from above. However, if a jack is used underneath the engine, make sure a piece of wood is positioned between the jack and oil pan to spread the load. **Caution:** *The pickup for the oil pump is very close to the bottom of the oil pan. If the pan is bent or distorted in any way, engine oil starvation could occur.*

3   The clutch fork and release bearing can remain attached to the transaxle housing for the time being.

4   To support the clutch disc during removal, install a clutch alignment tool through the clutch disc hub.

5   Carefully inspect the flywheel and pressure plate for indexing marks. The marks are usually an X, an O or a white letter. If they cannot be found, scribe marks yourself so the pressure plate and the flywheel will be in the same alignment during installation **(see illustration)**.

6   Turning each bolt only 1/4-turn at a time, loosen the pressure plate-to-flywheel bolts. Work in a criss-cross pattern until all spring pressure is relieved. Then hold the pressure plate securely and completely remove the bolts, followed by the pressure plate and clutch disc.

Inspection
Refer to illustrations 3.9, 3.11a and 3.11b

7   Ordinarily, when a problem occurs in the clutch, it can be attributed to wear of the clutch driven plate assembly (clutch disc). However, all components should be inspected at this time.

8   Inspect the flywheel for cracks, heat checking, grooves and other obvious defects. If the imperfections are slight, a machine shop can machine the surface flat and smooth, which is highly recommended regardless of the surface appearance. Refer to Chapter 2, Part A for the flywheel removal and installation procedure.

9   Inspect the lining on the clutch disc. There should be at least 1/16-inch of lining above the rivet heads. Check for loose rivets, distortion, cracks, broken springs and other obvious damage **(see illustration)**. As mentioned above, ordinarily the clutch disc is routinely replaced, so if in doubt about the condition, replace it with a new one.

10   The release bearing should also be replaced along with the clutch disc (see Section 4).

11   Check the machined surfaces and the diaphragm spring fingers of the pressure plate **(see illustrations)**. If the surface is grooved or

3.13   Center the clutch disc in the pressure plate with a clutch alignment tool

4.5   Drive out the spring pins with a small pin punch and hammer — use new pins for reassembly

Apply grease

4.7   Pack the inner groove of the release bearing with high-temperature grease

otherwise damaged, replace the pressure plate. Also check for obvious damage, distortion, cracking, etc. Light glazing can be removed with emery cloth. If a new pressure plate is required, new and factory-rebuilt units are available.

Installation

Refer to illustration 3.13

12   Before installation, clean the flywheel and pressure plate machined surfaces with lacquer thinner or acetone. It's important that no oil or grease is on these surfaces or the lining of the clutch disc. Handle the parts only with clean hands.

13   Position the clutch disc and pressure plate against the flywheel with the clutch held in place with an alignment tool **(see illustration)**. Make sure it's installed properly (most replacement clutch plates will be marked ''flywheel side'' or something similar — if not marked, install the clutch disc with the damper springs toward the transaxle).

14   Tighten the pressure plate-to-flywheel bolts only finger tight, working around the pressure plate.

15   Center the clutch disc by ensuring the alignment tool extends through the splined hub and into the pocket in the crankshaft. Wiggle the tool up, down or side-to-side as needed to center the disc. Tighten the pressure plate-to-flywheel bolts a little at a time, working in a criss-cross pattern to prevent distorting the cover. After all of the bolts are snug, tighten them to the specified torque. Remove the alignment tool.

16   Using high temperature grease, lubricate the inner groove of the release bearing (refer to Section 4). Also place grease on the release lever contact areas and the transaxle input shaft bearing retainer.

17   Install the clutch release bearing as described in Section 4.

18   Install the transaxle and all components removed previously. Tighten all fasteners to the proper torque specifications.

4   Clutch release bearing, fork and shaft – removal and installation

Refer to illustrations 4.5 and 4.7

Warning: *Dust produced by clutch wear and deposited on clutch components may contain asbestos, which is hazardous to your health. DO NOT blow it out with compressed air and DO NOT inhale it. DO NOT use gasoline or petroleum-based solvents to remove the dust. Brake system cleaner should be used to flush the dust into a drain pan. After the clutch components are wiped clean with a rag, dispose of the contaminated rags and cleaner in a labeled, covered container.*

1   Refer to Chapter 7, Part A and remove the transaxle.

2   Using a pair of pliers, pull the ends of the release bearing retaining clip (or return clip) out of the release fork **(see illustration 2.1)**.

3   Remove the release bearing from the clutch housing. Be careful not to lose the retaining clip (or return clip).

4   Hold the center of the bearing and turn the outer portion while applying pressure. If it doesn't turn smoothly or if it's noisy, it must

be replaced. It's a good idea to replace it anyway, when you consider the time and effort spent on removing the transaxle. However, if you elect to reinstall the old bearing, wipe it off with a clean rag. Don't immerse the bearing in solvent — it's sealed for life and would be ruined by the solvent.

5   Check the release fork ends for excessive wear. If the fork must be replaced, drive the spring pins out of the fork and shaft with a small pin punch and a hammer **(see illustration)**. Discard the spring pins, slide the shaft out of the clutch housing and remove the fork, spring and spacers.

6   Lubricate the release shaft bore in the clutch housing with high-temperature grease, slide the shaft part way into the housing and place the spacers, spring and fork in position. Continue to slide the shaft through the components and align the spring pin holes. Insert new spring pins and drive them into position.

7   Lubricate the release fork ends with a small amount of high-temperature grease (don't overdo it). Pack the groove in the inner diameter of the release bearing with the same grease **(see illustration)** and position it against the release fork.

8   Install the release bearing retaining clip. Make sure the clip is secured in the bearing groove and the ends are inserted into the release fork properly.

9   Install the transaxle.

5   Clutch cable – removal, installation and adjustment (1986 through 1989 models)

Refer to illustrations 5.3 and 5.4

Removal

1   Disconnect the negative battery cable (ground cable) from the battery.

8

5.3   The clutch cable is secured to the release shaft lever by a clevis pin and cotter pin – once they're removed, the cable housing and grommet can be pulled (or pryed, if necessary) out of the bracket

2   Unscrew the adjuster wheel completely to produce slack in the cable.
3   Remove the cotter pin from the clutch release lever, pull out the clevis pin and disconnect the cable housing from the bracket **(see illustration)**.
4   Working under the dash, disconnect the cable end from the top of the clutch pedal **(see illustration)**.
5   Pull the cable through the firewall from the engine side. If the rubber grommet sticks in the firewall, pry it out with a screwdriver.

Installation and adjustment
6   When installing the cable, lightly lubricate the ends with multipurpose grease. Install the cable by reversing the removal procedure, then adjust the clutch pedal free play by following the procedure in Chapter 1.

6   Clutch release cylinder – removal and installation (1990 and later models)

1   Disconnect the negative cable from the battery.
2   Raise the vehicle and support it securely on jackstands.
3   Loosen the bleed plug on the release cylinder (it's bolted to the transaxle) and place a drain pan under the bleed plug. Apply the clutch pedal several times to force the hydraulic brake fluid out of the system. Continue to apply the clutch pedal until all fluid is expelled. Tighten the bleed plug securely. **Caution:** *Don't allow hydraulic brake fluid to come into contact with paint, as it will damage the finish.*
4   Disconnect the hydraulic line at the release cylinder. Have a small can and rags handy, as some residual fluid will be spilled as the line is removed.
5   Remove the snap-ring and remove the clevis pin. Disconnect the pushrod from the transaxle lever.
6   Unbolt the release cylinder from the clutch housing and remove the release cylinder.
7   Installation is the reverse of the removal procedure. Bleed the system (see Section 8).

7   Clutch master cylinder – removal and installation (1990 and later models)

Refer to illustration 7.4
1   Disconnect the negative cable from the battery.
2   Raise the vehicle and support it securely on jackstands.
3   Loosen the bleed plug on the release cylinder and place a drain pan under the bleed plug. Apply the clutch pedal several times to force the hydraulic brake fluid out of the system. Continue to apply the clutch pedal until all fluid is expelled. Tighten the bleed plug securely. **Caution:** *Don't allow hydraulic brake fluid to come into contact with paint as it will damage the finish.*
4   Disconnect the hydraulic line at the master cylinder **(see illustration)**. Have a small can and rags handy, as some residual fluid will be spilled as the line is removed.
5   Working inside the vehicle, remove the cotter pin, washer and re-

5.4   Unhook the cable end from the top of the clutch pedal

7.4 Clutch master cylinder and reservoir (hydraulically actuated clutch models)

5   *Cap*
6   *Clamp*
7   *Reservoir*
8   *Master cylinder*

move the clevis pin. Disconnect the pushrod from the clutch pedal.
6   Working in the engine compartment, remove the nuts securing the master cylinder to the bulkhead and remove the maser cylinder. Installation is the reverse of removal. Be sure to bleed the system (see Section 8).

8   Clutch hydraulic system – bleeding (1990 and later models)

1   The hydraulic system should be bled to remove all air whenever any part of the system has been removed or if the fluid level has been allowed to fall so low that air has been drawn into the master cylinder. The procedure is very similar to bleeding a brake system.
2   Fill the master cylinder with new brake fluid conforming to DOT 3 specifications. **Caution:** *Do not re-use any of the fluid coming from the system during the bleeding operation or use fluid which has been inside an open container for an extended period of time.*
3   Raise the vehicle and place it securely on jackstands to gain access to the release cylinder, which is located on the side of the clutch housing.
4   Remove the dust cap which fits over the bleed plug and push a length of plastic hose over the plug. Place the other end of the hose into a clear container with about two inches of brake fluid. The hose end must be in the fluid at the bottom of the container.
5   Have an assistant depress the clutch pedal several times and keep it depressed. Open the bleeder valve on the release cylinder, allowing fluid to flow through the hose. Close the bleeder valve when your assistant signals that the clutch pedal is at the bottom of its travel. Once closed, have your assistant release the pedal. **Caution:** *The rapid-repeated operation of the clutch pedal may cause the release cylinder's piston to be forced out of the release cylinder body. Allow the clutch pedal to return to the fully raised position before depressing it again.*

10.1   With the vehicle on the ground, loosen the driveaxle hub nut

10.4b   Pull out on the steering knuckle and remove the driveaxle from the hub splines

10.4a   If the driveaxle won't slide out of the hub easily, a puller can be used to push it out – DO NOT hammer on the end of the driveaxle to force it out!

10.5   Be careful when prying the inner end of the axle out of the transaxle (the seal is very close to the edge of the joint and could be damaged if the pry bar is inserted too far)

6   Continue this process until all air is evacuated from the system, indicated by a solid stream of fluid being ejected from the bleed plug each time with no air bubbles in the hose or container. Keep a close watch on the fluid level inside the clutch master cylinder reservoir – if the level drops too low, air will be sucked back into the system and the process will have to be started all over again.

7   Install the dust cap and lower the vehicle. Check carefully for proper operation before placing the vehicle in normal service.

---

9   Driveaxles – general information and inspection

Power is transmitted from the transaxle to the wheels through a pair of driveaxles. The inner end of each driveaxle is splined to the differential. The outer ends of the driveaxles are splined to the axle hubs and locked in place by an axle nut.

The inner ends of the driveaxles are equipped with sliding double offset joints, which are capable of both angular and axial motion. Each inner joint assembly consists of an inner race, ball bearing and cage assembly and an outer race (housing) in which the inner bearing assembly is free to slide in and out as the driveaxle moves up and down with the wheel. The inner joints are rebuildable (Section 8).

Each outer joint, which consists of ball bearings running between an inner race and an outer cage, is capable of angular but not axial movement. The outer joints are neither rebuildable nor removable. Should one of them fail, a new driveaxle/outboard joint assembly must be installed.

The boots should be periodically inspected for damage, leaking lubricant and cuts. Damaged CV joint boots must be replaced immediately or the joints can be damaged. Boot replacement involves removal of the driveaxle (Section 7). **Note:** *Some auto parts stores carry "split" type replacement boots, which can be installed without removing the driveaxle from the vehicle. This is a convenient alternative; however, it's recommended that the driveaxle be removed and the CV joint disassembled and cleaned to ensure that the joint is free from contaminants such as moisture and dirt, which will accelerate CV joint wear.* The most common symptom of worn or damaged CV joints, besides

lubricant leaks, is a clicking noise in turns, a clunk when accelerating from a coasting condition or vibration at highway speeds.

To check for wear in the CV joints and driveaxle shafts, grasp each axle (one at a time) and rotate it in both directions while holding the CV joint housings, inspecting for movement, indicating worn splines or sloppy CV joints. Also check the driveaxle shafts for cracks, dents, twisting and bending.

---

10   Driveaxles – removal and installation

Refer to illustrations 10.1, 10.4a, 10.4b, 10.5 and 10.7

Removal

1   Remove the wheel cover and loosen the driveaxle hub nut **(see illustration)**. Loosen the wheel lug nuts, raise the front of the vehicle and support it securely on jackstands. Remove the front wheel.

2   Remove the driveaxle hub nut. To prevent the hub from turning, brace a screwdriver across two of the wheel studs, then remove the nut.

3   Remove the two balljoint-to-lower arm nuts and separate the lower arm from the balljoint (refer to Chapter 10 if necessary).

4   Push the driveaxle from the hub with a puller (if it's stuck), then pull out on the steering knuckle and remove the outer end from the hub splines **(see illustrations)**.

5   Carefully pry the inner end of the axle from the transaxle, using a large pry bar positioned between the transaxle housing and the CV joint housing **(see illustration)**.

6   Support the CV joints and carefully remove the driveaxle from the vehicle.

Installation

7   Pry the old circlip from the inner end of the driveaxle and install a new one **(see illustration)**. Lubricate the differential seal with multipurpose grease, raise the driveaxle into position while supporting the CV

8

10.7   Always replace the circlip on the inner CV joint stub shaft before reinstalling the driveaxle

11.3   Pry the boot clamp retaining tabs up with a small screwdriver and slide the clamps off the boot

11.4   Pry the wire ring ball retainer out of the outer race, . . .

11.5a   . . . then slide the outer race off the inner bearing assembly

joints and insert the splined end of the inner CV joint into the the differential side gear. Seat the shaft into the side gear by pushing firmly on the driveaxle.

8   Apply a light coat of multi-purpose grease to the outer CV joint splines, pull out on the strut/steering knuckle assembly and install the stub axle in the hub.

9   Connect the balljoint to the lower arm (Chapter 10).

10   Install the hub nut using a new large washer underneath it. Lock the disc so that it cannot turn and tighten the hub nut securely.

11   Grasp the inner CV joint housing (not the driveaxle) and pull out to make sure that the axle has seated securely in the transaxle.

12   Install the wheel and lower the vehicle.

13   Tighten the hub nut to the specified torque and install the wheel cover.

11   Driveaxle boot replacement and constant velocity (CV) joint overhaul

Refer to illustrations 11.3, 11.4, 11.5a, 11.5b, 11.6, 11.7, 11.8, 11.9, 11.10a, 11.10b, 11.11a, 11.11b, 11.13, 11.14, 11.17, 11.19, 11.20, 11.21a, 11.21b, 11.28, and 11.30

**11.5b   Driveaxle and CV joint components –
exploded view**

1   Circlip (always replace)
2   Inner CV joint outer race
3   Wire ring ball retainer
4   Snap-ring
5   Inner race
6   Cage
7   Balls
8   Inner boot
9   Boot clamp
10   Boot clamp
11   Boot clamp
12   Outer boot
13   Outer CV joint and axle assembly
14   Dynamic damper (left side only)
15   Dynamic damper clamp

Inner CV joint and boot

Disassembly

Note: *The inner CV joint on 1990 and later models cannot be disassembled. If worn or damaged, the entire assembly must be replaced.*

1   *Remove the driveaxle from the vehicle (Section 7).*

2   Mount the driveaxle in a vise. The jaws of the vise should be lined with wood or rags to prevent damage to the axleshaft.

3   Pry the boot clamp retaining tabs up with a small screwdriver and slide the clamps off the boot **(see illustration).**

4   Slide the boot back on the axleshaft and pry the wire ring ball retainer from the outer race **(see illustration).**

5   Pull the outer race off the inner bearing assembly (see illustrations).

6   Remove the snap-ring from the groove in the axleshaft with a pair of snap-ring pliers **(see illustration).**

7   Mark the inner race and cage to ensure that they are reassembled with the correct sides facing out **(see illustration).**

8   Slide the inner bearing assembly off the axleshaft.

9   Using a screwdriver or piece of wood, pry the balls from the cage **(see illustration).** Be careful not to scratch the inner race, the balls or the cage.

10   Align the inner race lands with the cage windows and pull the race out of the cage **(see illustrations).**

Inspection

11   Clean the components with solvent to remove all traces of grease. Inspect the cage and races for pitting, score marks, cracks and other signs of wear and damage. Shiny, polished spots are normal and will not adversely affect CV joint performance **(see illustrations).**

11.6   Remove the snap-ring from the end of the axle

11.7   Place match marks on the inner race and cage to identify which side must face the end of the shaft during reassembly

11.9   Pry the balls out of the cage with a screwdriver – be careful not to nick or scratch them

11.10a   Align the lands of the inner race with the windows of the cage, . . .

11.10b   . . . then remove the inner race from the cage

11.11a   Check the inner race lands and grooves for pitting and score marks

11.11b   Check the cage for cracks, pitting and score marks (shiny spots are normal and don't affect operation)

8

11.13   Press the balls into the cage through the windows using thumb pressure only

11.14   Wrap the splined area of the axle with tape to prevent damage to the boot when installing it

3.0 ± 0.040-inch
(75 ± 1mm)

11.19   Adjust the length of the CV joint (distance between the boot bands) before tightening the clamps

11.17   Pack the inner race and cage assembly full of CV joint grease (also note that the larger diameter side, or "bulge", is facing the axleshaft end)

Reassembly

12 Insert the inner race into the cage. Verify that the matchmarks are on the same side. However, it's not necessary for them to be in direct alignment with each other.

13 Press the balls into the cage windows with your thumbs **(see illustration)**.

14 Wrap the axleshaft splines with tape to avoid damaging the boot. Slide the small boot clamp and boot onto the axleshaft, then remove the tape **(see illustration)**.

15 Install the inner race and cage assembly on the axleshaft with the larger diameter side or "bulge" of the cage (and the previously applied marks) facing the axleshaft end.

16 Install the snap-ring in the groove. Make sure it's completely seated by pushing on the inner race and cage assembly.

17 Fill the outer race and boot with the specified type and quantity of CV joint grease (normally included with the new boot kit). Pack the inner race and cage assembly with grease, by hand, until grease is worked completely into the assembly **(see illustration)**.

18 Slide the outer race down onto the inner race and install the wire ring retainer.

19 Wipe any excess grease from the axle boot groove on the outer race. Seat the small diameter of the boot in the recessed area on the axleshaft. Push the other end of the boot onto the outer race and move the race in or out to adjust the joint to the proper length **(see illustration)**.

20 With the axle set to the proper length, equalize the pressure in the boot by inserting a dull screwdriver between the boot and the outer race **(see illustration)**. Don't damage the boot with the tool.

21 Install the boot clamps **(see illustrations)**.

22 Install a new circlip on the inner CV joint stub axle **(see illustration 7.7)**.

23 Install the driveaxle as described in Section 7.

11.20   Equalize the pressure inside the boot by inserting a small, dull screwdriver between the boot and the outer race

Outer CV joint and boot

Disassembly

24 Following Steps 1 through 10, remove the inner CV joint from the axleshaft and disassemble it.

25 If the left driveaxle outer CV joint is being serviced, pry open the dynamic damper clamp and slide the damper off the axleshaft.

26 Remove the outer CV joint boot clamps, using the technique described in Step 3. Slide the boot off the axleshaft.

Inspection

27 Thoroughly wash the inner and outer CV joints in clean solvent and blow them dry with compressed air, if available. **Note:** *Because the outer joint cannot be disassembled, it is difficult to wash away all the old grease and to rid the bearing of solvent once it's clean. But*

11.21a To install the new clamps, bend the tang down and . . .

11.21b . . . fold the tabs over to hold it in place

11.28 After the old grease has been rinsed away and the \solvent has been blown out with compressed air, rotate the outer joint housing through its full range of motion and inspect the bearing surfaces for wear and damage – if any of the balls, the race or the cage look damaged, replace the driveaxle and outer joint assembly

11.30 Position the dynamic damper the specified distance (A) from the outer CV joint, then tighten the clamp

A = 15-inches (383.5 mm)

it is imperative that the job be done thoroughly, so take your time and do it right.

28 Bend the outer CV joint housing at an angle to the driveaxle to expose athe bearings, inner race and cage (**see illustration**). Inspect the bearing surfaces for signs of wear. If the bearings are damaged or worn, replace the driveaxle.

Reassembly

29 Slide the new outer boot onto the driveaxle. It's a good idea to wrap vinyl tape around the spline of shaft to prevent damage to the boot (**see illustration 8.14**). When the boot is in position, add the specified amount of grease (included in the boot replacement kit) to the outer joint and the boot (pack the joint with as much grease as it will hold and put the rest into the boot). Slide lthe boot on the rest of the way and install the new clamps (**see illustrations 8.21a and 8.21b**).

30 If you are overhauling the left driveaxle, install the dynamic damper. Position it the specified distance from the outer CV joint housing (**see illustration**). Attach the damper clamp.

31 Proceed to clean and reassemble the inner CV joint by following Steps 11 through 22, then install the driveaxle as outlined in Section 7.

12 Clutch pedal – removal and installation

Refer to illustration 12.3

1   Disconnect the cable from the negative battery terminal.

2   On 1989 and earlier models, loosen the clutch cable adjuster wheel (Chapter 1) and unhook the end of the cable from the top of the clutch pedal (under the dash). On 1990 and later models, remove the cotter pin and pull out the clevis pin from the master cylinder pushrod.

12.3 Clutch pedal and related components – exploded view (1986 through 1989 models)

3   Remove the pedal shaft nut and washers, then slide the pedal off the shaft (**see illustration**). Wipe the old grease off the shaft.

4   Remove the bushings from the pedal and inspect them for wear. Install new ones if necessary. When installing the bushings in the pedal, lubricate them with multi-purpose grease. Also lubricate the hook at the top of the clutch pedal.

5   Install the clutch pedal by reversing the removal procedure, then adjust the free play as outlined in Chapter 1.

8

Chapter 9 Brakes

Contents

Specifications

General

Brake fluid type	See Chapter 1
Power brake booster pushrod-to-master cylinder piston clearance	0.016 to 0.031 in (0.40 to 0.80 mm)
Parking brake lever travel	5 to 7 clicks

Front brakes

Minimum brake pad thickness	See Chapter 1
Disc standard thickness	
Sumitomo front brake	0.512 in (13 mm)
Tokico front brake	0.750 in (19 mm)
Disc minimum thickness*	
Sumitomo front brake	0.450 in (11.4 mm)
Tokico front brake	0.670 in (17 mm)
Disc runout	0.006 in (0.15 mm) maximum

Refer to marks stamped on the disc (they supersede information printed here)

Rear brakes

Minimum brake shoe lining thickness	See Chapter 1
Drum standard diameter	7.1 in (180 mm)
Drum maximum diameter*	7.2 in (182 mm)
Drum out-of-round	0.0006 in (0.015 mm)

Refer to marks cast into drum (they supersede information printed here)

Torque specifications

	Ft-lbs	Nm
Caliper mounting bolts (Sumitomo)	43 to 58	59 to 78
Caliper inner-to-outer bolts (Sumitomo)	58 to 69	78 to 93
Caliper lower mounting bolt (Tokico)	16 to 23	22 to 31
Caliper torque plate-to-steering knuckle (Tokico)	47 to 54	64 to 74
Inlet fitting bolt (Tokico)	18 to 22	25 to 29
Wheel cylinder mounting bolts	5.8 to 8.7	7.8 to 12
Brake backing plate-to-axle bolts	36 to 43	49 to 59
Master cylinder-to-brake booster nuts	5.8 to 8.7	7.8 to 12
Brake booster-to-firewall nuts	5.8 to 8.7	7.8 to 12
Brake pedal support-to-firewall nuts	5.8 to 8.7	7.8 to 12
Disc-to-hub bolts	36 to 43	49 to 59
Wheel lug nuts	See Chapter 1	

1   General information

The vehicles covered by this manual are equipped with hydraulically operated front and rear brake systems. The front brakes are disc type and the rear brakes are drum type. Both the front and rear brakes are self adjusting. The front disc brakes automatically compensate for pad wear, while the rear drum brakes incorporate an adjustment mechanism which is activated when the parking brake is applied and released and the brake pedal is pumped, alternately.

Hydraulic system

The hydraulic system consists of two separate diagonally split circuits. The master cylinder has separate reservoirs for the two circuits and in the event of a leak or failure in one hydraulic circuit, the other circuit will remain operative. A visual warning of low fluid level is given by a warning light activated by a float switch in the master cylinder reservoir.

Proportioning valve

A proportioning valve, located in the engine compartment below the master cylinder, regulates outlet pressure to the rear brakes after a predetermined rear input pressure has been reached, preventing early rear wheel lock-up under heavy brake loads. The valve is also designed to assure full pressure to one brake system should the other system fail.

Power brake booster

The power brake booster, utilizing engine manifold vacuum and atmospheric pressure to provide assistance to the hydraulically operated brakes, is mounted on the firewall in the engine compartment.

Parking brake

The parking brake operates the rear brakes only, through a cable. It's activated by a lever mounted in the center console.

Service

After completing any operation involving disassembly of any part of the brake system, always test drive the vehicle to check for proper braking performance before resuming normal driving. When testing the brakes, perform the tests on a clean, dry flat surface. Conditions other than these can lead to inaccurate test results.

Test the brakes at various speeds with both light and heavy pedal pressure. The vehicle should stop evenly without pulling to one side or the other. Avoid locking the brakes because this slides the tires and diminishes braking efficiency and control of the vehicle.

Tires, vehicle load and front end alignment are factors which also affect braking performance.

2   Disc brake pads — replacement

Warning: *Disc brake pads must be replaced on both front wheels at the same time — never replace the pads on only one wheel. Also, the dust created by the brake system may contain asbestos, which is harmful to your health. Never blow it out with compressed air and don't inhale any of it. An approved filtering mask should be worn when work-*ing on the brakes. Do not, under any circumstances, use petroleum-based solvents to clean brake parts. Use brake cleaner or denatured alcohol only!

Note: *When servicing the disc brakes, use only high quality, nationally recognized brand name pads.*

1   Remove the cap from the brake fluid reservoir (see Chapter 1) and siphon off about two-thirds of the fluid from the reservoir. Failing to do this could result in the reservoir overflowing when the caliper pistons are pressed into their bores.

2   Apply the parking brake. Loosen the wheel lug nuts, raise the front of the vehicle and support it securely on jackstands. Place blocks behind the rear wheels.

3   Remove the front wheels. Work on one brake assembly at a time, using the assembled brake for reference, if necessary.

4   Inspect the brake disc carefully as outlined in Section 4. If machining is necessary, follow the information in that Section to remove the disc, at which time the pads can be removed from the calipers as well.

5   The pad replacement procedure varies, depending on whether your vehicle has Sumitomo or Tokico calipers. To check which type it has, see if the calipers have pad protectors like those shown in illustration 2.6a. If they do, your vehicle has Sumitomo calipers. If not, your vehicle has Tokico calipers.

Vehicles with Sumitomo calipers

Refer to illustrations 2.6a, 2.6b, 2.6c, 2.6d, 2.6e, 2.6f, 2.6g, 2.6h, 2.6i, 2.6j and 2.6k

6   To replace the pads on Sumitomo calipers, follow illustrations 2.6a through 2.6k, being sure to stay in order and read the caption with each illustration. Then proceed to Step 13.

2.6a   Pry the pad protector off of the pad retaining pins

2.6b   Before removing anything, wash the brake assembly with brake cleaner (spraying with an aerosol can of cleaner is shown here) and allow it to dry. Remember — NEVER blow off the brake dust with compressed air — asbestos dust is a health hazard!

2.6c   Pry the center of the M-clip out of the outer brake pad, . . .

2.6d . . . then pull the ends of the clip out of the pad retaining pins

2.6e   Using a pair of pliers, pull the K spring off of the inner brake pad and out from under the retaining pins

2.6f   Pull out both pad retaining pins

2.6g   Using a C-clamp (or a pair of large pliers), push the inner brake pad towards the inside of the caliper, which will bottom the caliper piston in its bore, making room for the new pads

2.6h Pull the brake pads straight out of the caliper

2.6i If the anti-squeal shim hasn't stuck to the brake pad, remove it from the caliper

2.6j Before installing the new brake pads, it's a good idea to apply an anti-squeal compound to the pad backing plates, following label instructions

2.6k Install the new pads and clips, referring, if necessary, to the assembled brake on the other side of the car. When installing the M-clip, insert one end into the hole in one of the retaining pins, then rotate the other retaining pin so its hole is properly angled to insert the other end of the clip. Push the center of the clip into the hole in the brake pad.

2.7 Unscrew the caliper lower mounting bolt (arrow) and pivot the caliper up for access to the brake pads

2.9 Bottom the caliper piston in the bore by prying it down with a hammer handle

Vehicles with Tokico calipers

Refer to illustrations 2.7, 2.9 and 2.11

7   Remove the caliper lower mounting bolt (**see illustration**) and swing the caliper up far enough to allow removal of the brake pads. Secure it in the raised position with a piece of wire.

8   Pull the brake pads out of the carrier. Remove the spring clips from each end of the torque plate, noting their installed positions. Inspect each clip for distortion, replacing it if necessary.

9   Depress the caliper piston into the bore by pushing on it with a wooden tool, such as a hammer handle (**see illustration**). This will provide room for the new pads.

10   Apply a coat of anti-squeal compound to the backing plates of the brake pads, following label instructions (**see illustration 2.6j**).

9

2.11   Clip the anti-squeal shim to the outer pad

11   Place the spring clips on the carrier plate. Clip the anti-squeal shim on the outer pad **(see illustration)** and insert the pads into the carrier.
12   Swing the caliper body down over the pads and install the lower mounting bolt, tightening it to the specified torque.

All Vehicles

13   After replacing the pads, firmly depress the brake pedal a few times to bring the pads into contact with the disc. The pedal should be at normal height above the floorpan and firm.
14   Check for fluid leakage and make sure the brakes operate normally before driving in traffic.

3   Disc brake caliper — removal, overhaul and installation

Warning: *Dust created by the brake system may contain asbestos, which is harmful to your health. Never blow it out with compressed air and don't inhale any of it. An approved filtering mask should be worn when working on the brakes. Do not, under any circumstances, use petroleum-based solvents to clean brake parts. Use brake cleaner or denatured alcohol only!*
Note: *If an overhaul is indicated (usually because of fluid leakage) explore all options before beginning the job. New and factory rebuilt calipers are available from auto parts stores on an exchange basis, which makes this job quite easy. If it's decided to rebuild the calipers, make sure a rebuild kit is available before proceeding. Always rebuild the calipers in pairs — never rebuild just one of them.*

Removal

1   Remove the cap from the brake fluid reservoir, siphon off about two-thirds of the fluid into a container and discard the fluid. Brake fluid will damage paint, so be careful not to spill any. **Note:** *The remainder of the removal procedure depends on whether your vehicle has Sumitomo or Tokico calipers. To check which type it has, see if the calipers have pad protectors like those shown in illustration 2.6a. If they do, your vehicle has Sumitomo calipers. If not, your vehicle has Tokico calipers.*
2   Apply the parking brake. Loosen the wheel lug nuts, raise the front of the vehicle and support it securely on jackstands. Remove the front wheels.

Vehicles with Sumitomo calipers
Refer to illustration 3.5

3   Remove the brake pads from the caliper following the procedure in Section 2.
4   Loosen the hose fitting at the frame bracket and remove the hose securing clip (see Section 9). The brake hose can now be unscrewed from the caliper. Plug the end of the hose to prevent excessive fluid loss.
5   If the caliper is going to be overhauled, loosen the two bolts that secure the caliper frame together **(see illustration)**. Remove the two mounting bolts and lift the caliper off the vehicle.

Vehicles with Tokico calipers
Refer to illustration 3.6

6   Disconnect the brake line from the caliper by removing the inlet fitting bolt **(see illustration)**. Plug the end of the line to prevent excessive brake fluid loss.

7   Remove the caliper lower mounting bolt **(see illustration 2.7)**, swing the caliper up until it clears the disc and slide it off of the upper pin by pushing it in (toward the engine). The brake pads can stay in the torque plate.

Overhaul
Refer to illustrations 3.9a, 3.9b, 3.9c, 3.10a, 3.10b, 3.11, 3.12, 3.13a, 3.13b, 3.18a, 3.18b, 3.18c, 3.19a, 3.19b, 3.20 and 3.21

8   Clean the exterior of the caliper with brake cleaner or denatured alcohol. **Warning:** *Never use gasoline, kerosene or petroleum-based cleaning solvents.* Place the caliper on a clean workbench.
9   If you are overhauling a Sumitomo-design caliper, remove the two bolts that secure the halves of the caliper frame together, then separate the halves **(see illustration)**. The torque plate can now be removed **(see illustrations)**.
10   Two different techniques are used to eject the piston from the caliper, depending on caliper design:
   a) On a Sumitomo caliper, place the caliper piston-side down on the workbench, then use compressed air to remove the piston from the caliper **(see illustration)**.
   b) On a Tokico caliper, place a block of wood or several shop rags in the caliper as a cushion **(see illustration)**, then apply compressed air to the inlet port to push the piston out.
Whichever method is used, apply only enough air pressure to ease the piston out of the bore. If the piston is blown out with much force, it could be damaged. **Warning:** *Never place your fingers in front of the piston in an attempt to catch or protect it when applying compressed air, as serious injury could occur.*

3.5   If the Sumitomo caliper is to be disassembled for overhaul, loosen the bolts that hold the inner and outer portions of the caliper together (A) — they are very tight and it's easier to break them loose before the caliper is removed. Remove the caliper mounting bolts (B) to detach the caliper from the vehicle.

3.6   On Tokico calipers, remove the inlet fitting bolt (arrow)

3.9a With the Sumitomo caliper held in a vise, remove the bolts that secure the inner and outer halves of the caliper frame together, then separate them

3.9b The inner half of the Sumitomo caliper can now be slid off of the torque plate

3.9c An exploded view of a Sumitomo disc brake caliper

3.10a On a Sumitomo caliper, place the caliper piston-side down and direct compressed air into the brake hose inlet port to eject the piston

3.10b When ejecting the piston on a Tokico caliper, place a block of wood between the piston and caliper to prevent damage to the piston

9

3.11   On a Sumitomo caliper, pry the wire retaining ring off of the dust boot, then remove the boot

11 Remove the dust boot. On Sumitomo calipers, pry the wire retaining ring off of the dust boot, then remove the boot **(see illustration)**.

12 Using a wood or plastic tool, remove the piston seal from the groove in the caliper bore **(see illustration)**. Metal tools may damage the caliper bore.

13 Remove the bleeder screw. On Sumitomo calipers, remove the torque plate pin bushing from the caliper housing **(see illustration)**. On Tokico-design calipers, remove the pin boot, sleeve boots and sleeve **(see illustration)**. Discard all rubber parts.

14 Clean the remaining parts with brake system cleaner or denatured alcohol then blow them dry with compressed air.

15 Carefully examine the piston for nicks and burrs. If surface defects are present, the parts must be replaced.

16 Check the caliper bore for nicks, burrs and corrosion. You can remove light corrosion and stains with crocus cloth. Discard the mounting bolts if they're corroded or damaged.

17 Lubricate the piston bore with clean brake fluid. Lubricate the new piston seal with the red silicone grease supplied in the repair kit, then position the seal in the caliper bore groove.

3.12   To avoid damaging the caliper bore or seal groove, remove the piston seal with a plastic or wooden tool — a pencil works well

3.13a   To remove the torque plate pin bushing, grab it with a pair of needle-nose pliers, twist it and push it through the caliper frame

3.13b   Exploded view of the Tokico-design caliper

Connecting bolt

Hose

Washer

Boots

Pin

Bolt

Cap

Bleeder

Bolt

Sleeve boot

Cylinder

Sleeve

Boots

Carrier

Seal

Piston

Boots

Spring

Pad

Shim

18 On Sumitomo calipers, lubricate the piston with clean brake fluid. Insert the piston squarely into the caliper bore, then push down with your fingers to bottom it in the bore (see illustration). Smear the piston groove with the silicone grease supplied in the repair kit, then stretch the dust boot over the top of the piston and install the retaining ring (see illustrations).

19 On Tokico calipers, lubricate the piston and piston boot lips with the silicone grease provided in the repair kit, then slide the piston boot onto the bottom (closed end) of the piston (see illustration). Lower the piston and boot assembly into the caliper bore and work the fluted portion of the dust boot into its groove in the bore (see illustration). Once the boot is seated around its entire circumference, the piston can be pushed into the bore.

20 On Sumitomo calipers, apply a coat of silicone grease to the torque plate pins and install the plate by sliding the pins through the inner half of the caliper body (see illustration). Place the caliper halves

3.18a On Sumitomo calipers, install the piston squarely in the caliper bore, then push it straight in until the dust boot groove is flush with the caliper face

3.18b Stretch the dust boot over the top of the piston, . . .

3.18c . . . then install the retaining ring

Piston   Piston boot

3.19a On Tokico calipers, place the piston boot onto the bottom of the piston, . . .

3.19b . . . then tuck the fluted portion of the boot into the upper groove of the caliper bore and bottom the piston in the bore

3.20 On Sumitomo calipers, lubricate the torque plate pins with silicone grease then assemble the plate and the inner portion of the caliper

9

Sleeve side

Caliper body

Sleeve

Pin side

Caliper body

Narrow Wide

Pin

3.21   On Tokico calipers, apply silicone grease to the sliding surfaces of the sleeve and pin, to the bores in the caliper body and to the lips of the rubber boots. On the sleeve side of the caliper, install the rubber boots first, then the sleeve.

together, install the bolts and tighten them to the specified torque.
21 On Tokico calipers, lubricate the sleeve, pin bore and boots with silicone grease, then install them in their proper locations in the caliper body **(see illustration)**.

Installation

22 On Sumitomo calipers, slide the caliper over the disc, aligning the threaded holes in the torque plate with the holes in the steering knuckle. Install the mounting bolts, tightening them to the specified torque. The brake hose and pads can now be installed.
23 On Tokico calipers, ensure the brake pads are in place, then slide the upper mounting hole over the pin. Pivot the caliper down over the pads and disc and install the lower mounting bolt, tightening it to the specified torque. Connect the brake hose, using new copper washers on each side of the inlet fitting bolt. Tighten the inlet fitting bolt to the specified torque.
24 Bleed the brakes following the procedure in Section 10.
25 Install the wheels and lower the vehicle. Tighten the lug nuts to the torque specifed in chapter 1.
26 Firmly depress the brake pedal a few times to bring the pads into contact with the disc.
27 Inspect the caliper for fluid leaks and check brake operation before driving the vehicle in traffic.

---

4 Brake disc — inspection, removal and installation

Refer to illustrations 4.2, 4.4a, 4.4b, 4.5a and 4.5b

1   Loosen the wheel lug nuts, raise the vehicle and support it securely on jackstands. Remove the wheel.
2   Remove the brake caliper as outlined in Section 3. It's not necessary to disconnect the brake hose. After removing the caliper, suspend it out of the way with a piece of wire **(see illustration)**.

4.2   Suspend the caliper with a piece of wire whenever you have to move it — don't let it hang by the brake hose!

4.4a   Check the disc runout with a dial indicator — if the reading exceeds the maximum allowable runout limit, the disc will have to be machined or replaced

Inspection

3   Visually inspect the disc surface for scoring and other damage. Light scratches and shallow grooves are normal after use and may not always be detrimental to brake operation, but deep scoring — over 0.015-inch (0.38 mm) — requires disc removal and refinishing by an automotive machine shop. Be sure to check both sides of the disc. If pulsating has been noticed during application of the brakes, suspect disc runout.
4   To check disc runout, place a dial indicator at a point about 1/2-inch from the outer edge of the disc **(see illustration)**. Set the indicator to zero and turn the disc. The difference between the highest and lowest indicator reading should not exceed the specified allowable runout maximum. If it does, the disc should be refinished by an automotive machine shop. **Note:** *Professionals recommend resurfacing of brake discs regardless of the dial indicator reading (to produce a smooth, flat surface that will eliminate brake pedal pulsations and other undesirable symptoms related to questionable discs). At the very least, if you elect not to have the discs resurfaced, deglaze them with medium-grit emery cloth (use a swirling motion to ensure a non-directional finish)* **(see illustration)**.
5   It is absolutely critical that the disc not be machined to a thickness under the specified minimum allowable thickness. This thickness is stamped onto the edge of the disc **(see illustration)**. The disc thickness can be checked with a micrometer **(see illustration)**.

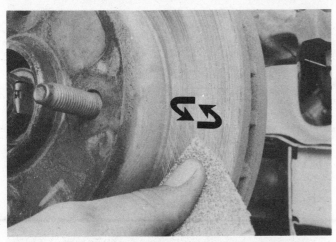

4.4b   Using a swirling motion, remove the glaze from the disc with emery cloth or sandpaper

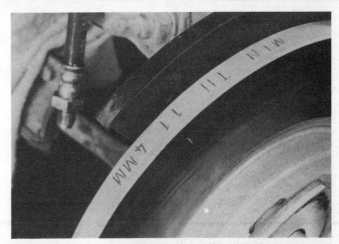

4.5a   The minimum allowable disc thickness is stamped on the edge of the disc

4.5b   Check the thickness of the disc with a micrometer, at several points around the outer edge

5.4a   Before removing any internal drum brake components, wash them off with brake cleaner and allow them to dry — position a drain pan under the brake to catch the residue — DO NOT USE COMPRESSED AIR TO BLOW THE BRAKE DUST FROM THE PARTS!

Removal and installation

6   Following the procedure outlined in Chapter 10, remove the steering knuckle and hub assembly from the vehicle.

7   Due to the need for special tools to remove and install the hub and disc on the steering knuckle and to properly adjust the hub bearing preload, the steering knuckle and hub assembly must be taken to a dealer service department or other shop equipped with the necessary tools.

8   Install the steering knuckle and hub assembly, referring to the procedure described in Chapter 10.

9   Install the caliper and brake pad assembly over the disc and position it on the steering knuckle (refer to Section 3 for the caliper installation procedure, if necessary). Tighten the caliper bolt(s) to the specified torque.

10   Install the wheel, then lower the vehicle to the ground. Depress the brake pedal a few times to bring the brake pads into contact with the disc. Bleeding of the system will not be necessary unless the brake hose was disconnected from the caliper. Check the operation of the brakes carefully before placing the vehicle into normal service.

5   Drum brake shoes — replacement

Warning: *Drum brake shoes must be replaced on both wheels at the same time — never replace the shoes on only one wheel. Also, the dust created by the brake system may contain asbestos, which is harmful to your health. Never blow it out with compressed air and don't*

inhale any of it. An approved filtering mask should be worn when working on the brakes. Do not, under any circumstances, use petroleum-based solvents to clean brake parts. Use brake cleaner or denatured alcohol only!

Caution: *Whenever the brake shoes are replaced, the shoe-to-shoe, automatic adjuster (if equipped) and hold-down springs should also be replaced. Due to the continuous heating/cooling cycle that the springs are subjected to, they lose their tension over a period of time and may allow the shoes to drag on the drum and wear at a much faster rate than normal. When replacing the rear brake shoes, use only high quality nationally recognized brand name parts.*

1   Loosen the wheel lug nuts, raise the rear of the vehicle and support it securely on jackstands. Block the front wheels to keep the vehicle from rolling.

2   Release the parking brake.

3   Remove the wheel and brake drum (see Chapter 1, Section 32, for the brake drum removal procedure). **Note:** *All four rear brake shoes must be replaced at the same time, but to avoid mixing up parts, work on only one brake assembly at a time.*

1986 through 1988 models
Refer to illustrations 5.4a through 5.4w

4   Refer to the accompanying illustrations **(5.4a through 5.4w)** for the inspection and replacement of the brake shoes. Be sure to stay in order and read the caption under each illustration. Then proceed to Step 19.

9

5.4b Exploded view of the left side drum brake assembly — 1986 through 1988 models

1 Backing plate	6 Piston	11 Shoe-to-shoe spring
2 Spring	7 Wheel cylinder body	12 Clip spring
3 Adjuster	8 Shoe hold-down spring pin	13 Bleeder screw
4 Parking brake lever	9 Shoe hold-down spring	14 Wheel cylinder boot
5 Brake shoe	10 Shoe retainer spring	

5.4c Pry the clip spring off the anchor point at the bottom of the brake shoes

5.4d Using a pair of needle-nose pliers, unhook the shoe retainer spring from the bottom of the shoes

5.4e   Pry the shoe-to-shoe spring out from the holes in the brake shoes

5.4f   Remove the shoe hold-down springs from each brake shoe — this is done by pushing the retainer cap down, turning it 90° to align the slot with the pin and then releasing it

5.4g   Remove the shoes and adjuster from the backing plate as an assembly

5.4h   Disconnect the parking brake cable from the parking brake lever. This is most easily accomplished by pulling the spring back on the cable with a pair of diagonal cutting pliers and gripping the cable lightly with the pliers, then disengaging the cable from the lever — be careful not to nick the cable.

5.4i   Separate the trailing shoe (the one with the parking brake lever attached) from the leading shoe

5.4j   Pry the C-clip off of the parking brake lever pivot pin (there's a clip on each side, but only remove the one on the side opposite the lever)

9

5.4k   Pry the spring off the adjuster actuator, . . .

5.4l . . . then remove the end of the adjuster strut

5.4m   Separate the parking brake lever from the trailing shoe.
Transfer the lever to the new trailing shoe and secure it in place
with the C-clip, crimping it closed with pliers. Attach the end of
the adjuster to the shoe and pry the spring back over the
actuator (reverse steps k and l).

5.4n   Pry the spring on the adjuster screw up and
over the screw

5.4o   Pry off the C-clip from the back side of the leading
shoe, then remove the adjuster screw

5.4p   Clean the adjuster screw and apply multi-purpose grease to
the threads and end. Attach the adjuster to the new leading shoe
and secure it by crimping the C-clip shut around the pivot pin. Pry
the spring over the adjuster so it's positioned on the under side.

5.4q Apply a LIGHT coat of multi-purpose grease to the brake shoe contact areas on the backing plate. Don't overdo it, though, as grease on the friction surface of the shoes will ruin them.

5.4r Attach the parking brake cable to the parking brake lever, once again holding the spring back on the cable with a pair of diagonal cutting pliers

5.4s Position the trailing shoe on the backing plate and install the hold-down spring — make sure the shoe engages properly with the wheel cylinder

5.4t Mount the leading shoe to the backing plate, connecting the adjuster screw with its other end (on the trailing shoe). Install the hold-down spring and ensure the shoe is properly engaged with the wheel cylinder.

5.4u Insert one end of the shoe-to-shoe spring into its hole, then push the other end into its corresponding hole — make sure the ends are pushed in completely

5.4v Connect the shoe retainer spring across the bottom of each shoe — it must be installed behind the anchor, as shown

9

1989 and later models

Refer to illustrations 5.6a, 5.6b and 5.17

5   Refer to illustration 5.4a and clean the brake assembly.

6   Using a pair of pliers, grip the automatic adjuster spring, unhook it from the adjuster lever, then remove the spring and lever **(see illustrations)**.

7   Spread the shoes apart and remove the adjuster.

5.4w   Hook the clip spring under the shoe anchor, then pull it up over the top of the anchor far enough for the tang on the anchor (arrow) to snap into the slot in the clip

8   Grip the shoe-to-shoe spring with a pair of pliers and unhook it.

9   Remove the hold-down springs from each shoe, using the technique shown in illustration 5.4f.

10   Remove the leading shoe from the brake backing plate, then unhook the parking brake cable from the parking brake lever.

11   Clean the adjuster screw and lubricate its threads with multi-purpose grease **(see illustration 5.4p)**.

12   Lubricate the brake shoe contact areas on the backing plate with multi-purpose grease **(see illustration 5.4q)**.

13   Transfer the parking brake lever from the old trailing shoe to the new one. It will be necessary to pry the C-clip from the lever pivot pin and crimp it into position once the lever is attached to the new shoe **(see illustration 5.4j)**.

14   Connect the parking brake lever to the parking brake cable and position the trailing shoe against the backing plate. Install the hold-down spring.

15   Place the leading shoe on the backing plate and install the hold-down spring.

16   Connect the shoe-to-shoe spring between the bottom of the two shoes.

17   Spread the tops of the shoes apart and install the adjuster. Make sure the slotted ends of the adjuster slide over the slots in the shoes **(see illustration)**.

18   Install the adjuster lever and automatic adjuster spring.

All models

Refer to illustration 5.19

19   Before reinstalling the drum it should be checked for cracks, score marks, deep scratches and hard spots, which will appear as small discolored areas. If the hard spots cannot be removed with fine emery cloth or if any of the other conditions listed above exist, the drum must be taken to an automotive machine shop to have it turned. **Note:** *Pro-*

5.6a   Exploded view of the right side drum brake assembly – 1989 and later models

1   *Automatic adjuster spring*
2   *Adjuster lever*
3   *Adjuster*
4   *Shoe-to-shoe spring*
5   *Shoe hold-down spring*
6   *Shoe, lining and pin assembly — leading*
7   *Backing plate*
8   *Parking lever and pin assembly*
9   *Shoe and lining assembly — trailing*
10 *Shoe hold-down spring pin*
11 *Wheel cylinder body*
12 *Bleeder screw*
13 *Bleeder screw cap*
14 *Boot*
15 *Piston*
16 *Wheel cylinder cup*
17 *Spring and expander cup assembly*

0070-H

5.6b Unhook the adjuster spring, then remove the spring and lever (arrows)

5.17 Make sure the slotted ends of the adjuster slide over the slots in the shoes

fessionals recommend resurfacing the drums whenever a brake job is done. Resurfacing will eliminate the possibility of out-of-round drums. If the drums are worn so much that they can't be resurfaced without exceeding the maximum allowable diameter (cast into the drum) **(see illustration)**, *then new ones will be required. At the very least, if you elect not to have the drums resurfaced, remove the glazing from the surface with medium-grit emery cloth using a swirling motion.*

20 Install the brake drum and adjust the rear wheel bearings (Chapter 1).
21 Mount the wheel, install the lug nuts, then lower the vehicle. Tighten the lug nuts to the torque specified in Chapter 1.
22 Alternately cycle the parking brake lever and pump the brake pedal several times to adjust the brake shoes to the drum.
23 Check brake operation before driving the vehicle in traffic.

---

6 Wheel cylinder — removal, overhaul and installation

Refer to illustration 6.4

Note: *If an overhaul is indicated (usually because of fluid leakage or sticky operation) explore all options before beginning the job. New wheel cylinders are available, which makes this job quite easy. If it's decided to rebuild the wheel cylinder, make sure that a rebuild kit is available before proceeding. Never overhaul only one wheel cylinder — always rebuild both of them at the same time.*

Removal

1 Raise the rear of the vehicle and support it securely on jackstands. Block the front wheels to keep the vehicle from rolling.
2 Remove the brake shoe assembly (Section 5).
3 Remove all dirt and foreign material from around the wheel cylinder.
4 Unscrew the brake line fitting from the inner side of the brake backing plate **(see illustration)**. Use a flare nut wrench, if available, to prevent rounding off the corners of the fitting. Don't pull the brake line away from the wheel cylinder.
5 Remove the wheel cylinder mounting bolts from the inner side of the brake backing plate.
6 Detach the wheel cylinder from the brake backing plate and place it on a clean workbench. Immediately plug the brake line to prevent fluid loss and contamination. **Note:** *If the brake shoe linings are contaminated with brake fluid, install new brake shoes.*

Overhaul

7 Remove the bleeder screw, pistons and boots from the wheel cylinder body **(see illustration 5.4b or 5.6a)**. Remove the cup seals from the pistons.
8 Clean the wheel cylinder with brake fluid, denatured alcohol or brake system cleaner. **Warning:** *Do not, under any circumstances, use petroleum based solvents to clean brake parts!*
9 Use compressed air to remove excess fluid from the wheel cylinder and to blow out the passages.

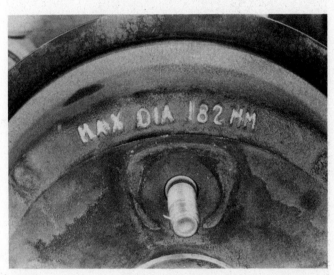

5.19 The maximum allowable diameter is cast into the drum

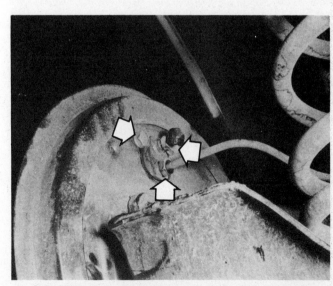

6.4 Unscrew the brake line fitting, then remove the two wheel cylinder mounting bolts (arrows)

9

7.4   Unscrew the brake line fitting tube nuts (arrows) with a flare nut wrench

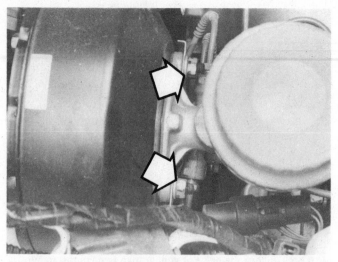

7.6   Unplug the brake fluid level indicator electrical connector, then remove the two master cylinder mounting nuts (arrows)

10   Check the cylinder bore for corrosion and score marks. Crocus cloth can be used to remove light corrosion and stains, but the cylinder must be replaced with a new one if the defects cannot be removed easily, or if the bore is scored.

11   Lubricate the new cup seals with brake fluid. Apply corrosion prevention compound (included in the repair kit) inside of the cylinder.

12   Assemble the wheel cylinder components. Make sure the cup lips face toward the center of the cylinder, or they won't seal **(see illustration 5.4b or 5.6a)**.

Installation

13   Apply a thin coat of silicone sealant to the backing plate where the wheel cylinder seats, place the cylinder in position and install the mounting bolts.

14   Connect the brake line and tighten the fitting, then tighten the wheel cylinder bolts. Install the brake shoe assembly.

15   Bleed the brakes (Section 10).

16   Check brake operation before driving the vehicle in traffic.

---

7   Master cylinder — removal, overhaul and installation

Refer to illustrations 7.4, 7.6, 7.8a, 7.8b, 7.9, 7.10, 7.11a, 7.11b and 7.11c

Note: *Before deciding to overhaul the master cylinder, check on the availability and cost of a new or factory rebuilt unit and also the availability of a rebuild kit.*

Removal

1   The master cylinder is located in the engine compartment, mounted to the power brake booster.

2   Remove as much fluid as you can from the reservoir with a syringe.

3   Place rags under the fluid fittings and prepare caps or plastic bags to cover the ends of the lines once they are disconnected. **Caution:** *Brake fluid will damage paint. Cover all body parts and be careful not to spill fluid during this procedure.*

4   Loosen the tube nuts at the ends of the brake lines where they enter the master cylinder **(see illustration)**. To prevent rounding off the flats on these nuts, the use of a flare nut wrench, which wraps around the nut, is preferred.

5   Pull the brake lines slightly away from the master cylinder and plug the ends to prevent contamination.

6   Disconnect the electrical connector at the master cylinder, then remove the two nuts attaching the master cylinder to the power booster **(see illustration)**. Pull the master cylinder off the studs and out of the engine compartment. Again, be careful not to spill the fluid as this is done.

Overhaul

7   Before attempting the overhaul of the master cylinder, obtain the proper rebuild kit, which will contain the necessary replacement parts and also any instructions which may be specific to your model.

8   Inspect the reservoir grommets for indications of leakage near the base of the reservoir. On 1986 through 1989 models, remove the screw securing the reservoir. On all models, remove the reservoir (see **illustrations**).

9   Place the cylinder in a vise and use a punch or Phillips screwdriver to depress the pistons until they bottom against the other end of the

7.8a   On 1986 through 1989 models, remove the reservoir mounting screw (arrow), . . .

7.8b . . . then pull the reservoir out of the grommets

7.9 Push the pistons all the way in and remove the piston stop screw

7.10 Push the pistons in and use snap-ring pliers to remove the snap-ring

7.11a Remove the primary piston assembly from the master cylinder bore

7.11b To remove the secondary piston assembly, tap the master cylinder firmly against a block of wood

master cylinder (**see illustration**). Hold the pistons in this position and remove the stop screw on the side of the master cylinder.

10 Carefully remove the snap-ring at the end of the master cylinder (**see illustration**).

11 The internal components can now be removed from the cylinder bore (**see illustrations**). Make a note of the proper order of the com-

ponents so they can be returned to their original locations. **Note:** *The two springs are of different tension, so pay particular attention to their order. Also, do not disassemble the piston components — they are serviced as an assembly.*

12 Carefully inspect the bore of the master cylinder. Any deep scoring or other damage will mean a new master cylinder is required.

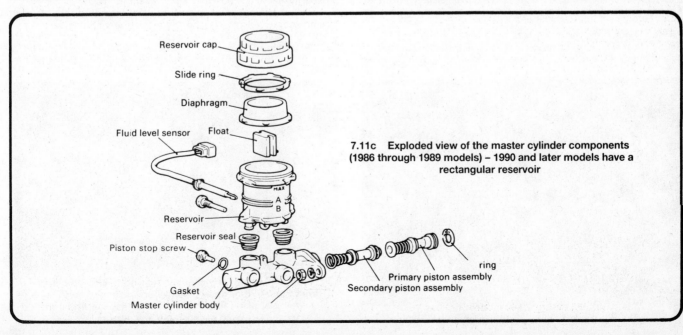

7.11c Exploded view of the master cylinder components (1986 through 1989 models) – 1990 and later models have a rectangular reservoir

Reservoir cap
Slide ring
Diaphragm
Float
Fluid level sensor
Reservoir
Reservoir seal
Piston stop screw
Gasket
Master cylinder body
ring
Primary piston assembly
Secondary piston assembly

9

13 Replace all parts included in the rebuild kit, following any instructions in the kit. Clean all reused parts with clean brake fluid or denatured alcohol. Do not use any petroleum-based cleaners. During assembly, lubricate all parts liberally with clean brake fluid.

14 Push the assembled components into the bore, bottoming them against the end of the master cylinder, then install the stop screw. Be sure to install a new gasket on the stop screw.

15 Install the new snap-ring, making sure it is seated properly in the groove.

16 Before installing the master cylinder it should be bench bled. Because it will be necessary to apply pressure to the master cylinder piston and, at the same time, control flow from the brake line outlets, it is recommended that the master cylinder be mounted in a vise, with the jaws of the vise clamping on the mounting flange. The master cylinder is aluminum, so be careful not to damage it.

17 Insert threaded plugs into the brake line outlet holes and snug them down so that there will be no air leakage past them, but not so tight that they cannot be easily loosened.

18 Fill the reservoir with brake fluid of the recommended type (see Chapter 1).

19 Remove one plug and push the piston assembly into the master cylinder bore to expel the air from the master cylinder. A large Phillips screwdriver can be used to push on the piston assembly.

20 To prevent air from being drawn back into the master cylinder the plug must be replaced and snugged down before releasing the pressure on the piston assembly.

21 Repeat the procedure until only brake fluid is expelled from the brake line outlet hole. When only brake fluid is expelled, repeat the procedure with the other outlet hole and plug. Be sure to keep the master cylinder reservoir filled with brake fluid to prevent the introduction of air into the system.

22 Since high pressure is not involved in the bench bleeding procedure, an alternative to the removal and replacement of the plugs with each stroke of the piston assembly is available. Before pushing in on the piston assembly, remove the plug as described in Step 19. Before releasing the piston, however, instead of replacing the plug, simply put your finger tightly over the hole to keep air from being drawn back into the master cylinder. Wait several seconds for brake fluid to be drawn from the reservoir into the piston bore, then depress the piston again, removing your finger as brake fluid is expelled. Be sure to put your finger back over the hole each time before releasing the piston, and when the bleeding procedure is complete for that outlet, replace the plug and snug it before going on to the other port.

Installation

23 Install the master cylinder over the studs on the power brake booster and tighten the attaching nuts only finger tight at this time.

24 Thread the brake line fittings into the master cylinder. Since the master cylinder is still a bit loose, it can be moved slightly for the fittings to thread in easily. Do not strip the threads as the fittings are tightened.

25 Fully tighten the mounting nuts and the brake fittings.

26 Fill the master cylinder reservoir with fluid, then bleed the master cylinder (only if the cylinder has not been bench bled) and the brake system as described in Section 10. To bleed the cylinder on the vehicle, have an assistant pump the brake pedal several times and then hold the pedal to the floor. Loosen the fitting nut to allow air and fluid to escape. Repeat this procedure on both fittings until the fluid is clear of air bubbles. Test the operation of the brake system carefully before placing the vehicle into normal service.

8   Proportioning valve — removal and installation

Removal

1 Although special test equipment is necessary to properly diagnose a proportioning valve malfunction, the home mechanic can remove and install it if it has been diagnosed faulty.

2 The proportioning valve is located below the master cylinder. Using a flare nut wrench to avoid rounding off the tube nuts, unscrew the tube nuts at the ends of the brake lines where they enter the valve. Gently pull the lines away from the valve and plug the ends of the lines or wrap plastic bags tightly around them to prevent excessive leakage and brake system contamination.

3 Remove the mounting nut from the center of the valve and maneuver the valve out from the brake lines.

Installation

4 Position the valve on the bracket and insert the brake lines into the holes. Screw all of the tube nuts into the valve by hand, being careful not to cross thread them. Install the mounting nut and tighten it securely.

5 Tighten the tube nuts securely, again using the flare nut wrench.

6 Bleed the entire brake system as described in Section 10. If the ends of the lines were not capped securely and all of the fluid in the master cylinder reservoir has drained out, the master cylinder will have to be bled first. The master cylinder bleeding procedure (on vehicle) can be found in Section 7, Step 26.

9   Brake lines and hoses — inspection and replacement

Refer to illustrations 9.4a and 9.4b

1 About every six months the flexible hoses which connect the steel brake lines with the rear brakes and front calipers should be inspected for cracks, chafing of the outer cover, leaks, blisters, and other damage (see Chapter 1).

2 Replacement steel and flexible brake lines are commonly available from dealer parts departments and auto parts stores. Do not, under any circumstances, use anything other than genuine steel lines or approved flexible brake hoses as replacement items.

3 When installing the brake line, leave at least 3/4-inch (19 mm) clearance between the line and any moving or vibrating parts.

4 When disconnecting a hose and line, first remove the spring clip **(see illustration)**. Then, using an open end wrench to hold the hose and a flare nut wrench to hold the tube, unscrew the fitting **(see il-**

9.4a   Pry the spring clip off the brake hose fitting

9.4b   A backup wrench must be used to keep the hose from turning, otherwise the steel brake line will twist — if available, use a flare nut wrench on the line fitting to prevent rounding off the corners lustration). Use the wrenches in the same manner when reconnecting the hose and line, then install a new clip. **Note:** *Make sure the tube passes through the center of its grommet.*

5   When disconnecting two hoses, use open end wrenches on the hose fittings. When connecting two hoses, make sure they are not bent, twisted or strained.

6   Steel brake lines are usually retained along their span with clips. Always remove these clips completely before removing a fixed brake line. Always reinstall these clips, or new ones if the old ones are damaged, when replacing a brake line, as they provide support and keep the lines from vibrating, which can eventually break them.

10   Brake system bleeding

Refer to illustration 10.8

Warning: *Wear eye protection when bleeding the brake system. If the fluid comes in contact with your eyes, immediately rinse them with water and seek medical attention.*

Note: *Bleeding the hydraulic system is necessary to remove any air that manages to find its way into the system when it's been opened during removal and installation of a hose, line, caliper or master cylinder.*

1   It will probably be necessary to bleed the system at all four brakes if air has entered the system due to low fluid level, or if the brake lines have been disconnected at the master cylinder.

2   If a brake line was disconnected only at a wheel, then only that caliper or wheel cylinder must be bled.

3   If a brake line is disconnected at a fitting located between the master cylinder and any of the brakes, that part of the system served by the disconnected line must be bled.

4   Remove any residual vacuum from the brake power booster by applying the brake several times with the engine off.

5   Remove the master cylinder reservoir cover and fill the reservoir with brake fluid. Reinstall the cover. **Note:** *Check the fluid level often during the bleeding operation and add fluid as necessary to prevent the fluid level from falling low enough to allow air bubbles into the master cylinder.*

6   Have an assistant on hand, as well as a supply of new brake fluid, a clear container partially filled with clean brake fluid, a length of 3/16-inch plastic, rubber or vinyl tubing to fit over the bleeder screw and a wrench to open and close the bleeder screw.

7   Beginning at the left rear wheel, loosen the bleeder screw slightly, then tighten it to a point where it is snug but can still be loosened quickly and easily.

8   Place one end of the tubing over the bleeder screw and submerge the other end in brake fluid in the container **(see illustration)**.

9   Have the assistant pump the brakes slowly a few times to get pressure in the system, then hold the pedal firmly depressed.

10   While the pedal is held depressed, open the bleeder screw just enough to allow a flow of fluid to occur. Watch for air bubbles to exit

the submerged end of the tube. When the fluid flow slows after a couple of seconds, tighten the screw and have your assistant release the pedal.

11   Repeat Steps 9 and 10 until no more air is seen leaving the tube, then tighten the bleeder screw and proceed to the right front wheel, the right rear wheel and the left front wheel, in that order, and perform the same procedure. Be sure to check the fluid in the master cylinder reservoir frequently.

12   Never use old brake fluid. It contains moisture which will deteriorate the brake system components.

13   Refill the master cylinder with fluid at the end of the operation.

14   Check the operation of the brakes. The pedal should feel solid when depressed, with no sponginess. If necessary, repeat the entire process.

Warning: *Do not operate the vehicle if you are in doubt about the effectiveness of the brake system.*

11   Power brake booster — check, removal and installation

Operating check

1   Depress the brake pedal several times with the engine off and make sure that there is no change in the pedal reserve distance.

2   Depress the pedal and start the engine. If the pedal goes down slightly, operation is normal.

Air tightness check

3   Start the engine and turn it off after one or two minutes. Depress the brake pedal several times slowly. If the pedal goes down farther the first time but gradually rises after the second or third depression, the booster is air tight.

4   Depress the brake pedal while the engine is running, then stop the engine with the pedal depressed. If there is no change in the pedal reserve travel after holding the pedal for 30 seconds, the booster is air tight.

Removal

Refer to illustration 11.7

5   Power brake booster units should not be disassembled. They require special tools not normally found in most automotive repair stations or shops. They are fairly complex and because of their critical relationship to brake performance it is best to replace a defective booster unit with a new or rebuilt one.

6   To remove the booster, first remove the brake master cylinder as described in Section 7. Pull the proportioning valve and bracket forward, being careful not to kink the lines.

7   Locate the pushrod clevis connecting the booster to the brake pedal **(see illustration)**. This is accessible from the interior in front of the passenger's seat, under the dash.

8   Remove the clevis pin cotter pin with pliers and pull out the

10.8   When bleeding the brakes, a hose is connected to the bleeder screw at the caliper or wheel cylinder and then submerged in brake fluid. Air will be seen as bubbles in the tube and container. All air must be expelled before moving on to the next wheel.

11.7   Remove the cotter pin and clevis pin, then unscrew the booster mounting nuts (arrows)

9

clevis pin.

9   Holding the clevis with pliers, disconnect the clevis locknut with a wrench. The clevis is now loose.

10 Disconnect the hose leading from the engine to the booster. Be careful not to damage the hose when removing it from the booster fitting.

11 Remove the four nuts and washers holding the brake booster to the firewall. You may need a light to see them, as they are under the dash **(see illustration 11.7)**.

12 Slide the booster straight out from the firewall until the studs clear the holes, and pull the booster, brackets and gaskets from the engine compartment area.

Installation

Refer to illustrations 11.14a and 11.14b

13 Installation procedures are basically the reverse of those for removal. Tighten the clevis locknut securely and the booster mounting nuts to the specified torque.

14 If the power booster unit is being replaced, the clearance between the master cylinder piston and the pushrod in the vacuum booster must be measured. Using a depth micrometer or vernier calipers, measure the distance from the seat (recessed area) in the master cylinder to the master cylinder mounting flange. Next, measure the distance from the end of the vacuum booster pushrod to the mounting face of the booster (including gasket) where the master cylinder mounting flange seats. Subtract the two measurements to get the clearance **(see illustration)**. If the clearance is more or less than specified, turn the adjusting screw on the end of the power booster pushrod until the clearance is within the specified limit **(see illustration)**.

15 A second method to measure the pushrod-to-piston clearance is to install the master cylinder to the vacuum booster with a small piece of modeling clay placed on the end of the pushrod. Make sure the gasket is in place when making this trial fit. Remove the master cylinder and measure the resulting impression left in the clay. Again adjust as needed to meet the Specification. This method may require several trial-and-error fits to reach the proper clearance.

16 After the final installation of the master cylinder and brake hoses and lines, the brake pedal height and free play must be adjusted and the system must be bled. See the appropriate Sections of this Chapter for the procedures.

12   Parking brake – adjustment

Refer to illustrations 12.3 and 12.4

1   Pull the parking brake lever up as far as possible, counting the number of clicks as you go. The travel should be five to seven clicks. If you are able to raise the lever higher, the parking brake might not hold the vehicle on an incline. If the travel is less than specified, the automatic adjusters on the rear brakes could be rendered useless. If the parking brake lever travel is not five to seven clicks, adjust the parking brake, as described below.

2   Remove the center console (see Chapter 11).

3   On 1986 through 1989 models, turn the cable adjusting nuts on the equalizer until the specified lever travel is obtained **(see illustration)**. Tighten the nuts evenly to avoid over-adjusting one cable, leaving the other slack. On 1990 and later models, turn the single cable adjusting nut on the equalizer until the specified lever travel is obtained.

4   If necessary, adjust the parking brake indicator light switch so the Brake light on the instrument panel is off when the parking brake lever is all the way down. To adjust the switch, loosen the switch mounting screw (directly in front of the lever quadrant teeth) and move the switch up or down, as necessary **(see illustration)**. After the switch has been adjusted, tighten the screw securely.

5   Check to make sure the rear brakes don't drag when the vehicle is driven.

11.14a The booster pushrod-to-master cylinder piston clearance must be as specified — if there is interference between the two, the brakes may drag; if there is too much clearance, there will be excessive brake pedal travel

11.14b To adjust the length of the booster pushrod, hold the serrated portion of the rod with a pair of pliers and turn the adjusting screw in or out, as necessary, to achieve the desired setting

12.3 The parking brake cable adjusting nuts are located under the center console. When adjusting the cables, turn each adjusting nut (arrows) an equal amount to obtain the correct lever travel.

12.4 To adjust the parking brake light switch, loosen the mounting screw (arrow) and, with the handle in the released position, move the switch as necessary to turn the light off. Tighten the mounting screw.

13.6 Pry off the parking brake E-clip, then push the cable through the backing plate

13.8 The rear seat cushion must be removed and the carpet peeled back to gain access to the cable clamp bolts (arrows) — you only need to remove the bolt that holds the cable being replaced

13 Parking brake cables – replacement

Refer to illustrations 13.6 and 13.8
Note: *This procedure applies to both the right and left cables.*
1 Remove the center console (see Chapter 11).
2 On 1986 through 1989 models, completely unscrew the cable adjusting nut from the cable to be removed. On 1990 and later models, turn the single cable adjusting nut on the equalizer to allow slack in the cable(s) to be removed.
3 Loosen the rear wheel lug nuts on the side of the vehicle on which the cable is to be removed. Raise the rear of the vehicle and support it securely on jackstands. Place blocks in front of the front wheels. Remove the wheel.
4 Remove the brake drum and shoes, following the procedure outlined in Section 5.
5 Unhook the cable end from the parking brake lever on the brake shoe.
6 Remove the E-clip that secures the cable to the brake backing plate **(see illustration)** and pull the cable through the plate.
7 Unhook the cable from the clips on the suspension trailing arm.
8 Remove the rear seat cushion. Lift up the carpet, unscrew the cable

clamp bolt and free the cable from the clamp **(see illustration)**. Pull the cable and grommet through the floorpan into the interior.
9 Installation is the reverse of the removal procedure. After the cable is installed, adjust the parking brake (see Section 12).

14 Brake pedal — removal and installation

Refer to illustration 14.4
1 Disconnect the cable from the negative terminal of the battery.
2 Remove the lower dash panel trim under the steering column (see Chapter 11).
3 Remove the steering intermediate shaft (see Chapter 10).
4 Unhook the brake pedal return spring from the pedal **(see illustration)**.
5 Remove the cotter pin from the brake booster operating rod clevis pin and pull out the clevis pin **(see illustration 11.7)**.
6 Pry off the stopper ring from the end of the brake pedal shaft and remove the washer.

14.4 Typical brake pedal assembly components – exploded view

Grease

Bushing

Washer

Stopper ring

Brake light switch

Pedal support

Return spring

Accelerator cover
(Vehicle without air conditioner)

Brake pedal
(with manual transaxle)

Brake pedal
(with automatic transaxle)

9

7   Remove the four nuts which secure the left end of the pedal support to the firewall. Two are accesible from under the dash, while the other two are reached from the engine compartment.

8   The pedal and shaft can now be slid to the left and maneuvered out from under the dash.

9   Inspect the bushings at each end of the shaft for wear and general deterioration, replacing them if necessary. Check the shaft and pedal for distortion, which will warrant replacement (DO NOT attempt to heat or straighten the pedal or the shaft if distortion is evident).

10 Before installing the pedal and shaft assembly, lubricate the bushings with multi-purpose grease. The remainder of the installation procedure is the reverse of removal. Be sure to tighten the brake pedal support-to-firewall nuts to the specified torque and install a new cotter pin on the operating rod clevis pin.

15   Brake light switch — removal, installation and adjustment

1   Remove the lower dash panel trim under the steering column (Chapter 11).

2   Locate the brake light switch, which is mounted at the top of the left side brake pedal support (see illustration 14.4). Follow the switch wiring to the electrical connector and unplug it.

3   Unscrew the locknut on the switch and unscrew the switch from its bracket.

4   Installation is the reverse of removal. To adjust the switch, loosen the locknut and turn the switch in or out to allow the switch plunger to be depressed when the brake pedal is at rest. Tighten the locknut when the correct adjustment is obtained.

Chapter 10   Suspension and steering systems

Contents

Specifications

Torque specifications	**Ft-lbs**	**Nm**
Front suspension		
Front strut/shock absorber upper mounting nuts	8 to 11	11 to 15
Strut/shock absorber piston rod-to-upper insulator	29 to 36	39 to 49
Balljoint-to-lower arm bolts/nuts	69 to 87	94 to 118
Balljoint-to-steering knuckle nut	43 to 52	58 to 71
Strut bar-to-lower arm bolts/nuts	69 to 87	94 to 118
Strut bar-to-crossmember nut	54 to 61	73 to 83
Steering knuckle-to-strut assembly bolts/nuts	54 to 65	73 to 88
Rear suspension		
Fixture-to-floorpan bolts	36 to 51	49 to 70
Fixture-to-suspension arm nut	36 to 51	49 to 70
Steering		
Tie-rod end-to-steering knuckle nut	11 to 25	15 to 34
Steering wheel nut	25 to 32	34 to 43
Steering gear-to-crossmember bolts	22 to 29	30 to 39
Intermediate shaft pinch bolts	11 to 14	15 to 19
Wheel lug nuts	See Chapter 1	

10

Front suspension and steering components

1 Stabilizer bar
2 Strut/shock absorber and coil spring assembly
3 Lower arm
4 Balljoint
5 Tie-rod end
6 Tie-rod
7 Steering gear boot
8 Steering gear

Rear suspension components

1 Trailing (suspension) arm
2 Stabilizer bar
3 Coil spring

10

1 General information

The front suspension is a MacPherson strut design. The steering knuckle is located by a lower arm which is triangulated by a strut bar. A stabilizer bar, mounted to the front crossmember and connecting the lower arms, minimizes body lean.

The rear suspension consists of trailing arms with integral spindles, coil springs and telescopic shock absorbers. Some models are equipped with a stabilizer bar.

The rack-and-pinion steering gear is located behind the engine/trans-axle assembly on the firewall and actuates the steering arms, which are integral with the steering knuckles. The steering column is designed to collapse in the event of an accident.

Frequently, when working on the suspension or steering system components, you may come across fasteners which seem impossible to loosen. These fasteners on the underside of the vehicle are continually subjected to water, road grime, mud, etc., and can become rusted or ''frozen,'' making them extremely difficult to remove. In order to unscrew these stubborn fasteners without damaging them (or other components), be sure to use lots of penetrating oil and allow it to soak in for a while. Using a wire brush to clean exposed threads will also ease removal of the nut or bolt and prevent damage to the threads. Sometimes a sharp blow with a hammer and punch is effective in breaking the bond between a nut and bolt threads, but care must be taken to prevent the punch from slipping off the fastener and ruining the threads. Heating the stuck fastener and surrounding area with a torch sometimes helps too, but isn't recommended because of the obvious dangers associated with fire. Long breaker bars and extension, or ''cheater,'' pipes will increase leverage, but never use an extension pipe on a ratchet — the ratcheting mechanism could be damaged. Sometimes, turning the nut or bolt in the tightening (clockwise) direction first will help to break it loose. Fasteners that require drastic measures to unscrew should always be replaced with new ones.

Since most of the procedures that are dealt with in this Chapter involve jacking up the vehicle and working underneath it, a good pair of jackstands will be needed. A hydraulic floor jack is the preferred type of jack to lift the vehicle, and it can also be used to support certain components during various operations. **Warning:** *Never, under any circumstances, rely on a jack to support the vehicle while working on it. Whenever any of the suspension or steering fasteners are loosened or removed they must be inspected and, if necessary, replaced with new ones of the same part number or of original equipment quality and design. Torque specifications must be followed for proper reassembly and component retention. Never attempt to heat or straighten any suspension or steering components. Instead, replace bent or damaged parts with new ones.*

2 Front stabilizer bar — removal and installation

Refer to illustrations 2.2 and 2.3

Warning: *Whenever any of the suspension or steering fasteners are loosened or removed, they must be inspected and, if necessary, replaced with new ones of the same part number or of original equipment quality and design. Torque specifications must be followed for proper reassembly and component retention.*

Removal

1   Raise the front of the vehicle and support it securely on jackstands. Apply the parking brake and position blocks behind the rear wheels.
2   Remove the stabilizer bar-to-lower arm bolts and clamps, noting how the clamp halves are positioned **(see illustration)**.
3   Remove the stabilizer bar bracket bolts and detach the bar from the vehicle **(see illustration)**.
4   Pull the brackets off the stabilizer bar and inspect the bushings for cracks, hardening and other signs of deterioration. If the bushings are damaged, replace them.

Installation

5   Position the stabilizer bar bushings on the bar with the slits facing the front of the vehicle.
6   Insert the lower ends of the brackets into their slots, push the brackets over the bushings and raise the bar up to the frame. Install

the bracket bolts but don't tighten them completely at this time.
7   Install the stabilizer bar-to-lower arm rubber bushings, clamps and bolts. Tighten the bolts finger tight.
8   Tighten the bracket bolts.
9   Lower the vehicle and tighten the clamp bolts securely.

3 Strut bar — removal and installation

Refer to illustrations 3.3a, 3.3b and 3.6

Warning: *Whenever any of the suspension or steering fasteners are loosened or removed, they must be inspected and, if necessary, replaced with new ones of the same part number or of original equipment quality and design. Torque specifications must be followed for proper reassembly and component retention.*

Removal

1   Loosen the wheel lug nuts, raise the front of the vehicle and support it securely on jackstands. Apply the parking brake and position blocks behind the rear wheels. Remove the front wheel.
2   Remove the stabilizer bar-to-strut bar clamp (refer to the previous Section if necessary).
3   Remove the strut bar-to-front crossmember nut and the two bolts and nuts that secure the other end of the bar to the lower arm **(see illustrations)**.
4   Remove the large washer and rubber bushing from the front of the bar, then pull the bar straight back out of the crossmember.
5   Check the bar for cracks and distortion. If the bar is bent more

2.2 Remove the bolt (arrow) from the clamp, then pry the clamp off the stabilizer bar and strut bar

2.3 Remove the bolt (arrow) from each stabilizer bar bracket, swing the brackets down and maneuver the bar out from under the vehicle

3.3a To remove the strut bar, first unscrew the large nut
at the front of the crossmember and remove the
washer and bushing, . . .

3.3b . . . then remove the two bolts and nuts (arrows)
that secure the bar to the lower arm

than 0.120-inch (3 mm) it must be replaced. Inspect the bushings for
wear, cracks, hardness and general deterioration, replacing them if
necessary.

Installation

6   Before installing the bar, or if installing a new one, thread the inner
locknuts onto the bar the specified distance **(see illustration)**.
7   Assemble the inner washer, rubber bushing and sleeve on the bar
and insert it into the hole in the crossmember. Install the two bolts
and nuts that secure the bar to the lower arm and tighten them to the
specified torque.
8   Install the outer rubber bushing, washer and nut on the front of
the bar, but don't tighten the nut with a tool yet.
9   Install the stabilizer bar-to-strut bar clamp and bolt. Lower the vehicle and tighten the clamp bolt securely.
10   Tighten the outer strut bar nut to the specified torque.
11   It would be a good idea to drive the vehicle to an alignment shop
to have the front wheel alignment checked and, if necessary, adjusted.

**4   Front strut/shock absorber and coil spring
assembly — removal, inspection and installation**

Refer to illustrations 4.2, 4.3, 4.4, and 4.5
Warning: *Whenever any of the suspension or steering fasteners are
loosened or removed, they must be inspected and, if necessary, re-*

80.5 mm
(3.17 in.)

3.6 Thread the inner locknuts onto the strut bar until the
outer face of the outer nut is 3.17-inches (3-11/64 inches
should be close enough) from the end of the bar — this will
provide the proper caster angle

*placed with new ones of the same part number or of original equipment
quality and design. Torque specifications must be followed for proper
reassembly and component retention.*

Removal

1   Loosen the wheel lug nuts, raise the front of the vehicle and support
it securely on jackstands. Apply the parking brake and position blocks
behind the rear wheels. Remove the front wheel.
2   Unbolt the brake hose bracket from the strut **(see illustration)**.
3   Remove the strut-to-knuckle nuts and knock the bolts out with
a hammer and punch **(see illustration)**.

4.2 Unbolt the brake hose bracket (arrow) from the strut

4.3 Remove the two strut-to-knuckle nuts and bolts
(arrows) — if the bolts won't pull out easily, knock
them out with a hammer and punch

10

4.4   Pry the steering knuckle out of the strut flanges

4.5   Be sure to support the strut while removing the four strut-to-body nuts — the strut will fall if you don't

4   Separate the strut from the steering knuckle **(see illustration)**. Be careful not to overextend the inner CV joint. It's a good idea to wire the top of the steering knuckle to the body to prevent this from happening.

5   Support the strut and spring assembly with one hand and remove the strut-to-body nuts **(see illustration)**. Remove the assembly out through the fender well.

Inspection

6   Check the strut body for leaking fluid, dents, cracks and other obvious damage which would warrant repair or replacement.

7   Check the coil spring for chips or cracks in the spring coating (this will cause premature spring failure due to corrosion).

8   If any undesirable conditions exist, proceed to Section 5 for the strut disassembly procedure.

Installation

9   Guide the strut assembly up into the fender well and insert the upper mounting studs through the holes in the body. Once the studs protrude through the body, install the nuts so the strut won't fall back through. This may require an assistant, as the strut is quite heavy and awkward.

10 Slide the steering knuckle into the strut flange and insert the two bolts. Install the nuts and tighten them to the specified torque.

11 Position the brake hose bracket on the strut and install the bolt, tightening it securely.

12 Install the wheel, lower the vehicle and tighten the lug nuts to the specified torque.

13 Tighten the upper mounting nuts to the specified torque.

5   Strut cartridge — replacement

Refer to illustrations 5.4, 5.5a, 5.5b, 5.7, 5.9, 5.13, 5.17a, 5.17b and 5.17c

1   If the struts exhibit the telltale signs of wear (leaking fluid, loss of dampening capability) explore all options before beginning any work. The strut cartridges can be replaced. However, rebuilt strut assemblies (some complete with springs) are available on an exchange basis which eliminates much time and work. Whichever route you choose to take, check on the cost and availability of parts before disassembling the vehicle. **Warning:** *Disassembling a strut assembly is a dangerous undertaking and extreme care must be taken during the procedure or serious bodily injury may result. Use only a high quality spring compressor and carefully follow the manufacturer's instructions furnished with the tool. After removing the coil spring from the strut assembly, set it aside in a safe, isolated area (a steel cabinet is preferred).*

2   Remove the strut and spring assembly following the procedure described in Section 4. Mount the strut assembly in a vise with the jaws of the vise cushioned with rags or blocks of wood.

3   Following the tool manufacturers instructions, install the spring

compressor (which can be rented at most auto parts stores or equipment yards on a daily basis) on the spring and compress it sufficiently to relieve all pressure from the spring seat. This can be verified by wiggling the spring seat.

4   Unscrew the piston rod nut while using a large pair of pliers on the spring seat to prevent it from turning **(see illustration)**.

5   Lift the insulator and upper spring seat off the damper shaft **(see illustrations)**. Inspect the bearing in the insulator for smooth operation and replace it if necessary.

6   Carefully remove the compressed spring assembly and set it in a safe place, such as inside a steel cabinet. **Warning:** *Never place your head near the end of the spring!* Slide the bump rubber up off the piston rod.

7   Unscrew the oil seal nut **(see illustration)** and discard it.

8   Remove the strut from the vise and pour the damper fluid into an approved oil container.

9   Place the strut back in the vise and remove the O-ring from the strut body **(see illustration)**. Pull the piston rod out of the strut.

10 Wash the strut tube out with solvent and blow it dry with compressed air, if available. If the old piston rod is to be reinstalled, wash it too.

11 Lubricate the shock absorber cylinder and piston with clean damper fluid. Install the piston rod in the shock absorber cylinder. Assemble the cylinder and piston unit to the strut tube, after lubricating all parts with damper fluid.

12 Fill the strut tube with 240 cc's of damper fluid. Do this slowly, taking time to pump the piston rod up and down to expel any air from under the piston.

5.4   Hold the collar on the spring seat with a large pair of pliers while loosening the piston rod nut

Cap

Insulator

Spring seat

Bump rubber

Piston

Oil seal nut

Square section O—ring

Spring

Strut

5.5a Exploded view of the strut/shock absorber and coil spring assembly components

5.5b Remove the insulator and upper spring seat from the piston rod

13 Slide the piston guide over the piston rod, with the flange facing up (see illustration).

14 Install a new O-ring between the piston guide and the strut tube.

15 Coat the oil seal lips and the threads of the oil seal nut with damper fluid and install the nut. Tighten it securely.

16 Stroke the damper shaft up and down a few times to verify proper operation.

17 Fully extend the damper shaft. Assemble the strut beginning with the bump rubber, coil spring and upper spring seat. Make sure the spring is properly positioned and the upper seat is installed so the flat side of the hole in the seat mates with the flat on the piston rod (see illustrations).

18 Install the insulator and a new piston rod nut, tightening it to the specified torque. Remove the spring compressor.

19 Install the strut and spring assembly on the vehicle as outlined in Section 4.

5.7 Unscrew the oil seal nut, then pour out the fluid

5.9 Remove the square section O-ring from the strut body

5.13 Lubricate the piston rod and install the guide with the flange facing up

Piston guide

O-ring

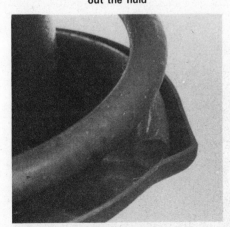

5.17a The tail on the bottom of the coil spring must be positioned in the seat pocket in the strut

5.17b When installing the upper seat, note that the flat side of the hole in the seat must mate with the flat on the piston rod (arrows)

5.17c The upper spring tail must seat in the recessed area of the upper seat (arrow)

10

6.3   Remove the lower arm nut (arrow) and pivot bolt — if the bolt is difficult to remove, drive it out with a hammer and punch

6   Lower arm – removal, inspection and installation

Refer to illustration 6.3
Warning: *Whenever any of the suspension or steering fasteners are loosened or removed, they must be inspected and, if necessary, replaced with new ones of the same part number or of original equipment quality and design. Torque specifications must be followed for proper reassembly and component retention.*

Removal

1   Loosen the wheel lug nuts on the side to be dismantled, raise the front of the vehicle, support it securely on jackstands, apply the parking brake and place blocks behind the rear wheels. Remove the wheel.
2   On 1989 and earlier models remove the strut bar–to–lower arm bolts and nuts **(see illustration 3.3b)** and the remaining balljoint–to–lower arm bolt and nut.
3   On 1989 and earlier models remove the bolt and nut from the lower control arm pivot **(see illustration).** Pry the arm from the crossmember if it is stuck. On 1990 and later models, detach the lower arm bracket and remove the lower arm mounting shaft bolts and bracket to separate the control arm from the chassis.

Inspection

4   Check the lower arm for distortion and the bushings for wear, damage and deterioration. Replace a damaged or bent control arm with a new one. If the inner pivot bushing is worn, take the lower arm to a dealer service department or a repair shop, as special tools are required to replace it.

7.6   The balljoint is fastened to the lower arm by two bolts and nuts (arrows)

Installation

5   Place the lower arm into the crossmember. Install the bolt and nut, but don't tighten them completely yet.
6   Connect the outer end of the arm to the balljoint and strut bar, tightening the three nuts to the specified torque.
7   Place a jack under the balljoint, with a block of wood on the jack head as a cushion. Raise the lower arm to simulate normal ride height, then tighten the pivot bolt nut to the specified torque.
8   Install the wheel and lug nuts, lower the vehicle and tighten the lug nuts to the specified torque.

7   Balljoints – check and replacement

Refer to illustrations 7.6 and 7.7
Warning: *Whenever any of the suspension or steering fasteners are loosened or removed, they must be inspected and, if necessary, replaced with new ones of the same part number or of original equipment quality and design. Torque specifications must be followed for proper reassembly and component retention.*

Check

1   Raise the vehicle and support it securely on jackstands.
2   Visually inspect the rubber boot for cuts, tears or leaking grease. If any of these conditions are noticed, the balljoint should be replaced.
3   Place a large pry bar under the balljoint and attempt to push the balljoint up. Next, position the pry bar between the steering knuckle and the lower arm and apply downward pressure. If any movement is seen or felt during either of these checks, a worn out balljoint is indicated.
4   Have an assistant grasp the tire at the top and bottom and shake the top of the tire in an in–and–out motion. Touch the balljoint stud nut. If any looseness is felt, suspect a worn out balljoint stud or a widened hole in the steering knuckle boss. If the latter problem exists, the steering knuckle should be replaced as well as the balljoint.

Replacement

5   Loosen the wheel lug nuts, raise the vehicle and support it securely on jackstands. Remove the wheel.
6   Break the balljoint–to–lower arm bolts loose, but don't remove them yet **(see illustration).**
7   Loosen the balljoint stud nut a couple of turns. Separate the balljoint from the steering knuckle with a balljoint separator **(see illustration),** then remove the nut.
8   Unscrew the two balljoint–to–lower arm bolts and remove the balljoint.
9   To install the balljoint, position it on the lower arm and install the two bolts, but don't tighten them yet.
10   Insert the balljoint stud into the steering knuckle and install the nut, tightening it to the specified torque.
11   Tighten the balljoint–to–lower arm bolts to the specified torque.
12   Install the wheel and lug nuts. Lower the vehicle and tighten the lug nuts to the specified torque.

7.7   Use a ''pickle-fork'' type balljoint separator to break the balljoint loose from the steering knuckle — boot damage can be minimized by applying grease to the boot first

10 Insert the balljoint stud into the steering knuckle and install the nut, tightening it to the specified torque.
11 Tighten the balljoint-to-lower arm bolts to the specified torque.
12 Install the wheel and lug nuts. Lower the vehicle and tighten the lug nuts to the specified torque.

8 Steering knuckle and hub assembly — removal and installation

Warning: *Whenever any of the suspension or steering fasteners are loosened or removed they must be inspected and, if necessary, replaced with new ones of the same part number or of original equipment quality and design. Torque specifications must be followed for proper reassembly and component retention. Dust created by the brake system may contain asbestos, which is harmful to your health. Never blow it out with compressed air and don't inhale any of it. Do not, under any circumstances, use petroleum-based solvents to clean brake parts. Use brake cleaner or denatured alcohol only.*

Removal

1 Remove the wheel cover and unscrew the hub nut (see Chapter 8).
2 Loosen the wheel lug nuts, raise the vehicle and support it securely on jackstands. Remove the wheel. Remove the brake caliper and support it with a piece of wire as described in Chapter 9.
3 Loosen, but do not remove the strut-to-steering knuckle bolts/nuts **(see illustration 4.3)**.
4 Separate the tie-rod from the steering knuckle arm as outlined in Section 18.
5 Separate the balljoint from the steering knuckle (Section 7). The strut-to-knuckle bolts can now be removed.
6 Remove the steering knuckle and hub assembly from the strut, balljoint and driveaxle. If the driveaxle sticks in the hub splines, push it from the hub as described in Chapter 8. Support the end of the driveaxle with a piece of wire.

Installation

7 Guide the knuckle and hub assembly into position, inserting the driveaxle into the hub.
8 Push the knuckle into the strut flange and install the bolts, but don't tighten them yet.
9 Insert the balljoint stud into the steering knuckle hole and install the nut, but don't tighten it yet.
10 Attach the tie-rod to the steering knuckle arm as described in Section 18. Tighten the strut bolt nuts, the balljoint nut and the tie-rod nut to the specified torque.
11 Install the caliper as outlined in Chapter 9.
12 Install the hub nut and tighten it securely (Chapter 9).
13 Install the wheel and lug nuts.
14 Lower the vehicle and tighten the lug nuts to the specified torque.
15 Tighten the hub nut to the specified torque.

9 Front axle hub and bearing — replacement

Due to the need for special tools to replace the hub and bearing assembly in the steering knuckle and to properly adjust the hub bearing preload, the steering knuckle and hub assembly must be taken to a Hyundai dealer service department or a repair shop equipped with the necessary tools for this procedure. Refer to Section 8 for the steering knuckle removal procedure.

10 Rear stabilizer bar — removal and installation

Refer to illustration 10.2

Warning: *Whenever any of the suspension or steering fasteners are loosened or removed, they must be inspected and, if necessary, replaced with new ones of the same part number or of original equipment quality and design. Torque specifications must be followed for proper reassembly and component retention.*

1 Remove the rear axle assembly as outlined in Section 13.
2 Using white paint or a scribe, place match marks on the stabilizer bar aligned with the punch marks on the stabilizer bar brackets **(see**

Punch mark   Aligning mark

10.2 Before removing the stabilizer bar, make marks on the bar that are aligned with the punch marks on the bar brackets

illustration). This will ensure proper alignment of the stabilizer bar splines during installation.
3 Pull the trailing arms apart far enough to allow the stabilizer bar to slide out of the splines.
4 Check the bar for cracks and distortion. Install a new one if necessary.
5 Installation is the reverse of the removal procedure.
6 Install the rear axle assembly.

11 Rear coil spring — removal and installation

Refer to illustrations 11.3 and 11.7

Warning: *Whenever any of the suspension or steering fasteners are loosened or removed, they must be inspected and, if necessary, replaced with new ones of the same part number or of original equipment quality and design. Torque specifications must be followed for proper reassembly and component retention.*

Removal

1 Loosen the rear wheel lug nuts, raise the rear of the vehicle and support it securely on jackstands. The jackstands must be placed under the vehicle at the lifting points, not under the rear axle assembly. Remove the wheel.
2 Position a floor jack under the spring pocket area of the suspension arm and raise it just enough to feel resistance from the spring. Remove the shock absorber lower mounting bolt (see Section 12 if necessary).
3 Slowly lower the jack until the coil spring is fully extended, then guide the spring out of the mounts **(see illustration)**.

11.3 Once the coil spring is fully extended, it can be removed from the seat — it may be necessary to push down on the suspension arm to obtain adequate clearance for removal

10

11.7   The upper end of the coil spring must be positioned in the upper seat as shown

Installation

4   Before installing the coil spring, check the upper seat for cracks, hardening and general deterioration. Replace it if necessary.
5   Check the bump stop on the suspension arm for cracks and wear and replace it if necessary. It's retained to the arm by one nut on the under side of the arm.
6   Check the coil spring for cracks, chips, excessive rust and deformation. Replace the spring if any of these conditions exist.
7   Place the coil spring in the seat on the suspension arm. Install the upper seat, making sure that it is positioned properly **(see illustration)**.
8   Raise the floor jack high enough to enable the lower end of the shock absorber to be reconnected. Tighten the bolt securely.
9   Install the wheel and lower the vehicle. Tighten the lug nuts to the specified torque.

12   Rear shock absorber — removal and installation

Refer to illustrations 12.2 and 12.3

Warning: *Whenever any of the suspension or steering fasteners are loosened or removed, they must be inspected and, if necessary, replaced with new ones of the same part number or of original equipment quality and design.*

1   Loosen the rear wheel lug nuts, raise the rear of the vehicle and support it securely on jackstands. Position blocks in front of the front wheels. Remove the rear wheel(s).
2   Position a floor jack under the rear suspension arm and raise it just enough to take some of the spring pressure off the shock absorber. Remove the shock absorber lower mounting bolt **(see illustration)**.
3   Remove the upper mounting bolt and nut **(see illustration)** and

detach the shock absorber.
4   Installation is the reverse of the removal procedure. Be sure to tighten the fasteners securely.

13   Rear Axle assembly — removal, overhaul and installation

Warning: *Whenever any of the suspension or steering fasteners are loosened or removed, they must be inspected and, if necessary, replaced with new ones of the same part number or of original equipment quality and design. Torque specifications must be followed for proper reassembly and component retention.*

Removal

Refer to illustrations 13.9a and 13.9b

1   Loosen the rear wheel lug nuts (both wheels), raise the rear of the vehicle and support it securely on jackstands placed underneath the lifting points, not under the axle assembly. Position blocks in front of the front wheels.
2   Remove the brake drums following the rear wheel bearing servicing procedure in Chapter 1.
3   Disconnect the brake hydraulic lines from the rear wheel cylinders. Refer to Chapter 9 if necessary.
4   Detach the brake backing plates from the rear axle by removing the bolts. Disconnect the parking brake cables from the suspension arms and reposition the brake assemblies out of the way. Note the asbestos warnings stated in Chapter 9.
5   Unbolt the brake line clamps from the under sides of the suspension arms, then disconnect the lines from the flexible hoses at the brakets on the front of each suspension arm. After removing the brake lines, plug the ends to keep contaminants out.
6   Remove the rear section of the exhaust system (refer to Chapter 4 if necessary).
7   Remove the rear shock absorbers (see Section 12).
8   Support the rear axle with a floor jack positioned under the center of the assembly where the two suspension arms meet. If two floor jacks are available, support the assembly on each side, just inside the mounting points.
9   Unbolt the mounting fixtures from the floorpan **(see illustrations)**. Slowly lower the axle assembly, making sure nothing is left connected.

Overhaul

Refer to illustrations 13.11, 13.15, 13.16 and 13.20

10   The rear axle assembly is composed of two separate suspension arms which may be separated for servicing. The arms contain bushings that can be replaced if they're worn out.
11   Using a sharp scribe or paint, apply match marks to the fixtures and the suspension arms **(see illustration)**.
12   Remove the nuts that retain the fixtures to the suspension arms, then pull the fixtures off the arms. Check the rubber bushings on each fixture for wear, cracks and deterioration. If they must be replaced, drive them out with a hammer and drift and drive the new ones in (lubricate them with soapy water first).

12.2   Support the suspension arm with a jack before removing either shock absorber mounting bolt

12.3   Two wrenches are needed to remove the upper mounting bolt and nut

Suspension arm, right

Shock absorber

Dust cover

Clamp

Bushing A

Spring upper seat

Coil spring

Bump stopper

Suspension arm, left

Stabilizer bar

Bushing B

Rubber stopper

Fixture

Washer

Rubber bushing

13.9a   Rear suspension components — exploded view

13.9b   The rear axle assembly mounting fixtures are retained to the floorpan by two bolts (arrows)

Fixture   Rubber bushing

Nut

Mating aligning marks

13.11   Make match marks on the fixtures and suspension arms before separating them

10

13.15   Tap around the outer edge of the bushing when removing it, so it doesn't become cocked in the tube

13.16   Use a hammer and drift punch to drive bushing B out of the left suspension arm

13.20   The fixtures must be positioned as shown here during installation

13   If the vehicle is equipped with a rear stabilizer bar, mark the relationship of the bar to the bar brackets (see Section 10).

14   Remove the dust cover clamp and pull the two arms apart.

15   Mount the right suspension arm in a vise lined with rags, remove the rubber stopper, then tap the bushing out of the end of the tube **(see illustration)**.

16   Mount the left suspension arm in the vise and drive out the bushing from inside the tube **(see illustration)**.

17   Lubricate the new bushings and seats with chassis grease and install them with a bushing driver. If a bushing driver isn't available, use a large socket or a piece of pipe.

18   Apply chassis grease to the surface of the right suspension arm. Install the rubber stopper.

19   Push the right and left suspension arms together and install the stabilizer bar, if equipped. Make sure the marks on the stabilizer bar line up with the marks on the brackets.

20   Install the mounting fixtures on the suspension arms (line up the marks made in Step 11). Make sure the fixtures and the washers are installed properly **(see illustration)**. Don't tighten the fixture nuts completely yet.

21   Pack grease into the dust cover and lips and tighten the clamp.

Installation

22   Install the axle assembly by reversing the removal steps. Be sure to tighten the fixture-to-floorpan bolts to the specified torque. Lower the vehicle to the ground and tighten the fixture nuts to the specified torque.

23   Bleed the brake system (Chapter 9).

14   Steering system — general information

All models are equipped with rack-and-pinion steering. The steering gear is bolted to the crossmember at the firewall and operates the steering arms via tie-rods. The inner ends of the tie-rods are protected by rubber boots which should be inspected periodically for secure attachment, tears and leaking lubricant.

The power assist system consists of a belt-driven pump and associated lines and hoses. The power steering pump reservoir fluid level should be checked periodically (Chapter 1).

The steering wheel operates the steering shaft, which actuates the steering gear through universal joints. Looseness in the steering can be caused by wear in the steering shaft universal joints, the steering gear, the tie-rod ends and loose retaining bolts.

15   Steering wheel — removal and installation

Refer to illustrations 15.3 and 15.4

Warning: *Whenever any of the suspension or steering fasteners are*

loosened or removed, they must be inspected and, if necessary, replaced with new ones of the same part number or of original equipment quality and design. Torque specifications must be followed for proper reassembly and component retention.

1   Disconnect the cable from the negative terminal of the battery.

2   Pull the horn pad from the steering wheel.

3   Remove the steering wheel retaining nut then mark the relationship of the steering shaft to the hub to simplify installation and ensure steering wheel alignment **(see illustration)**.

15.3   After removing the steering wheel nut, make alignment marks on the steering column shaft and the steering wheel hub — this will ensure correct steering wheel alignment during installation

15.4 Use a steering wheel puller to separate the steering wheel from the shaft — DO NOT hammer on the shaft in an attempt to remove the wheel!

4   Use a steering wheel puller to disconnect the steering wheel from the shaft **(see illustration)**.
5   To install the wheel, align the mark on the steering wheel hub with the mark on the shaft and slip the wheel onto the shaft. Install the hub nut and tighten it to the specified torque.
6   Install the horn pad.
7   Connect the negative battery cable.

16 Intermediate shaft — removal and installation

Refer to illustrations 16.2 and 16.4
Warning: *Whenever any of the suspension or steering fasteners are loosened or removed, they must be inspected and, if necessary, replaced with new ones of the same part number or of original equipment quality and design. Torque specifications must be followed for proper reassembly and component retention.*

1   Turn the front wheels to the straight ahead position. Raise the vehicle and support it securely on jackstands.
2   Using white paint, place alignment marks on the upper universal joint, the steering shaft, the lower universal joint and the steering gear input shaft **(see illustration)**.
3   Remove the upper and lower universal joint pinch bolts.
4   Remove the three dust cover bolts **(see illustration)** and pull the cover into the driver's compartment.
5   Pry the intermediate shaft universal joint off the steering gear input shaft. Separate the shaft from the steering column and pull the assembly into the driver's compartment.
6   Installation is the reverse of the removal procedure. Be sure to align the marks and tighten the pinch bolts to the specified torque.

17 Steering gear — removal and installation

Refer to illustrations 17.2 and 17.5
Warning: *Whenever any of the suspension or steering fasteners are loosened or removed, they must be inspected and, if necessary, replaced with new ones of the same part number or of original equipment quality and design. Torque specifications must be followed for proper reassembly and component retention.*

Note: *This procedure applies to both power and manual steering gear assemblies. When working on a vehicle equipped with a manual steering gear, simply ignore any references made to the power steering system.*

Removal

1   Raise the front of the vehicle and support it securely on jackstands. Apply the parking brake.
2   Place a drain pan under the steering gear (power steering only).

16.2 Make alignment marks on the intermediate shaft and the steering column shaft (do the same to the other end of the intermediate shaft, at the steering gear input shaft)

16.4 The dust cover is fastened to the inner firewall with three bolts

17.2 Remove the power steering pressure (1) and return (2) lines — (3) is the intermediate shaft lower pinch bolt

Remove the power steering pressure and return lines and cap the ends to prevent excessive fluid loss and contamination **(see illustration)**.
3   Mark the relationship of the lower intermediate shaft universal joint to the steering gear input shaft (see Section 16). Remove the lower intermediate shaft pinch bolt.

10

17.5   Remove the two bolts from each steering gear housing clamp

18.2a   Loosen the jam nut while holding the tie-rod with a wrench (or a pair of locking pliers) on the flat portion of the rod to prevent it from turning

18.2b   The relationship of the tie-rod end to the tie-rod can be marked with white paint

4   Separate the tie-rod ends from the steering knuckle arms (see Section 18).

5   Support the steering gear and remove the steering gear housing clamp bolts **(see illustration)**. Lower the unit, separate the intermediate shaft from the steering gear input shaft and remove the steering gear from the vehicle.

Installation

6   Raise the steering gear into position and connect the intermediate shaft, aligning the marks.

7   Install the gear housing clamps and bolts and tighten the bolts to the specified torque.

8   Connect the tie-rod ends to the steering knuckle arms (Section 18).

9   Install the intermediate shaft lower pinch bolt and tighten it to the specified torque.

10   Connect the power steering pressure and return hoses to the steering gear and fill the power steering pump reservoir with the recommended fluid (Chapter 1).

11   Lower the vehicle and bleed the steering system as outlined in Section 21.

---

18   Tie-rod ends — removal and installation

Refer to illustrations 18.2a, 18.2b and 18.4

Warning: *Whenever any of the suspension or steering fasteners are loosened or removed, they must be inspected and, if necessary, replaced with new ones of the same part number or of original equipment quality and design. Torque specifications must be followed for proper reassembly and component retention.*

Removal

1   Loosen the wheel lug nuts. Raise the front of the vehicle, support it securely, block the rear wheels and apply the parking brake. Remove the front wheel(s).

2   Hold the tie-rod with a pair of locking pliers or a wrench and loosen the jam nut enough to mark the position of the tie-rod end in relation to the threads **(see illustrations)**.

3   Remove the cotter pin and loosen the nut on the tie-rod end stud.

4   Disconnect the tie-rod from the steering knuckle arm with a puller **(see illustration)**. Remove the nut and separate the tie-rod.

5   Unscrew the tie-rod end from the tie-rod.

Installation

6   Thread the tie-rod end on to the marked position and insert the tie-rod stud into the steering knuckle arm. Tighten the jam nut securely.

7   Install the castellated nut on the stud and tighten it to the specified torque. Install a new cotter pin.

18.4   A gear puller works well for separating the tie-rod end from the steering knuckle arm — note that the nut hasn't been removed (leaving it in place will prevent the two from separating violently)

20.4 To detach the power steering pump, remove the pressure line fitting nut (1), the return line hose (2), the pressure line bracket (3), the adjuster bolt (4) and the pivot bolt (not visible in this photo) — have a container ready to catch spilled fluid when removing the pump

8   Install the wheel and lug nuts. Lower the vehicle and tighten the lug nuts to the specified torque.
9   Have the alignment checked by a dealer service department or an alignment shop.

19   Steering gear boots — replacement

1   Loosen the lug nuts, raise the vehicle and support it securely on jackstands. Remove the front wheel(s).
2   Refer to Section 18 and remove the tie-rod end and jam nut.
3   Remove the steering gear boot clamps and slide the boot off.
4   Before installing the new boot, wrap the threads and serrations on the end of the steering rod with a layer of tape so the small end of the new boot isn't damaged.
5   Slide the new boot into position on the steering gear until it seats in the groove in the steering rod and install new clamps.
6   Remove the tape and install the tie-rod end (Section 18).
7   Install the wheel and lug nuts. Lower the vehicle and tighten the lug nuts to the specified torque.

20   Power steering pump — removal and installation

Refer to illustration 20.4
Warning: *Whenever any of the suspension or steering fasteners are loosened or removed, they must be inspected and, if necessary, replaced with new ones of the same part number or of original equipment quality and design. Torque specifications must be followed for proper reassembly and component retention.*

1   Disconnect the cable from the negative battery terminal.
2   Loosen the tension on the pump drivebelt (Chapter 1) and remove the belt.
3   Using a suction gun, suck out as much fluid from the power steering fluid reservoir as possible. Place a drain pan under the vehicle to catch any fluid that may spill out when the hoses are disconnected.
4   Disconnect the pressure and return lines from the pump **(see illustration)**. Unbolt the high pressure line bracket from the pump.
5   Remove the adjuster bolt and pivot bolt from the pump **(see illustration 20.4)** and detach the pump from the vehicle.
6   Installation is the reverse of the removal procedure. Be sure to adjust the power steering pump drivebelt tension and top up the power steering fluid reservoir (Chapter 1).
7   Bleed the power steering system as described in Section 21.

21   Power steering system — bleeding

1   Following any operation in which the power steering lines have been disconnected, the power steering system must be bled to remove all air and obtain proper steering performance.
2   With the front wheels in the straight ahead position, check the power steering fluid level and, if low, add fluid (see Chapter 1).
3   Start the engine and allow it to run at fast idle. Recheck the fluid level and add more if necessary.
4   Bleed the system by turning the steering wheel from side-to-side, without hitting the stops. This will work the air out of the system. Keep the reservoir full of fluid as this is done.
5   When the air is out of the system, return the wheels to the straight ahead position and leave the vehicle running for several more minutes before shutting it off.
6   Road test the vehicle to be sure the steering system is functioning normally and noise free.
7   Recheck the fluid level to be sure it's correct. Add fluid if necessary (see Chapter 1).

22   Wheels and tires — general information

Refer to illustration 22.1
   All vehicles covered by this manual are equipped with metric-sized fiberglass or steel belted radial tires **(see illustration)**. Use of other size or type of tires may affect the ride and handling of the vehicle. Don't mix different types of tires, such as radials and bias belted, on the same vehicle as handling may be seriously affected. It's recommended that tires be replaced in pairs on the same axle, but if only one tire is being replaced, be sure it's the same size, structure and tread design as the other.
   Because tire pressure has a substantial effect on handling and wear, the pressure on all tires should be checked at least once a month or before any extended trips (see Chapter 1).

22.1   Metric tire size code

10

Wheels must be replaced if they are bent, dented, leak air, have elongated bolt holes, are heavily rusted, out of vertical symmetry or if the lug nuts won't stay tight. Wheel repairs that use welding or peening are not recommended.

Tire and wheel balance is important in the overall handling, braking and performance of the vehicle. Unbalanced wheels can adversely affect handling and ride characteristics as well as tire life. Whenever a tire is installed on a wheel, the tire and wheel should be balanced by a shop with the proper equipment.

23   Front end alignment — general information

A front end alignment refers to the adjustments made to the front wheels so they are in proper angular relationship to the suspension and the ground. Front wheels that are out of proper alignment not only affect steering control, but also increase tire wear. The only front end adjustment normally required on this vehicle is toe-in. Caster angle is slightly adjustable.

Getting the proper front wheel alignment is a very exacting process, one in which complicated and expensive machines are necessary to perform the job properly. Because of this, you should have a technician with the proper equipment perform these tasks. We will, however, use this space to give you a basic idea of what is involved with front end alignment so you can better understand the process and deal intelligently with the shop that does the work.

Toe-in is the turning in of the front wheels. The purpose of a toe specification is to ensure parallel rolling of the front wheels. In a vehicle with zero toe-in, the distance between the front edges of the wheels will be the same as the distance between the rear edges of the wheels. The actual amount of toe-in is normally only a fraction of an inch. Toe-in adjustment is controlled by the tie-rod end position on the tie-rod. Incorrect toe-in will cause the tires to wear improperly by making them scrub against the road surface.

Caster is the tilting of the front steering axis from the vertical. A tilt toward the rear is positive caster and a tilt toward the front is negative caster. Caster is adjusted by changing the position of the adjusting nuts on the strut bar.

Camber angle is not adjustable on this vehicle.

Chapter 11 Body

Contents

Specifications

Front door bolt hole-to-rear of glass

	Inches	mm
1989 3-door vehicles only	11-5/32	283.2
All others	2-39/64	65

Torque specifications

	Ft-lbs	Nm
Seat bolt	11 to 13	16 to 18

1 General information

These models feature a "unibody" layout, using a floor pan with front and rear frame side rails which support the body components, front and rear suspension systems and other mechanical components.

Certain components are particularly vulnerable to accident damage and can be unbolted and repaired or replaced. Among these parts are the body moldings, bumpers, hood and trunk lids and all glass.

Only general body maintenance practices and body panel repair procedures within the scope of the do-it-yourselfer are included in this Chapter.

2 Body — maintenance

1   The condition of your vehicle's body is very important, because the resale value depends a great deal on it. It's much more difficult to repair a neglected or damaged body than it is to repair mechanical components. The hidden areas of the body, such as the wheel wells, the frame and the engine compartment, are equally important, although they don't require as frequent attention as the rest of the body.

2   Once a year, or every 12,000 miles, it's a good idea to have the underside of the body steam cleaned. All traces of dirt and oil will be removed and the area can then be inspected carefully for rust, damaged

brake lines, frayed electrical wires, damaged cables and other problems. The front suspension components should be greased after completion of this job.

3   At the same time, clean the engine and the engine compartment with a steam cleaner or water soluble degreaser.

4   The wheel wells should be given close attention, since undercoating can peel away and stones and dirt thrown up by the tires can cause the paint to chip and flake, allowing rust to set in. If rust is found, clean down to the bare metal and apply an anti-rust paint.

5   The body should be washed about once a week. Wet the vehicle thoroughly to soften the dirt, then wash it down with a soft sponge and plenty of clean soapy water. If the surplus dirt is not washed off very carefully, it can wear down the paint.

6   Spots of tar or asphalt thrown up from the road should be removed with a cloth soaked in solvent.

7   Once every six months, wax the body and chrome trim. If a chrome cleaner is used to remove rust from any of the vehicle's plated parts, remember that the cleaner also removes part of the chrome, so use it sparingly.

3 Vinyl trim — maintenance

Don't clean vinyl trim with detergents, caustic soap or petroleum-based cleaners. Plain soap and water works just fine, with a soft brush to clean dirt that may be ingrained. Wash the vinyl as frequently as the rest of the vehicle.

After cleaning, application of a high quality rubber and vinyl protectant will help prevent oxidation and cracks. The protectant can also be applied to weatherstripping, vacuum lines and rubber hoses, which often fail as a result of chemical degradation, and to the tires.

4 Upholstery and carpets — maintenance

Every three months remove the carpets or mats and clean the interior of the vehicle (more frequently if necessary). Vacuum the upholstery and carpets to remove loose dirt and dust.

5 Body repair — minor damage

See photo sequence

Repair of minor scratches

1   If the scratch is superficial and does not penetrate to the metal of the body, repair is very simple. Lightly rub the scratched area with a fine rubbing compound to remove loose paint and built-up wax. Rinse the area with clean water.

2   Apply touch-up paint to the scratch, using a small brush. Continue to apply thin layers of paint until the surface of the paint in the scratch is level with the surrounding paint. Allow the new paint at least two weeks to harden, then blend it into the surrounding paint by rubbing with a very fine rubbing compound. Finally, apply a coat of wax to the scratch area.

3   If the scratch has penetrated the paint and exposed the metal of the body, causing the metal to rust, a different repair technique is required. Remove all loose rust from the bottom of the scratch with a pocket knife, then apply rust inhibiting paint to prevent the formation of rust in the future. Using a rubber or nylon applicator, coat the scratched area with glaze-type filler. If required, the filler can be mixed with thinner to provide a very thin paste, which is ideal for filling narrow scratches. Before the glaze filler in the scratch hardens, wrap a piece of smooth cotton cloth around the tip of a finger. Dip the cloth in thinner and then quickly wipe it along the surface of the scratch. This will ensure that the surface of the filler is slightly hollow. The scratch can now be painted over as described earlier in this section.

Repair of dents

4   When repairing dents, the first job is to pull the dent out until the affected area is as close as possible to its original shape. There is no point in trying to restore the original shape completely as the metal in the damaged area will have stretched on impact and cannot be re-

stored to its original contours. It is better to bring the level of the dent up to a point which is about 1/8-inch below the level of the surrounding metal. In cases where the dent is very shallow, it is not worth trying to pull it out at all.

5   If the back side of the dent is accessible, it can be hammered out gently from behind using a soft-face hammer. While doing this, hold a block of wood firmly against the opposite side of the metal to absorb the hammer blows and prevent the metal from being stretched.

6   If the dent is in a section of the body which has double layers, or some other factor makes it inaccessible from behind, a different technique is required. Drill several small holes through the metal inside the damaged area, particularly in the deeper sections. Screw long, self-tapping screws into the holes just enough for them to get a good grip in the metal. Now the dent can be pulled out by pulling on the protruding heads of the screws with locking pliers.

7   The next stage of repair is the removal of paint from the damaged area and from an inch or so of the surrounding metal. This is done with a wire brush or sanding disk in a drill motor, although it can be done just as effectively by hand with sandpaper. To complete the preparation for filling, score the surface of the bare metal with a screwdriver or the tang of a file, or drill small holes in the affected area. This will provide a good grip for the filler material. To complete the repair, see the subsection on filling and painting later in this Section.

Repair of rust holes or gashes

8   Remove all paint from the affected area and from an inch or so of the surrounding metal using a sanding disk or wire brush mounted in a drill motor. If these are not available, a few sheets of sandpaper will do the job just as effectively.

9   With the paint removed, you will be able to determine the severity of the corrosion and decide whether to replace the whole panel, if possible, or repair the affected area. New body panels are not as expensive as you may think and it is often quicker to install a new panel than to repair large areas of rust.

10   Remove all trim pieces from the affected area except those which will act as a guide to the original shape of the damaged body, such as headlight shells, etc. Using metal snips or a hacksaw blade, remove all loose metal and any other metal that is badly affected by rust. Hammer the edges of the hole inward to create a slight depression for the filler material.

11   Wire brush the affected area to remove the powdery rust from the surface of the metal. If the back of the rusted area is accessible, treat it with rust inhibiting paint.

12   Before filling is done, block the hole in some way. This can be done with sheet metal riveted or screwed into place, or by stuffing the hole with wire mesh.

13   Once the hole is blocked off, the affected area can be filled and painted. See the following subsection on filling and painting.

Filling and painting

14   Many types of body fillers are available, but generally speaking, body repair kits which contain filler paste and a tube of resin hardener are best for this type of repair work. A wide, flexible plastic or nylon applicator will be necessary for imparting a smooth and contoured finish to the surface of the filler material. Mix up a small amount of filler on a clean piece of wood or cardboard (use the hardener sparingly). Follow the manufacturer's instructions on the package, otherwise the filler will set incorrectly.

15   Using the applicator, apply the filler paste to the prepared area. Draw the applicator across the surface of the filler to achieve the desired contour and to level the filler surface. As soon as a contour that approximates the original one is achieved, stop working the paste. If you continue, the paste will begin to stick to the applicator. Continue to add thin layers of paste at 20-minute intervals until the level of the filler is just above the surrounding metal.

16   Once the filler has hardened, the excess can be removed with a body file. From then on, progressively finer grades of sandpaper should be used, starting with a 180-grit paper and finishing with 600-grit wet-or-dry paper. Always wrap the sandpaper around a flat rubber or wooden block, otherwise the surface of the filler will not be completely flat. During the sanding of the filler surface, the wet-or-dry paper should be periodically rinsed in water. This will ensure that a very smooth finish is produced in the final stage.

17   At this point, the repair area should be surrounded by a ring of

bare metal, which in turn should be encircled by the finely feathered edge of good paint. Rinse the repair area with clean water until all of the dust produced by the sanding operation is gone.

18   Spray the entire area with a light coat of primer. This will reveal any imperfections in the surface of the filler. Repair the imperfections with fresh filler paste or glaze filler and once more smooth the surface with sandpaper. Repeat this spray-and-repair procedure until you are satisfied that the surface of the filler and the feathered edge of the paint are perfect. Rinse the area with clean water and allow it to dry completely.

19   The repair area is now ready for painting. Spray painting must be carried out in a warm, dry, windless and dust free atmosphere. These conditions can be created if you have access to a large indoor work area, but if you are forced to work in the open, you will have to pick the day very carefully. If you are working indoors, dousing the floor in the work area with water will help settle the dust which would otherwise be in the air. If the repair area is confined to one body panel, mask off the surrounding panels. This will help minimize the effects of a slight mismatch in paint color. Trim pieces such as chrome strips, door handles, etc., will also need to be masked off or removed. Use masking tape and several thicknesses of newspaper for the masking operations.

20   Before spraying, shake the paint can thoroughly, then spray a test area until the spray painting technique is mastered. Cover the repair area with a thick coat of primer. The thickness should be built up using several thin layers of primer rather than one thick one. Using 600-grit wet-or-dry sandpaper, rub down the surface of the primer until it is very smooth. While doing this, the work area should be thoroughly rinsed with water and the wet-or-dry sandpaper periodically rinsed as well. Allow the primer to dry before spraying additional coats.

21   Spray on the top coat, again building up the thickness by using several thin layers of paint. Begin spraying in the center of the repair area and then, using a circular motion, work out until the whole repair area and about two inches of the surrounding original paint is covered. Remove all masking material 10 to 15 minutes after spraying on the final coat of paint. Allow the new paint at least two weeks to harden, then use a very fine rubbing compound to blend the edges of the new paint into the existing paint. Finally, apply a coat of wax.

6   Body repair — major damage

1   Major damage must be repaired by an auto body shop specifically equipped to perform unibody repairs. These shops have the specialized equipment required to do the job properly.

2   If the damage is extensive, the body must be checked for proper alignment or the vehicle's handling characteristics may be adversely affected and other components may wear at an accelerated rate.

3   Due to the fact that all of the major body components (hood, fenders, etc.) are separate and replaceable units, any seriously damaged components should be replaced rather than repaired. Sometimes the components can be found in a wrecking yard that specializes in used vehicle components, often at considerable savings over the cost of new parts.

9.2   Use paint or a permanent marker to mark on the hinge plate around the hood bolts – mark around the entire hinge plate before adjusting the hood (early models)

7   Hinges and locks — maintenance

Once every 3000 miles, or every three months, the hinges and latch assemblies on the doors, hood and trunk should be given a few drops of light oil or lock lubricant. The door latch strikers should also be lubricated with a thin coat of grease to reduce wear and ensure free movement. Lubricate the door and trunk locks with spray-on graphite lubricant.

8   Fixed glass — replacement

Replacement of the windshield and fixed glass requires the use of special fast-setting adhesive/caulk materials and some specialized tools. It is recommended that these operations be left to a dealer or a shop specializing in glass work.

9   Hood – removal, installation and adjustment

Refer to illustrations 9.2, 9.10, and 9.11
Note: *The hood is heavy and somewhat awkward to remove and install – at least two people should perform this procedure.*
Note: *This procedure is shown on an early model where the hood is hinged at the front by the radiator. On later models, the hood is hinged at the rear by the base of the windshield. This procedure pertains to all models.*

Removal and installation

1   Use blankets or pads to cover the cowl area of the body and fenders. This will protect the body and paint as the hood is lifted free.

2   Use paint or a permanent marker to make alignment marks around the bolt heads to ensure proper alignment upon installation **(see illustration).**

3   Disconnect any cables or electrical connectors which will interfere with removal.

4   Have an assistant support the weight of the hood. Remove the hinge-to-hood screws or bolts.

5   Lift off the hood.

6   Installation is the reverse of removal.

Adjustment

7   Front-and-rear and side-to-side adjustment of the hood is made by moving the hinge plate slot after loosening the bolts or nuts.

8   Mark a line around the entire hinge plate so you can judge the amount of movement **(see illustration 9.2)**

9   Loosen the bolts and move the hood into correct alignment. Move the hood only a little at a time. Tighten the hinge bolts and carefully lower the hood to check the position.

10   If necessary after installation, the entire hood latch assembly can be adjusted up-and-down as well as side-to-side on the firewall so the hood closes securely, with the hood flush with the fenders. To perform this adjustment, mark around the hood latch mounting screws to provide a reference point, then loosen them and reposition the latch assembly, as necessary **(see illustration).** Following adjustment, retighten the mounting bolts.

9.10   To adjust the hood latch, mark lines around the hood latch mounting screws (arrows), loosen the screws, position the latch where required and retighten the screws (early models)

11

These photos illustrate a method of repairing simple dents. They are intended to supplement *Body repair - minor damage* in this Chapter and should not be used as the sole instructions for body repair on these vehicles.

1   If you can't access the backside of the body panel to hammer out the dent, pull it out with a slide-hammer-type dent puller. In the deepest portion of the dent or along the crease line, drill or punch hole(s) at least one inch apart . . .

2   . . . then screw the slide-hammer into the hole and operate it. Tap with a hammer near the edge of the dent to help 'pop' the metal back to its original shape. When you're finished, the dent area should be close to its original contour and about 1/8-inch below the surface of the surrounding metal

3   Using coarse-grit sandpaper, remove the paint down to the bare metal. Hand sanding works fine, but the disc sander shown here makes the job faster. Use finer (about 320-grit) sandpaper to feather-edge the paint at least one inch around the dent area

4   When the paint is removed, touch will probably be more helpful than sight for telling if the metal is straight. Hammer down the high spots or raise the low spots as necessary. Clean the repair area with wax/silicone remover

5   Following label instructions, mix up a batch of plastic filler and hardener. The ratio of filler to hardener is critical, and, if you mix it incorrectly, it will either not cure properly or cure too quickly (you won't have time to file and sand it into shape)

6   Working quickly so the filler doesn't harden, use a plastic applicator to press the body filler firmly into the metal, assuring it bonds completely. Work the filler until it matches the original contour and is slightly above the surrounding metal

7 Let the filler harden until you can just dent it with your fingernail. Use a body file or Surform tool (shown here) to rough-shape the filler

8 Use coarse-grit sandpaper and a sanding board or block to work the filler down until it's smooth and even. Work down to finer grits of sandpaper - always using a board or block - ending up with 360 or 400 grit

9 You shouldn't be able to feel any ridge at the transition from the filler to the bare metal or from the bare metal to the old paint. As soon as the repair is flat and uniform, remove the dust and mask off the adjacent panels or trim pieces

10 Apply several layers of primer to the area. Don't spray the primer on too heavy, so it sags or runs, and make sure each coat is dry before you spray on the next one. A professional-type spray gun is being used here, but aerosol spray primer is available inexpensively from auto parts stores

11 The primer will help reveal imperfections or scratches. Fill these with glazing compound. Follow the label instructions and sand it with 360 or 400-grit sandpaper until it's smooth. Repeat the glazing, sanding and respraying until the primer reveals a perfectly smooth surface

12 Finish sand the primer with very fine sandpaper (400 or 600-grit) to remove the primer overspray. Clean the area with water and allow it to dry. Use a tack rag to remove any dust, then apply the finish coat. Don't attempt to rub out or wax the repair area until the paint has dried completely (at least two weeks)

9.11 Adjust the rear of the hood vertically using the hood bumpers — there's one on each side of the cowl at the rear corner of the hood

10.2 Locations of 1986 radiator grille mounting screws

11   Finally, adjust the hood bumpers on the cowl so that the hood, when closed, is flush with the fenders **(see illustration)**.
12   The hood latch assembly, as well as the hinges, should be periodically lubricated with white lithium base grease to prevent sticking or jamming.

10   Radiator grille – removal and installation

Refer to illustrations 10.2 and 10.4

1986 models
1   Remove the parking light assemblies (Chapter 12).
2   Remove the mounting screws and detach the grille from the vehicle **(see illustration)**.
3   Installation is the reverse of removal.

1987 through 1989 models
4   Disengage the six grille retaining clips with a small screwdriver **(see illustration)**.
5   Once all of the retaining clips are disengaged, pull the grille out sharply and remove it.
6   To install the grille, press it in place until the clips lock it into position.

10.4 Use a small screwdriver to disengage the radiator grille retaining clips (1987 through 1989 models)

1990 and later models
7   Open the hood.
8   Unscrew the grille at the top, pull up slightly and remove the grille.

11.1 Typical bumper component details (1986 through 1989 models shown)

Front bumper
Retaining bolts
Bumper plate
Bumper rail
Bumper stay nuts
Energy absorber
Front bumper cover
Bumper cover-to-body bolts

Rear bumper
Bumper rail
Energy absorber
Rear bumper cover
Retaining bolts
Bumper stay nuts
Bumper cover-to-body bolts

12.2a Pull out the door handle for access to the screw that secures the handle bezel

12.2b The armrest retaining screws are hidden under covers which can be pried off using a small screwdriver

12.2c Don't forget the screws along the bottom of the panel

11 Bumpers — removal and installation

Refer to illustration 11.1
Note: *This procedure applies to either the front or rear bumper.*
1 Remove the bumper cover-to-body bolts **(see illustration).**

12.3a On 1986 and 1987 vehicles, work a cloth back and forth behind the window handle until the clip is dislodged

12.3b On 1988 and later vehicles, push the clip off with a screwdriver

2 Disconnect any wiring or other components which would interfere with removal of the bumper.
3 Support the bumper's weight with a jack or jackstand. Alternatively, have an assistant support the bumper.
4 Remove the retaining bolts and detach the bumper.
5 Installation is the reverse of removal.
6 Tighten the retaining bolts securely.
7 Install the bumper cover bolts and any other components which were removed.

12 Door trim panel – removal and installation

Refer to illustrations 12.2a, 12.2b, 12.2c, 13.3a, 13.3b, 13.3c and 12.6
1986 through 1989 models
1 Disconnect the negative cable from the battery. Place the cable out of the way so it cannot accidentally come in contact with the negative terminal of the battery, as this would once again allow power into the electrical system of the vehicle.
2 Remove the door handle bezel, armrest and screws along the bottom of the panel **(see illustrations).**
3 Remove the window crank by working a cloth back and forth behind the handle to dislodge the clip or push it off with a screwdriver **(see illustrations).** On 1990 and later models, remove the mirror trim panel on the inside of the door, then remove the three screws and remove the outside mirror.
4 Insert a large putty knife or a thin pry bar between the trim panel and the door and disengage the retaining clips, working around the outer edge until the panel is free of the door.
5 Once all of the clips are disengaged, unscrew the lock knob, detach the trim panel, lift it away, unplug any electrical connectors and remove the trim panel from the vehicle.
6 For access to the inner door, peel back the plastic service hole cover, taking care not to tear it **(see illustration).** To install, place the service hole cover in position and press it in place.

12.3c Snap the clip back into the groove — the window handle is now ready to be reinstalled by pushing it onto the shaft

12.6 Be very careful when pulling the plastic service hole cover off — don't tear or distort it

11

13.1   Dashboard component details (1986 through 1989 models)

7   Prior to installation of the door panel, make sure to reinstall any clips in the panel which may have come out during the removal procedure and remain in the door itself.

8   Plug in any electrical connectors and place the panel in position in the door. Press the door panel into place until the clips are seated and install any retaining screws and armrest/door pulls. Install the manual regulator window crank.

---

13   Dashboard trim panels – removal and installation

Refer to illustrations 13.1, 13.3 and 13.13

1986 through 1989 models

Lower crash pad side assembly

1   Remove the retaining screws (including the two hood release

handle mounting screws), lower the assembly, unplug the electrical connector and remove the lower crash pad side assembly **(see illustration)**.

2   Installation is the reverse of removal.

Steering column shroud under cover

3   Remove the two retaining screws **(see illustration)**.

4   Swing the cover down and detach it from the dashboard.

Lower crash pad

5   Remove the steering column cover (Section 14)

6   Pry out the screw covers.

7   Remove the screws and detach the cover.

8   Installation is the reverse of removal.

13.3   Remove the two cover retaining screws (arrows)

13.13   Use a small screwdriver to pry off the cover surrounding the radio

Instrument cluster housing

9   Remove the retaining screws, lift the housing up and turn it over.
10   Unplug the electrical connectors and remove the housing.
11   Installation is the reverse of removal.

Main fascia panel assembly

12   Remove the screws at the top of the assembly.
13   Pry off the radio cover for access to the two lower retaining screws **(see illustration)**.
14   Remove the screws and lift the fascia panel off.
15   Installation is the reverse of removal.

Lower crash pad main assembly

16   Remove the center console (see Section 15).
17   Remove the retaining screws, detach the assembly, lower it sufficiently for access to the electrical connectors and unplug them. Remove the assembly.
18   Installation is the reverse of removal.

1990 and later models

Refer to illustration 13.21

Lower fascia panel and audio unit

19   Remove the steering column cover (see Section 14).
20   Remove the hood release handle mounting screws.
21   Remove the screws, pull the panel out and unhook the antenna and electrical connectors and remove the lower fascia panel **(see illustration)**.
22   Installation is the reverse of removal.

Lower crash pad side assembly

23   Remove the screws and remove the lower crash pad side assembly.
24   Installation is the reverse of removal.

Lower crash pad main assembly

25   Remove the screws and remove the glove box assembly.
26   Remove the retaining screws, detach the assembly, lower it sufficiently for access to the electrical connectors and unplug them. Remove the assembly.
27   Installation is the reverse of removal.

Instrument cluster housing

28   Remove the retaining screws and unclip the housing.
29   Installation is the reverse of removal.

13.21   Dashboard component details (1990 and later models)

1   *Speaker grille*
2   *Crash pad upper cover*
3   *Crash pad main assembly*
4   *Cluster housing*
5   *Steering column shroud*
6   *Lower crash pad side assembly*
7   *Lower fascia*
8   *Crash pad center support bracket*
9   *Cigar light mounting protector*
10   *Ash tray*
11   *Lower crash pad main assembly*
12   *Lower crash pad main center bracket*

11

0591H

15.3   Center console component layout (1986 through 1989 models)

Crash pad main assembly

30   Remove all previously described components attached to the crash pad main assembly.

31   Remove the front speaker grilles. Unbolt the speakers, pull them up, disconnect the electrical connectors and remove both speakers.

32   Remove the retaining screws and carefully pull the crash pad main assembly toward the rear. With the help of an assistant, remove the assembly from the vehicle.

33   Installation is the reverse of removal.

14   Steering column cover – removal and installation

1   Remove the steering wheel (see Chapter 10).

2   Remove the retaining screws on the lower side of the steering column.

3   Carefully pry the halves of the cover apart. Unplug any electrical connectors and remove the cover halves from the steering column.

4   Installation is the reverse of removal.

15   Center console – removal and installation

1986 through 1989 models

Refer to illustration 15.3

1   Disconnect the negative cable at the battery. Place the cable out of the way so it cannot accidentally come in contact with the negative terminal of the battery, as this would once again allow power in the electrical system of the vehicle.

15.7   Center console compartment layout (1990 and later models)

1   *Front console*
2   *Front console cassette box*
3   *Shift lever boot*
4   *Shift lever indicator*
5   *Shift lever boot retainer*
6   *Rear console*
7   *Rear console mounting bracket*
8   *Front console mounting bracket*

16.5a   A cranked wrench such as this one is required to reach the hinge-to-body bolts when adjusting the doors

16.5b   Adjust the door lock striker by loosening the retaining screws and tapping the striker in the desired direction with a plastic mallet

17.3 Scribe or paint around the hinge bolt mounting flange (1) so you can re-install the trunk lid in its proper location – unscrew or loosen the lid-to-hinge bolts (2) to remove or adjust the trunk lid

2 Remove the shift knob or handle.
3 Remove the retaining screws **(see illustration).** If necessary, move the seats forward for access to the rear screws.
4 Detach the console and lift it from the vehicle.
5 Installation is the reverse of removal.

1990 and later models

Refer to illustration 15.7

7 Slide the front seats forward. Remove the retaining screws and remove the rear console **(see illustration).**
8 Remove the shift knob or handle.
9 Remove the retaining screws and remove the front console.
10 Installation is the reverse of removal.

---

16 Door – removal, installation and adjustment

Refer to illustrations 16.5a and 16.5b

1 Remove the door trim panel. Disconnect any electrical connec-

18.3 Paint or scribe around the hinge bolts (arrows) so you can return the liftgate to the same position when you install it – there's a hinge on each side of the liftgate, so make sure you mark the bolts on each of them

18.8a To adjust the engagement of the liftgate, loosen the three liftgate latch mounting bolts . . .

17.7 After loosening the bolts, you can move the striker to adjust the trunk lid position (1986 through 1989 models shown)

tors and push them through the door opening so they won't interfere with door removal.
2 Place a jack or stand under the door or have an assistant on hand to support it when the hinge bolts are removed. **Note:** *If a jack or stand is being used, place a rag between it and the door to protect the door's painted surfaces.*
3 Mark around the hinge-to-door bolts so you can return the door to its proper adjustment when installing it.
4 Remove the hinge-to-door bolts and carefully lift off the door. Installation is the reverse of removal.
5 Following installation of the door, check that it is in proper alignment and adjust it, if necessary, as follows:
  a) Up-and-down and forward-and-backward adjustments are made by loosening the hinge-to-body bolts and moving the door, as necessary. A special cranked tool may be required to reach some of the bolts **(see illustration).**
  b) The door lock striker can also be adjusted both up-and-down and sideways to provide a positive engagement with the locking mechanism. This is done by loosening the retaining screws and moving the striker, as necessary **(see illustration).**

18.4 Use a small screwdriver to pry up on the lock, and then detach the support strut end from the tailgate

18.8b . . . and/or the lock striker screws (arrows) and move the component(s) as necessary

11

17   Trunk lid – removal, installation and adjustment

Refer to illustrations 17.3 and 17.7

1   Open the trunk lid and cover the edges of the trunk compartment with pads or cloths to protect the painted surfaces when the lid is removed.

2   Disconnect any cable or electrical connectors which are attached to the trunk lid and would interfere with removal.

3   Scribe or paint alignment marks around the hinge bolt mounting flanges **(see illustration)**.

4   While an assistant supports the lid, remove the lid-to-hinge bolts on both sides and lift off the lid **(see illustration 17.3)**.

5   Installation is the reverse of removal. **Note:** *When reinstalling the trunk lid, align the lid-to-hinge bolts with the marks made during removal.*

6   After installation, close the lid and check that it is in proper alignment with the surrounding panels. Front and rear and side-to-side adjustments of the lid are controlled by the position of the lid-to-hinge bolts in their slots. To adjust, loosen the lid-to-hinge bolts, reposition the lid and retighten the bolts **(see illustration 17.3, if necessary)**.

7   The height of the lid in relation to the surrounding body panels when closed can be adjusted by loosening the striker bolts, repositioning the striker and tightening the bolts **(see illustration)**.

18   Liftgate – removal, installation and adjustment

Refer to illustrations 18.3, 18.4, 18.8a and 18.8b

1   Open the liftgate and cover the upper body area around the opening with pads or cloths to protect the painted surfaces when the liftgate is removed.

2   Disconnect any cables, hoses or electrical connectors which would interfere with removal of the liftgate.

3   Paint or scribe around the hinge bolts **(see illustration)**.

4   While an assistant supports the liftgate, detach the support struts **(see illustration)**.

5   Remove the hinge bolts and detach the liftgate from the vehicle.

6   Installation is the reverse of removal.

7   After installation, close the liftgate and check that the door is in proper alignment with the surrounding panels. Adjustments to the liftgate are made by moving the position of the hinge bolts in their slots. To adjust, loosen the hinge bolts and reposition them either side–to–side or front-to-rear the desired amount and retighten the bolts **(see illustration 18.3, if necessary)**.

8   The engagement of the liftgate can be adjusted by loosening the latch mounting bolts and/or the lock striker screws, repositioning the latch and/or striker and tightening the screws **(see illustrations)**.

**19.3a   Front door component details
(1986 through 1989 models)**

19.3b   Rear door component details
(1986 through 1989 models)

19   Door latch, lock cylinder and handle – removal
     and installation

1   Remove the door trim panel and service hole cover (Section 12).
2   Remove the door window glass (Section 20).

Door latch

Refer to illustrations 19.3a , 19.3b and 19.3c

3   Reach in through the door service hole and disconnect the door
safety rod and the door inside handle rod from the latch **(see illustrations)**.
4   Remove the three door latch retaining screws from the end of the
door. Remove the door lock.
5   Installation is the reverse of removal.

19.3c Typical 1990 and later
door component details
(rear door shown, front
door similar)

3   *Division channel*
4   *Fixed glass*
5   *Weatherstrip*
6   *Door glass*
7   *Pad*
8   *Glass run*
9   *Regulator*

11

19.6   Disconnect the lock cylinder rod (1) from the lock cylinder, then use pliers to slide the retaining clip (2) off the lock cylinder (3)

Inside   Outside

20.5a   On front doors, pry out the trim strips before removing the glass

20.5b   Tilt the door glass as shown when lifting it out of the opening

20.7   Make sure to install the glass in the run with the specified distance between the rear bolt hole and the edge of the glass

19.9   Remove the inside handle retaining screws (arrows) — when re-installing the front door handle, adjust the position of the handle assembly so the handle has a full stroke travel of about 48°, and then tighten the screws securely

Lock cylinder

Refer to illustration 19.6

6   Disconnect the lock cylinder rod from the lock cylinder (**see illustration**).
7   Use pliers to slide the retaining clip off and remove the lock cylinder from the door (**see illustration 19.6**).
8   Installation is the reverse of removal.

Inside handle

Refer to illustration 19.9

9   Remove the retaining screw(s) (**see illustration**).
10   Rotate the handle away and detach it from the door.
11   Installation is the reverse of removal. On front doors, before tightening the retaining screws, adjust the position of the handle assembly so the handle stroke travel is approximately 48° (**see illustration 19.9**).

Outside handle

12   Disconnect the control link(s) from the handle.
13   Remove the nuts from inside the door and detach the handle from the door.
14   Installation is the reverse of removal.

---

20   Door window glass — removal and installation

Refer to illustrations 20.5a, 20.5b, and 20.7

1   Remove the door trim panel and service hole cover (see Section 12).
2   Lower the window glass.
3   On rear doors, remove the retaining screws, pull the glass run and division channel out of the door and remove the fixed glass assembly (**see illustration 19.3b**).
4   Scribe or paint marks on the two window-to-glass run bolts and remove them.
5   On front doors, use a screwdriver to pry out the trim strips at the top of the door (**see illustration**). Remove the window glass by tilting it to detach the glass from the glass channel studs and then sliding the glass up and out of the door (**see illustration**).
6   If necessary, remove the regulator retaining bolts and then slide the regulator out of the opening in the door.
7   Installation is the reverse of removal. On front doors, if the glass has been removed from the glass run, make sure to reinstall it with the rear edge of the glass the specified distance from the rear glass run bolt hole (**see illustration**).

21.1   Use a small screwdriver to pry off the mirror adjusting lever cover

21.2a   Remove the screw and adjusting lever . . .

21.2b   . . . and rotate the trim cover off

21   Outside mirror — removal and installation

Refer to illustrations 21.1, 21.2a, 21.2b and 21.3

1   Use a screwdriver to pry off the adjusting lever trim cover (**see illustration**).
2   Remove the screw and adjusting lever and lift off the mirror trim cover (**see illustrations**).
3   Remove the three retaining screws and lift off the mirror (**see illustration**).
4   Installation is the reverse of removal.

22   Seats — removal and installation

Refer to illustrations 22.1a, 22.1b and 22.1c

1   On front seats, remove the mounting bolts, unplug any electrical connectors and lift the seat(s) from the vehicle (**see illustration 22.1a**). For instructions on removing the rear seat, refer to illustrations 22.1b and 22.1c.

21.3   The mirror is retained by three screws

11

22.1a   Front seat installation details

Head rest

Front seat back

Recliner handle

Front seat recliner assy

Front seat shield cover

Front seat cushion

RH SIDE

LH SIDE

Mounting bolts

Mounting bolts

Front seat track

Front seat track (Passive system)

22.1b   When removing the rear seat, unscrew the two bolts that attach the bottom of the lower seat cushion to the floorpan and remove the lower seat cushion . . .

22.1c   . . . then fold down the seat back, remove the side bracket mounting bolts (arrows), and slide the seat back off the mounting bracket that holds the center of the seat back on the floorpan

2   Installation is the reverse of removal. Tighten the mounting bolts to the specified torque.

23   Front fender inner panels — removal and installation

Refer to illustration 23.2

1   Raise the vehicle, support it securely and remove the front wheel(s).
2   Remove the bolts and lower the panel(s) from the fender well **(see illustration)**.
3   Installation is the reverse of removal.

24   Seat belt check

1   Check the seat belts, buckles, latch plates and guide loops for any obvious damage or signs of wear.
2   Check that the seat belt reminder light comes on when the key is turned to the On or Start positions. A chime should also sound.
3   The seat belts are designed to lock up during a sudden stop or impact, yet allow free movement during normal driving. Check that the retractors return the belt against your chest while driving and rewind

23.2   Front fender inner panel details

the belt fully when the buckle is unlatched.
4   If any of the above checks reveal problems with the seat belt system, replace parts as necessary.

Chapter 12 Chassis electrical system

Contents

Specifications

Light bulb application   Wattage
Exterior
Headlight (bulb type)	65/45
Front turn signal light	27
Front parking light	8
Brake/tail light	27/8
Back-up light	27
License plate light	8
Rear side marker light	3.8
Rear turn signal light	27

Interior
Glove compartment light	3.4
High mounted brake light	17
Interior light	10
Luggage compartment light	5
Parking light	3.8

12

1 General information

The electrical system is a 12-volt, negative ground type. Power for the lights and all electrical accessories is supplied by a lead/acid-type battery which is charged by the alternator.

This Chapter covers repair and service procedures for the various electrical components not associated with the engine. Information on the battery, alternator, distributor and starter motor can be found in Chapter 5.

It should be noted that when portions of the electrical system are serviced, the cable should be disconnected from the negative battery terminal to prevent electrical shorts and/or fires.

2   Electrical troubleshooting — general information

A typical electrical circuit consists of an electrical component, any switches, relays, motors, fuses, fusible links or circuit breakers related to that component and the wiring and connectors that link the component to both the battery and the chassis. To help you pinpoint an electrical circuit problem, wiring diagrams are included at the end of this book.

Before tackling any troublesome electrical circuit, first study the appropriate wiring diagrams to get a complete understanding of what makes up that individual circuit. Trouble spots, for instance, can often be narrowed down by noting if other components related to the circuit are operating properly. If several components or circuits fail at one time, chances are the problem is in a fuse or ground connection, because several circuits are often routed through the same fuse and ground connections.

Electrical problems usually stem from simple causes, such as loose or corroded connections, a blown fuse, a melted fusible link or a bad relay. Visually inspect the condition of all fuses, wires and connections in a problem circuit before troubleshooting it.

If testing instruments are going to be utilized, use the diagrams to plan ahead of time where you will make the necessary connections in order to accurately pinpoint the trouble spot.

The basic tools needed for electrical troubleshooting include a circuit tester or voltmeter (a 12-volt bulb with a set of test leads can also be used), a continuity tester, which includes a bulb, battery and set of test leads, and a jumper wire, preferably with a circuit breaker incorporated, which can be used to bypass electrical components. Before attempting to locate a problem with test instruments, use the wiring diagram(s) to decide where to make the connections.

Voltage checks

Voltage checks should be performed if a circuit is not functioning properly. Connect one lead of a circuit tester to either the negative battery terminal or a known good ground. Connect the other lead to a connector in the circuit being tested, preferably nearest to the battery or fuse. If the bulb of the tester lights, voltage is present, which means that the part of the circuit between the connector and the battery is problem free. Continue checking the rest of the circuit in the same fashion. When you reach a point at which no voltage is present, the problem lies between that point and the last test point with voltage. Most of the time the problem can be traced to a loose connection. **Note:** *Keep in mind that some circuits receive voltage only when the ignition key is in the Accessory or Run position.*

Finding a short

One method of finding shorts in a circuit is to remove the fuse and connect a test light or voltmeter in its place to the fuse terminals. There should be no voltage present in the circuit. Move the wiring harness from side to side while watching the test light. If the bulb goes on, there is a short to ground somewhere in that area, probably where the insulation has rubbed through. The same test can be performed on each component in the circuit, even a switch.

Ground check

Perform a ground test to check whether a component is properly grounded. Disconnect the battery and connect one lead of a self-powered test light, known as a continuity tester, to a known good ground. Connect the other lead to the wire or ground connection being tested. If the bulb goes on, the ground is good. If the bulb does not go on, the ground is not good.

Continuity check

A continuity check is done to determine if there are any breaks in a circuit — if it is passing electricity properly. With the circuit off (no power in the circuit), a self-powered continuity tester can be used to check the circuit. Connect the test leads to both ends of the circuit (or to the "power" end and a good ground), and if the test light comes on the circuit is passing current properly. If the light doesn't come on, there is a break somewhere in the circuit. The same procedure can be used to test a switch, by connecting the continuity tester to the power in and power out sides of the switch. With the switch turned On, the test light should come on.

Finding an open circuit

When diagnosing for possible open circuits, it is often difficult to locate them by sight because oxidation or terminal misalignment are hidden by the connectors. Merely wiggling a connector on a sensor or in the wiring harness may correct the open circuit condition. Remember this when an open circuit is indicated when troubleshooting a circuit. Intermittent problems may also be caused by oxidized or loose connections.

Electrical troubleshooting is simple if you keep in mind that all electrical circuits are basically electricity running from the battery, through the wires, switches, relays, fuses and fusible links to each electrical component (light bulb, motor, etc.) and to ground, from which it is passed back to the battery. Any electrical problem is an interruption in the flow of electricity to and from the battery.

3   Fuses — general information

Refer to illustrations 3.1 and 3.3

The electrical circuits of the vehicle are protected by a combination of fuses, circuit breakers and fusible links. The fuse block is located on the left side of the dashboard under a pull-down cover **(see illustration)**.

Each of the fuses is designed to protect a specific circuit, and the various circuits are identified on the fuse panel itself.

Miniaturized fuses are employed in the fuse block. These compact fuses, with blade terminal design, allow fingertip removal and replacement. If an electrical component fails, always check the fuse first. A blown fuse is easily identified through the clear plastic body. Visually inspect the element for evidence of damage **(see illustration)**. If a continuity check is called for, the blade terminal tips are exposed in the fuse body.

Be sure to replace blown fuses with the correct type. Fuses of different ratings are physically interchangeable, but only fuses of the

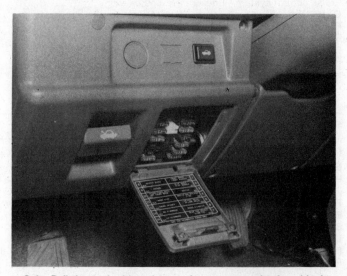

3.1   Pull down the hinged cover for access to the fuse block

Good

Burned out

3.3   The fuses used on these models can be easily checked visually to determine if they are blown

proper rating should be used. Replacing a fuse with one of a higher or lower value than specified is not recommended. Each electrical circuit needs a specific amount of protection. The amperage value of each fuse is molded into the fuse body.

If the replacement fuse immediately fails, don't replace it again until the cause of the problem is isolated and corrected. In most cases, this will be a short circuit in the wiring caused by a broken or deteriorated wire.

4 Fusible links — general information

Refer to illustrations 4.3a and 4.3b

Some circuits are protected by fusible links. The links are used in circuits which are not ordinarily fused, such as the ignition circuit.

The fusible links on later models are similar to fuses in that they can be visually checked to determine if they are melted. On 1986 models, check the fusible links with an ohmmeter to verify that they aren't burned out.

To replace a fusible link, first disconnect the negative cable from the battery. Unplug the burned out link and replace it with a new one (available from your dealer) (see illustrations). Always determine the

4.3a 1986 model fusible link details

4.3b On later models, simply unplug the fusible link and replace it with a new one — always determine the cause of the circuit overload before replacement

cause for the overload which melted the fusible link before installing a new one.

5 Relays — general information

Refer to illustration 5.2

Several electrical accessories in the vehicle use relays to transmit the electrical signal to the component. If the relay is defective, the component will not operate properly.

The various relays are grouped together in several locations under the dash, adjacent to the component, or in the engine compartment for convenience in the event of needed replacement (see illustration).

If a faulty relay is suspected, it can be removed and tested by a dealer service department or a repair shop. Defective relays must be replaced as a unit.

6 Turn signal/hazard flashers — check and replacement

1 The turn signal/hazard flasher, a small black plastic canister shaped unit located under the dash in the wiring harness, flashes the turn signals.
2 When the flasher unit is functioning properly, and audible click can be heard during its operation. If the turn signals fail on one side or the other and the flasher unit does not make its characteristic clicking sound, a faulty turn signal bulb is indicated.
3 If both turn signals fail to blink, the problem may be due to a blown fuse, a faulty flasher unit, a broken switch or a loose or open connection. If a quick check of the fuse box indicates that the turn signal fuse has blown, check the wiring for a short before installing a new fuse.
4 To replace the flasher, simply pull it out of the fuse block or wiring harness.
5 Make sure that the replacement unit is identical to the original. Compare the old one to the new one before installing it.
6 Installation is the reverse of removal.

7 Ignition switch and lock cylinder — removal and installation

Refer to illustration 7.5

1 Disconnect the negative cable from the battery.
2 Remove the steering wheel (Chapter 10).
3 Remove the under cover panel and the steering column cover (Chapter 11).
4 Unplug the switch electrical connector.

5.2 On later models, the relays for the horn, headlights, tail lights and choke are located on the firewall in the engine compartment

12

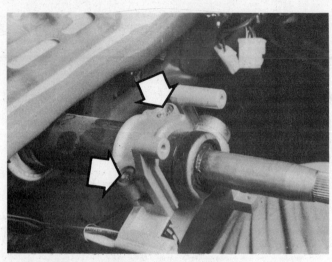

7.5   Drill out the heads of the special screws (arrows) retaining the igniton switch clamp

5   Drill out the heads of the special screws securing the clamp bracket to the ignition switch assembly **(see illustration)**.
6   Separate the ignition switch from the clamp. It may be necessary to use a punch and hammer to drive the screws out. Remove the ignition switch assembly.
7   Installation is the reverse of removal. Be sure to use new special screws when installing the new switch.

8   Combination switch — removal and installation

Refer to illustration 8.4
1   Disconnect the negative cable from the battery.
2   Remove the steering wheel (Chapter 10).
3   Remove the under cover panel and steering column cover (Chapter 11).
4   Remove the retaining screws **(see illustration)**.
5   Trace the wiring harness down the steering column to the connector. Cut the wiring tie-strap (if equipped), unplug the connector and slide the switch up off the column.
6   Installation is the reverse of removal.

9   Radio — removal and installation

1   Disconnect the negative cable from the battery.
2   Remove the instrument panel main fascia panel (Chapter 11).
3   Remove the radio mounting screws or bolts.
4   Pull the radio out, reach behind it and unplug the electrical connector and the antenna lead.
5   Detach the radio from the instrument panel.
6   Installation is the reverse of removal.

10   Headlights — removal and installation

1   Disconnect the negative cable from the battery.

Sealed-beam type

2   Remove the radiator grille (Chapter 11).
3   Remove the headlight retainer screws, taking care not to disturb the adjustment screws.
4   Remove the retainer and pull the headlight out far enough to unplug the connector.
5   Remove the headlight.
6   To install the headlight, plug the connector in, place the headlight in position and install the retainer and screws. Tighten the screws securely.
7   Install the radiator grille.

8.4   Combination switch retaining screw locations (arrows)

Bulb type

Refer to illustrations 10.8, 10.9 and 10.10
Warning: *The halogen gas filled bulbs used on these models are under pressure and may shatter if the surface is scratched or the bulb is dropped. Wear eye protection and handle the bulbs carefully, grasping only the base whenever possible. Do not touch the surface of the bulb with your fingers because the oil from your skin could cause it to overheat and fail prematurely. If you do touch the bulb surface, clean it with rubbing alcohol.*
8   Open the hood. Unplug the electrical connector **(see illustration)**.

10.8   Pry up on the locking tab and unplug the connector from the bulb type headlight holder

10.9   Turn the retainer counterclockwise to remove it, . . .

10.10 . . . then pull the bulb holder straight out to gain access to the bulb

9   Reach behind the headlight assembly, grasp the retainer and turn it counterclockwise to remove it **(see illustration)**. Pull the holder assembly out for access to the bulb.

10 Push in and rotate the bulb counterclockwise to remove it **(see illustration)**.

11 Insert the new bulb into the holder and turn it clockwise to seat it in the holder.

12 Install the bulb holder in the headlight assembly.

13 Install the retainer and turn it clockwise to lock it in place.

14 Plug in the electrical connector.

11 Headlights — adjustment

Refer to illustrations 11.6a and 11.6b

Note: *It is very important to have the headlights adjusted correctly. If adjusted incorrectly they could blind the driver of an oncoming vehicle and cause a serious accident or seriously reduce your ability to see the road. The headlights should be checked for proper aim every 12*

11.6b On bulb type headlights, the upper adjusting screw (H) moves the beam horizontally and the lower screw (V) moves it vertically

0075-H

11.6a Sealed beam headlight adjusting screw locations

months and any time a new headlight is installed or front end body work is performed. It should be emphasized that the following procedure is only an interim step which will provide temporary adjustment until the headlights can be adjusted by a properly equipped shop.

1   Headlights have two adjusting screws, one on the top controlling up and down movement and one on the side controlling left and right movement.

2   There are several methods of adjusting the headlights. The simplest method requires a blank wall 25 feet in front of the vehicle and a level surface in front of the wall.

3   Attach masking tape vertically to the wall in reference to the vehicle centerline and the centerlines of both headlights.

4   Position a horizontal tape line in reference to the centerline of all the headlights. **Note:** *It may be easier to position the tape on the wall with the vehicle parked only a few inches away.*

5   Adjustment should be made with the vehicle sitting level, the gas tank half-full and no unusually heavy load in the trunk or cargo area.

6   Starting with the low beam adjustment, position the high intensity zone so it is two inches below the horizontal line and two inches to the right of the headlight vertical line. Adjustment on sealed beam equipped models is made by turning the top adjusting screw *clockwise* to raise the beam and *counterclockwise* to lower the beam **(see illustration)**. The adjusting screw on the side should be used in the same manner to move the beam left or right. On bulb-type headlights, the upper adjusting screw moves the headlight assembly right or left and the lower one moves it up and down **(see illustration)**.

7   With the high beams on, the high intensity zone should be vertically centered with the exact center just below the horizontal line. **Note:** *It may not be possible to position the headlight aim exactly for both high and low beams. If a compromise must be made, keep in mind that the low beams are the most used and have the greatest effect on driver safety.*

8   Have the headlights adjusted by a dealer service department or service station at the earliest opportunity.

12 Bulb replacement

Refer to illustrations 12.3a, 12.3b, 12.4a and 12.4b

1   The lenses of many lights are held in place by screws, which makes it a simple procedure to gain access to the bulbs.

2   On some lights, the lenses are held in place by clips. On these, the lenses can either be removed by unsnapping them or by using a small screwdriver to pry them off.

12

12.3a   The front parking light bulb is accessible after releasing the spring and rotating the housing out of the fender

12.3b   Pull the holder out of the side marker housing for access to the bulb

3   Several types of bulbs are used. Some are removed by pushing in and turning counterclockwise **(see illustrations)**. Others can simply be unclipped from the terminals or pulled straight out of the socket.
4   To gain access to the instrument panel illumination lights **(see illustrations)**, the instrument cluster will have to be removed as described in Section 14.

---

13   Wiper motors — removal and installation

Refer to illustrations 13.2, 13.3, 13.5a, 13.5b, 13.7a, 13.7b, 13.8 and 13.9
1   Disconnect the negative cable from the battery.

Windshield wiper motor
2   Disconnect the washer hoses **(see illustration)**.
3   Remove the wiper arms and the cowl top cover retaining screws, then detach the cover for access to the motor **(see illustration)**.
4   Detach the wiper arm spindle link from the motor.
5   Remove the screws from the wiper motor mounting plate **(see illustrations)**. Unplug the electrical connector and remove the assembly from the vehicle.
6   Installation is the reverse of removal.

12.4a   Remove the switch housing from the cluster and turn the holder counterclockwise for access to the bulb

12.4b   After removing the instrument cluster, turn the bulb holders, lift them out and withdraw the bulbs

13.2   Disconnect the washer hoses

13.3 Remove the wiper arms and the cowl cover retaining screws (arrows)

13.5a Remove the wiper mounting plate screws in the cowl area . . .

13.5b . . . and the engine compartment

Rear window wiper motor

7   Remove the wiper arm, spindle nut and washers **(see illustration)**. Note the order in which the wiper spindle washers are arranged for installation **(see illustration)**.

8   Open the liftgate and remove the trim panel **(see illustration)**.

9   Unplug the electrical connector, remove the three mounting screws and lower the motor from the liftgate **(see illustration)**.

10 Installation is the reverse of removal.

13.7a Lift the cover up for access to the rear window wiper retaining nut

13.7b Rear window wiper components — exploded view

13.8 Liftgate trim panel details

13.9 Unplug the connector, remove the mounting screws (arrows) and lower the wiper motor from the liftgate

12

14.4a   The instrument cluster is retained by four screws

14.4b   Squeeze the clip together to disconnect the cable from the speedometer (cluster removed for clarity)

14   Instrument cluster — removal and installation

Refer to illustrations 14.4a, 14.4b and 14.5

1   Disconnect the negative cable from the battery.
2   Remove the steering wheel (Chapter 10).
3   Remove the steering column cover and the cluster housing (Chapter 11).
4   Remove the retaining screws, then pull out the instrument cluster and disconnect the wiring connectors and speedometer **(see illustrations)**.
5   To replace any faulty components within the cluster, simply unbolt or unscrew them and replace them with new units **(see illustration)**.
6   Installation is the reverse of removal.

15   Instrument panel — removal and installation

Refer to illustration 15.3

1   Disconnect the negative cable from the battery.
2   Remove the steering wheel (Chapter 10).
3   Remove the steering column covers, dashboard finish panels, instrument cluster, heater register ducts, radio, heater controls and any other components which would interfere with removal **(see illustration 15.3)**.
4   Remove the retaining bolts, nuts and screws, unplug any electrical connectors and pull the instrument panel up and to the rear to detach it **(see illustration 15.3)**.
5   Installation is the reverse of removal.

16   Cruise control system — description and checking

The cruise control system maintains vehicle speed through a vacuum actuated servo motor located in the engine compartment, which is connected to the throttle linkage by a cable. The system consists of the servo motor, clutch switch, brake light switch, control switches, a relay and associated vacuum hoses.

14.5   Instrument cluster details

1 Lens assembly
2 Fuel and temperature gauges
3 Tachometer
4 Housing
5 Display prism
6 Prism color lens
7 Printed circuit board
8 Bulb
9 Bulb holder
10 Speedometer

Cluster housing assembly

Identification plate

main assembly

Glove box mirror

Glove box housing

Cluster gauge mounting bracket

Crash pad main facia panel assembly

Glove box lock striker

Radio mounting bracket

Lower crash pad main center bracket

Steering column covers

Lower crash pad mounting bracket

Shroud under cover

Lower crash pad main assembly

Cigar light mounting protector

Fuse box cover

Ash tray

Lower crash pad side assembly

15.3 Instrument panel components — exploded view

12

Because of the complexity of the cruise control system and the special tools and techniques required for diagnosis and repair, it should be left to a dealer service department or properly equipped shop. However, it is possible for the home mechanic to make simple checks of the wiring and vacuum connections for minor faults which can be easily repaired. These include:
a) Inspecting the cruise control actuating switches and wiring for broken wires or loose connections.
b) Checking the cruise control fuse.
c) Checking the hoses in the engine compartment for tight connections, cracked hoses and obvious vacuum leaks. The cruise control system is operated by vacuum so it is critical that all vacuum switches, hoses and connections be secure.

17 Power window system — description and checking

The power window system operates the electric motors mounted in the doors, which lower and raise the windows. The system consists of the control switches, the motors (regulators), glass mechanisms and associated wiring.

Because of the complexity of the power window system and the special tools and techniques required for diagnosis and repair, it should be left to a dealer service department or properly equipped shop. However, it is possible for the home mechanic to make simple checks of the wiring connections and motors for minor faults which can be easily repaired. These include:
a) Inspecting the power window actuating switches and wiring for broken wires or loose connections.
b) Checking the power window fuse and/or circuit breaker.
c) Removing the door panel(s) and checking the power window motor wiring connections for looseness and damage, and inspecting the glass mechanisms for damage which could cause binding.

B = Black
L = Blue
W = White
Br = Brown
G = Green
R = Red
Y = Yellow

18.4 Wiring diagram color codes (if more than one color is indicated on the diagram — for example, R-G — it means the wire is red with a green stripe)

18 Wiring diagrams — general information

Refer to illustration 18.4

Since it isn't possible to include all wiring diagrams for every year covered by this manual, the following diagrams are those that are typical and most commonly needed.

Prior to troubleshooting any circuits, check the fuse and circuit breakers (if equipped) to make sure they are in good condition. Make sure the battery is properly charged and has clean, tight cable connections (Chapter 1).

When checking the wiring system, make sure that all connectors are clean, with no broken or loose pins. When unplugging a connector, do not pull on the wires, only on the connector housings themselves.

Refer to the accompanying illustration for the wire color codes applicable to your vehicle.

Front exterior lights, engine compartment and instrument panel wiring diagram

0076-H

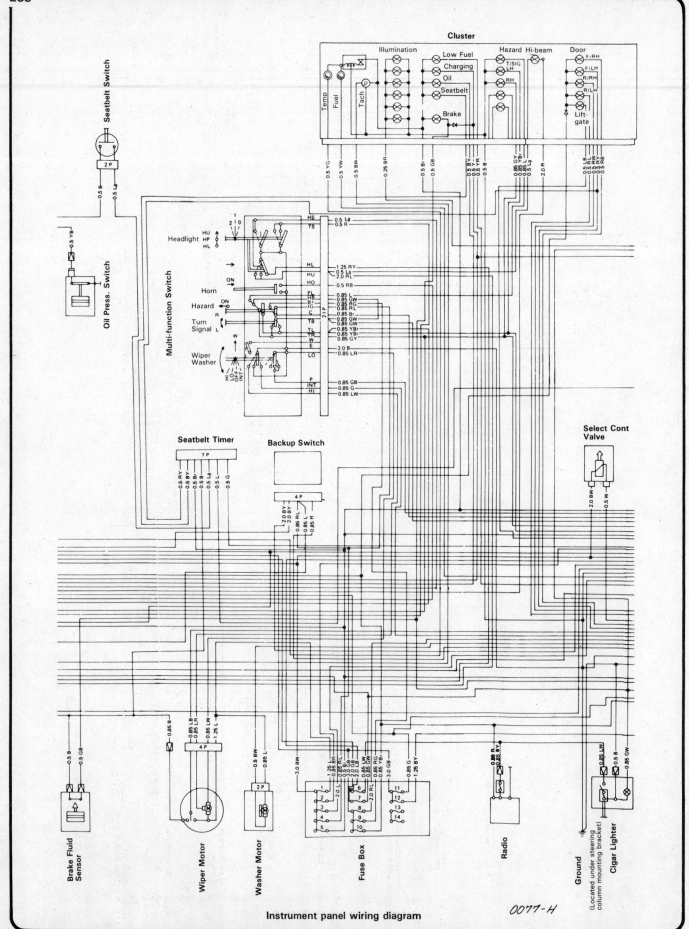

Instrument panel wiring diagram

0077-H

Vehicle interior wiring diagram

0078-H

0079-H

Vehicle interior and rear light wiring diagram

Index

Haynes Automotive Manuals

NOTE: New manuals are added to this list on a periodic basis. If you do not see a listing for your vehicle, consult your local Haynes dealer for the latest product information.

ACURA
*1776 Integra '86 thru '89 & Legend '86 thru '90

AMC
Jeep CJ - *see JEEP (412)*
694 Mid-size models, Concord, Hornet, Gremlin & Spirit '70 thru '83
934 (Renault) Alliance & Encore '83 thru '87

AUDI
615 4000 all models '80 thru '87
428 5000 all models '77 thru '83
1117 5000 all models '84 thru '88

AUSTIN-HEALEY
Sprite - *see MG Midget (265)*

BMW
*2020 3/5 Series not including diesel or all-wheel drive models '82 thru '92
276 320i all 4 cyl models '75 thru '83
632 528i & 530i all models '75 thru '80
240 1500 thru 2002 except Turbo '59 thru '77

BUICK
Century (front wheel drive) - *see GM (829)*
*1627 Buick, Oldsmobile & Pontiac Full-size (Front wheel drive) all models '85 thru '95
Buick Electra, LeSabre and Park Avenue; Oldsmobile Delta 88 Royale, Ninety Eight and Regency; **Pontiac** Bonneville
1551 Buick Oldsmobile & Pontiac Full-size (Rear wheel drive)
Buick Estate '70 thru '90, Electra'70 thru '84, LeSabre '70 thru '85, Limited '74 thru '79
Oldsmobile Custom Cruiser '70 thru '90, Delta 88 '70 thru '85,Ninety-eight '70 thru '84
Pontiac Bonneville '70 thru '81, Catalina '70 thru '81, Grandville '70 thru '75, Parisienne '83 thru '86
627 Mid-size Regal & Century all rear-drive models with V6, V8 and Turbo '74 thru '87
Regal - *see GENERAL MOTORS (1671)*
Riviera - *see GENERAL MOTORS (38030)*
Skyhawk - *see GENERAL MOTORS (766)*
Skylark '80 thru '85 - *see GM (38020)*
Skylark '86 on - *see GM (1420)*
Somerset - *see GENERAL MOTORS (1420)*

CADILLAC
*751 Cadillac Rear Wheel Drive all gasoline models '70 thru '93
Cimarron - *see GENERAL MOTORS (766)*
Eldorado - *see GENERAL MOTORS (38030)*
Seville '80 thru '85 - *see GM (38030)*

CHEVROLET
*1477 Astro & GMC Safari Mini-vans '85 thru '93
554 Camaro V8 all models '70 thru '81
866 Camaro all models '82 thru '92
Cavalier - *see GENERAL MOTORS (766)*
Celebrity - *see GENERAL MOTORS (829)*
24017 Camaro & Firebird '93 thru '96
625 Chevelle, Malibu & El Camino all V6 & V8 models '69 thru '87
449 Chevette & Pontiac T1000 '76 thru '87
550 Citation all models '80 thru '85
*1628 Corsica/Beretta all models '87 thru '96
274 Corvette all V8 models '68 thru '82
*1336 Corvette all models '84 thru '91
1762 Chevrolet Engine Overhaul Manual
704 Full-size Sedans Caprice, Impala, Biscayne, Bel Air & Wagons '69 thru '90
Lumina - *see GENERAL MOTORS (1671)*
Lumina APV - *see GENERAL MOTORS (2035)*
319 Luv Pick-up all 2WD & 4WD '72 thru '82
626 Monte Carlo all models '70 thru '88

241 Nova all V8 models '69 thru '79
*1642 Nova and Geo Prizm all front wheel drive models, '85 thru '92
420 Pick-ups '67 thru '87 - Chevrolet & GMC, all V8 & in-line 6 cyl, 2WD & 4WD '67 thru '87; Suburbans, Blazers & Jimmys '67 thru '91
*1664 Pick-ups '88 thru '95 - Chevrolet & GMC, all full-size pick-ups, '88 thru '95; Blazer & Jimmy '92 thru '94; Suburban '92 thru '95; Tahoe & Yukon '95
831 S-10 & GMC S-15 Pick-ups '82 thru '93
*24071 S-10 & GMC S-15 Pick-ups '94 thru '96
*1727 Sprint & Geo Metro '85 thru '94
*345 Vans - Chevrolet & GMC, V8 & in-line 6 cylinder models '68 thru '96

CHRYSLER
25025 Chrysler Concorde, New Yorker & LHS, Dodge Intrepid, Eagle Vision, '93 thru '96
2114 Chrysler Engine Overhaul Manual
*2058 Full-size Front-Wheel Drive '88 thru '93
K-Cars - *see DODGE Aries (723)*
Laser - *see DODGE Daytona (1140)*
*1337 Chrysler & Plymouth Mid-size front wheel drive '82 thru '95
Rear-wheel Drive - *see Dodge (2098)*

DATSUN
647 200SX all models '80 thru '83
228 B - 210 all models '73 thru '78
525 210 all models '79 thru '82
206 240Z, 260Z & 280Z Coupe '70 thru '78
563 280ZX Coupe & 2+2 '79 thru '83
300ZX - *see NISSAN (1137)*
679 310 all models '78 thru '82
123 510 & PL521 Pick-up '68 thru '73
430 510 all models '78 thru '81
372 610 all models '72 thru '76
277 620 Series Pick-up all models '73 thru '79
720 Series Pick-up - *see NISSAN (771)*
376 810/Maxima all gasoline models, '77 thru '84
Pulsar - *see NISSAN (876)*
Sentra - *see NISSAN (982)*
Stanza - *see NISSAN (981)*

DODGE
400 & 600 - *see CHRYSLER Mid-size (1337)*
*723 Aries & Plymouth Reliant '81 thru '89
1231 Caravan & Plymouth Voyager Mini-Vans all models '84 thru '95
699 Challenger/Plymouth Saporro '78 thru '83
Challenger '67-'76 - *see DODGE Dart (234)*
610 Colt & Plymouth Champ (front wheel drive) all models '78 thru '87
*1668 Dakota Pick-ups all models '87 thru '96
234 Dart, Challenger/Plymouth Barracuda & Valiant 6 cyl models '67 thru '76
*1140 Daytona & Chrysler Laser '84 thru '89
Intrepid - *see CHRYSLER (25025)*
*30034 Neon all models '94 thru '97
*545 Omni & Plymouth Horizon '78 thru '90
*912 Pick-ups all full-size models '74 thru '93
*30041 Pick-ups all full-size models '94 thru '96
*556 Ram 50/D50 Pick-ups & Raider and Plymouth Arrow Pick-ups '79 thru '93
2098 Dodge/Plymouth/Chrysler rear wheel drive '71 thru '89
*1726 Shadow & Plymouth Sundance '87 thru '94
*1779 Spirit & Plymouth Acclaim '89 thru '95
*349 Vans - Dodge & Plymouth V8 & 6 cyl models '71 thru '96

EAGLE
Talon - *see Mitsubishi Eclipse (2097)*
Vision - *see CHRYSLER (25025)*

FIAT
094 124 Sport Coupe & Spider '68 thru '78
273 X1/9 all models '74 thru '80

FORD
10355 Ford Automatic Trans. Overhaul
*1476 Aerostar Mini-vans all models '86 thru '96

268 Courier Pick-up all models '72 thru '82
2105 Crown Victoria & Mercury Grand Marquis '88 thru '96
1763 Ford Engine Overhaul Manual
789 Escort/Mercury Lynx all models '81 thru '90
*2046 Escort/Mercury Tracer '91 thru '96
*2021 Explorer & Mazda Navajo '91 thru '95
560 Fairmont & Mercury Zephyr '78 thru '83
334 Fiesta all models '77 thru '80
754 Ford & Mercury Full-size, Ford LTD & Mercury Marquis ('75 thru '82); Ford Custom 500,Country Squire, Crown Victoria & Mercury Colony Park ('75 thru '87); Ford LTD Crown Victoria & Mercury Gran Marquis ('83 thru '87)
359 Granada & Mercury Monarch all in-line, 6 cyl & V8 models '75 thru '80
773 Ford & Mercury Mid-size, Ford Thunderbird & Mercury Cougar ('75 thru '82); Ford LTD & Mercury Marquis ('83 thru '86); Ford Torino,Gran Torino, Elite, Ranchero pick-up, LTD II, Mercury Montego, Comet, XR-7 & Lincoln Versailles ('75 thru '86)
231 Mustang II 4 cyl, V6 & V8 models '74 thru '78
357 Mustang V8 all models '64-1/2 thru '73
*654 Mustang & Mercury Capri all models Mustang, '79 thru '93; Capri, '79 thru '86
*36051 Mustang all models '94 thru '97
788 Pick-ups & Bronco '73 thru '79
*880 Pick-ups & Bronco '80 thru '96
649 Pinto & Mercury Bobcat '75 thru '80
1670 Probe all models '89 thru '92
*1026 Ranger/Bronco II gasoline models '83 thru '92
*36071 Ranger '93 thru '96 & Mazda Pick-ups '94 thru '96
*1421 Taurus & Mercury Sable '86 thru '95
*1418 Tempo & Mercury Topaz all gasoline models '84 thru '94
1338 Thunderbird/Mercury Cougar '83 thru '88
*1725 Thunderbird/Mercury Cougar '89 and '96
344 Vans all V8 Econoline models '69 thru '91
*2119 Vans full size '92-'95

GENERAL MOTORS
*10360 GM Automatic Transmission Overhaul
*829 Buick Century, Chevrolet Celebrity, Oldsmobile Cutlass Ciera & Pontiac 6000 all models '82 thru '96
*1671 Buick Regal, Chevrolet Lumina, Oldsmobile Cutlass Supreme & Pontiac Grand Prix front wheel drive models '88 thru '95
*766 Buick Skyhawk, Cadillac Cimarron, Chevrolet Cavalier, Oldsmobile Firenza & Pontiac J-2000 & Sunbird '82 thru '94
38020 Buick Skylark, Chevrolet Citation, Olds Omega, Pontiac Phoenix '80 thru '85
1420 Buick Skylark & Somerset, Oldsmobile Achieva & Calais and Pontiac Grand Am all models '85 thru '95
38030 Cadillac Eldorado '71 thru '85, Seville '80 thru '85, Oldsmobile Toronado '71 thru '85 & Buick Riviera '79 thru '85
*2035 Chevrolet Lumina APV, Olds Silhouette & Pontiac Trans Sport all models '90 thru '95
General Motors Full-size Rear-wheel Drive - *see BUICK (1551)*

GEO
Metro - *see CHEVROLET Sprint (1727)*
Prizm - '85 thru '92 see CHEVY Nova (1642), '93 thru '96 see TOYOTA Corolla (1642)
*2039 Storm all models '90 thru '93
Tracker - *see SUZUKI Samurai (1626)*

GMC
Safari - *see CHEVROLET ASTRO (1477)*
Vans & Pick-ups - *see CHEVROLET (420, 831, 345, 1664 & 24071)*

(Continued on other side)

---

* Listings shown with an asterisk (*) indicate model coverage as of this printing. These titles will be periodically updated to include later model years - consult your Haynes dealer for more information.

Haynes North America, Inc., 861 Lawrence Drive, Newbury Park, CA 91320 • (805) 498-6703

HONDA
351	**Accord CVCC** all models '76 thru '83
1221	**Accord** all models '84 thru '89
2067	**Accord** all models '90 thru '93
42013	**Accord** all models '94 thru '95
160	**Civic 1200** all models '73 thru '79
633	**Civic 1300 & 1500 CVCC** '80 thru '83
297	**Civic 1500 CVCC** all models '75 thru '79
1227	**Civic** all models '84 thru '91
*2118	**Civic & del Sol** '92 thru '95
*601	**Prelude CVCC** all models '79 thru '89

HYUNDAI
*1552	**Excel** all models '86 thru '94

ISUZU
*1641	**Trooper & Pick-up,** all gasoline models Pick-up, '81 thru '93; Trooper, '84 thru '91
	Hombre - *see CHEVROLET S-10 (24071)*

JAGUAR
*242	**XJ6** all 6 cyl models '68 thru '86
*49011	**XJ6** all models '88 thru '94
*478	**XJ12 & XJS** all 12 cyl models '72 thru '85

JEEP
*1553	**Cherokee, Comanche & Wagoneer Limited** all models '84 thru '96
412	**CJ** all models '49 thru '86
50025	**Grand Cherokee** all models '93 thru '95
50029	**Grand Wagoneer & Pick-up** '72 thru '91 Grand Wagoneer '84 thru '91, Cherokee & Wagoneer '72 thru '83, Pick-up '72 thru '88
*1777	**Wrangler** all models '87 thru '95

LINCOLN
2117	**Rear Wheel Drive** all models '70 thru '96

MAZDA
648	**626** (rear wheel drive) all models '79 thru '82
*1082	**626/MX-6** (front wheel drive) '83 thru '91
370	**GLC Hatchback** (rear wheel drive) '77 thru '83
757	**GLC** (front wheel drive) '81 thru '85
*2047	**MPV** all models '89 thru '94
	Navajo - *see Ford Explorer (2021)*
267	**Pick-ups** '72 thru '93
	Pick-ups '94 thru '96 - *see Ford Ranger (36071)*
460	**RX-7** all models '79 thru '85
*1419	**RX-7** all models '86 thru '91

MERCEDES-BENZ
*1643	**190 Series** four-cyl gas models, '84 thru '88
346	**230/250/280** 6 cyl sohc models '68 thru '72
983	**280 123 Series** gasoline models '77 thru '81
698	**350 & 450** all models '71 thru '80
697	**Diesel 123 Series** '76 thru '85

MERCURY
See FORD Listing

MG
111	**MGB** Roadster & GT Coupe '62 thru '80
265	**MG Midget, Austin Healey Sprite** '58 thru '80

MITSUBISHI
*1669	**Cordia, Tredia, Galant, Precis & Mirage** '83 thru '93
*2097	**Eclipse, Eagle Talon & Plymouth Laser** '90 thru '94
*2022	**Pick-up** '83 thru '96 & **Montero** '83 thru '93

NISSAN
1137	**300ZX** all models including Turbo '84 thru '89
*72015	**Altima** all models '93 thru '97
*1341	**Maxima** all models '85 thru '91
*771	**Pick-ups** '80 thru '96 **Pathfinder** '87 thru '95
876	**Pulsar** all models '83 thru '86
*982	**Sentra** all models '82 thru '94
*981	**Stanza** all models '82 thru '90

OLDSMOBILE
	Achieva - *see GENERAL MOTORS (1420)*
	Bravada - *see CHEVROLET S-10 (831)*
	Calais - *see GENERAL MOTORS (1420)*
	Custom Cruiser - *see BUICK RWD (1551)*
*658	**Cutlass** V6 & V8 gas models '74 thru '88
	Cutlass Ciera - *see GENERAL MOTORS (829)*
	Cutlass Supreme - *see GM (1671)*
	Delta 88 - *see BUICK Full-size RWD (1551)*
	Delta 88 Brougham - *see BUICK Full-size FWD (1551), RWD (1627)*
	Delta 88 Royale - *see BUICK RWD (1551)*
	Firenza - *see GENERAL MOTORS (766)*
	Ninety-eight Regency - *see BUICK Full-size RWD (1551), FWD (1627)*
	Ninety-eight Regency Brougham - *see BUICK Full-size RWD (1551)*
	Omega - *see GENERAL MOTORS (38020)*
	Silhouette - *see GENERAL MOTORS (2035)*
	Toronado - *see GENERAL MOTORS (38030)*

PEUGEOT
663	**504** all diesel models '74 thru '83

PLYMOUTH
	Laser - *see MITSUBISHI Eclipse (2097)*
	For other PLYMOUTH titles, see DODGE.

PONTIAC
	T1000 - *see CHEVROLET Chevette (449)*
	J-2000 - *see GENERAL MOTORS (766)*
	6000 - *see GENERAL MOTORS (829)*
	Bonneville - *see Buick FWD (1627), RWD (1551)*
	Bonneville Brougham - *see Buick (1551)*
	Catalina - *see Buick Full-size (1551)*
1232	**Fiero** all models '84 thru '88
555	**Firebird** V8 models except Turbo '70 thru '81
867	**Firebird** all models '82 thru '92
	Firebird '93 thru '96 - *see CHEVY Camaro (24017)*
	Full-size Front Wheel Drive - *see BUICK, Oldsmobile, Pontiac Full-size FWD (1627)*
	Full-size Rear Wheel Drive - *see BUICK, Oldsmobile, Pontiac Full-size RWD (1551)*
	Grand Am - *see GENERAL MOTORS (1420)*
	Grand Prix - *see GENERAL MOTORS (1671)*
	Grandville - *see BUICK Full-size (1551)*
	Parisienne - *see BUICK Full-size (1551)*
	Phoenix - *see GENERAL MOTORS (38020)*
	Sunbird - *see GENERAL MOTORS (766)*
	Trans Sport - *see GENERAL MOTORS (2035)*

PORSCHE
*264	**911** except Turbo & Carrera 4 '65 thru '89
239	**914** all 4 cyl models '69 thru '76
397	**924** all models including Turbo '76 thru '82
*1027	**944** all models including Turbo '83 thru '89

RENAULT
141	**5 Le Car** all models '76 thru '83
	Alliance & Encore - *see AMC (934)*

SAAB
247	**99** all models including Turbo '69 thru '80
*980	**900** all models including Turbo '79 thru '88

SATURN
2083	**Saturn** all models '91 thru '96

SUBARU
237	**1100, 1300, 1400 & 1600** '71 thru '79
*681	**1600 & 1800** 2WD & 4WD '80 thru '89

SUZUKI
*1626	**Samurai/Sidekick & Geo Tracker** '86 thru '96

TOYOTA
1023	**Camry** all models '83 thru '91
92006	**Camry** all models '92 thru '95
935	**Celica Rear Wheel Drive** '71 thru '85
*2038	**Celica Front Wheel Drive** '86 thru '93
1139	**Celica Supra** all models '79 thru '92
361	**Corolla** all models '75 thru '79

961	**Corolla** all rear wheel drive models '80 thru '87
1025	**Corolla** all front wheel drive models '84 thru '92
*92036	**Corolla & Geo Prizm** '93 thru '96
636	**Corolla Tercel** all models '80 thru '82
360	**Corona** all models '74 thru '82
532	**Cressida** all models '78 thru '82
313	**Land Cruiser** all models '68 thru '82
*1339	**MR2** all models '85 thru '87
304	**Pick-up** all models '69 thru '78
*656	**Pick-up** all models '79 thru '95
*2048	**Previa** all models '91 thru '95
2106	**Tercel** all models '87 thru '94

TRIUMPH
113	**Spitfire** all models '62 thru '81
322	**TR7** all models '75 thru '81

VW
159	**Beetle & Karmann Ghia** '54 thru '79
238	**Dasher** all gasoline models '74 thru '81
96017	**Golf & Jetta** all models '93 thru '97
*884	**Rabbit, Jetta, Scirocco, & Pick-up** gas models '74 thru '91 & Convertible '80 thru '92
451	**Rabbit, Jetta & Pick-up** diesel '77 thru '84
082	**Transporter 1600** all models '68 thru '79
226	**Transporter 1700, 1800 & 2000** '72 thru '79
084	**Type 3 1500 & 1600** all models '63 thru '73
1029	**Vanagon** all air-cooled models '80 thru '83

VOLVO
203	**120, 130 Series & 1800 Sports** '61 thru '73
129	**140 Series** all models '66 thru '74
*270	**240 Series** all models '76 thru '93
400	**260 Series** all models '75 thru '82
*1550	**740 & 760 Series** all models '82 thru '88

TECHBOOK MANUALS
2108	**Automotive Computer Codes**
1667	**Automotive Emissions Control Manual**
482	**Fuel Injection Manual, 1978 thru 1985**
2111	**Fuel Injection Manual, 1986 thru 1996**
2069	**Holley Carburetor Manual**
2068	**Rochester Carburetor Manual**
10240	**Weber/Zenith/Stromberg/SU Carburetors**
1762	**Chevrolet Engine Overhaul Manual**
2114	**Chrysler Engine Overhaul Manual**
1763	**Ford Engine Overhaul Manual**
1736	**GM and Ford Diesel Engine Repair Manual**
1666	**Small Engine Repair Manual**
10355	**Ford Automatic Transmission Overhaul**
10360	**GM Automatic Transmission Overhaul**
1479	**Automotive Body Repair & Painting**
2112	**Automotive Brake Manual**
2113	**Automotive Detailing Manual**
1654	**Automotive Eelectrical Manual**
1480	**Automotive Heating & Air Conditioning**
2109	**Automotive Reference Manual & Dictionary**
2107	**Automotive Tools Manual**
10440	**Used Car Buying Guide**
2110	**Welding Manual**
10450	**ATV Basics**

SPANISH MANUALS
98903	**Reparación de Carrocería & Pintura**
98905	**Códigos Automotrices de la Computadora**
98910	**Frenos Automotriz**
98915	**Inyección de Combustible 1986 al 1994**
99040	**Chevrolet & GMC Camionetas** '67 al '87 Incluye Suburban, Blazer & Jimmy '67 al '91
99041	**Chevrolet & GMC Camionetas** '88 al '95 Incluye Suburban '92 al '95, Blazer & Jimmy '92 al '94, Tahoe y Yukon '95
99042	**Chevrolet & GMC Camionetas Cerradas** '68 al '95
99055	**Dodge Caravan & Plymouth Voyager** '84 al '95
99075	**Ford Camionetas y Bronco** '80 al '94
99077	**Ford Camionetas Cerradas** '69 al '91
99083	**Ford Modelos de Tamaño Grande** '75 al '87
99088	**Ford Modelos de Tamaño Mediano** '75 al '86
99095	**GM Modelos de Tamaño Grande** '70 al '90
99118	**Nissan Sentra** '82 al '94
99125	**Toyota Camionetas y 4-Runner** '79 al '95

---

* Listings shown with an asterisk (*) indicate model coverage as of this printing. These titles will be periodically updated to include later model years - consult your Haynes dealer for more information.

Over 100 Haynes motorcycle manuals also available

5-97

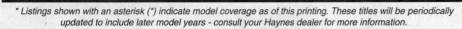